Recovering International Relations

Recovering International Relations

The Promise of Sustainable Critique

DANIEL J. LEVINE

OXFORD
UNIVERSITY PRESS

OXFORD
UNIVERSITY PRESS

Oxford University Press is a department of the University of Oxford.
It furthers the University's objective of excellence in research,
scholarship, and education by publishing worldwide.

Oxford New York
Auckland   Cape Town   Dar es Salaam   Hong Kong   Karachi
Kuala Lumpur   Madrid   Melbourne   Mexico City   Nairobi
New Delhi   Shanghai   Taipei   Toronto

With offices in
Argentina   Austria   Brazil   Chile   Czech Republic   France   Greece
Guatemala   Hungary   Italy   Japan   Poland   Portugal   Singapore
South Korea   Switzerland   Thailand   Turkey   Ukraine   Vietnam

Oxford is a registered trade mark of Oxford University Press
in the UK and certain other countries.

Published in the United States of America by
Oxford University Press
198 Madison Avenue, New York, NY 10016

© Oxford University Press 2012

Library of Congress Cataloging-in-Publication Data
Levine, Daniel J.
Recovering international relations : the promise of sustainable critique / Daniel J. Levine.
p. cm.
Includes bibliographical references and index.
ISBN 978-0-19-991606-1 (hardback : alk. paper) –
ISBN 978-0-19-991608-5 (pbk. : alk. paper)   1. International relations –
Philosophy.   I. Title.
JZ1242.L49 2012
327.101 – dc23
2012006946

ISBN 978-0-19-991606-1
ISBN 978-0-19-991608-5

For Aaron, Frank, Rhoda, and Susan,
who made this possible

Contents

List of Tables/Figures

Tables

Figures

Acknowledgments

THIS BOOK WOULD not have been written without the benefit of several scholarly communities, together with numerous contributions from coworkers, friends, and family. Compiling this list is thus a pleasant obligation; in acknowledging each act of kindness, I am drawn into grateful, pleasant recollection. I am lucky to have had the company of so many interlocutors.

To Daniel Deudney, Jane Bennett, and Renée Marlin-Bennett go my greatest thanks. Daniel has shepherded this project since its beginning, encouraging my intuitions and fostering a deep appreciation of theory's possibilities. He also delineated, and insisted upon, a degree of logical rigor that made clear the distinction between the free play of big ideas, on the one hand, and carefully made, close-knit arguments on the other. Though there have been many others, this lesson remains his greatest. I have tried to make good on it.

Jane Bennett joined this project at a difficult time. She looked beyond the page, seeing not merely what I had *done* but what I had *tried to do*, and then helping trace a path that would connect the two. It is a gift I can never wholly repay. For her part, Renée Marlin-Bennett was a careful, demanding, and scrupulous reader. Her knowledge of international theory would brook no careless generalizations. At the same time, her own deeply felt normative commitments—equal parts Hayward Alker and Abraham Joshua Heschel—gave her both sympathy for and concrete insight into the aims and limitations of sustainable critique.

At Johns Hopkins, William E. Connolly and Siba N'Zatioula Grovogui were constant friends and remarkable teachers. Mark Blyth read many early drafts with a sharp pen; so did Waleed Hazbun and Mimi Keck. Paola Marratti was a wonderful teacher, as were Jennifer Culbert and the late Giovanni Arrighi. Thanks, too, go to Michael Hanchard, Steven David, Adam Sheingate, Sam Chambers, Steve Teles, Kellee Tsai, Ruth Leys, Hent de Vries, Dick Katz, Ken Moss, Marc Caplan, Ron Walters, and Sarah Berry. My initial years of study were also sustained in part thanks to the generosity of the Stulman Jewish Studies program; thanks go to the Stulman family and to David Nirenberg and to Steven David. I was also sustained by grants of summer funding, thanks to Matt Crenson and to the Marshall-Baruch Foundation.

At Colgate, particular thanks are due to Daniel Monk and Nancy Ries: fine mentors and good friends. Fred Chernoff, Noah Dauber, Dan Epstein, Ed Fogarty, Constance Harsh, Michael Johnston, Xan Karn, Jacob Mundy, Rob Nemes, Krisjon Olson, Jenna Reinbold, Ben Stahlberg, and Manny Teodoro were challenging interlocutors and supportive colleagues. At the University of Alabama, thanks must go to the departments of History and Political Science, to the Honors and New Colleges, and in particular to Carmen Burkhalter, Ellen Cutrone, Naomi Choi, Kari Fredrickson, Doug Gibler, Rich Fording, Jim Hall, Mike Innis-Jiménez, Heather Kopelson, Utz McKnight, Ted Miller, Emily Ritter, Steve Schwab, Steve Bunker, and Jacqueline Morgan.

This project began with study and work in which I was engaged in the 1990s. At Tel Aviv University, my deepest thanks go to Ilai Alon, Shai Feldman, and Shlomo Giora Shoham. I also learned much from Azar Gat, Zeev Maoz, Shimon Naveh, Reuven Pedhazur, Aharon Shai, and Dov Tamari. Meron Benvenisti of the Truman Institute was generous in giving a young scholar a much-needed chance. At the Jaffee Center for Strategic Studies (now the INSS), I owe many debts to Shlomo Brom, Ram Erez, Moshe Grundman, Anat Kurz, Emily Landau, Tamir Magal, Tamar Malz-Ginsburg, and Yiftah Shapir. My former colleagues at the Foreign and Commonwealth Office also played a key role in thinking through the initial problems that actuated this project; thanks are due to Andrew Ayre, Francis Cornish, Alisa Helbitz, Jumana Jaouni, Cath Jenkins, David Manning, Simon Pease, Menna Rawlings, Greg Shapland, Robert Watson, Elizabeth Scholes, and Ruti Winterstein. Special thanks go to Ron Skolnik and to Amir Tadmor: *she-asu li bet sefer*, in the best sense.

More recently, I have benefited from comments and suggestions from a broad array of readers. To Jeremy Arnold, Alex Barder, Shlomit Barnea, Elisabetta Brighi, Tony Burke, Sergio Catignani, Raffaella del Sarto, Bill Dixon, Bud Duvall, Blake Etheridge, Stef Fishel, Simon Glezos, Jairus Grove, Misgav Har-Peled, Alex Lefebvre, Dan Nexon, Ido Oren, Rose Shinko, Laura Sjoberg, Brent Steele, Joan Tronto, and Mabel Wong, I owe more thanks than I can properly convey. Rameez Abbas, Erin Ackerman, Alexander Alden, Sam Barkin, Roger Berkowitz, Stephen Biddle, Sarah Clark, Tom

Donahue, Amitai Etzioni, Josh Gold, Harry Gould, Jake Greear, Cemal Hasimi, Meghan Helsel, Ryan Holston, Morgan Hitzig, Anatoli Ignatov, Piki Ish-Shalom, Isaac Kamola, Lili Knorr, Marjo Koivisto, Hitomi Koyama, Dot Kwek, Jennifer Lalonde, Jennifer Lin, Jenny Lobasz, Noora Loori, Leandro Mendonça, David Marshall, Michael McCarthy, David McCourt, Terukazu Morikawa, Paulina Ochoa-Espejo, George Oppel, Nobutaka Otobe, Sumita Pahwa, Deganit Paikowski, Benjamin Periello, Chas Phillips, Luke Plotica, Jeff Pugh, Smita Rahman, Andrew A. G. Ross, Ariel Ilan Roth, Mort Schoolman, Nils Schott, Rudy Sil, Jill Stauffer, Ty Solomon, Hannah Son, Mina Suk, Lars Tønder, Sunil Vaswani, Juan Wang, Toby Weatherall, Lauren Wilcox, and Tom Williams were also generous with time and ideas. Patrick Thaddeus Jackson has been an unstinting friend and mentor; so were Ned Lebow and Nick Onuf. At OUP, Dave McBride has been a kind (and patient!) editor; thanks also to Peter Mavrikis, Joy Matkowski and Alexandra Dauler. Teresa and Ilai Cribelli leavened my work, and my life, with love and imagination.

There are also gifts of another sort. My parents, Aaron and Rhoda Levine, were generous in both financial support and care. Frank and Susan Cribelli welcomed me into their family and gave another gift—help caring for our newborn son—without which this book would never have been finished. In gratitude, I dedicate it to them.

Recovering International Relations

Introduction

Sustainable Critique and the Lost Vocation of International Relations

We have replaced decency by reason.
—ARTHUR KOESTLER[1]

The Lost Vocation

The first academic chair in international politics was established at the University of Aberystwyth, Wales, in 1919, and the discipline of International Relations (IR) has existed in something like its present form since about the end of the Second World War.[2] The life of the contemporary discipline— as distinct from the normative traditions on which it draws—thus spans some six to eight decades. What work is it understood to be doing? What,

---

1. Koestler (1941), p. 173.

2. Schmidt (1998), p. 155. For additional broad-based disciplinary surveys of IR, see Bayliss, Smith, and Owens (2008), Dougherty and Pfaltzgraff (2001), Doyle (1997), Griffiths (2007), Guilhot (2008, 2011), Guzzini (1998), Halliday (1994), Haslam (2002), Hinsley (1967), Hoffmann (1977), Holsti (1985), Kahler (1997), Knutsen (1997), Molloy (2006), Olson and Groom (1991), Oren (2003), Robin (2001), Smith, Booth, and Zalewski (1996), Spegele (1996), Vasquez (1998), and Walker (1992). Gunnell (2006), Somit and Tanenhaus (1967), and Ross (1991) are useful for a broader perspective. But see also Holden (2002).

A few notes on terminology. Following what is increasingly the academic norm, International Relations (or IR) refers to the academic discipline. Events in world politics will generally be denoted as such. The term *paradigm* refers to particular theoretical constructs in IR, formed when long-standing normative political theory (or fact-value) traditions are parsed through particular methodologies. Hence, neorealism and neoliberalism are paradigms that draw on longer running realist and liberal normative-political traditions, parsed through middle-range methodological approaches. This can lead to some confusion, as some paradigms in IR are named with reference to the fact-value tradition from which they are adapted (Waltzian neorealism, a paradigm drawn from the realist tradition, parsed through a behaviorist methodology), and others with reference to the dominant methodology they employ (IR constructivism, at turns an adaptation of the realist or liberal tradition but parsed through a combination of constructivist language philosophy and poststructural philosophy of science). This "loose" usage draws on Vasquez (1998), pp. 22–23, and Etzioni (2001), p. 2: "more than a perspective," as the latter put it, "but less than a theory," a means by which preexisting political-social-normative

as Alexander Wendt provocatively asked, is International Relations *"for"*?[3] To speak very broadly, one finds an answer in the cataclysms of its early years: two world wars, the development and use of nuclear weapons, cycles of economic depression and upheaval, and numerous acts of genocide. The events of the twentieth century dealt a sharp blow to the hopes of the Scottish and German enlightenments, to the effect that an increasingly complex world might, with sufficient ingenuity, be made automatically self-sustaining and that technical progress and moral progress moved hand in glove. Over several centuries, a series of distinct and largely disconnected political systems had been brought, or forced, into a kind of global commons.[4] Many observers, most famously Immanuel Kant, though not unmoved by the violence that accompanied the creation of that commons, saw in its emergence a hopeful sign: the first flowering of a better world to come.[5] By the mid-twentieth century, however, such optimism came under intense pressure. Human-generated violence

---

sensibilities are stretched and fitted to a complex, indeterminate, vital world by the application of methodology. Like Thomas Kuhn, I understand paradigms to be "normalized" research programs in which incommensurable fact-value consensuses harden into disciplinary divisions. Like Robert Merton, my use of the term is as much critical as constructive: to "bring out into the open air…the assumptions, concepts and basic propositions" of a given theoretical construct (Merton [1963], p. 13). Compare to more formal borrowings: Lijphart (1974) with regard to Kuhn, and Allison (1971) with regard to Merton. On the term's contested nature, see Jackson and Nexon (2009).

My use of the term *tradition* draws idiosyncratically on the work of Larry Laudan (1977, 1996) and R. B. J. Walker (1992). Like Laudan, I see a tradition as consisting of "a set of beliefs about what sorts of entities and processes make up the domain of inquiry"; unlike him, however, I hold these to be distinct from "epistemic and methodological norms about how the domain is to be investigated" (1996, p. 83; see also 1977, pp. 71–72 and 78ff.). Also problematically for the present work, Laudan's approach makes no firm distinction between scientific pursuits and nonscientific ones (1977, pp. 13–15, 79–80, 104–105, 189–192, and ch. 7; 1996, p. 85); in particular—given the concerns of international theory—he seems unconcerned with the problem of mass violence and the ways in which a particular scientific tradition might interconnect with, or serve, agendas that rely on or justify such violence. On this point, Walker's (1992) observations as to the existence of normative carryovers between "theories of international relations" and "other areas of social and political enquiry" through which a "universalist aspiration is…entwined with the legitimation of domination" (29) are crucial. Traditions, as argued here, are *always* normative at bottom. This being so, the question then becomes: what ought we to do, given our reliance on them to make sense of world politics?

3. Wendt (2001). See also Smith (1995).

4. Deudney (2007), ch. 1; Buzan and Little (2000), especially part 4. See also Arrighi (1994), McNeill (1982), Parker (1996), Rosenberg (1994), Sassen (2006), Spruyt (1994), Teschke (2003), Tilly (1992), Wallerstein (1974), Wolf (1997), and Van Creveld (1999). For the term *global commons*, see Posen (2003) and Morse (1977); more distantly, Hardin (1968) and Schelling (1978), pp. 110–115.

5. See the essays in Kant (2001); also Doyle (1997), ch. 8, and Yovel (1980).

had, it seemed, outstripped its creative potential, threatening to destroy the commons rather than complete it.

Preventing such destruction would require active management. The job of IR—one might go so far as to call it a vocation—was to create the kind of practical, theoretically informed expertise by which to effect that sort of management: to build a cumulative reservoir of knowledge for stewarding an increasingly dense, heavily armed, and persistently diverse world, whether by the creation of new capabilities, institutions, or procedures.[6] The technical challenge of this effort has been considerable, owing to complicating material developments endemic to world politics since at least the middle of the twentieth century. These include an ever-growing global population with attendant problems of scarcity, poverty, and competition; an increasingly dense network of global interdependencies that create new and unanticipated points of friction and competition; and the growth and diffusion of the means for mass destruction. These same developments, however, also created new possible configurations of interest, community, and solidarity. The hope of IR theory as a practical, knowledge-building enterprise has been the possibility of learning to leverage the latter against the former, whether by preserving stable balances of power, crafting durable international institutions, or propagating peaceable international norms.[7]

Though this claim—that a sense of vocation unites the discipline of International Relations across the decades—may carry an odd ring to some contemporary theorists, it is neither new nor unprecedented. Since the Second World War, Ira Katznelson has argued, such "vocational" sensibilities have been shared across political science as a whole. "Scholar-sentinels" like Hannah Arendt, Karl Polanyi, Robert Dahl, Harold Lasswell, and Charles Lindblom "combined the deduction of politics from norms with its extrapolation from facts, affiliating engaged social criticism with disinterested social science to discover truth about how things work. Social science furnished their pathway to ethics."[8] Mid-century studies in political economy (Polanyi), totalitarianism (Arendt), urban politics and social welfare (Dahl and Lindblom), or power and social planning (Lasswell, Mannheim)

---

6. Wendt (2001), in the previously cited essay, refers to this as "steering," though he admits that this begs a series of near-imponderables: who should be steering the global order and toward what? On the notion of vocation employed here, see Barkawi (1998), Keohane (2009), Norton (2004), and Wolin (1972). Gunnell (2006), Strauss (2007), and Bender (1993) are also of interest.

7. Reus-Smit and Snidal (2008); Shapcott (2004).

8. Katznelson (2003), p. 3. See also Jackson (2008) and Prewitt (2009).

were driven by more than scholarly inquisitiveness. They sought to lay the foundations for a new political science, first imagined by Hegel but sharpened by the horrors of the early and mid-twentieth century.

Even if political scientists did not know precisely what to call that horror that animated their shared project (terms like "the Holocaust" were still some ways away, to say nothing of a consensual understanding of the events to which they alluded), they still knew that it was something to be avoided.[9] What Edward Hallett Carr called the "twenty years' crisis" amply illustrated both the dangers latent in industrial-era mass politics and how much work needed to be done if concepts of freedom drawn from earlier eras were to be reconciled to the unforgiving political and economic conditions to which it gave rise. Whatever their methodological differences, political science and political scientists—from Albert Hirschman to Harold Laski, from Friedrich Hayek's *Road to Serfdom* to Robert Dahl and Charles Lindblom's *Politics, Economics and Welfare* to Jürgen Habermas's *Structural Transformation of the Public Sphere*—largely shared these broad aims. Whatever critiques are to be made within it and of it, the traumas of contemporary history are deeply imprinted in the scholarly identity of political science: the need to contain what historian Alan Milward aptly called the "inherent fissile tendencies" of the late-modern European political system.[10]

International Relations was no different. Such concerns animated all its major traditions, from classical realism to communitarianism and neofunctionalism and the work of theorists as diverse as Hans Morgenthau, Carr, David Mitrany, Karl Deutsch, and Ernst Haas.[11] Even the numerous "second debate" theorists, lamenting the primitive state of IR theory and expressing a desire to replace its rambling tradition of "wisdom literature" (Acton, Bolingbroke, Treitschke) with scientific rigor, shared in

---

9. Haidu (1992); Kiernan (2007). Though this consensus is not without its critics, namely, Snyder (2009).

10. Milward (2000), p. 25; also Waever (1996), pp. 122–125. Or as Tony Judt (2005) explained: "Post-national, welfare-state, cooperative, pacific Europe was not born of the optimistic, ambitious, forward-looking project imagined in fond retrospect by today's Euro-idealists. It was the insecure child of anxiety. Shadowed by history, its leaders implemented social reforms and built new institutions as a prophylactic, to keep the past at bay" (p. 6). Compare to Mannheim, writing in 1940: "Those who have first-hand knowledge of the crisis [in which Western states and societies find themselves], even if they are keen opponents of dictatorship, are united in the belief that both the social order and the psychology of human beings are changing through and through, and that if this is an evil it is an evil that is bound to spread. They are convinced moreover that we should not let ourselves be duped by this momentary lull, but should use it to acquire the new techniques, without which it is impossible to face the new situation" (pp. 3–4).

11. On classical realism, see the lengthy discussion in chapter 3. For a discussion of postnational liberalism beginning with Mitrany, Carr's "utopian" writings, Deutsch, and Haas, see chapters 4 and 5.

it.[12] Scientific methods were not adopted for their own sake; they reflected a deeply humanistic desire to play a role in the postwar reconstructive project, to plumb the depths "of the crater which is yawning beneath our western society."[13] To paint, as some critics have, all of neopositivist IR with the same brush—as either an organized scholarly conspiracy to suppress "welling transnationalist outcries" by means of the "scientifically inscrutable ideological connotations" of structuralism, or as evidence of scholars' fascination for "puzzles" at the expense of "problems"—is to overlook this.[14] Following Katznelson, it is to perpetuate the most widespread of intradisciplinary fallacies: that the gap between "speculative, semi-philosophical, brooding texts" and "doggedly empirical, social science treatises" is so vast "that they inhabit separate universes."[15] It is also to forget the role such knowledge plays in very real improvements in the human condition. For good or ill, the last of Marx's *Theses* aptly describes the vocation to which IR theory has aspired, in both its normative and positive inflections not to merely understand the world but also to change it.[16] As Robert Keohane noted: "we study politics not because it is beautiful or easy to understand, but because it is so important to all fields of human endeavor"; there is no neutrality "with respect to order vs. chaos [or] war vs. peace."[17] And for David Lake, IR scholarship includes the duty to, if possible, "identify levers that when manipulated can facilitate progress toward more humane and normatively desirable ends." This, he avers, is society's due: payback for the "relatively prosperous and ... desirable lifestyle" accorded the academic.[18]

Critique and the Loss of Vocation

If so, then a degree of consensus surrounding the ultimate aims of IR theory can be assumed: "the search for peace, the maintenance of order, the avoidance

---

12. The term *wisdom literature* is Riker's (1972), p. viii. See, for example, the essays in Fox (1959), Knorr and Rosenau (1969), Wight and Bull (1966), and Wolfers (1962), as well as Hoffmann (1958–59, 1977), Deutsch (1960, 1971), Morgenthau (1967a), Bull (1966), and Kaplan (1966).

13. Mannheim (1940), p. 5.

14. Ashley (1984), p. 232; on this point, see Navon (2001). This holds even if one acknowledges, with Crawford, a sustained effort to marginalize these critiques: "not taking Ashley seriously has become a bit of an industry in its own right." Here cited in Hamati-Ataya (2011b), p. 270. On the problems/puzzles distinction, see Mosser (2010).

15. Katznelson (2003), p. 117; also Shepsle (2009) and Deutsch (1971).

16. Cox (2008).

17. Keohane (2009), pp. 362–363.

18. Lake (2011), p. 465.

of war and the establishment of community."[19] Yet even so, basic divisions existed within the discipline. "Our...modern mentors in IR theory," noted Ernst and Peter Haas, "did not differ over values: realists and idealists preferred peace to war, life to death, wealth to poverty. They differed over the question of freedom of the will, or what we now call the agency-structure problem."[20] That is, the basic divisions among the theoretical traditions in IR persisted owing to basic assumptions that were essentially metaphysical in nature: irrefutable in one another's terms and both logically and morally incommensurate.[21] What is freedom? What rights appertain to it? What is the good life?

Given these basic divisions, practical reason could not suffice on its own. To live up to its vocation, students of international theory have long realized, IR's practical, theory- and knowledge-building effort would require a parallel effort in the opposite direction: a set of practices for reflecting on the interconnections between facts and values in international theory. Absent this second—critical-reflexive—form of theory, any one line of practical reason would naturally reify into social domination, notwithstanding the intentions of its promulgators. This is the thesis that Theodor Adorno and Max Horkheimer first set out in the *Dialectic of Enlightenment* (1947): "Enlightenment, understood in the widest sense as the advancement of thought, has always aimed at liberating human beings from fear and installing them as masters."[22] Yet mastery had not in fact liberated humanity from fear; "the wholly enlightened earth" had become "radiant with triumphant calamity."[23] Practical theory, it turned out, had unanticipated real-world effects when not chastened by critique. Its priests and advocates in the academy—consciously or otherwise, willingly or otherwise—had been partners in catastrophe.

The relationship of the dialectic of enlightenment thesis to IR theory is complex and is set out in some detail in chapter 1. Its basic outline, however, can be compactly summarized. In constructing theories about world politics, IR has drawn on traditions of normative social and political thought that came to maturity in nineteenth-century Europe, traditions such as nationalism, liberalism, Marxism, and corporatism. For theorists writing in the immediate

---

19. Jarvis (2000), p. 12.

20. Haas and Haas (2002), p. 581.

21. Bleiker (2000).

22. Adorno and Horkheimer (2002), p. 1.

23. Adorno and Horkheimer (2002), p. 1.

aftermath of the Second World War, this inheritance posed a problem, for each of these traditions had shown both its insufficiency in the face of twentieth-century challenges and its potential to reify into murderously total-itarian "coercive utopias."[24] The very worldviews that had brought humanity to catastrophe were now, clothed in new scholarly-theoretical idiom, expected to keep it *from* catastrophe. It seemed to be impossible to think—whether as a theorist or as a practitioner—about world politics except by reifying some normative prism or another whose historical legacy was deeply suspect: real-ism had ties to realpolitik, nationalism, and hypernationalism; laissez-faire liberalism had ties to social upheaval at home and imperialism abroad; and the humanism of early Marxist thought did not undo its complicity, even as a perversion of itself, in the terrors of Stalin.[25] A by-product of both theory in the "covering law" tradition and conceptual thinking more generally, reifica-tion is not unique to such late-modern problems or concerns.[26] However, the conditions that complicated world politics at mid-century rendered it more acutely problematic in the context of IR theory than in studies of domestic

---

24. A useful interim definition (more on this later) of *reification* can be found in Berger and Luckmann (1967), p. 89: "the apprehension of the products of human activity *as if* they were something other than human products—such as facts of nature, results of cosmic laws, or man-ifestations of divine will. Reification implies that man is capable of forgetting his own author-ship of the human world, and further, that the dialectic between man, the producer, and his products, is lost to consciousness." To this should be added a second meaning, drawing upon Marion Levy (1969): "the confusion of analytical structures with concrete structures...what one ordinarily distinguishes as aspects of an object with the parts of the object. We would commit it with regard to the physical universe if we referred to the shape and mass of a table as though those aspects were in no way different from the top or the legs of the table" (p. 99). The term *coercive utopias* comes from Brzezinski (1993).

25. Carr (1964): "Every political judgment helps to modify the facts on which it is passed. Political thought is itself a form of political action. Political science is the science not only of what is, but of what ought to be" (p. 5).

26. By "covering law" theory, I mean social-scientific approaches in which a phenomenon to be explained is "deduced from a set of premises that includes a universal law" (Glynos and Howarth [2007], p. 21). Also Hollis (1994), Hollis and Smith (1991), Chernoff (2005, 2007), and Jackson (2010). By "late modernity," I mean several things at once. Like Anthony Giddens and Ulrich Beck, my usage fuses multiple "classic" narratives of modernization: as a process in which capitalism, industrialization, rationalization, market economics, and "civilizational processes" (à la Norbert Elias and Freud) are together radically transforming human existence. Also like Beck and Giddens, I understand late-modern life to be predi-cated on a sense of the constantly changing and the permanently unfinished. My usage here, however, places a particular emphasis on shared anguish or solemnity; there is a *mourning quality* to late modernity. It is that era in which the entire world has become subject to human agency and human shortsightedness and in which the dangers of that subjection have become generally—albeit hazily and inconsistently—understood. For a compact sur-vey of these themes, see Heaphy (2007); for a sprawling one, see Berman (1982), especially pp. 290–312.

politics.[27] This, in turn, complicated the discipline's ability to make good on its vocational aspirations.

How and to what degree particular IR theorists were aware of the specific arguments and peculiar idiom of the *Dialectic of Enlightenment* may be debated.[28] Not so its more general sensibilities, which were widely shared throughout twentieth-century social and political theory. No less a figure than Max Weber, one of the objects of Adorno and Horkheimer's critique, expressed a variant of them in the closing lines of "Science as a Vocation," more than two decades before the publication of the *Dialectic*.[29] Obscured by a reliance on prophetic language drawn from the book of Isaiah, this aspect of Weber's thought is easily overlooked:

> He calleth to me out of Seir, Watchman, what of the night? The watchman said, The morning cometh, and also the night: if ye will enquire, enquire ye: return, come.[30]

The "night" to which Isaiah referred was the long night of Israel's exile, whose redemption was God's promise: the reward of those who kept their faith even in its darkest hours. For Weber, it was the long night of traditional and

---

27. Mitrany (1975b): "Today we are in the early stages of a wholly new political society .... The situation is new but the ideological ingredients are those laid down by democratic liberalism and Marxism, both products of the social transition of the nineteenth century... it is all a battle of ideologies drained of ideas: no concepts fresh to our time, no political theory to have absorbed and make sense of the new problems and conditions" (p. 27). See also Carr (1942, 1945). Catastrophic, hyperviolent conflict is not in any sense unique to late modernity, as Bell (2007); Gat (2006), ch. 6; and the figures in Luard (1987, p. 247) show. It is rather the confluence of ideology, despair, and mass destruction that is so terrifying. In late modernity, ideologies command the loyalty they do despite, or even in part because of, their apparent bankruptcy.

28. Direct connections are few but important. Morgenthau spent time in Frankfurt and recalled attending seminars at Horkheimer's Institute for Social Research. While he later dismissed their seminars as "futile hair-splitting," his biographer suggests that their debates had a formative effect on the young scholar. See Morgenthau (1984), pp. 13–14; Frei (2001), pp. 38–39; and, more broadly, Scheuerman (2009b). Carr's link to this scholarship comes from his interest in Mannheim's *Ideology and Utopia*; on this point, see Gismondi (2004) and Jones (1998), ch. 6. A less direct connection is through Carl Schmitt. In addition to Morgenthau's (1933) extended discussion of the "concept of the political" and his "hidden dialogue" (Scheuerman: 1999, 2007a) with Schmitt, Herz (1959) includes an extended theorization based on the *Nomos of the Earth*. For surveys tracing the influence of Frankfurt School scholarship in the United States, see Jay (1973/1996, 1984b), Jenemann (2007), Wheatland (2009), and Wiggershaus (1994).

29. For a detailed comparative reading of Weber's disenchantment thesis and the *Dialectic of Enlightenment*, see Habermas (1984–87), Vol. 1, pp. 345–365.

30. Weber (1958a), p. 156. Weber is paraphrasing from Isaiah 21:11–12.

charismatic forms of tyranny, from which reason had promised to liberate mankind. Yet note the ambivalence of the prophecy: even when the "morning" of reason comes, still it shall be "night"! The ever more rationalized society was proving no less oppressive than what it was replacing. Dislocation, anomie, and exploitation were spreading. Many had already retreated from reason, into the arms of old superstitions or new ideologies. "The people to whom this [prophecy] was said," Weber noted, speaking of the ancient Israelites and their descendants, "has enquired and tarried for more than two millennia, and we are shaken when we realize its fate."[31] Weber, it will be recalled, died in 1920. The fate to which he refers is not the gas chambers, but collective dispossession: the "Jewish Question" in its liberal-nationalist nineteenth-century variant, not its genocidal twentieth-century one. He was issuing a warning: that modern society risked turning its members into a tribe of latter-day exiles, wandering the deserts of disenchantment.[32] It would not do to wait patiently as the Israelites had done: these dangers demanded purposeful but also reflective action.[33]

It should not therefore be surprising that IR theorists like Morgenthau, Mitrany, John Herz, Stanley Hoffmann, and Carr appreciated both theory's positive and critical moments and understood that each was needed to temper the other.[34] Hans Morgenthau's work testifies to this dual appreciation with particular clarity. On the one hand, *Politics among Nations* offered "six principles of political realism." On the other, Morgenthau affirmed that "politics [was] an art, and not a science," which "yield[ed] only to that intricate combination of moral and material pressures which the art of the statesman create[d] and maintain[ed]."[35] Thus was an analytical-deductive sensibility matched to a synthetic, morally reflective one: the quality of drawing eclectically upon distinctive normative-political traditions, with an eye to balancing fact-value constructions against one another.[36]

---

31. Weber (1958a), p. 156.

32. See also Weber's notion of "iron cage" in (1958b), pp. 181–182; also Gismondi (2004) and Freund (1968), pp. 17–24.

33. On this point, see the essays in Jaspers (1989).

34. See Williams (2005, 2007), Lebow (2003), and Craig (2003) on Morgenthau; M. Cox (2000), Jones (1998), and Haslam (1999) on Carr; and Ashley (1981) on Herz.

35. Respectively, Morgenthau (1967b), p. 4, and (1946), p. 10.

36. Morgenthau (1966): "While political science must thus come to terms with the problems of power, it must adapt its emphasis to the ever-changing circumstances of the times. When the times tend to depreciate the elements of power, it must stress its importance. When the times incline toward a monistic conception of power in the general scheme of things, it must show its limitations. When the times conceive of power primarily in military terms, it must

Yet despite both awareness of and appreciation for critique, a sustained balance between theory's positive and critical moments would prove elusive. Although the positive, knowledge-building side of IR flourished, its critical-reflexive side grew only in irregular fits and starts. A space for critique had been *posited*, but it could not be *sustained*—there was nothing onto which it could anchor. Certainly, there have been moments of critical introspection within IR theory as regards the reification of particular facts and values. The various "great debates" in IR can be understood in retrospect as moments when contestation over particular such reifications has come to a head. However, these have been intermittent in duration, and inconsistent with regard to depth. Viewed over six decades, IR theory has striven unceasingly toward greater analytical sophistication but has turned to critical self-account only hesitantly, eclectically, and irregularly. Morgenthau himself was as responsible for this as anyone. "A political science which is true to its moral commitment," he wrote in 1955, "ought at the very least to be an unpopular undertaking."[37] Such Delphic pronouncements beg more questions than they answer. "Unpopularity" is hardly a stable perch for critique, unless one can show that all popular positions are perforce demotic and that all dissident ones are virtuous.

Stanley Hoffmann's still widely read critique of IR as an "American social science" showed a similar lacuna. "The discipline of international relations is...too close to the fire," he argued. It needed "triple distance": moving away "from the contemporary, toward the past; from the perspective of a super-power...toward that of the weak and the revolutionary...; from the glide into policy science, back to the steep ascent toward...traditional political philosophy."[38] Hoffmann would locate IR among a cluster of ideas, values, and principles—in Adornian-Weberian terms, a *constellation* in which each element both informs and constrains the others.[39] "This would...be a way of putting the fragments into which the discipline explodes, if not together, at

---

call attention to the variety of factors which go into the power equation.... When the reality of power is being lost sight of over its moral and legal limitations, it must point to that reality. When law and morality are judged as nothing, it must assign them their rightful place" (p. 77). Here cited from Lebow (2003), p. 238.

37. Morgenthau (1955), p. 446. See also Morgenthau (1967a), p. 213, and Cozette (2008).

38. Hoffmann (1977) p. 59; here cited from Vitalis (2005). See also Crawford and Jarvis (2001).

39. As shall become apparent, *constellation* is a term of art both in this work and in Adornian-inflected critical theory generally: following Martin Jay, it denotes "a juxtaposed rather than integrated cluster of changing elements that resist reduction to a common denominator, essential core, or generative first principle" (here from Bernstein (1991), p. 8). Its application here, however, is mine, rather than Hoffmann's. A noteworthy earlier attempt to combine constellar

least in perspective."⁴⁰ The idea is intriguing, but Hoffmann does not follow up on it: *how* might this be done, in practice? Similar calls have been reiterated many times, both before and since: by Charles Beard in the 1920s and recently in Monteiro and Ruby's call for an "IR without foundations" and Markus Kornprobst's call for an ever-renewing "rhetorical discipline."⁴¹ Yet to argue the need for a thing is not the same as setting out its intellectual conditions of possibility.⁴²

Admittedly, sustaining a balance between practical and reflexive theory is difficult. International Relations works with static concepts that posit implicit ontologies within which they work and to which they refer. How can such thinking be rendered "without foundations"? Over the past decades, theorists as varied as Arnold Wolfers, Barry Buzan, Jens Bartelson, Chris Brown, Raymond Duvall and Michael Barnett, Daniel Deudney, Robert Gilpin, Bill McSweeney, David Baldwin, Stefano Guzzini, Ben Rosamond, and Jef Huysmans have acknowledged this difficulty, suggesting that various core concepts in IR, like security and power, are in some sense "essentially contested"—indefinable without smuggling in some kind of ideological and/ or metaphysical baggage and implicated in various forms of political work.⁴³ If that is true, the ramifications are profound. It implies that all IR theory is in some sense ideologically or politically agentic—that it does partisan work. This, in turn, implies obligations on the part of the theorist to systematic self-disclosure, for—here quoting Keohane and Nye—"academic pens leave marks in the minds of statesmen, with profound results for policy."⁴⁴ The

---

thinking and IR may be found in Wyn Jones (2001). That said, the application to which the constellation is put in the present work differs from Wyn Jones materially. This point is made at length in chapter 2.

40. Hoffmann (1977), p. 59.

41. Beard (1927): "We do not know whether man, long the victim of natural forces and many delusions, can emancipate himself from the involution of life and environment...and assume the Jovian role of interpreter and director. But perhaps it will not be amiss to bring together in a kind of mosaic some of the ideas that lie scattered in broken fragments in the path of experience" (pp. 9–10). See Monteiro and Ruby (2009a, 2009b), Kornprobst (2009) and *infra* Hellmann (2009).

42. On Monteiro and Ruby, see Bohman (2009), Chernoff (2009), Jackson (2009), and Mercado (2009); more generally, see Hamati-Ataya (2011b).

43. Ayoob (1995), Bartelson (1998), Baldwin (1997), Brown (1994), Buzan (1991), Dalby (1997), Deudney (1990), Barnett and Duvall (2005), Gilpin (1984, 1996), Guzzini (2005), Huysmans (1998), McSweeney (1999), Rosamond (2000), pp. 4–9, Waever (1995, 1996), and Wolfers (1962). The term *essentially contested concepts* originates in Gallie (1955–56), as read by Connolly (1983).

44. Keohane and Nye (1977), p. 4.

theorist of world politics might be forgiven for believing that she is forced to choose between the Scylla of smuggling in ideological or otherwise tendentious views under the guise of value-free social science and the Charybdis of retreating into the technically recondite or the morally otherworldly.[45]

Moving past this point, however, will not be accomplished merely by the periodic rediscovery and refurbishment of forgotten methodologies: turning away from rational choice to rediscover interpretive language games or lifeworlds or from neoliberal theories of the state as an economic firm to studies emphasizing states' socially constructed and/or historically contingent institutional development. Certainly, these are all valuable perspectives, with each capturing important aspects of a reality that confounds simple cause-and-effect explanations. But though emerging from critiques of past orthodoxies, the research programs in IR to which they have given rise are not themselves *sustainably critical*. Critique is not merely something to be directed outward, against specific value constructs that particular IR theorists may dislike. It must also be directed *inward*, against the limitations of thought itself: addressing not merely *particular* reifications, but reification *as such*. When critique fails in this latter aspect, it cannot sustain itself over time. It becomes merely an extension of practical reason, a means by which one partisan agenda hacks away at competing ones. *IR needs forms of critique in which theory's ideologically agentic nature is accepted even as theorists continue to strive for "value freedom."*

This calls, admittedly, for a degree of theoretical doublethink: a kind of conceptual shotgun wedding. Uncomfortable though this may be, however, it cannot be avoided: the need for it inheres in the contradictions that arise from attempting to conceptualize politics. World politics in the late-modern era admits of—even if it must never be entirely reduced to—the specter of catastrophic violence: "what for political theory is the extreme case (as revolution or civil war) is for international theory the regular case."[46] As such, these problematics carry with them what the theorists of the C.A.S.E. collective have termed "a special kind of responsibility."[47] A sustainably critical IR would address itself to living up to that responsibility. "Critique would not have the power to break up false consciousness if it were not impelled by a *passion for critique*," observed Jürgen Habermas in 1971.[48] Yet that passion must

---

45. Wendt and Friedheim (1995), p. 695.

46. Here in Koskenniemi (2002), p. 466. The original quotation is attributed to Martin Wight.

47. C.A.S.E. Collective (2006), p. 473.

48. Habermas (1971), p. 234; here cited from Bernstein (1976), p. 201; emphasis as in Bernstein.

neither blind itself to the possibility of new reifications and acts of exclusion nor become a basis for its own transcendent counterorthodoxies. This holds *even as* the potential for the practical study of global justice, human rights, economic development, and new forms of community is to be acknowledged, and the growing prominence of these areas in the discipline celebrated. As well as methodologies, then, ethics constitutes a necessary term in this equation.

This book aims to develop a basis for sustaining such a form of "double-think," working in three steps. First, I aim to *exhume* those moments of critical reflexivity that have always been present in international theory, whether in its speculative, interpretive, or positivist articulations. That is, I aim to show that *consensus on the need for critical reflexivity has long existed and that such consensus spans the gap between avowedly normative and ostensibly value-free international theory*. To do that, I find and unpack moves or gestures toward such reflexivity from a broad array of theoretical traditions and research programs and strip them of the divergent and often incompatible idioms that too often conceal them. Second, I seek to *identify* trends, moments, and dynamics that frustrate such gestures: if the aforementioned consensus exists, *why does the discipline seem to be constantly debating it*? Why have students of IR so little to show for their efforts? The answer lies in tendencies that are specific to conceptual theory and its problematic interaction with politics; these must be identified. Third, I aim to *lay a foundation* for sustaining critical reflexivity within IR theory: developing new research practices, with an eye toward the discipline's historic sense of vocation and with fresh awareness of the challenges that sensibility faces.

The first two of these aims shall be met by two sets of arguments, working in tandem. First, in chapters 1 and 2, the challenges facing sustainable critique are set out in broad theoretical and philosophical terms. *Calling* for sustainable critique cannot succeed on its own, I mean to suggest; the conditions of its intellectual possibility must also be considered, and problems bracketed or overcome. Close rereadings of three major traditions in IR follow in chapters 3 through 5. I hope to demonstrate in concrete terms how those challenges have foiled past attempts: why critique has proven difficult to sustain (despite near-universal understanding of the need for it) and how this difficulty has affected IR's ability to meet its larger vocational aspirations.

My third aim, building on the pincerlike action of those two sets of arguments, is more amorphous but also more ambitious. Drawing on insights from postwar classical Frankfurt School theory, and in particular from a reexamination of the writings of Theodor Adorno, I argue that a free-standing faculty of critique within international theory is both possible and needed.

Following this, I set out basic values and concepts on which such critique might be sustained. The ultimate aim, begun in this work but not confined to it, is an approach to IR in which normative reflexivity is as sustained, rigorous, and intellectually uncompromising as practical theory building, in which knowledge building and critical self-reflection coexist *in real time*. Put another way, I aim to sustain *both* critique *and* practical theory in the same intellectual moment. Each, I mean to show, has a continuous, ongoing need for the other. This is not a postfoundational form of IR so much as an attempt to balance foundationalisms against one another. A first cut of this approach is set out in the later sections of chapter 2, using existing approaches in IR as a model. The conclusion returns to it at greater length.

The remainder of this chapter develops these aims, explains them conceptually, and then lays out the plan of the subsequent chapters. It proceeds in four key moves. First, the notion of sustainable critique is developed through a broad conceptual discussion of reification and a discussion of why methodological debates in IR theory cannot, on their own, meet the dangers reification poses. Following this, I offer a 'rogues' gallery' of the forms reification has taken in contemporary international theory. I do so with an eye to how the dominant fact-value traditions of IR, on the one hand, and the dominant methodological approaches on the other have combined to make reification's potential dangers difficult to both see and check. Third, I develop a conceptual ideal-type of my own—chastened reason—as a kind of idealized mind-set by which a sustainably critical approach to international theory might be possible.[49] Finally, I survey the coming chapters of the book, laying out the theoretical account of reification detailed in chapters 1 and 2, the case studies of it developed in chapters 3 through 5, and the possibility of adapting Adorno's concept of a constellation to the problem of managing it in the conclusion.

Sustainable Critique (1): The Problem of Reification

The concept of reification, central to this project, requires some additional elucidation before the path to sustainable critique can be cleared. Social sciences describe human-constructed realities through analogies, whose artificiality is progressively naturalized—lost to intellectual understanding and theoretical consideration—until they come finally to appear "as facts of nature, results of cosmic laws, or manifestations of divine will."[50] Different moments in

---

49. This notion of chastening owes much to Flathman (1993).

50. Berger and Luckmann (1967), p. 89. See also Marks (2011).

theorizing, as chapters 3 through 5 show, set out to undo or criticize an existing theoretical or political common sense, combining long-standing fact-value traditions (captured in IR by the traditions of realism, liberalism, and the like but drawn from normative political-theory traditions of much older vintage) with particular methodological approaches to produce paradigmatic research programs. Each does so by positing its own particular reifications in distinction to others; over time, these, too, are lost to intellectual understanding and theoretical consideration. Assumptions that emerged in dynamic interaction with and in response to a changing political and scholarly reality take on the qualities of received wisdom. They thus come to be conflated with the world they were meant to describe—"merge[d] with the world of nature," as Berger and Luckmann put it, equated with things-in-themselves that cannot disclose themselves otherwise.[51]

The term *reification* itself has a complicated heritage. Its usage here derives from Karl Marx's notion of commodity fetishism and from the subsequent work of Hungarian Marxist theorist Georg Lukács.[52] Yet as Gillian Rose has observed, the term has "no canonical source, and has become prominent and debased as much by insinuation as by scrupulous examination."[53] Certainly, contemporary social-scientific and social-theoretic usages vary widely. Deployed loosely, it often appears as a synonym for a class of logical conflations akin to Alfred North Whitehead's "fallacy of misplaced concreteness."[54] Yet that looseness, Timothy Bewes has recently noted, has an ironic effect: it renders the term "susceptible to the problem it denotes"; reification takes on precisely the sort of pseudoscientific agency that its promulgators ostensibly meant to critique.[55]

Here, reification is construed as a highly particular kind of forgetting: of the distinction between theoretical concepts and the real-world things they mean to describe or to which they refer.[56] All theory—including this

---

51. Berger and Luckmann (1967), p. 91.

52. See Marx (1976), pp. 163–177, and Lukács (1971). Also Arato and Breines (1979); Goldmann (1976), chs. 2–3; Ollman (1971), pp. 198–204; Parkinson (1977), pp. 55–57; and West (1991), ch. 6.

53. Rose (1978), p. 28.

54. Whitehead (1925): "the accidental error of mistaking the abstract for the concrete" (pp. 74–75; see also pp. 85–86; Thompson [1997]; Whitehead [1978], pp. 7–8; and Marcuse [1964], chs. 8–9). For examples of such usage (in economics, race, and sociology, respectively), see Bernard (1995), Duster (2005), and the "reification" entry in Scott and Marshall (2009).

55. Bewes (2002), p. 3.

56. Adorno and Horkheimer (2002): "Loss of memory is the transcendental condition of science. All reification is forgetting" (p. 191).

one—relies to some degree on such forgetting, as it inheres in the particular ways in which the former can, and cannot, adequately describe the latter. Yet that forgetting has a distinctive chain of potential analytical and normative effects. The sanctity of sentient life is frequently an unintended casualty of it; left to its own devices, reification "thingifies" sentient beings, blurring the moral separations traditionally made between them and inanimate objects. The same intellectual process that transforms a stand of trees into lumber or a hilltop into coal—that is, transforms them into fungible commodities or factors in economic production—can transform human beings as well: men and women become *labor* in economic terms or *force assets* in military-strategic ones. The "instruments or means of thought," initially meant to pave the road to human betterment, thereby "become independent of the purpose of thought."[57]

This process of forgetting has distinctive consequences for IR, given the vocation earlier described for it. Theory's reliance on reification suggests that theorists are not merely *describing* the world when they fit complex events into paradigmatic research traditions. Rather, they are *redacting* it. As King, Keohane, and Verba observe:

> Even the most comprehensive description done by the best cultural interpreters with the most detailed contextual understanding will drastically simplify, reify, and reduce the reality that has been observed....No description, no matter how thick...comes close to capturing the full "blooming and buzzing" reality of the world.[58]

Given the proximity of IR's policy analyses to the use of extreme and deadly force, this reliance upon "drastic simplification and reduction" presents a dilemma.[59] Without it, there would be no hope of creating practical knowledge, no hope of intelligently stewarding a world that presents real and abiding challenges.[60] Yet with it, one risks naturalizing the ontological assumptions of

---

57. Adorno (2000), p. 76. See also Horkheimer (2004), pp. 14–15.

58. King, Keohane, and Verba (1994), p. 43, here cited from Sil (2004), pp. 313–314. "Thick description" is from Clifford Geertz.

59. Adorno (1973) "Coming to light in this is the fact that subjectification and reification do not simply diverge. They are correlates.... The reduction of the object to pure material, which precedes all subjective syntheses as its necessary condition, sucks the subject's own dynamics out of it: it is disqualified, immobilized and robbed of whatever would allow motion to be predicated at all" (p. 91).

60. Goldmann (1976): "Professional skill is one domain where a rather high minimal level of intellectual life is absolutely essential to the functioning of society" (p. 48).

particular fact-value traditions and their derived scholarly research programs, such that these take on an "objective" imprimatur. Theory, it would seem, can live neither with reification nor without it. Some mode of managing or checking its effects must therefore be found, if IR's historic vocation is to be made good upon.

Such management requires a shift in the way in which IR theorists do their work. Even conceding the field's growing commitment to both scholarly pluralism and normative theory, existing forms of academic discourse and dialogue are insufficient.[61] The norms of the academy are such that, once having achieved a certain degree of intellectual achievement, theorists write and research according to their own scholarly-normative lights. A variety of shorter and longer term processes of give-and-take, most notably peer review and open debate, are trusted to shake out errors of all sorts.[62] This image of a grand conversation runs deep in scholarly tradition and self-understanding, part of the labor of love by which the isolation of research and writing can be sustained as theorists rework recalcitrant drafts and mountains of data. It is also part of the way in which disciplines and subdisciplines self-organize.

Their other virtues notwithstanding, however, such processes do not serve as sufficient critical firebreak for the dangers of unchecked reification, given the potential for contemporary world politics to rapidly produce extreme destruction. Theory remains the "slow drilling of hard boards." The speed at which late modern politics proceeds stands in sharp relief against the pace of such work. It places IR theorists before a dilemma: either work on the fly—uncritically perpetuating the reifications of an existing discourse—or confine themselves to purely technical (or else morally otherworldly) questions at the

---

61. On the growing pluralism of IR and the hopes attached to such pluralism, see Snidal and Wendt (2009) and the essays in Reus-Smit and Snidal (2008). On the problems attached to such pluralism, Koskenniemi (2002) is nonpareil: "The interdisciplinary call cannot be divorced from the *kinds* of sociology and ethics that are being advocated. The suggested sociology is always already normatively loaded, and loaded so as to underwrite the constellation already produced through power" (pp. 488–9, emphasis in original).

62. On this point in IR, see Cox (1996a), pp. 144–146. For a broader social-scientific phrasing, Diesing (1991) is nonpareil. "How can a [scholarly] community maintain a middle ground? The basis for a healthy science is (1) a definite social interest and commitment, including political action, plus (2) some detachment and self-skepticism, and (3) some moderate professionalism.... A community with a shared concern maintains itself by emphasizing a collective research process" (pp. 353–354). Diesing is correct insofar as he goes: academia exists to *slow down ideas*; to subject them to ponderous reflection through various means and methods. Perhaps, he suggests, academia itself needs to slow down, if it is to discharge the social functions expected of it. Well and good, but how this is to be done? To declare the need for a thing is not the same as defining a means by which to do it. IR is "fast" for a reason.

margins. Nonacademic discourse, too, suffers from this state of affairs, and many have considered what this means for policy making.[63] The present work does so inwardly for IR, as a discipline that is ethically accountable to itself and to the multiple and overlapping social, economic, and political communities within which its practitioners live and work. Owing to the particular nature of what they do and the era in which they do it, the vocation of IR requires tools by which theorists can critique *themselves in real time*, that *internalize* dialogue and debate. The absence of such tools has made critique harder to sustain, and with it, that longer term vocation.

The present work does not, then, advance a theory of international relations in the widely accepted sense of this term.[64] Sustainable critique is a philosophical-normative sensibility: a set of ideas about thinking, superimposed onto an understanding of the material conditions in which world politics is nested. It assumes that social science is profoundly limited in its ability to make sense of the political world, notwithstanding the demand for the knowledge it produces. Given this limitation, and given the connections between the academic study of IR and the real-world deployment of deadly (sometimes even catastrophically deadly) force, sustainable critique holds first, that students of IR have particular ethical obligations to reflective self-regard, and second, that fostering such self-regard can give their work a new kind of purchase. It thus combines the explicit normativity and sense of political urgency that characterized post-1945 classical realism with the deep skepticism and "dissident" sensibilities that animate critical, feminist, and postpositivist IR's discussions of the normative and methodological deficits of the existing theoretical mainstream.[65]

---

63. See, inter alia, Bauman (1998), Castells (2000), Connolly (2002, 2005), Deibert (1999), Harvey (1990), Rosa (2003), Scheuerman (2005), Sennett (1998), Virilio (1986), and Wolin (1997). On war in this context, there is, of course, an enormous literature, from the futuristic (Toffler and Toffler [1993]), to the technical (Owens [2001], O'Hanlon [2000], Rumsfeld [2002], Arquilla and Ronfeldt [1997]), to the critical-sociological and historical (Latham [2002], Der Derian [1992, 2001], Moskos et al. [2000], Van Creveld [2007]). An older line of thinking is captured in Wright (1942/1965), pp. 3–4, and passim.

64. That is, it is not a theory in the sense that Raymond Aron (1967) explained it: "a hypothetical, deductive system consisting of a group of hypotheses whose terms are strictly defined, and whose relationships…are most often given a mathematical form" (p. 186). But there is, Aron noted, a more ancient sense of the term that would suit present purposes: as observation and faithful representation of the affairs of the polis. In the Greek from which it is borrowed, a *theor* was an ambassador, or representative of another city-state, whose function was to bear witness to official events of public or ritualistic concern or interest. On this point, see also Habermas (1971), p. 301, and Deutsch (1971).

65. Glynos and Howarth (2007), p. 6. On "dissident" IR, see Ashley and Walker (1990) and Hamati-Ataya (2011a).

Asserting the limits of social science in politics and the role that ideas have in constituting the political realm does *not* deny the existence of a world that is antecedent to particular moments of human thought. It is not the political world's *unreality* that makes it so difficult to characterize without reification, but the particular quality of its *reality*: the essentially complex, interconnected, "lumpy" quality of real-world things that generalizing typologies so often and so easily elide, the fact that individuals encounter that world as a unitary given (even if it is constituted by human action in the aggregate), and the complex, stochastic way in which ideas become material.[66] Since the 1990s, this position has become increasingly well known to IR through "middle ground/*via media*" constructivism, neoclassical realism, feminist critical moral ethnographies, and a new generation of security studies that stresses complexity, history and contingency.[67] Yet in different ways, all of these have underestimated the extent to which the limitations of theory come into play in understanding political realities. This underestimation can be seen in ongoing attempts to use arguments drawn from the philosophy of science—from Karl Popper to Roy Bhaskar—to delimit a space for systematic inquiry into global politics to the effect that the world is multilayered and that some of those layers are either invisible to reason or resistant to it.[68] In themselves, such claims are correct. Some aspects of deep structure—whether linguistic, systemic, material, or ideational—are present in any complex thing and impede its analysis or comprehension by means of static or antecedently given conceptual schemas. To the extent that theory grows to accommodate these limitations, the knowledge it produces grows in nuance and sophistication.

---

66. The term *lumpy* in this sense I take from Sassen (2006), pp. 382–383; see also North (1990), p. 16.

67. On "middle ground" or "via media" constructivism, see Adler (1997), Dessler (1999), and Wendt (1999). On neoclassical IR, see Friedberg (1988), Lobell et al. (2009), Rose (1998), Schweller (2006), and Zakaria (1998). On feminist moral ethnographies, see Robinson (1999, 2006). On security studies, see Lyall and Wilson (2009) and Biddle (2004).

68. This, for example, is the argument made in Bhaskarian critical realist approaches to IR: see Joseph and Wight (2010), Kurki (2008), Patomäki (2002, 2003), Patomäki and Wight (2000), Wendt (1999), and Wight (2006); also see Brown (2007) and Lebow (2011) for partial rejoinders. Certainly, there is much in critical realism that parallels the approach outlined here; Bhaskar adopts Adorno's critique of identitarian thinking and marries it to what he calls "the epistemic fallacy" ("that ontological questions can always be reparsed in epistemological form"). What Bhaskar draws from this, moreover—his application of Lockean "underlaboring" and of the relationships between particular concrete forms of life and the reification of particular kinds of social or political theory—certainly aligns with I call chastened reason. But the sustainable critique would still suspect the claim that that "reality" can be reclaimed thereby, at least in the context of world politics; that an emancipatory pot of gold (or as Patomäki calls it, a "concrete utopia") can be squared with postfoundationalism. It seems to me—more on this later—that concepts like freedom and utopia are *always* absolutist in scope when used in the

Yet such methods need to go further. The complexity of politics differs from that of the natural world or the ontological instability of "social kinds" owing to "looping effects."[69] It is more than the randomness of friction;[70] more than the complexity captured by concepts like political ecology,[71] emergent properties, and system effects[72] or turbulence and "fragmegration."[73] Politics involves the struggle for power, and—as Machiavelli first explained—that has involved the knowing manipulation of falsehood, of appearances against realities. This is not lost on the crafty political entrepreneur, whether a sixteenth-century Italian prince, a World Bank or UN technocrat, or a grassroots activist who sees in new information technologies a way to leapfrog political borders.[74] Conceptual and discursive subterfuge and unequal access to information are *actively engaged* when political entrepreneurs do their work.[75]

In the face of this, appeals to philosophies of science or social science can go only so far.[76] The discovery attributed to Clausewitz by Carl Schmitt—that

context of sovereign politics and violent death. Bhaskar (1989), p. 13; on Bhaskar's approach to Adornian thinking, see Norrie (2000, 2003).

69. Hacking (1995), Wendt (1999), ch. 2.

70. Clausewitz (1984), pp. 119–120, 585, and passim.

71. Sprout and Sprout (1965).

72. Jervis (1997).

73. Rosenau (1997).

74. Machiavelli (1961); Sewell (1966), pp. 255–263, 320–332; Haas (1964), pp. 119–125; Finnemore (1996); Keck and Sikkink (1998). On this point, see Bernstein, Lebow, Stein, and Weber (2000). The family resemblance between their "scenario-based forward thinking" and sustainable critique should become apparent in the forthcoming.

75. Not without reason do King et al. (1994) specify that "[social] scientific research uses explicit, codified, and *public* methods to generate and analyze data whose reliability can therefore be assessed" (p. 8, emphasis in original). See also Brady and Collier (2004), pp. 22, 44–46. Compare to Wolin (2004): "The prevalence of illusions did not lead Machiavelli into a crusade for a science which would dispel them. Instead, the aim of the new science was to unmask those illusions which interfered with the proper ends of political action, and at the same time, to teach the political actor how to create and exploit the illusions which served those ends" (p. 191).

76. Hence Patomäki and Wight (2000, p. 223), citing Roy Bhaskar, note that all forms of social knowing presuppose their own ontologies. This is so, and the consequence is frequently that the full moral import of particular ontologies will not be apparent to those who deploy them "social-scientifically." But is that a problem of scientific *discovery* or of political *sagacity*? Both they and, before them, Guzzini (1993, pp. 446–447) have observed how Kuhnian "incommensurability" theses would become used by IR theorists to "legitimate...a stagnant conservatism" (Patomäki and Wight [2000], p. 226). But this is not a new observation. Richard Bernstein (1976, pp. 84–114) argued as much—well before the rise of neorealist IR—against the appropriations of Kuhnian thinking made by David Truman, Gabriel Almond, and Sheldon Wolin. Nor would it have surprised Popper: the core of his objection to Kuhnian paradigmatism was

war has no "brain" save for politics—runs very deeply indeed.[77] Part of the distinctiveness of international relations as a field of inquiry lies in the possibility that *political* relations are essentially different from *social* ones. For IR to be IR, that is, it may necessitate ideal-typical concepts of identity and difference that are more theological than rationalist and are bound up in transcendent yearnings that—as Weber noted—reason can undermine, but not ultimately satisfy.[78] If so, then in an important sense, although politics takes place *in* the world, it may not be *of the world*: its moral content may come from beyond. Any attempt to reduce it to scientific principles would simply drive such yearnings in new directions.

---

that, in positing science as a series of incommensurate fact-value constructions, "paradigms" were none other than the dreaded "historicist" Hegelianism, reentering politics through the "back door." Paradigms, Popper feared—a point aptly made by Elman and Elman (2002, p. 234)—would render claims in social science "unfalsifiable." This, in turn, would throw Popper's larger project—using "falsification" to protect the "open society" from its "enemies"—into the breach. On this point, see also Barber (2006); Diesing (1991), pp. 31–34; Mayo (1996), p. 22; Sil (2000b), pp. 361–362; Lakatos and Musgrave (1970), pp. 52–53; and Walker (2010).

On this latter point, Chernoff's (2005) attempt to reground IR in "Duhemian conventionalism" is noteworthy. Chernoff defends the idea that "a set of rational criteria of policy choice" (p. 211) can help IR theory in "fulfilling the historical mission of the discipline" (p. 207). But Chernoff's understanding of IR's "historical mission" is telling: "aiding policy makers by providing a rational basis for the attempt to control future outcomes" (p. 207). But *which* policy makers, and which policies? Embedded in what baseline political order? Chernoff draws his examples from the contemporary system of states, that is, by naturalizing an existing normative-political order. But surely contesting this naturalization—without falling into nihilism—was the project that Popperian falsification, however well or badly, undertook to sustain. See also Chernoff (2007).

77. Schmitt (1996), p. 34. See also Strauss (2007) [1942].

78. Schmitt (2005) [1985]: "All significant concepts of the modern theory of the state are secularized theological concepts not only because of their historical development—in which they were transferred from theology to the theory of the state, whereby, for example, the omnipotent God became the omnipotent lawgiver—but also because of their systematic structure, the recognition of which is necessary for a sociological consideration of these concepts. The exception for jurisprudence is analogous to the miracle in theology" (p. 36). See Guilhot (2010), Huysmans (2008), Margalit (2005), McCormick (1998), Ochoa-Espejo (2010), Odysseos and Petito (2007), and Luoma-Aho (2009).

From a different tack, Gershom Scholem and Aviezer Ravitzky have explored the possibility that terms like *freedom*, *emancipation*, and *truth* contain what Scholem called an "apocalyptic sting," which social science ignores at its peril. See Ravitzky (1996), pp. 3–4, and Scholem (1997), pp. 27–30. Scholem and Ravitzky speak specifically of the Hebrew language and its ostensibly unmediated connection to revealed biblical concepts of redemption, sovereignty, judgment, and so forth. The immediate concern of such investigations was to uncover the potential for something like a messianically fueled fascism to emerge in the modern-day state of Israel. Granted that doing so would require a fuller argument than can be offered here *in nuce*, generalizing this concern to politics more broadly is not unwarranted. For analogous discussions vis-à-vis Christian realism, see Butterfield (1950), Niebuhr (1944) and Patterson (2008).

It is important to tread carefully here. The point is that IR, to the extent that it is distinct from sociology or public policy, must be able to accommodate the possibility of relationships that are essentially *political*, defined on the basis of friends and enemies. This does not mean that particular instantiations of the "friend-enemy distinction" are necessarily objectively true in any deep or metaphysical sense, that human relations must always *everywhere* be political in nature, or even, necessarily, that they *ever* are.[79] Such distinctions, to take the first of these objections, can certainly be predicated on falsehoods— as in the context of Schmitt, the theologian Jacob Taubes has convincingly shown.[80]

Meanwhile, the possibility that the international arena has been (or could be) transformed from a political order into a social one is an ongoing theoretical and empirical question: from Ulrich Beck's ostensible "reinvention of politics" to discussions of global governance and the notion of transnational lifeworlds and public spheres.[81] But the question here is one of ideal types, not observed or empirical realities. What comes of jettisoning concepts for defining political relations in favor of social ones? Let it be stipulated that amity has replaced enmity in particular international relationships: along the U.S.-Canadian border or among the Norden states, to pick two widely cited examples.[82] Does this suggest a deeper set of processes by which enmity is in retreat within a particular class of International Relations? Let that point, too, be stipulated. Does that mean it is in retreat *everywhere* or that the essential nature of international relations is changing?

The move from the former question to the latter involves a very deep, essentially metaphysical argument, effectively a communitarian retreading

---

79. Morgenthau (1933): "Schmitt's doctrine of the political is a metaphysical one that makes only a distant appeal to historical or psychological realities," and one "cannot presume to 'refute' a metaphysical conception by proving that its affirmations find no concordance with known empirical facts" (p. 46). Rather, Morgenthau continues, one must either appeal to a competing, equally transcendent but incommensurable one or seek contradictions in how that position has been derived, interpreted, and/or applied. The opposition of "social" relations with "political" ones must be understood as an attempt at the former: to replace a primordial friend-enemy relationship with another one, rooted in some form of cosmopolitanism. On the Schmitt-Morgenthau connection, see Brown (2007), Frei (2001), Honig (1995–96), Pichler (1998), Huysmans (1999), Scheuerman (1999, 2007a), Koskenniemi (2002), and the essays in Williams (2007).

80. Taubes (2004), p. 51.

81. Beck (1997); Barnett and Sikkink (2008). On appropriations of the Habermasian notions of lifeworld and public sphere into IR, see the lengthy discussion in chapter 2. For Schmitt, this would simply be the creation of a new "nomos of the earth"; see Ochoa-Espejo (2010).

82. Inter alia, Deutsch (1957, 1967), Shore (1998), Waever (1995, 1996, 1998), Hansen and Waever (2002), Guzzini and Jung (2004), and Andersson (2010).

of Francis Fukuyama's "end of history."[83] The danger lies in failing to see the connection between such arguments and the kind of vulgar messianism into which they have slipped, and do slip, when the reifications on which they rely are left unchecked.[84] Given their proximity to ideological reductionism, some obligation must be incumbent on theorists to recognize their true metaphysical depth. Alternatively, such theorists must actively work to avoid such slippage by counterbalancing these metaphysical assumptions with others. Either way, an intervening scholarly ethos is needed, cultivating what Mitchell Dean has called "a certain modesty and self-awareness."[85] That is what sustainable critique aims at.

Such modesty has a double edge. In accepting the notion of sustainable critique developed here, the coming chapters need to develop a careful, mediate position between the assumptions of IR theory and the Frankfurt School–informed critique it develops in response to them. Adorno's sociological writings—best known through *The Authoritarian Personality* and his and Horkheimer's discussion of the culture industry—are not without their own stipulated ontologies. Society, on Adorno's account, is a totality that constitutes a single, integrated system of economic and cultural production.[86] "Official" political differences are nested within a field of reified ideological mystifications so encompassing as to leave no one wholly outside.

In itself, that position is not a problem; it is a metaphysical-cum-ontological claim—albeit an unrelievedly pessimistic one—that is as good as any other, pieces of which are mirrored in a variety of neo- and post-Marxist discussions of power and interest. That said, two provisos must be borne in mind. First, Adornian critique is not—and does not claim to be—ideologically free-floating in the Mannheimian sense.[87] One is smuggling in an ontology that takes a partisan position on a key debate within both academic IR and world politics more generally—the primacy of the political. Second, that ontology is tragic: it negates any possibility of escape, mandating instead our reluctant acceptance. We are trapped in a world of our own reified mediations. As such, the only forms of thinking, feeling, and knowing that are not wholly suspect take place within a kind of self-made intellectual diaspora in

83. Fukuyama (1992).

84. Aradau (2004), Bigo and Walker (2007), Ish-Shalom (2009), Jackson and Kaufman (2007), Koskenniemi (2009) – and in particular, Waever (2011).

85. Dean (2007), p. 256.

86. See Adorno (1969–70), (1974), pp. 193–194, and (2000), pp. 22ff.

87. On this point, see Adorno (1983).

which our own finitude and fallibility are constantly foregrounded; there is no space for being "at home in the world." That position has its own dangers. For these reasons, IR theory inflected with an Adornian notion of reflexivity must *itself* be brought under the ambit of sustainable critique. Its reifications, too, require continued management.

Sustaining such a mediate position means treading lightly between social science, with its appeals to truths grounded in some version of reason, and political theories that *begin* as the expression of partisan sensibilities. The origins, methods, and forms of knowing characteristic of the latter, although no less historically contingent than the former, are nonetheless quite independent of them. Contact between the two may enrich or deepen each, but their basic distinctness remains unaltered.[88] Certainly, it is a mistake to reduce *all* forms of power-knowledge to the conscious manipulation of ideological false consciousness.[89] Even so, the imperfect understanding of the nexus of ideology and knowledge is a standing political opportunity for the would-be political entrepreneur. Politics—the practical art of "doing the right thing at the right time in view of the particular historical circumstances"—presents genuine and enduring challenges for research projects based on theoretical conceptualization and generalized description.[90] The paradigms of IR—neorealism and neoliberalism, Wendt's systemic constructivism, liberal and intergovernmental institutionalism, and so on—are constructs of fact and value; as such, they do political as well as analytical work. If theory is to avoid reification's pitfalls, awareness of the essential limitations of thinking about world politics

---

88. The point is best made in an unsuspected source: Alfred Lord Tennyson's "Ulysses." To conquer and to govern, Ulysses discovers, are different—and not complementary—skill sets. Tennyson's hero makes no apologies for this; he delegates the latter job and returns to what he knows: "This is my son, mine own Telemachus, / To whom I leave the sceptre and the isle,— / Well-loved of me, discerning to fulfill / This labor, by slow prudence to make mild / A rugged people, and thro' soft degrees / Subdue them to the useful and the good.... He works his work, I mine" (Tennyson [1976], pp. 265–266). For a contrary view—that a cosmopolitan social science can be sustained in a world that is not politically cosmopolitan—see Beck (2004). Ultimately, Beck must assume ontology by intellectual fiat: that whatever the world "really is" is other than what official political institutions, or scholarly-disciplinary analyses, have made of it. But does that not merely assume what would otherwise need to be demonstrated?

89. As Wendt (1999) argues, p. 60. See also Connolly (1981).

90. Kratochwil (2006), p. 6. Bhaskar (1989) notes: "*values must be immanent* (as latent or partially manifested tendencies) in the practices in which we engage, or normative discourse is utopian or idle. I think that Marx...grasped this. And it is on this feature that Habermas' deduction of speech-constitutive universals also turns" (pp. 113–4, emphasis in original). What should the IR theorist make of this? Can, as Bhaskar supposes, a language of *freedom* be thus sustained, without making appeal (even if unconsciously) to transhistorical claims of truth? There is no simple answer. On the complex relationship between Bhaskar's thinking and that of Habermas, see Norrie (2003) and Patomäki (2002), ch. 6.

in the late-modern era must be constant and continuous. That, precisely, is why IR theory requires *sustainable* forms of critique. What is sought here is not the reconciliation of mutually incommensurate accounts of reality, but the tools by which to preserve those accounts alongside one another in their full irreducibility: "to *reactivate* a crisis in the social sciences" and sustain it, at least insofar as this applies to the study of world politics.[91] If IR can do this, it stands a chance of balancing its practical and critical moments and thereby meeting its larger vocation.

Sustainable Critique (2): Reification in International Theory

Critique is not made sustainable, however, merely by explaining why it needs to be so. Meeting the challenge of reification requires specialized tools. For that, one must be in a position to observe how reification has worked "in the trenches" of theory. Describing *what reification is* in general terms is one task; understanding *how it has gone unchecked in IR* is quite another. The latter requires an appreciation both of different theoretical and normative contexts and of political contingencies. A sustainably critical IR would have to account for the ways in which particular disciplinary traditions—realism, liberalism, and the like—are complex unions of fact and value, how those unions parse the complicated world of human social and political interaction, and how they are connected to methodologies to form paradigmatic research programs. From there, a rough descriptive typology of reification within IR theory—the 'rogues' gallery' promised above—could be drawn out. Such a typology is set out in the coming paragraphs to guide and inform the discussions of the coming chapters.

Given the aims of this book, the move to set out such a typology is not made lightly. A certain performative contradiction attends the attempt, for all such schematic representations are themselves reifications. IR theory cannot be reduced to the immanent movements of "pure" or "noumenal" ideas, outside either high or academic politics. Numerous environmental considerations play a role that is difficult to characterize within top-down conceptual schemas but are clearly of great importance in how paradigms and research programs become hegemonic. By way of example, it is surely not a coincidence that early IR realism and realpolitik sustained a persistent theme of tragedy and finitude and early post–Cold War constructivist IR showed tremendous

---

91. Glynos and Howarth (2007), p. 2, emphasis in original.

optimism regarding the possibilities of discourse and the potential of culture, society, and community to flower even on the harsh ground of international anarchy. Both are reactions to events and to broader cultural and historical moods. Similarly, studies by Nicolas Guilhot, Ido Oren, Ron Robin, Ben Rosamond, and Brian Schmidt have shown how academic politics—personalities, institutional ideologies, and access to funding—play a role in how particular ideas or turns of theory become hegemonic.[92] To propose a deductive typology is to sever these contexts. Yet at the same time, some point of entry must be found if sustainable critique is to be developed conceptually.

In short, my work is no more immune to reification than those it critiques in the coming chapters. The typology developed here must therefore strive to critique itself; its connection to sustainable critique and the larger vocation of IR must be continuously foregrounded.[93] The aim is not to produce a checklist against which particular theories might be immunized against this or that form of ideological bias. Rather, it is to produce what legal scholars sometimes call an "exhaustion" argument. I argue in the next chapter that all theories of international politics *must* rely on reification to some degree, owing to a particular idealism inherent in thought. Obviously, one cannot demonstrate a claim of this sort with any kind of deductive certainty.[94] One can, however, adopt a second best approach: showing that *the major paradigms and traditions in IR do so rely and that the discipline seems not to have drawn from that reliance the necessary conclusions.* Given the pervasiveness of reification extensively documented, it shall then be argued, IR theorists *ought* to contribute to a project whereby all can learn to reframe their thinking along sustainably reflexive lines. The typology offered here, then, frames the case studies in chapters 3 through 5 that make that second best case. It is not an end, but a means. However insufficient these provisos, they will have to do—at least until the concluding chapter of this book, when they can themselves be brought within the ambit of sustainable critique.

With those provisos in mind, reification in IR theory can be delineated with reference to two sets of factors: first, the fact-value tradition from which a body of theory emerges and, second, the methodological approaches through which they are parsed into research paradigms, to wit:

---

92. Guilhot (2008, 2011), Oren (2003), Robin (2001), Rosamond (2000), and Schmidt (1998).

93. Jackson (2008).

94. Such a conclusion, as Deutsch (1963) noted, would be impossible without "either metaphysical convictions or a sweeping prediction of the entire future course of social science" (p. 14).

Table 0.1   Typologizing Reifications in IR Theory

	Fact-Value Tradition
Methodological Approach	Paradigmatic IR Theory, and associated reification

Three methodological approaches—the vertical axis in table 0.1—are treated in this book: metaphysical approaches, middle-range approaches, and third-way approaches. These are detailed in Table 0.2. *Metaphysical* methodologies make reference to essential or transcendent categories or classes, which are at bottom unknowable except in highly intuitive or eclectic ways that go beyond what can be directly observed or experienced.[95] These may be either openly eschatological in character (as when particular nations are held to possess divine favor or privileged historical destinies) or entirely intramundane (as when ostensibly natural forces, such as evolution and natural selection or the declining rate of profit, are held to drive the political world to particular outcomes). *Middle-range* approaches, which emerged historically in part as a response to the reifications on which metaphysical approaches rely, attempted a radical separation of theories and reality, the idea that "research design," as Most and Starr put it, need not "be logically consistent with the empirical phenomena and related theory it is supposed to study."[96] Such methodologies are often—though not always, as the case of Karl Deutsch will show—grounded on combinations of as-if assumptions about actors and structures, with an eye to developing falsifying tests for those assumptions as a bar to their reification. Yet as Fred Chernoff and Kenneth Waltz have variously noted, "crucial experiment" notions of scientific discovery are not easily applied to IR, for "it is impossible to treat a single hypothesis in isolation from the totality of principles, background assumptions and beliefs" on which it is predicated.[97] Absent such tests, nothing prevents these as-if assumptions from

---

95. See the valuable discussion in Kurki (2008), pp. 33–40.

96. Most and Starr (1989), p. 4; or following Kenneth Waltz: "Explanatory power is gained by moving away from 'reality.'" Here cited infra Onuf (2009), p. 187. On the term *middle range*, see Merton (1963): "theories intermediate to the minor working hypotheses evolved in abundance during the day-by-day routines of research, and the all-inclusive speculations comprising a master conceptual scheme from which it is hoped to derive a very large number of empirically informed uniformities of social behavior" (pp. 5–6).

97. Chernoff (2005), p. 104. Also Waltz (1986): "Because of the interdependence of theory and fact, we can find no Popperian crucial experiment, the native results of which would send a theory crashing to the ground. The background knowledge against which to test a theory is as problematic as the theory itself" (p. 334). The foregoing benefits from the valuable discussion in Molloy (2006).

Table 0.2 Three Methodological Approaches in IR Theory

Name	Definition	Effect of Unchecked Reification
Metaphysical	Grounding IR theory in forces or forms that are essentially unknowable except in highly intuitive and/or eclectic ways.	Essentialism; that is, attributing real-world agency or materiality to these forms or forces.
Middle-range	Grounding IR theory in as-if assumptions about world politics, whose correspondence to real-world events and processes is held to be subject to particular factual "tests."	Conflating as-ifs with reality as such, owing to no means of chastening them.
Third-way	Balancing the systematicity of middle-range methodologies with the essentialism of metaphysical ones, by selective synthesis.	The "pluralist fallacy": the uncritical assumption that theoretical or discursive syntheses can dissolve political contestations.

being conflated with the reality they were originally purported to describe. Finally, *"Third-way"* methodologies attempt to balance the systematicity of middle-range methodologies with the essentialism of metaphysical ones by means of selective synthesis: in effect, to develop a third way between agency and structure, as this debate has played out across five decades and three (or four) great debates. Here, reification becomes dangerous when the power of discourse to dissolve incommensurate value positions in *theory* is uncritically extended to its ability to do so in *politics*, forgetting that the latter may be made of different stuff than the former.

Two key points must be remembered. The first is that although the methodological approaches outlined here roughly parallel those historical break points in IR known as the great debates, those connections are only approximated by the historical record. Outliers—like neoclassical realism, surveyed in chapter 3—exist and are significant. Moreover, while methodologies emerge partly in response to one another and may grow in sophistication, no progressivist or cumulativity of knowledge argument of the sort put forward by positivists or neopositivists is here understood to be at work.[98] That theories respond to one another does not mean that they advance in any absolute sense.

The reifying character of these methodologies, however, varies greatly according to the fact-value traditions into which they are read. These traditions provide each paradigm with the antecedent "moral ethnography" that gives it its normative shape.[99] Obviously, there are a great many of these. Owing to limitations of space, the present work explores only three: a *realist* tradition and two branches of what is broadly referred to as the liberal IR tradition: a *communitarian* tradition and an *individualist* one. These are summarized in table 0.3. Through these, IR makes connections between longer traditions in normative political theory and particular real-world problematics; the lines of these appropriations are set out at some length in the coming chapters. In table 0.4, the methodologies are then superimposed onto these traditions. The arguments summarized in table 0.4 are set out in detail in chapters 3 through 5.

Sustainable Critique (3): Chastened Reason

Sustainable critique, then, does not take issue with any particular methodological approach or normative tradition or any with one paradigm emerging from their conjunction. Barring egregious mistakes of logic, argument, or fact, which can be ascertained only through close readings of individual arguments, any of these is as good or as bad as any other. What matters is the manner in which the theorists using them incorporate sensitivity to reification, checking the latter's potentially dangerous excesses. If IR theory necessarily derives from, or trails out into, normative-political sensibilities, then in so managing them, its practitioners would be poised to make a signal contribution to a wider world of political discourse and policy. By thinking in both positive and critical terms at once, IR could create a sustainably critical perspective on world politics that might then be turned back onto, and made to inform, ongoing policy debates and discourses. International Relations theory might thus square a complex circle, mindful both of events in the real world and of the political ideologies that set out the bounds of debate by which that world is known. This would be *sustainably managing reification*: accepting its centrality to conceptual thinking and actively devising tactics and practices by which to remember its effects and contain them.

---

98. See, for example, Walt (1991).

99. Robinson (1999, 2006).

Table 0.3 Three Fact-Value Traditions in IR Theory

Name	Defining Fact-Value Assumptions	Key Theorists
Realism	Sovereign political affiliations, i.e., states, moderate an a priori state of war. The vocation of international theory is to help states manage their interrelations.	Hans Morgenthau, Kenneth Waltz, Alexander Wendt, Randall Schweller, Richard Ned Lebow
Communitarianism	Similar to realism, but the "state of war" is not moderated solely by sovereign power. When interlinked through satisfying networks of community, sovereign power can be complemented or attenuated. The vocation of international theory lies in developing such insights to work in global contexts.	H. G. Wells, David Mitrany, E. H. Carr, Karl Deutsch, Ernst Haas (later work), Emanuel Adler
Individualism	Political life defined by individuals, whose liberty and interests are logically prior and ontologically stable and can thus be balanced to produce order by the creation of appropriate institutions. The vocation of international theory lies in adapting or extending such institutions to global contexts.	Ernst Haas (early work), Keohane and Nye, Legro and Moravcsik, Katzenstein and Sil (?)

Table 0.4 Partial Typology of Reification in IR Theory, by Fact-Value Tradition and Methodological Approach

		Fact-Value Tradition		
		Realism	Communitarianism	Individualism
		(Ch. 3)	(Ch. 4)	(Ch. 5)
Methodological Approach	Metaphysical	*Classical realism* Key reification: "Dutch boy syndrome" —social/political order faces imminent decline into irrationalism; scholarly vocation to use "finger" of theory to shore up the "dyke" of reason.	*(Paleo)Functionalism* Key reification: "The great universe whose children we are" —belief in the existence of an a priori or emergent universal human community, whose realization is limited only by false consciousness or narrowness of view; the vocation of theory is to overcome these.	*Neofunctionalism* Key reification: Providentialism—belief that reason and interest are a priori givens and provide a stable basis for the creation of self-regulating institutions and structures. Vocation of theory is to map out the structure and function of such institutions and structures.[a]
	Middle-range	*Structural neorealism* Key reification: "normative smuggling" —defining key analytics or terms such that ontological-political differences are enfolded into them sub rosa.	*Transactionalism & security communities* Key reification: "The wise android" —belief in the power of cybernetic modes of control and feedback to remake political life and thus transcend the agency-structure divide.	*Liberal institutionalism* Key reification: "Disharmonious cooperation" —belief that a felicitous balancing of interests and orders will obviate the need for agreed-upon notions of amity, justice, etc.

(Continued)

Table 0.4 (Continued)

	Fact-Value Tradition		
	Realism	Communitarianism	Individualism
	(Ch. 3)	(Ch. 4)	(Ch. 5)
Third-way	*Systemic constructivism* Key reification: "Epistemological lowballing"—belief that theory can solve essential and/or ontological questions through improved modes of discourse.	*Communitarian constructivism* Key reification: "Primacy of vision"— proceeding backward from identified, idealized end states to present-day practices or concerns, with an eye to marking a path between them.	*Multiparadigmatism/eclecticism* Key reification: The "Pirandello problem"—multiple methodologies in search of a unifying ethos.

ᵃ*Viner (1972)*.

Chastened reason is advanced as the theoretical mind-set that could inform this perspective. To chasten reason, in this context, means to confront the limitations inherent in *all* conceptual thought—its reliance on reification—by positing them a priori.[100] It is to assume that ideas or concepts are abstractions of real-world things that are, as Adorno understood, never identical with things in themselves.[101] Theorists are not outside the world they wish to understand; they are parents and children, citizens, members of academic and political communities, participants in economies and societies. Their thinking is defined through subjective experience. To chasten thought is to see knowledge as emerging from historically contingent convergences of interest, identity, and understanding. It is to assume that the appearance of reality, while significant, remains distinct from reality as such; it understands such appearances, and their diffusion, as phenomena to be studied in their own right. Martin Hollis and Steve Smith's hermeneutic circle does not bind theorists merely when they work or when they speak ex cathedra; they—we—"are always already embedded in a social and political world that constructs the boundaries of what can be said or done."[102] Given that state of affairs, the ability to speak meaningfully about political life is a derivative function of the hermeneutic circle: theorists need to be attuned to their location within it, to its associated social functions, and to the perspectives that emerge from these.[103]

Taken specifically in the context of IR, chastened reason assumes a priori the existence of reification as the basis on which thinking about world politics is predicated, even if the outline of *particular* reifications is not immediately evident. It assumes further that sensitivity to reification is progressively lost over time and that dangers attend that loss. So, just as safecrackers once used sandpaper to increase the sensitivity of their fingertips to the tumblers falling in a combination

---

100. And in this sense, it bears noting, the notion of reification used here is closer to that of Adorno and Honneth than to that of Lukács. For Lukács, reification was a mutilation of thought that could be met through revolutionary or critical practices that returned human social existence to an original harmony. This point would become the basis for deontological critiques of Lukács by Adorno and Horkheimer (2002), Habermas (1984), and Honneth (2008), all of whom held that reification was inherent in thinking.

101. This point—the critique of what Theodor Adorno (1973, pp. 146–151) calls *identitarian* or *identity thinking*—is developed in chapter 1.

102. Fierke (1998), p. xi. Hollis and Smith (1991); Hollis (1994).

103. Glynos and Howarth (2007), indeed, speak not of a *hermeneutic* circle, but of a *retroductive* one. "By a retroductive circle we aim to capture the necessary 'to and fro' movement of retroductive reasoning that can extend to the practice of persuading a wider community of scholars and practitioners that they *should* accept our explanations" (p. 40, emphasis in original).

lock, chastened reason points theorists toward seeking tools by which to enhance and preserve sensitivity to reification in its encounter with world politics.

That there is a need for such intellectual-normative sandpaper may surprise those who had hoped that postpositivist IR—the third debate as defined by Yosef Lapid—might on its own sustain a kind of conceptual "permanent revolution."[104] It has not done so. The devil remains in the details, the ways in which constructivism has been connected to events in world politics. These vary from V. O. Quine's "tribunals of experience" as taken up by Hollis and Smith, to Stephen Toulmin's "population selectionist tests" as used by Ernst and Peter Haas, to speech-act theory, structuration, and system and lifeworld, as taken up by theorists like Wendt, Emanuel Adler, Thomas Risse, and Marc Lynch.[105] The move they share is to base claims of constructivist "world-making" on commonsense notions of lived experience: observable scientific, linguistic, or cultural practices. As such, these approaches have an intuitive, appealing quality—especially emerging in the years when globalization, the signing of the Maastricht treaty, the fall of apartheid, and the emergence of the World Wide Web created both new forums for postnational forms of community and new potential mechanisms for global governance.[106]

Yet when viewed from a longer *durée*, such "non-capital-P-pragmatism" loses much of its appeal.[107] The radical nature of late-modern experience places (at the very least) an extraordinarily high burden on it—perhaps even dooming such pragmatism from the outset. If truth is to be held up to tribunes of experience or found in knowledge practices, would not those experiences or practices have to submit themselves before the defining horrors of the age? If it is attributable to practices, must it not include the practices of genocide, nuclear bomb dropping, ethnic cleansing, strategic manipulation of human hunger—and the intellectual, social, and cultural practices implicated in them or propaedeutic to them? No progressive agenda for the study of world politics worthy of the name would seriously claim otherwise.

---

104. See Hoffman (1987), Rengger (1988), Lapid (1989a), and Neufeld (1993) for contrasting views on this point.

105. For broad surveys, see Sil (2000a) and Onuf (2002). On Quine, see Hollis (1994), pp. 77–83; Hollis and Smith (1991), pp. 55–57; on Toulmin, see Haas (1991), restated in Haas and Haas (2002); on speech act theory, see Kratochwil (1991) and Onuf (1989); on structuration, see Adler (1997), Checkel (1998), Dessler (1989), Gould (1998), and Wendt (1987). On the use of Habermasian concepts of system and lifeworld, see Risse (2000, 2004), Lynch (1999, 2006a & b), and the discussion in chapter 2.

106. Barder and Levine (2012).

107. Albert and Kopp-Malek (2002).

Yet there are serious obstacles facing such inclusions. How exactly are such experiences, in anything like their full, actual horror, to be conceptualized and transmitted? To dig a mass grave with the others of one's village and then be executed with them in it; to be vaporized in a mushroom cloud; to be killed with one's family by one's former neighbors, wielding machetes is also to be placed beyond the reach of interrogation. Perhaps it takes one beyond the reach of empiricism. One cannot prepare questionnaires for the dead, and to interrogate the living with an eye to fitting their responses into rubrics seems to diminish the inexpressible nature of their suffering. The very concept of testimony is beggared in such contexts, as political theorist Giorgio Agamben has evocatively shown.[108] If so, what becomes of empiricism—at bottom, a glorified form of theoretical witnessing? If capable only of a distant echo of late modernity's full horror, how can its analyses fail to skew toward idealism? Even in conflicts where such possibilities are not directly implicated, the fact that such horrors have and do take place, that such realities have entered into the political-cultural lexicon, urgently points to the insufficiency of contemporary empiricism. While nothing is impossible—the Bhaskarian critical realist approaches alluded to before bear noting—the difficulties facing its improvement must be born in mind,[109] all the more so considering that mainstream constructivists are only beginning to consider the philosophical problems it entails.[110]

Failing that, one must admit of at least the *possibility* that such horrors remain unspeakable and incommunicable in the most literal sense: there is simply no utterance that conveys them in their fullness. Any attempt to do so must be viewed with suspicion—must chasten itself.[111] Holocaust survivor, author, and chemist Primo Levi agreed: having survived a machine so effective in the mass production of death, he argued, *perforce* made him a statistical outlier.[112] Levi was not demeaning his own experience or engaging in false modesty; he was insisting on preserving the integrity of an event that even his

---

108. Agamben (2002); also Haidu (1992) and the discussion in Katznelson (2003), pp. 26–27.

109. Note that the term *critical realism* is here a methodological term derived from the philosophy of science and should not be conflated with the realist IR tradition or its derived paradigms (neorealism, etc.). See Kurki (2008), Patomäki (2002, 2003), Patomäki and Wight (2000), and Wight (2006).

110. See, for example, the essays in Price (2008).

111. Or as Agamben (2002) put it, must "submit...every word to the test of an impossibility of speaking" (p. 157).

112. Levi (1988): "At a distance of years one can today definitively affirm that the history of the *Lagers* has been written almost exclusively by those who, like myself, never fathomed them to the bottom" (p. 17).

experience could not fathom. Everyday linguistic processes of banalization—as when terms like *awesome, extreme,* and *radical* increasingly apply to objects of mass consumption (pizza, movies)—demonstrate the acuteness of the problem facing theory in this context. Theoretical parlance, no less than ordinary language, seems unable to maintain a lexicon of inexpressible terms or unthinkable concepts; over time, these become domesticated and diminished.[113] Even if no one consciously intends harm, this both deeply injures the dignity of the dead and gravely endangers the living. By "thinking about the unthinkable"—or as others have more recently put it, "dispensing with the super-empirical"—one perhaps also cultivates the illusion of "the unthinkable's" tractability and becomes accustomed to it.[114] Perhaps one even helps bring it about. Hence the necessity of chastening reason is remembering its manifest inadequacy to the task facing IR. Without chastened reason, IR risks tracing out events in world politics in artificially and dangerously optimistic hues of comprehensibility, regularity, and predictability. For all its dispassionate hardheadedness, the discipline would become dangerously idealistic, despite itself.

Ideally, given the radical nature of late-modern violence, any tribunal of reason—whether Quine's and Hollis's figurative one, the tribunal of analytical reason to which social science makes its ultimate appeal, or the court of public opinion in which mass politics is played out—would simply recuse itself, as do judges when asked to preside over a case for which they lack jurisdiction. But in a world defined by very real fears, this seems unrealistic. Men and women, fearing death, will try to muddle through—to think their way out of the dangers they believe they face.[115] But could one not—again, as second best—acknowledge the limited reach of those efforts and find ways to keep it constantly present to mind? Perhaps that could be the work of IR theorists. Trained in both the uses and blind alleys of thinking, they would be best suited to manning the barricades that could hold reification at bay, that chasten reason. This would be a means to institutionalize and internalize the discipline's enduring debates, to "deflate the dogmatic pretensions" that come

---

113. This should not be read as a kind of Luddite moral outrage. The instability potential of language also gives it the potential for transformation or self-reinvention, as when terms of abuse—*queer* is a widely studied example—become terms of empowerment. It does, however, raise complexities for the discussion of things that one might hope could be socially, normatively, or historically intransitive—as many hold the Holocaust should be. See Knowlton and Cates (1993) and Hopgood (2009); Denich (1994) is also illuminating.

114. Respectively, Kahn (1962), Jackson, infra Hellmann (2009), p. 656. See also Rapoport (1964).

115. Huysmans (1998), pp. 236ff.

with theories that codify, and thus conceal the tendentiousness of, subjective beliefs and value preferences.[116]

Plan of the Work

The remainder of this book develops the "exhaustion" argument put forward here, in two parts. Chapter 1 reviews the distinction between positive and critical theory, a foreshortened discussion of the distinction Max Horkheimer first made in the 1930s, adapted to the particular problems of IR. It then discusses how this distinction, while an effective tool for theoretical pluralization, does not solve the problem of reification, which is deeply rooted in the incompatibilities between conceptual thought and politics. Chapter 2 compares the sustainable critique argument developed in chapter 1 to other appropriations of Frankfurt School theory in IR—in particular, the critical IR theory and critical security studies approaches emerging from the work of Robert Cox, Andrew Linklater, and fourth debate Habermasian approaches to IR. Finding such appropriations wanting, it also suggests a reconsideration of pre-Habermasian Frankfurt theory, in particular through the writings of Adorno, and takes some initial steps toward such reconsideration.

Chapters 3 through 5 undertake focused critiques of three fact-value traditions in IR theory. Each chapter tells an essentially similar story: it sees paradigmatic research programs—neorealism, neofunctionalism, transactionalism, and so on—as fusions of methodological approaches and fact-value traditions, animated by a vocational impulse and motivated by critical dissatisfaction with earlier instances of theoretical reification. In effect, it will be argued, all of the major research programs in IR theory have dealt, however momentarily and implicitly, with the challenge reification poses to the broad vocation of IR. Yet each failed to sustain the reflexive moment that animated it. Rather than adopting chastened reason as a positive value, each has used critique instrumentally, to clear the ground for its own alternative political commitments. Given the problem of reification defined here, it will be argued, this is not enough.

In chapter 3, this argument is brought to bear against the realist tradition, first in its metaphysical instantiation (chiefly the work of Hans Morgenthau), then in its middle-range (Waltzian) turn, and finally in its third-way form in the systemic constructivism of Alexander Wendt. Chapters 4 and 5 undertake a parallel reconstruction of two dominant liberal IR traditions. In chapter 4,

---

116. Spegele (1996), p. 244.

communitarian theory—David Mitrany and the Fabians, Karl Deutsch's cybernetic transactionalism, and Emanuel Adler's communitarian IR theory—is explored in close readings. In chapter 5, this same tack is applied to individualist traditions—from the early work of Ernst Haas to Keohane and Nye. The attempt to balance individualism and communitarianism is then explored through a recent turn to multiparadigmatic approaches from Legro and Moravcsik to the analytical eclecticism of Rudra Sil and Peter Katzenstein. In each of these reconstructions, the same narrative-theoretical line is stressed: my aim is to bring out the distinctive reifications that have emerged, and gone unheeded, when these normative traditions are parsed through the metaphysical, middle-range, and third-way methodologies that have dominated the field over the last six decades.

Following this, I attempt in the conclusion to develop a concrete approach that might preserve the chastened mind-set to which sustainable critique aspires. This will be done through the application of Theodor Adorno's and Max Weber's notion of a *constellation*, alluded to in the Hoffmann discussion above. That is, by arranging multiple theoretical perspectives around a particular event or cluster of events in world politics, revealing IR theory to be a dynamic hybrid of traditional social science reductionism and intuitive philosophical hermeneutics. By deploying multiple paradigms in hybrid and overlapping fashions around complex, uncertain events, I argue, "constellar" explanations raise the prospect of polyvocal, highly pluralist, and mutually critical narratives that both enrich and chasten one another. "By gathering concepts round the central one that is sought, they attempt to express what that concept aims at, not to circumscribe it to operative ends."[117] Thus Adorno hoped to find "a third possibility beyond the alternatives of positivism and idealism."[118]

There is a tragic sensibility that animates such an approach. The positive and the critical must coexist because both are necessary and neither is sufficient; as Wendt and Duvall have recently noted, since science or the state "can never fully achieve 'the' truth, defined as an apolitical, objective representation of the world."[119] All knowledge is predicated on reification, and government policy, in the era of the modern administrative state, is the application of such knowledge. But all this means is that, following Sheldon Wolin, Weber

---

117. Adorno (1973), pp. 165–166.

118. Adorno (1973), p. 166.

119. Wendt and Duvall (2008), p. 619.

might have misstated the movement of modernity somewhat.[120] Perhaps reason need not vanquish myth in some grand, Clausewitizian battle of demystification. Reason and myth need only check and tame one another; reason tames myth by offering possibilities for creating wealth and welfare that the latter cannot, and myth tames reason by recalling that politics is never merely or wholly the exercise of reason.

Though this is tragedy, it is tragedy of a different sort than that to which IR has been traditionally treated: that of human *finitude*, not the inevitability of human *nature*. It lies at the intersection of what Whitehead called "the remorseless working of things" and Leo Strauss's recognition of "how terribly difficult it is to secure those minimums of decency, humanity, [and] justice" that free societies take for granted.[121] It summons up compassion for one's fellow creatures, recalling humanity's common sensitivity to pain and its common vulnerability in the face of death. Theory, as Anthony Burke has powerfully argued, cannot dictate what will come of such compassion; it can only assert its necessity and negate all countervailing claims that would make apology for inflicting suffering on others.[122] This turn deepens and reinvigorates the practical aims of IR: shielding it from moralizing self-righteousness or fatalistic ressentiment but also blocking its retreat into technical or scholastic nit-picking.

In 1966, Martin Wight argued that "international theory is marked, not only by paucity but also by intellectual and moral poverty." The reasons for this, Wight argued, were "first, the intellectual prejudice imposed by the sovereign state, and secondly, the belief in progress."[123] Some four decades later, Colin Wight would come to a similar conclusion: "politics is the terrain of competing ontologies." It cannot therefore be divorced "from competing visions of how the world is and how it should be."[124] We seem to have come full circle: between transcendent truth claims about the universe and appearances of truth that lie within particular culturally, historically, or politically contingent forms of life is a space of chastened reason that is enormously

---

120. Wolin (2008): "Not only did Weber underestimate the staying power of credulity; he could not foresee that the great triumphs of modern science would themselves provide the basis for technological achievements which, far from banishing the mythical, would unwittingly inspire it" (p. 12).

121. Whitehead (1925), pp. 16–17; Strauss (2007), p. 527. See the valuable discussions in Lebow (2003) and Mercado (2009).

122. A. Burke (2007).

123. Wight and Bull (1966), p. 20.

124. Wight (2006), p. 2.

difficult to sustain. Many live their entire lives never seeing it, and in most cases, no harm is done. But IR is specifically the study of how enduringly different political orders might coexist even (perhaps) in the midst of violence and anarchy. Coexistence in the present era may mean creating broad coalitions dedicated to *negative* ideals—more simply, to letting others be.[125] These are *negative* alliances, based on the will *not to destroy*. That, the present work argues, is an understanding of the vocation of IR that appreciates the full, historic aims of the discipline. Chastened reason suggests the space in which such negative alliances might emerge within the mind of the theorist. Only once such space becomes *sustainably conceivable*—with all the paradoxes and tensions this entails—might it bear fruit concretely or politically.

---

125. Schneck (2006).

"For We Born After": The Challenge of Sustainable Critique

Remember
When you speak of our failings
The dark time too
Which you have escaped.
—BERTOLT BRECHT[1]

THIS CHAPTER RETURNS to the problems stemming from of the dialectic of enlightenment, raised briefly in the introduction: connecting it both to the vocation of IR in particular and to more general questions regarding reification and sustainable critique. The claim put forward in the introduction—that while IR theorists have consistently appreciated the need for critique, they have failed to meet the challenge of sustaining it no less consistently—forms the basis of this discussion. That unchecked reification has been an abiding problem in IR for some seven decades is held to be a consequence of this failure. Reification is not the result of theorists simply choosing en bloc to encode political ideology within the idiom of "value-free" social science. It is rather a process of forgetting held to be inherent to thinking politically: to the tensions of trying to apply systematic theory to politics. Although many acknowledge this difficulty, such acknowledgments do not, on their own, suffice. Sustainable critique requires both an account of reification and specialized tools that can meet the challenges posed by that account. The aim of this chapter is to provide the former, laying the groundwork for the latter.

Neither of these tasks is easy; they involve a shift in theoretical gestalt. This may explain why, in the introduction, the discipline of IR was cast in historical-vocational terms. Because the challenge of sustaining critique is considerable, the importance of the attempt must be kept in mind as a firebreak against despair or resignation. With that in mind, this chapter will make an explicitly normative argument: what IR theorists *ought* to do to, given the ethical commitments of their vocation and the limits of

---

1. Brecht (2003), p. 75.

conceptual theory. It will plumb the insights of the same scholars whose work did so much to diagnose the dialectical nature of enlightenment reason in the first place: Max Horkheimer, Herbert Marcuse, and especially Theodor Adorno. If sustainable critique can in fact be married to IR—if, that is, the kind of "triple distance" to which Stanley Hoffmann was understood to have alluded in the previous chapter is possible—clues may be found by following their lead.

This chapter contains six sections. First, the "dialectic of enlightenment" thesis set out briefly in the introduction will be traced in greater detail, with particular emphasis on the Comtean-positivist tradition against which it emerged. Second, it will show how the legacy of Comtean positivism, combined with the technological transformations associated with late modernity—transformations that culminate in the extreme violence of the first and second world wars—created the need for chastened reason and sustainable critique. Taking a rhetorical cue from Hans Morgenthau, it will give the ethos animating such critique a name: the *animus habitandi*—the "will to dwell within, or to abide." In the third section, it seeks to demonstrate how the absence of such an ethos hinders theorists seeking to address their reliance on reification, drawing on examples from both ostensibly value-free and avowedly normative IR theory: recent work by Marc Trachtenberg, Mervyn Frost, and Richard Price.

The next three sections then change direction. Why is it, I ask in section four, that IR has struggled to fully address the problem of reification? Why is the obligation summed up in the *animus habitandi* so hard to parse out in concrete methodological terms? The answer lies in understanding how deeply IR's reliance on reification runs. To show this, I offer a foreshortened account of how it has traditionally been understood and critiqued in IR theory, contrasting that understanding with the sensibility set out here. Section five lays out the notions of negative dialectics and non-identity, upon which sustainable critique is predicated. Finally, section six considers the claim that some have made as to the essentially unworkable nature of such thought—the claim that the critique of reification set out here cuts so deeply as to make systematic social science impossible.

The chapters of this book work in a pincerlike motion. The present chapter and the next demonstrate reification as a *theoretical* challenge to sustainable critique, using the work of the Frankfurt School to show how it is inherent to the limitations of theory when applied to politics, the difficulty of characterizing those limitations, and the failure of existing critical traditions within IR to address this problem fully. Chapters 3 through 5 show how it has played out *concretely* over seven decades of research in IR, through a series of close contextual readings. The concluding chapter returns to the issues raised here: how, given the limitations and challenges facing both social science and late-modern politics, might a sustainably critical IR be possible?

Between Comte and Catastrophe

In his *Course on Positive Philosophy* (1830–42), Auguste Comte suggested that the collective capabilities of human thought passed through three states, or developmental stages. In the first of these—the theological stage—human consciousness seeks the causes of observable phenomena by resort to "the immediate actions of supernatural beings"—divine will, fairies, demigods. In the second stage, the metaphysical, human consciousness outgrows this, seeking causes in personified abstractions, which are held to inhere in being: forces of nature, of history, of spirit. In its third and final form, human consciousness gives over "the vain search after absolute notions, the origin and destination of the universe, and the causes of phenomena." Instead, the mind addresses itself to the discovery of natural laws, to "the establishment of a connection between single phenomena and some general facts, the number of which continually diminishes with the progress of science."[2]

This was a progressivist scientific project, nested within a larger normative one. Understanding would advance as parsimony and empiricism grew in its possible application to the study of ever-wider slices of the human and natural world. Different problem sets, to be sure, might lend themselves to such application with varying degrees of difficulty: those of mathematics, astronomy, and physics with relative ease; society and politics with greater difficulty. But Comte remained confident that "a wholly new order of scientific conceptions" would emerge, whereby even those fields most resistant to such reductionism—human society and politics—could be made rigorous. Such a science, he believed, would serve both "our most urgent intellectual necessities" and "the

---

2. Comte (1896), Vol. I, p. 2. In returning to Comte, I have (hesitantly) bypassed the extensive debates surrounding positivism's various reincarnations: the work of the early Wittgenstein, Carnap, etc.; the "critical realism" of Karl Popper; and Imre Lakatos's MSRP. These connections can be found in Neufeld (1995), ch. 2; Diesing (1991); Elman and Elman (2002); Tellis (1994), ch. 1; Chernoff (2005); Kurki (2008); and Jackson (2008).

3. Comte (1896), Vol. II, pp. 138–139. For a useful discussion of Comte's three-phase model, see Hobhouse (1967), pp. 59–79.

most imperative needs of immediate social practice."³ It would also provide a basis for new forms of political, spiritual, and social solidarity:

> The great political and moral crisis that societies are now undergoing...arise[s] out of intellectual anarchy. While stability in fundamental maxims is the first condition of genuine social order, we are suffering under an utter disagreement which may be called universal. Till a certain number of general ideas can be acknowledged as a rallying-point of social doctrine, the nations will remain in a revolutionary state, whatever palliatives may be devised; and their institutions can only be provisional. But whenever the necessary agreement on first principles can be obtained...the causes of disorder will have been arrested by the mere fact of the agreement. It is in this direction that those must look who desire a natural and regular, a normal state of society.⁴

Comte's claim is twofold. First, that social life can be reduced, as Herbert Marcuse put it, to "a more or less definite complex of facts governed by more or less general laws," such that it can be controlled by practical reason.⁵ Second, that once so reduced, social and political life would discover a true and universal basis for consensus and harmony: a "normal state" of society based on a consensus of facts and values. Society's reduction to a rational schematic, on this account, is its liberation from superstition and medievalism.

The *philosophie positive* did not emerge from an intellectual vacuum. Its meliorism refined and extended an intellectual project as old as the enlightenment itself: Bacon's and Descartes's aim to dispel mystification and make reason the master of nature, that it might "perfect and govern" the natural world and "endow the human family with new mercies."⁶ However cavalier this approach may have seemed to their contemporaries, Bacon and Descartes had even so limited their systematic philosophy chiefly to the natural world.⁷ By contrast, Comte

---

4. Comte (1896), Vol. I, pp. 15–16.

5. Marcuse (1960), p. 340; also Holborn (1968).

6. Bacon (1960) [1620], pp. 15, 29. Comte (1896): "It is difficult to assign a precise date to this [positivist] revolution....But if we must fix upon some marked period to serve as a rallying point, it must be said that—about two centuries ago—when the human mind was astir under the precepts of Bacon, the conceptions of Descartes, and the discoveries of Galileo. Then it was that the spirit of the Positive philosophy rose up" (Vol. I, p. 7). See Adorno and Horkheimer (2002), pp. 1–34.

7. Whitehead (1925) captures the mixed reception accorded this sensibility through a witticism attributed to the physician William Harvey, a contemporary of Bacon. The latter, Harvey

sought to extend reason into social and political affairs, too.[8] Just as the laws of nature provided a universal order for the natural world, so, too, would social laws give stability to a society then in the midst of wrenching transformations.

Viewed from the perspective of a century, it appeared to the scholars of the Frankfurt School that the development of positivism's social-scientific agenda had not brought with it Comte's hoped-for moral and spiritual regeneration. The extension of reason into human life had, without doubt, utterly transformed it. But its advances did not come unalloyed; reason had a dialectical nature, which Comte had failed to fully appreciate.[9] "We have no doubt," Theodor Adorno and Max Horkheimer wrote in the *Dialectic of Enlightenment*, "...that freedom in society is inseparable from enlightenment thinking." That said—

> We believe we have perceived with equal clarity, however, that the very concept of that thinking, no less than the concrete historical forms, the institutions of society with which it is intertwined, already contain the germ of the regression which is taking place everywhere today.[10]

The dialectical nature of reason and its tendency to "regression" are not, for Adorno and Horkheimer, simply reducible to positivism.[11] Their core lay in

---

asserted, "wrote of science like a Lord Chancellor" (63). Bacon was made lord chancellor of England in 1618.

8. Linklater (1990a): "Positivism emulates the method of the natural sciences. Its exponents employ what they regard as the more advanced methodological techniques of the social sciences in their attempt to construct an equally rigorous science of society.... Positivism therefore resembles the physical sciences which produce knowledge that enables human beings to acquire mastery of nature" (9). Also Wernick (2001), pp. 36ff.

9. Though, it can be argued, he sensed them. In this vein, the more bizarre aspects of Comte's undertakings—namely, his now all-but-forgotten Religion of Humanity, with its eclectic mix of social theory, Catholic iconography, and the canonization of Clotilde de Vaux—might be viewed with some sympathy. The Religion of Humanity, on this account, was Comte's attempt to give back what practical reason took away, avoiding precisely the regression to premodern superstition that Adorno and Horkheimer were, a century later, seeking to understand. "Like Nietzsche's madman in the marketplace," the sociologist and cultural theorist Andrew Wernick (2001) explained, "Comte was 'seeking God'...in the very midst of [His] cultural demise" (6; also Adorno et al. [1977], p. 121). See also Cole (1950), pp. 157–169; Manuel (1962); and Wright (1986). A fictional, but devastating, satire of Comte's Religion of Humanity is Assis (1997) [1881].

10. Adorno and Horkheimer (2002) [1944–47], p. xvi; Marcuse (1964), ch. 7. Or as Zygmunt Bauman (1989) has more recently put it: "We suspect...that the Holocaust could merely have uncovered another face of the same modern society whose other, more familiar face we so admire...that each of the two faces can no more exist without the other than can the two sides of a coin" (7).

11. The exact nature of their interaction and its effects for what is now called the "public sphere" are complex, and a full account exceeds present purposes. Some sense of their understanding may be gleaned from the following: "A moral system, with axioms, corollaries, and iron logic, and reliable application to every moral dilemma—that is what is demanded of philosophers.

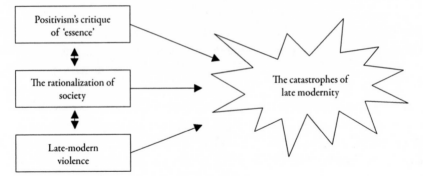

FIGURE 1.1 The Dialectic of Enlightenment Thesis

the reifying tendency of reason, as discussed in the introduction: that form of forgetting that allowed the instrumentalization of natural "kinds" to be turned unproblematically onto sentient beings. That potential, they hold, preceded Comte by at least several centuries; positivism simply amplified and extended its effects.[12] Not only did it extend such reason more deeply into the human and social spheres but also it constrained critical attempts to track or critique its regressive tendencies.

To speak very broadly, there were three interconnected reasons for this (see figure 1.1). First, positivism replaced metaphysical notions of essence with empirical notions of appearance—it conflated seeing with believing. In so doing, it tended to undermine the broadly humanistic aims of its promulgators by (perhaps inadvertently) calling those aims into question. Second, a moral-psychological effect issued from that initial conflation: a kind of gleeful exploitation of others that came from the mounting pressures of rationalized society, on the one hand, and the erosion of humanistic notions of moral obligation on the other. Third, when these factors were married to the technological break-throughs of late modernity—breakthroughs that positivist-enlightenment reason had itself helped ignite—the conditions for catastrophe were set. In the remainder of this section, each of these is taken in turn.

The first of these factors is positivism's critique of essence. As has been noted, positivism's reliance on empiricist forms of knowing confined human

---

As a rule they have fulfilled the expectation. Even when they have not set up a practical system or a fully developed casuistry, they have managed to derive obedience to authority from their theories. Usually they have justified once again the whole scale of values already sanctioned by public praxis, with all the comforts of sophisticated reasoning, demonstration and evidence" (Adorno and Horkheimer [2002], p. 197).

12. Adorno and Horkheimer (2002): "Bacon well understood the scientific temper which was to come after him" (2).

understanding to observable moments of cause and effect, dismissing as mere superstition the possibility of "immanent powers or hidden properties" that might inhere in people or things.[13] In the process, Adorno and Horkheimer argued, such forms of knowing inadvertently placed their humanistic aims into great jeopardy. If one was to be wholly consistent in one's empirical rigor, would one not have to concede that humanism *itself*—those doctrines holding that human beings were always to be treated as ends and never as means—was just another essentialist "superstition"? Root that humanism in whatever foundational axiom one might choose (human sentience, the soul, God's love of man), one must still appeal to some or another form of metaphysical abstraction of the sort with which Comte and his inheritors had no truck. In this sense, "[e]nlightenment is totalitarian" and has a tendency to self-destruct: it deconstructs the very values that actuate it.[14]

Within this critique of essence, moreover, Adorno discerned a tendency to what he would come to call *identity*, or *identitarian* thinking: a practice of reasoning that led to a conflation between concepts and categories, on the one hand, and real-world things on the other. By focusing entirely on observables and rejecting notions of essence, reason classified and ordered things on the basis of their outward likeness: "absorb[ing] experience into mental categories and ultimately…reduc[ing] reality to a set of concepts," as Fred Dallmayr explained.[15] This reduction carried risks. Identitarian thinking made "unlike things alike"—provisionally sacrificing their uniqueness to make them fungible.[16] "To think," Adorno asserted, "is to identify. Conceptual order is content to screen what thinking seeks to comprehend. The semblance and truth of thought entwine."[17] What if one forgot that this sacrifice was merely provisional? What if the concept became wholly conflated with the thing it was meant to describe? Roland Bleiker has aptly summarized the effects of that forgetting: to "subsume the particular under the general, force subjective and idiosyncratic identities into one unitary system of thought, one universal point of reference, one truth that silences all others."[18]

No less problematic is that such forgetting covers its tracks, becoming extremely difficult to keep present to mind. A limited awareness of this problem has long been present in both political science and IR. Ernst Haas and colleagues, by way

---

13. Adorno and Horkheimer (2002), p. 3.

14. Adorno and Horkheimer (2002), p. 4; see also Adorno et al. (1977), pp. 121–122.

15. Dallmayr (1994), p. 21.

16. Rose (1994), p. 157.

17. Adorno (1973) p. 5.

18. Bleiker (2000), p. 140. See also Rose (1978), pp. 46–48.

of example, captured some aspects of it in 1977: "modern man is 'in science,' not just a user of it...scientific culture has become conterminous with political life. The claims to truth associated with science, if not objectively 'true,' have the function of being socially true and compelling because modern man has put himself in the position, by dint of his political values, of being unable to do otherwise."[19]

Haas and colleagues write of losing the ability to distinguish between that which is "objectively true" and that which is "socially true": precisely to the challenge of checking or "tracking" reification's moments of forgetting. Adorno and Horkheimer shared this concern, but they saw the problem as both deeper and wider. Concerns of the sort Haas and colleagues raised captured only the tip of the dialectical iceberg; the state of "being unable to do otherwise" was symptomatic of a broader dysfunction. The reduction of things and people to ideal types—and from there to instrumentalities on the basis of their subjective use-value—was deeply woven into a culture that demanded constant profit and ever-greater efficiency:

> Science stands in the same relationship to nature and human beings in general as insurance theory stands to life and death in particular. Who dies is unimportant; what matters is the ratio of incidences of life and death to the liabilities of the company.[20]

The pressures placed on particular political orders, no matter how initially humanistic in outlook, were therefore bound to be legion. Such "metaphysical" abstractions as life, dignity, and freedom would inevitably find themselves pressed by more tangible concerns. As Horkheimer explained:

> Reason has become completely harnessed to the social process. Its operational value, its role in the domination of men and nature, has been made the sole criterion. Concepts have been reduced to summaries of the characteristics that several specimens have in common.... They are thought of as mere abbreviations of the items to which they refer.... *It is as if thinking itself had been reduced to the level of industrial processes, subjected to a close schedule—in short, made part and parcel of production.*[21]

---

19. Haas, Williams, and Babai (1977), p. 355; also Morgenthau (1972). See chapter 5 or Haas (1997).

20. Adorno and Horkheimer (2002), p. 66. See also Adorno (1973), pp. 126–127.

21. Horkheimer (2004), p. 15, emphasis mine. On this point, Lukács (1971) is apropos: "In consequence of the rationalization of the work-process, the human qualities and idiosyncrasies of

It is not, on this account, that reason produces untrue outcomes in any simple or falsifiable sense; it still possesses the means, following Horkheimer, to facilitate efficient production. It is rather that, in the process, "reason itself destroys the humanity which it had made possible in the first place."[22] Lacking the space, the time, or the resources for careful reflection, or a framework within which to act meaningfully on the basis of such reflection, reason had been loosed from its humanistic moorings. It had become a free-floating asset, to be appropriated to partisan advantage. Thus it was that the world could be made ever richer in comforts and diversions yet ever more shot through with angst and fear. One example of this was to be seen in totalitarianism, with showpiece public welfare projects built by slave laborers; another was the image of the 1950s-era suburban fallout shelter, with its array of "modern" appointments (wall-to-wall carpeting, foldout beds, board games—but alongside stocks of canned water and food, radiation filters, and a battery-operated civil defense radio). In both, material comfort and ease sat cheek by jowl with existential terror.[23]

The second of the three factors contributing to reason's "regression" derived from the first. The identitarian tendencies latent in reason and amplified by positivism's reliance on empiricism had distinct moral-psychological effects when combined with the increasing rationalization of society.[24] The tension between outward prosperity and inward anxiety recalls the desperation that (as surveyed in the introduction) Max Weber had described in his *Science as a Vocation* lecture: it drove men and women from the vocation of reason back into the arms of superstition and ideology. Yet Weber, it will be recalled, had retained the hope that enlightenment reason might someday close the circle and fulfill itself: that while the "night" of unreason had proven longer than anticipated, a "morning" of freedom was still to be worked and hoped for. Adorno and Horkheimer dismissed such hopes as Panglossian. This dismissal is in part explained by the perfected rationalization of mass murder, a development Weber had not lived to see. That said, there was more to the

---

the worker appear increasingly as *mere sources of error*…he is a mechanical part incorporated into a mechanical system" (p. 89, emphasis in original).

22. Habermas (1994), p. 39.

23. See, for example, Ghamari-Tabrizi (2005); also Marcuse (1964).

24. Horkheimer (1950). For a discussion of Adorno's appropriation of psychological theory, in particular the work of Freud, for his social analysis, see Sherratt (2002), pp. 24–49. For a compact discussion of Marcuse's *Eros and Civilization*, see Wiggershaus (1994), pp. 496–507.

story. Looking backward, these pressures could be discerned at the very roots of modernity, and even before it. The orgiastic humiliation documented in such "dark writers of the bourgeoisie" as the Marquis de Sade was one aspect of such tendencies. Another was the self-interested cunning lionized in the Homeric narratives.

Their discussion of Sade is particularly apposite. It is not the sexual acts *themselves* depicted in Sade that are important to Adorno and Horkheimer, but rather the way in which his characters appropriate one another's bodies: as use-values, bits of business, "entirely functionalized reason."[25] In a sense, Sade's protagonists were simply heeding Kant's call to the *aufklärers: sapere aude!* ("dare to know!"), even if in so daring, one penetrated realms traditionally forbidden or violated long-standing social conventions and orders. However, their path to personal understanding was marked by an unrepentant exploitation of one another's bodies as means to their own ends.[26] Each participant emancipates himself or herself by instrumentalizing the others. "For Sade, enlightenment was not so much an intellectual as a social phenomenon. He carried forward the dissolution of bonds... and the critique of solidarity with society, office, family, to the point of declaring anarchy."[27] Such "anarchic dissolution," it is true, gave rise to orgies of pleasure seeking rather than the fires of Auschwitz and Hiroshima. But in the former, Adorno and Horkheimer asserted, were planted the seeds of the latter. "Each of the Ten Commandments is declared void before the tribunal of reason... revealed without exception as ideologies."[28] The lesser offenses of Sade's antiheroes were merely harbingers of worse offenses yet to come.

---

25. Adorno and Horkheimer (2002): "More than a century before the emergence of sport, Sade demonstrated empirically what Kant grounded transcendentally: the affinity between knowledge and planning which has set its stamp of inescapable functionality on a bourgeois existence rationalized even in its breathing spaces. The precisely coordinated modern sporting squad, in which no member is in doubt over his role and a replacement is held ready for each, has its exact counterpart in the sexual teams of Juliette, in which no moment is unused, no body orifice neglected, no function left inactive" (69).

26. Compare this, incidentally, to Kant's account of sexual relations in the *Metaphysics of Morals*: "Sexual union *(commercium sexuale)* is the reciprocal use that one human being makes of the sexual organs and capacities of another.... For the natural use that one sex makes of another's sexual organs is *enjoyment*, for which one gives itself up to the other. In this act a human being makes himself into a thing, which conflicts with the right of humanity is his own person." See Vol. I, §24–25; here cited in Kant (1996b), pp. 426–427. From the discussion in Lukács (1971), p. 100.

27. Adorno and Horkheimer (2002), pp. 90–91. Or as Habermas (1984–87) succinctly summarized it: "victories over outer nature are paid for with defeats of inner nature" (Vol. I, p. 380).

28. Adorno and Horkheimer (2002), p. 91.

This brings the discussion to the third factor leading to the regressive potential of enlightenment reason. In the foregoing, Adorno and Horkheimer were said to have suggested that while "the germ of... regression" lay in the concept of enlightenment thinking, that germ had required the "concrete historical forms, the institutions of society with which it is intertwined," to strike root.[29] This refers to the material conditions that had come to prevail in late modernity, in particular the nexus of speed and what Daniel Deudney has helpfully called *violence interdependence*.[30] Technical innovation, itself an outgrowth of practical reason and its dialectical quality, would drastically extend and intensify the dangers of a practical reason now increasingly unchecked by sustainable critique. The resistance that natural forces had historically exercised on human will, dampening or diffusing its effects—what Clausewitz in the nineteenth century had called friction, and Machiavelli in the cinquecento had called Fortune—constrained denizens of late modernity far less than those living in earlier times.[31] Linked to new forms of political *virtù*, petty bigotries, simplistic understandings of society or politics, or even personal jealousies could give rise to enormous violence with unprecedented rapidity. Critique would have less time to work, even as it now had more to do.

Attached to the dialectical nature of reason, Adorno and Horkheimer held, the technical innovations of late modernity and the intellectual and moral-psychological effects of positivism's identitarian tendencies had helped produce catastrophe. Even as moral philosophy had promised to use reason to give human beings the reflective tools by which to free themselves from oppression and servitude, the rationalization of society neutralized the potential efficacy of such reflection. The latter now "offer[ed] no place from which theory... might be concretely convicted of the anachronisms it [was] suspected of[.]"[32] Unequal to the challenges that faced it, critique increasingly seemed a self-indulgent and irrelevant pursuit: at best a distraction, at worst a betrayal.

Sustainable Critique as an Ethical Commitment: The Animus Habitandi

In the context of IR, just such an indictment of critique is made in the opening pages of Herman Kahn's *Thinking about the Unthinkable* (1962). Kahn, a

---

29. Adorno and Horkheimer (2002) [1944–47], p. xvi; Marcuse (1964), ch. 7.

30. Following Deudney (2007): "The capacity of actors to do violent harm to one another" (35).

31. On friction, see Clausewitz (1984), pp. 119–120; on fortune, see Machiavelli, *Discourses*, Vol. II, p. 29.

32. Adorno (1973), p. 3.

contemporary of Adorno and Horkheimer, had argued that nuclear war, while certainly destructive and horrific, must be prepared for. Moreover, if fought, it could—and therefore had to be—won.[33] Provided certain practical measures (stockpiling water, dispersing population and industrial capacity, keeping strontium 90 out of children's milk) were taken, such wars would not, as was commonly reckoned, be the end of all things. Given that this was so, Kahn asserted, *Americans had no choice but to think carefully and strategically*—their enemies were doing so and would certainly exploit any hint of squeamishness or self-indulgent moralizing to the hilt. Self-chastising reflection was a luxury that could not be afforded: there was important work to be done, and all hands were needed on deck. "Unlike the lady in the cartoon," Kahn explained, "we cannot say 'stop the world, I want to get off.' We cannot get off. Even the most utopian of today's visionaries will have to concede that the mere existence of modern technology involves a risk to civilization that would have been unthinkable twenty-five years ago."[34] One simply *had no choice* but to plan for nuclear genocide. To do otherwise, Kahn asserted, was to betray reason's vocation, whether by giving in to moral cravenness, being misled by inadequate understanding, or indulging in cynically populist moral posturing.[35]

In one sense at least, Adorno and Horkheimer on the one hand and Kahn on the other were in general agreement. However regrettably, the conditions of postwar politics did not allow one to stop the world and get off. Yet that world remained, even so, the work of human beings. Surely, the scholars of the Frankfurt School held, there must be additional choices besides those Kahn offered: between accepting the unthinkable as an inevitable and necessary part of existence, on the one hand, and retreating into the moralizing, the populist, or the woolly-headed on the other.[36] Could one not argue that Kahn's "defense of thinking" had reified the crisis prevailing in late modernity by reducing the "nuclear revolution" to technical questions about single integrated operational plans (SIOPs) and children's milk? Without inquiring as to that revolution's origins or to the constitutive problems it opened up, how might political thinkers move past the immediate problem of survival?

---

33. Kahn (1962), pp. 29ff.

34. Kahn (1962), p. 23; Gray (1979).

35. Kahn (1961), pp. 9–27, and (1984), ch. 1. For a strong condemnation of Kahn, see Morgenthau (1972), pp. 121ff, also (1970), pp. 279–82. That said, Morgenthau's reply—as chapter 3 will show—is insufficient. Albeit inadvertently, he actually *advances* Kahn's argument.

36. For recent efforts in this vein, see Burke (2009), Perkovitch and Acton (2009), and Evans and Kawaguchi (2009).

Perhaps there was a pressing need to counter missiles and warheads with like, but that need existed because human beings helped create it. In at least a loose sense, any political order is a cooperative enterprise: missiles exist because men and women agree to build them. In that sense at least, a choice exists, and other choices are possible—even if the reality of late modern life is such that to express this possibility through simplistic notions like "choice" and "agreement" are clearly inadequate. In failing to understand these choices *as* choices, Kahn forgets this—and invites his readers to do likewise. That forgetting has normative and political consequences. Any other approach to the "unthinkable" becomes foolishness, as easily derided as "the lady in the cartoon."

Thinking about ways in which such choices might actually become workable—that is, creating thinking spaces in which one neither accepted the hopelessness of late modern international politics uncritically nor fled from it—would on this account be the work of critique, its definite social vocation. Yet even so, such critique needed to be chastened, for given the ease with which reification obscured the ideological content of thinking, *critique was as prone to oppressive turns of thought as was any other form of reason.*

A tragic sensibility pervades this realization—a recognition that, in the wake of the catastrophes of the twentieth century, *all* moments of thought had been made suspect. Critique did not go far enough simply by observing, in the well-known formulation, how all that was holy had become profane. When Marx and Engels took their next step, calling on "man" to consider "with sober senses, his real conditions of life and his relations with his kind," they had failed to account for those dystopias (Stalinist, Maoist) that might come out of such consideration: not a revolution that *freed* the masses but one that yoked them further still.[37] Or to put this in the terms developed earlier, all reification may well lie in forgetting, yet if one makes a fetish of remembering, one winds up romanticizing lost utopias that never existed. Critique alone is thus not enough; *sustainable* critique is needed.

The aim of sustainable critique is thus to slow down thought; to create the conditions of possibility for the "thinking space" that enlightenment reason had made both possible and impossible, by virtue of its dialectical character. As Adorno explained:

Perspectives must be fashioned that displace and estrange the world, reveal it to be, with its rifts and crevices, as indigent and distorted as

---

37. Here from, Tucker (1978), p. 476.

it will appear one day in the messianic light. To gain such perspectives without velleity or violence, entirely from felt contact with its objects—this alone is the task of thought.[38]

Such critique takes aim squarely at the problem of reification: it seeks to combat precisely those intellectual dynamics that cause theorists to naturalize particular ontological, epistemological, or normative assumptions, such that their ideological quality is no longer visible. Elsewhere and more aphoristically, Adorno asserted that "the splinter in your eye is the best magnifying-glass": those tools are to be valued that scatter, disrupt, or diffract one's perspective precisely because of the fact of that scattering, disruption, or diffraction.[39] However dangerous any particular notion of freedom or progress might be, given thought's tendency to reify into dangerous ideology, it remained the case that to jettison such notions altogether would be akin to submitting to an inhuman present.[40] Balance was key: without a tragic sensibility, critique became prone to its own forms of virulent counterreification. With too much of it, one retreated into precisely the kind of navel-gazing that Kahn had denounced with such vigor. Only a delicate equipoise could keep faith with a world "in which the unreasonable becomes reasonable and, as such, determines the facts; in which unfreedom is the condition of freedom, and war the guarantor of peace."[41] It would aim to produce a change of scholarly affect: chastening both the theorist and the consumer of theory by weighing hope against despair, faith against skepticism.

A simple anecdote illustrates the need. Imagine a family—two adults and two children—taking a trip to Disneyland. The younger child is enchanted: he sees a castle, life-size cartoon characters, eye-popping illusions—in short, a magical kingdom. The older child regards her younger sibling's enchantment with some derision. The "magic" does not fool *her*: she informs her brother that the castle is a plaster-and-stucco fake, that the various "illusions" are in fact sophisticated animatronic displays, that the cartoon characters are

---

38. Adorno (1974), p. 247.

39. Adorno (1974), p. 50.

40. Zuidervaart (2007a): "So the issue Adorno poses…is twofold: whether societal evil is inevitable, and whether a good society is historically possible. He wants to reject such inevitability while looking societal evil squarely in the face. And he wants to affirm the historical possibility of a good society, while demolishing premature affirmations of the goodness of contemporary society. In each case the 'goodness' or 'truth' of society is indexed both to the remembrance and the elimination of suffering" (145).

41. Marcuse (1960), p. vii.

costumed workers who enter and exit by means of concealed doors, and so on. Whose perception is the correct one? The younger child, who relies on the report of his senses, or the older child, whose antecedently given knowledge of how the world works makes her able to look past what her eyes and ears tell her?

Now consider the parents, who watch solicitously as the family vacation budget dwindles more rapidly than they expected. *Disneyland*, they conclude, *may well be a magic kingdom. But it's also a rip-off.* They may correlate the high price of the admission tickets and their children's strong desire to visit the place with the fact that many products marketed to children (films, school supplies) contain embedded advertisements for Disney parks and products. They might observe a strategic sensibility in how rides and lines are placed near souvenir or food concessions. Perhaps the parents feel some resentment at this; they may resolve henceforth to allow their children to watch only public television and to take future vacations in national parks. Alternatively, perhaps they feel pride at having been able to give their children what they asked for, despite (or because of) the expense.

Either way, it is apparent that direct, unmediated experience and understandings of context, meaning, or essence undermine each other, at more than one level. Either Disneyland is a magic kingdom, or it is a fake. Logically, it cannot easily be both—even if common sense suggests that each position captures something important. Moreover, each position takes a polemical stance vis-à-vis the others. The older sister derides her younger brother, who in turn may resent having his illusions shattered. The parents are not simply worrying about their vacation budget; they are discovering the outlines of a complex system of desires that plays both upon their children and upon their hopes and aspirations for them.

The claim to mutual exclusivity in any one of these worldviews—and the degree to which particular normative commitments may be bound up in them—is precisely what sustainable critique seeks to chasten. In his *Discourse on Method*, Descartes's third rule was "to think in an orderly fashion...beginning with the things which were simplest and easiest to understand and gradually and by degrees reaching more complex knowledge."[42] Or as Stephen Walt put it, IR must seek *"cumulative knowledge."* To obtain it, "the field must follow the standard canons of scientific research: careful and consistent use of terms, unbiased measurement of critical concepts, and public documentation of theoretical and empirical claims."[43] Only accepting ideas or theories in

---

42. Descartes (1960) [1637], p. 15. On this point, see Rose (1978) pp. 14ff.

43. Walt (1991), p. 222, emphasis in original; see also Most and Starr (1989).

their finished form—giving up a critical purview over the interests that inform their constitution—can advance instrumental understanding. These must be accepted as the younger child accepts the reality of Disneyland. Perspectives that subject that outwardly finished form to critique—whether (like the older daughter) by asserting that seeing is not always believing or (like the parents) by interpreting them in terms of complex socioeconomic relationships that "break through their surface existence"—subvert this process, for knowledge can only progress if each layer builds sequentially on the last.[44] Pull out any one link, and the chain comes undone. Hence the tendency for practical and critical theorizing on social and political problems to each makes the other its nemesis.[45]

The fact remains, however, that neither approach is *inherently* more valid or useful than the other, nor can either entirely encompass reality as a whole. There are different forms of knowing, and each captures a slice of a complex reality that is irreducible to thinking. Those who cannot appreciate Disneyland as a magical kingdom will never understand its undying attraction for children who beg to go and parents who save up to take them; those who cannot see it as a profit center will never understand how such desires interconnect with commerce, technology, and control. Both lend themselves to reifying simplifications. "Within this wide realm of what men know," wrote Karl Deutsch in 1958, "scientific and humanistic knowledge are as inseparable as the intellectual processes of synthesis and analysis, or as the presentational and the discursive views of symbols and language." The two are "situated along a single more or less continuous spectrum of human activities."[46] They can, and ought to be, mutually informative—if, that is, all parties both understand the need to chasten their various pretensions to truth and feel the tug of moral obligation to do so.

That sense of obligation requires a name. The *animus habitandi*—"the will to dwell within, or to abide"—might suffice for such a name. The term (from the Latin *habitare*, "to live within, inhabit, or dwell") takes its rhetorical cue from Hans Morgenthau's well-known *animus dominandi*: the "will to dominate," which he held to be a basic fact of political life that must be accepted a priori. A sustainably critical IR would have an obligatory a priori of its own. True to IR's historic sense of vocation, it would oblige theorists to

---

44. Adorno (2006), p. 138.

45. See Adorno (1983), pp. 4–10; Hoffman (1987), p. 232–233; Linklater (1990a), ch. 1.; Lukács (1971), pp. 10–18.

46. Deutsch (1958), p. 4.

accept their own vulnerability to reification as given: to assume, that is, that their concepts and understandings of the world are abstractions, the limits of which can never be entirely known, and whose outlines are constantly in danger of being forgotten. Hence the *animus habitandi*: IR theorists must strive to dwell *within the world*, rather than in their own *thoughts*, and to abide in its undifferentiated complexity and indeterminacy. It thus shares a family resemblance with the "sense of wonderment" that anchors Blaney and Inayatullah's critical turn, with Jane Bennett's "sense of enchantment," William Connolly's "faith," Christine Sylvester and Laura Sjoberg's "empathy," and Brent Steele's "irony."[47] Like them, it is an affective-intellectual disposition—a blend of the reasoned and the intuitive—that "allows us a 'critical distance' from our subject without requiring us to abandon our emotions."[48]

The argument for an *animus habitandi* is thus not wholly new, nor—as chapter 3 will show—is the recognition that Morgenthau's realism strove for something like it. Both claims lie at the core of Richard Ashley's (1984) "poverty of neo-realism" argument, and these would be repeated throughout the first wave of poststructuralist and "third-debate" IR.[49] And yet the question must be asked: beyond identifying the reifications of others, are these forms of IR *sustainably critical*—that is, do they themselves resist their own forms of reification? If reification inheres in thinking *itself*, it will infect all theories to some degree: it speaks to "structures" of thinking that constrain, at least partly, scholarly "agents," notwithstanding the latters' intention.[50] While some reifications might be more dangerous than others, the question of which ideas are "taken up" into political movements or policy shifts is to at least some degree a matter of contingent circumstance. The links between Giddensian "structuration" and Tony Blair's "new Labour," or between Edward Said's *Orientalism* and critical reexaminations of U.S. foreign policy—to pick two well-known examples—may now appear self-evident and indeed inevitable. This, however,

---

47. Blaney and Inayatullah (2004), Bennett (2001), Connolly (2004), Sylvester (1994, 2002), Sjoberg (2006), and Steele (2010).

48. Steele (2010).

49. Ashley (1984). For a trenchant analysis of Ashley's argument, see Connolly (1991), ch. 2.

50. Consider here Ashley's (1989) and Bleiker's (2000) concept of "transversal dissent." Such dissent, Bleiker notes, is meant to open up theory to various multinational, postnational, and transnational political constellations and assemblages. But why would these new assemblages be any freer of the temptation or predilection to dominate than any other? Here Hardt and Negri's (2004) concept of a multitude, united in love, comes to mind. The multitude might be loving, or it might be an oppressive mob. Or it might begin as the former and end as the latter.

is with benefit of hindsight: many ideas, no less potentially valuable, fail to hit political paydirt. The "uptake" of academic theory into policy is as contingent as any other sphere of politics. An a priori obligation thus exists to temper all of them, in real time.

For IR, the absence of an *animus habitandi* has direct, immediate effects. The tendency to reify the assumptions of one paradigm—to view, say, the anarchical states-system not as a useful conceit for organizing thought, but as an authentic reflection of human nature, *or* as a form of class rule to be deconstructed, *or* as a set of social constructions, *or* as a space for facilitating market interactions—both frames the problems of late-modern life and ensures their full complexity remains forever out of reach. Particular epistemologies perpetuate the myth of what Petersen has aptly called the "harmonious ontology": the assumption that "ultimately the diversity of the empirical world is reducible" to this or that "single principle" or characterization.[51] The effect is to conflate particular constructs through which reality is glimpsed with reality itself. If those constructs have ties to particular moral philosophies or political ideologies—and essentially contested concepts must by definition have such ties—IR theory will become a *party* to political debate, locating itself within larger political-normative discourses rather than critiquing them. In an era in which decentering views are ever more needed, they become harder and harder to sustain. A conscious commitment to something like the *animus habitandi* must therefore be made.

The Ethical Lacuna in IR: Three Examples

This obligation, however, has not been fully internalized: neither in IR theory's ostensibly value-free orientations nor in its normatively inflected ones. Marc Trachtenberg's (2006) recent *Craft of International History* illustrates this, with regard to the former. Historical and political knowledge, Trachtenberg acknowledges, is never absolute; there is no way even to prove that the external world exists in philosophically rigorous terms. But once stated, he argues, that point becomes trivial. It means simply, Trachtenberg asserts,

> that everything we do of an intellectual nature is premised on the assumption that we are not being systematically misled: we take as our point of departure the assumption that our basic beliefs about reality— about the existence of an external world knowable through the mind

---

51. Petersen (1999).

and through the senses, acting in tandem—are in fact correct.... The skeptic is not refuted; the basic epistemological problem is recognized, but the normal assumptions—about the existence of reality and the possibility of knowledge—are made, *and we just move on from there.*[52]

Trachtenberg's decision to "just move on from there" is perfectly understandable: he has a job to do. Even so, his judgment is quite explicitly an ethical-normative one: that a certain action (scholarship) is worthwhile, despite the risks entailed (the perpetuation of falsehood). The "normal assumptions" are therefore good enough, and no special or additional precautions need to be taken.

At first glance, Trachtenberg's position seems reasonable and perhaps even appealing. "There can be no living science," wrote the philosopher of science Alfred North Whitehead, "unless there is a widespread instinctive conviction in the existence of an *order of things.*" And yet, Whitehead quickly added, that conviction was predicated rather more on faith than on evidence: a faith "impervious to the demand for a consistent rationality."[53]

Two points now suggest themselves. First, unlike other disciplines, IR deals with questions of mass violence, war, and death not as limit cases, but as part of its everyday *problematique.* Second, for some two millennia, the careful observations of scores of independent researchers of stellar movements seemed to confirm the claim that the sun revolved around the earth. *The report of "the mind and the senses, acting in tandem," it turns out, is— sometimes—systematically misleading.* Trachtenberg's position does not seem to do justice to the potential costs of being misled in an era of constantly impending political-military catastrophe. All the more so when one considers that the "things we do of an intellectual nature" may have either direct effects on policy or indirect, trickle-down effects on the discourses from which policies emerge.[54] Theorists are protected by the institution of the academy, bound neither to the constitutional checks of policy makers nor even to the norms of

---

52. Trachtenberg (2006), pp. 13–14, emphasis mine.

53. Whitehead (1925), pp. 5–6; on process philosophy in IR, see Lebow (2008).

54. Consider Stanley Milgram's (1963) "obedience" experiments as a possible case in point: subjects were asked to administer what they believed to be fatal electric shocks to another person in the service of a scientific study. The assumption was that most would refuse to do so. In fact, depending on the subject's proximity to a perceived source of legitimate authority and his distance from those on whom the shocks were to be administered, at least a considerable plurality complied. Milgram's point: that one's individual predisposition to acts of extreme violence mattered less than the circumstances prevailing when that violence was carried out. To the question: Could Americans do the same terrible things Germans did during the war, Milgram's a

public discourse that constrain (however weakly) pundits and policy wonks. Surely this greater protection from without requires greater obligations from within, lest academics turn into public policy free riders, using their position to engage in advocacy. On this, Trachtenberg is silent. By defending his acceptance of IR's "normal assumptions," he acknowledges, if only pro forma, the obligation to sustainable reflexivity. Yet no further discussion ensues; no examination of what that obligation might mean is undertaken.

Indeed, even IR theory specifically geared to the study of normative problems and resting firmly on interpretive-critical foundations often fails to fully appreciate the need for such an ethos. Consider the work of theorists like Mervyn Frost and Richard Price. For Frost, normative IR theory is meant to provide the means to unlock dense nets of conflicting values—the "tug of principles" that complicates moral judgment and stymies ethical political action. Since the various parties to an entrenched conflict (he uses the Bosnian case) may all have tenable claims within a "settled body of norms in international relations," some method for sorting through such claims must be developed.[55] Normative theory, for Frost, is a practical enterprise, intended to answer the following question: "what ought we, as people more or less well constituted within free states, to do" in the face of this or that event?[56] He hopes, thereby, to identify and foster such new practices ("certain forms of encouragement, certain forms of facilitative practice, material aid and educational measures") as can best harmonize partisan claims with cosmopolitan values.[57]

Even accepting for the sake of argument Frost's claim that many international conflicts do not involve mutually exclusive or incommensurable value positions, at least three objections can be raised.[58] First, what stands surety for

---

nswer was unambiguous: "yes we could...and we still may, if conditions are right" (Bauman [1989], p. 152). Now consider: a key node in the "revolution in military affairs" (O'Hanlon [2000], Owens [2001]) of the 1990s was the use of information technology to create standoff weapons that could be precisely deployed by controllers many miles distant from the battlefield. The interfaces used by these controllers distance them from their targets, while tying them closely to a source of legitimate authority—the chain of command. The effect is to create what Cummings (2003, 2006)—citing Milgram—calls a "moral buffer," which "diminishes controllers' sense of responsibility and autonomy" regarding the violence they administer and the people on whom it is administered. (2003, p. 14). Milgram's conclusions, it appears, have been operationalized to *facilitate* obedience—quite the opposite of what he appears to have intended. Trachtenberg seems not to have considered such possibilities or the ethical questions they raise.

55. Frost (1996), pp. 205 and 105–112, respectively; see also Frost (1998).

56. Frost (1996), p. 207.

57. Frost (1996), p. 211.

58. Frost (2000): "We do not confront one another at international conferences as mutually uncomprehending tribes of scholars.... Life in our discipline is not like this" (5).

the actual content of his "settled core of agreed norms?"[59] Frost has delinked morality from the interests of the state and relocated them within some larger cosmopolitan normative common sense. But what makes the values of a *cosmopolis*—here recall the Melian dialogue from the perspective of the Melians, or French Revolutionary ideology from the perspective of the German romantics—any less potentially oppressive than those of a *polis*?[60] Second, there is the normative effect of assembling norms and redacting them, itself not an act innocent of political consequences. Third, one wonders how well Frost's reasoning would stand up in situations where the conflicts in question are not among third parties. Frost might find, as Herman Kahn did, that while "we, the people in this world, do not have the option of remaining in some sphere outside" of the action of world politics, one's space of reflection changes according to where *in particular* one is within that sphere of action.[61] The mode of reflective repose available to a theorist who is considering relatively distant wars not be sustainable when the fear of violence hits closer to home. One cannot know, of course, but that is precisely the point. One chastens reason precisely *because* one cannot know how well one's sense of duty will bear up in moments of weakness, fear, or exigency.

For his part, Richard Price believes that constructivist IR may be used to "help adjudicate between ethical accounts" by "accounting for the existence, origins and durability of international norms"; he seeks a means of "taking the prevalence of power seriously without precluding the possibility of meaningful progressive moral change."[62] Thus, he hopes, IR theory might avoid the twin dangers of relativism, on the one hand, and continental philosophy's "relentless identification of every new social formation as yet another form of domination" on the other.[63]

Yet Price's own logic betrays him: how would one presume to know moral progress in anything but a provisional and commonsense manner? It is one thing to recognize (as Price does) that real and ideal types must not be conflated.[64] It is quite another to know what that means "all the way down." Are not *all* unchastened notions of moral progress—as theorists

---

59. Frost (1996), p. 112.

60. Shilliam (2006).

61. Frost (2000), p. 2.

62. Price (2008), p. 17, 41.

63. Price (2008), p. 38. See also Reus-Smit's contribution (2008) in the same volume.

64. "You don't confirm or disaffirm the ideal type. You use it as a standard to measure the closeness or remoteness of empirical phenomena" (Deitelhoff and Müller, in Price [2008], p. 43).

from Molly Cochran to Hayward Alker have pointed out—potentially ide-alist?[65] One would need to do more than repeat Weberian truisms about real and ideal types; one would need methods that enforce their separation. It *might*, after all, be the case that the continental philosophers are right, and that all social forms *do* involve some measure of domination. If so, and if this or that new social form then gets called "progress," then the theorist following in Price's footsteps is apt to be providing ideological fodder, however uninten-tionally, for those who do harm to others. Barrington Moore's warning against those who condemned the violence of the French Revolution but ignored the excesses of the ancien régime applies here, if in reverse: structural violence is still violence, even if its static nature makes it more difficult to discern.[66]

Pace Price, that warning is not answered merely by allowing that "ethical standards applied in any given case may not be embraced by all others," or that "disparate cultural contexts" complicate ethical judgments.[67] One would need an active commitment of the sort characterized by the *animus habitandi*, anchored in specific practices.[68] Even when a consensus of values exists, there is an inherent epistemological uncertainty that attends all conceptual reduc-tions of world politics. That concepts like war, peace, amity, and oppression have a certain commonsense, transhistorical quality does *not* mean that theo-rists will automatically know how to trace out their specific configurations in any particular place and time.[69] If one is to assert that *moral progress occurs and is knowable* in any "universal" sense, one must do more than document how a particular violent practice has fallen into desuetude.[70] One must show that *an*

---

65. Alker (2005). Cochran (1999), to be sure, does not use this language; but it is why, in her idiom, "weak foundations" must not be construed to "yield non-contingent ethical claims" (16 and passim).

66. Moore (1993): "To dwell on the horrors of revolutionary violence while forgetting that of 'normal' times is merely partisan hypocrisy" (104). On structural violence, see Galtung (1969).

67. Price (2008), p. 40. Nor is it answered by his and Reus-Smit's (1998) observation that theo-rists "cannot help putting forth truth claims about the world. The individual who does not can-not act, and the genuinely unhypocritical relativist...struggles for something to say and write" (272). This is a claim of necessity, not of right. Perhaps, if the choices are that stark, one ought to devote oneself to ways of speaking and writing that sustainably critique themselves. If that is the only "genuinely nonhypocritical" way to speak, should one not seek after it?

68. This does beg the question: what practices in particular? I will be specifying these later on in chapter 2 and more fully still in the conclusion. The present discussion focuses on developing the claim that such practices are needed, as distinct from how they might be realized.

69. Namely, the "old war/new war" literature, as with Kaldor (2007).

70. Recall Mueller (1990) or Lebow (2010). Are these studies describing a decline in a *par-ticular kind* of violence? Or do they hold that an *absolute decline* in violence has taken place, implying some or another form of moral progress?

absolute decline in the quantity of violence and suffering in the world has taken place. Demonstrating such a claim convincingly is a problem of some magnitude. Given this difficulty, addressing the danger of unintentionally apologizing for new, as-yet undefined forms of oppression would have to be central to Price's project. No such effort is made.

What sustainable critique seeks to *sustain* are multiple and mutually incompatible ways of seeing. Each of these three examples shows how difficult this is: there are many ways in which concepts elide the world, and hence reification can run amok through many variations of forgetting. Yet if one accepts the ethos of the *animus habitandi*, the need for it cannot be denied: only such a perspective might preserve ambiguity—that is, the memory that things are never quite as we have sorted them out—in the face of pressures for peremptory clarity.

What this means in concrete methodological terms is complex, and will be dealt with at some length later. A compact—if somewhat cryptic—summary of it is captured by what Adorno has called "a doubled mode of conduct: an inner one, the immanent process which is the properly dialectical one, and a free, unbound one like a stepping out of dialectics."[71] This will be unpacked more fully later. Briefly, however, it can be summarized thus: the affective position set forth in the previous section—the *animus habitandi*'s constant oscillation between positions of despair and hope among theorists and their readers—must find its methodological counterpart in a series of oscillations between different paradigms within IR theory: buffeting the same event from numerous perspectives. The aim is not synthesis, but mutual chastening: the narratives would be "linked by criticizing one another, not by compromising."[72] Such an approach—as it were, agonism without antagonism—would find some of its initial inspiration in recent turns to regionalist, multiparadigmatic, and eclectic approaches in IR and to complexity theory.[73] Yet, as the coming chapters will show, it must considerably deepen and extend these turns by tying them to the ethical-vocational aspirations for IR set out in the foregoing. To borrow the language of political theorist Bonnie Honig, thus might IR theory *illuminate* politics rather than *displace* it.[74]

---

71. Adorno (1973), p. 31.

72. Adorno (1973), p. 31.

73. See, for example, Buzan and Waever (2003), Harrison (2006), Katzenstein (2005), Katzenstein and Sil (2004, 2008), Sil and Doherty (2000), Legro and Moravcsik (1999, 2001), Zürn and Checkel (2005), and Pempel (2005). The phrase "agonism without antagonism" I owe to an anonymous reader.

74. Honig (1993).

From Critique to Sustainable Critique

The previous two sections argued that the failure to evince and sustain an ethos akin to the *animus habitandi* has left IR continually vulnerable to unchecked reification. That granted, it is not the case that IR has remained wholly unaware of the problem: as the introduction noted, the need for critique has long been understood, and critical turns have been undertaken. Yet these turns proved short-lived; managing reification in an ongoing fashion has proven difficult. How might sustainable critique fare better? By way of answer, the present section summarizes the various ways in which reification has been conceived of, and dealt with, in IR. The aim is to illustrate sustainable critique by contrast. With due consideration for the fact that such typologies are *themselves* reifications, which must be brought under the ambit of their own form of critique, such a classification might help clarify what sustainable critique proposes to do differently.

With that in mind, attempts to check reification in IR can be grouped into three distinct sets of approaches: *analytical, normative*, and *vocational*. Each speaks to a different theoretical moment—or "level of analysis"—during which reification's distinctive form of forgetting may take place. Table 1.1 describes these moments briefly and then describes the ways in which IR's various reflective turns have sought to address them. My larger claim will proceed as follows: I shall argue that IR's past reflective turns have focused on reification only at the analytical and normative levels. If the discipline's historic vocation is to be made good upon, reflexivity must be deepened to accommodate the vocational one as well: to facilitate the kind of ongoing engagement described in the bottom-right rubric of table 1.1 and developed in the coming pages.

Analytical reification is that first-order moment of forgetting that erases the distinction between concepts and things in themselves—the real world of interactions and social processes that lies beyond any single reductive characterization. It is through such forgetting that a human-constructed order or a given fact-value tradition can appear to possess natural—or recalling Weber's comments on Isaiah from the introduction, supernatural—validity or moral legitimacy. The effect is to "rationally reenchant" the world: to accord primacy to a worldview in which relations of cause and effect are identifiable and tractable, and to accord agency, causality, or materiality to the concepts and traditions through which those relationships are parsed out.

Analytical reification is thus closely tied to what Paul Lazarsfeld, writing in 1941, called "administrative" theory, or what is nowadays sometimes

Table 1.1 Reification and Reflexivity in IR: Three "Levels of Analysis"

Level	Effect of Unchecked Reification at This Level	Key Reflective Countermove
Analytical	Conflates concepts or fact-value traditions with real-world things, reenchants rationalized social order by fetishizing "value-free" social science.	Targeted debunking: demonstrating the artificiality of a naturalized concept or fact-value tradition.
Normative	Accords privileged or universal normative legitimacy to particular configurations or narratives of world politics. May result from critiques of analytical reification.	Targeted debunking: demonstrating that a particular naturalized concept or fact-value tradition serves contestable political or fractional interests.
Vocational	Alienates theorist from larger world by obscuring ongoing connections between theory and practice; interferes with discipline's vocational aspirations.	Sustainable critique: since all thinking is given to reification, an ongoing mode of critical self-reflection is needed to chasten reason.

called value-free social science: academic studies or social planning efforts that divorce targeted theoretical problem solving "from the total historical situation in which such planning and studying goes on."[75] This covers an extremely broad swath of theory, for such isolation is often necessary to produce useful information; as Kenneth Waltz once observed, "in reality, everything is related to everything else."[76] It should not therefore be surprising that critical interventions at the analytical level number prominently among the field's numerous and widely read "classics": Waltz on images, Arnold Wolfers (and later, Barry Buzan and David Baldwin) on security, Helen Milner on anarchy, Patrick Morgan on deterrence, Ernst Haas on the balance of power, Hedley Bull and Stanley Hoffmann on theory and

---

75. Lazarsfeld (1941), p. 9. Lazarsfeld and Adorno, it should be noted, were collaborators for a time, and Lazarsfeld's distinction borrows heavily from Horkheimer's essay "Traditional and Critical Theory." See Adorno (2000), p. 138, and Jenemann (2007).

76. Waltz (1979), pp. 8–9. See also Waltz (1992): "Theory is artifice. A theory is an intellectual construction by which we select facts and interpret them" (22).

politics, Graham Allison on national-security decision making, and so on.[77] The key aim of such interventions is to reconstruct (i.e., remember) the framework from which a given conceptual construct or fact-value tradition has emerged, its generative provenance. The concept or tradition is thus returned to its proper sense and proportions. Practical theorizing can then resume.

Normative reification is a second-order mode of forgetting, which often—though not always—follows from the critique of analytical reification. This is because critique is often grounded in normative counterclaims as to what constitutes "the good"; it aims to reassert, or contest, the normative a prioris on which a given analytical concept or fact-value tradition is predicated.[78] Such critiques may further argue that the obfuscation of these a prioris, whether intentional or otherwise, serves fractional or partisan interests: that their naturalization induces support for (or at least fosters complacency toward) particular sets of policies by endowing them with a veil of legitimacy or inevitability—helping sustain whatever inequities they might suborn.[79] As at the analytical level, the critique of normative reification also focuses on specific acts or moments of debunking—albeit with a different end in mind. It aims "to puncture the social illusion" that unchecked reifications sustain—stripping them of their timelessness or inevitability, thereby opening them up to political contestation.[80] This work is explicitly emancipatory, and scholars engaging in such critique are generally unambiguous on that score: consider the work of Richard Ashley, Robert Cox, Andrew Linklater, Mark Neufeld, and Ken Booth.[81]

Yet that emancipatory aim contains its own reifying potential. Chapter 2 discusses this point in some detail, but briefly: what a priori conception of

---

77. Allison (1971), Bull (1966), Baldwin (1997), Buzan (1991), Haas (1953a, 1953b), Hoffmann (1958–59, 1977), Milner (1991), Morgan (1977, 2003), Wolfers (1962), and Waltz (2001), esp. pp. 230 to the end.

78. Lukács (1971): "Thus philosophy stands in the same relation to the special [i.e., social] sciences as they do with respect to empirical reality. The formalistic conceptualization of the special sciences become for philosophy an immutable substratum and this signals the final and despairing renunciation of every attempt to cast light on the reification that lies at the root of this formulation" (110). See also Bernstein (1976), Glynos and Howarth (2007), Habermas (1984, Vol. I, ch. 4), and Honneth (2008).

79. Adorno (2000), p. 138.

80. Lukács (1971), pp. 5–6.

81. Ashley (1981, 1984, 1989), Cox (1981, 1996a, 2008), Linklater (1990a, 1990b, 1998, 2007), Neufeld (1995), Booth (1991a, 1991b, 2005, 2007).

emancipation, however capacious, is wholly immunized from turning oppressive? The problem lies in an unresolved paradox that goes all the way back to Lukács: if the illusion that perpetuates reified social orders is as powerful as he suggests, how does he account for his own ability to see it? Further, what defines the reality that emerges from this or that critical intervention as *the* true and valid one? Even were we to stipulate this, how would such a reality be translated into programmatic politics without being rereified in some new, no less potentially repressive, normative-conceptual framework?[82] What resources exist to check that subsequent rereification? Political thinkers from Anne Norton to Cornel West have repeatedly warned of such problems.[83] Yet even avowedly normative approaches to IR theory—as the previous section showed—have not systematically accounted for it.

Vocational reification emerges from this lacuna. As the Frankfurt School social theorist Axel Honneth has recently noted, the challenge that unchecked reification poses is not merely one of methods or politics: it must include *ethics* as well if it is to be sustainably met. When human beings forget their role in authoring the world, they also lose a sense of their own responsibility for events that take place in it: of themselves as stakeholders. The individual, Honneth suggests, ceases to feel bound to and answerable for her actions as they affect the well-being of others and the world as a whole: "no longer empathetically engaged in interaction with [her] surroundings, but... instead placed in the perspective of a neutral observer, psychically and existentially untouched by [her] surroundings."[84]

Adapting this insight to IR, it suggests that *when theorists of world politics forget that political institutions and social realities are constituted—as well as described—by human ideas and actions, and that academic knowledge plays a particular (and occasionally important) role within that constitution, they forget their own obligations as stakeholders and moral agents.* Without that felt

---

82. Adorno (1973): "The meaningful times for whose return the early Lukács yearned were as much due to reification, to inhuman institutions, as he would later attest it only to the bourgeois age" (191). See also Adorno (1974), pp. 228–231; Habermas (1984), Vol. I, pp. 357–365; and the extended discussions in Arato and Breines (1979), chs. 8–9; Honneth (2008); and West (1991), ch. 6.

83. Norton (2004); West (1989).

84. Honneth (2008): "as soon as an agent permanently takes up the role of an exchange partner, he becomes a 'contemplative' 'detached observer,' while his own existence 'is reduced to an isolated particle and fed into an alien system.' With this conceptual shift of perspective, the concepts of contemplation and detachment become essential to the explanation of what takes place in the modus of reification at the level of social agency. Here, the subject is no longer empathetically engaged in interaction with his surroundings, but is instead placed in the perspective of a neutral observer, psychically and existentially untouched by his surroundings" (24).

obligation, IR's vocation cannot survive; given the difficulty of the "intellectual doublethink" it entails, why go to the trouble of trying to sustain it? Thus does it get lost in a welter of intramural debates: IR's "constant oscillation between the scientific and the metaphysical, the normative and the factual, the descriptive and the prescriptive."[85]

As the bottom-right rubric of table 1.1 suggests, addressing vocational reification obliges a different approach to critique than does addressing reification at its analytical and normative levels. In the former two, reification is conceived of as a fallacy to be exploded through bounded acts of conceptual debunking. Critique is a necessary but secondary task; the priority is to return to practical theory as quickly as possible. In vocational critique, reification is a necessary consequence of *all thinking*—including itself. Grounded in the ethos of the *animus habitandi*, vocational critique requires IR theorists to be constantly vigilant—toward the insufficiencies *of their own thinking* no less than to that of others—and suggests that ongoing, free-standing critical methods must be developed to meet that requirement. Given that reification results from the use of concepts to mediate between human thought and real-world processes, and that only by such mediation is thinking possible, it is not a one-off problem to be fixed and then moved past. It is rather an enduring, ineluctable fact to be accepted and managed in its effects.[86] One has, on this account, no unmediated experience of anything save (if one remains vigilantly self-aware) one's own mediations.[87] It is this negative move, back onto itself, that renders vocational critique sustainable over time.

This conception of critique has deep philosophical roots in the successes, and the failures, attributed to idealist philosophy since Kant. Why was it, Kant asked, that ideas about reality and reality itself never seemed to mesh as precisely as post-Cartesian philosophy seemed to expect? Often, he allowed, this could be chalked up to observer error—to faulty premises or data. But this was not always the case. There were certain antinomies—certain enduring logical paradoxes—that inhered in how human reason grasped the world. For example, Kant observed, it was possible to frame contradicting propositions that were logically unassailable in their own terms and yet mutually exclusive. One could, to use some of Kant's own examples, demonstrate logically *both*

---

85. Guilhot (2008), p. 301.

86. Adorno (2000): "There is nothing under the sun, and I mean absolutely nothing, which in being mediated through human intelligence and human thought is not also socially mediated" (15–16).

87. This formulation is from Daniel Bertrand Monk.

that the universe is bounded in time and space *and* that it is infinite; *both* that living things have free will *and* that their behavior is determined by nature; *both* that everything in nature exists contingently *and* that it is the will of a "necessary being."[88] These antinomies existed in a kind of logical limbo: each presented two elements that could not both simultaneously be true and yet could not each be disproved.[89]

In the context of the present argument, Kant's substantive positions regarding the infinity of the universe, freedom of the will, or the existence of God need not be specifically addressed. The key point is this: *concepts that represent abstract ideas in the mind*—through terms like *universe, infinite, necessary*, and *contingent*—*are constructs of meaning that originate in the mind*. The rules of logic by which they relate to one another *also* originate in the mind. For Kant, Herbert Marcuse explained, the world "is not immediately and already rational but must rather be brought into reason"; it must be "comprehended by thought and defined as a concept."[90] To get one's head around a problem is to imprint a conceptual-logical structure onto it.[91] Those imprints cannot be wholly traced out from within their own confines; that is, we cannot easily see the limits of a structure of thought from within that structure. Kant was aware of this. "One can tinker around with metaphysics in sundry ways," he warned, "without even suspecting that one might be venturing into untruth."[92]

To be clear, Kant is *not* suggesting that the material world is a figment of humanity's collective imagination. There are certain foundational realities whose certainty he believes he can establish. Moreover, there is a common human experience of the world, a shared perception of it that individuals are able to communicate to one another, and on which they can build. But that

---

88. See the *Critique of Pure Reason* [1781–87], hereafter Kant (1996a), pp. 454–485 (Ak. A426/ B454-A460/B488); and the *Prolegomena to Any Future Metaphysics*, hereafter Kant (2004), pp. 80–92 (Ak. 4:338–339). For helpful introductory essays, see Guyer and Wood (1998) and Kitcher (1996). For useful introductions into Kantian critical philosophy as it relates to IR, Williams and Booth (1996), Kratochwil (2007), Shilliam (2006), and Hutchings (1996, 2001) are helpful.

89. Kant (1996a), pp. 496–501 (Ak. A477/B505-A484/B512); Kant (2004), pp. 102–115 (Ak. 4:350–365).

90. Marcuse (1988), pp. 135–136; also Bleiker (2009), pp. 23–25.

91. Kant (1996a), pp. 94–95 (Ak. A42/B59); Kant (2004), pp. 46–47 (Ak. 4:294–295). Pippin (1982), chapter 2 is also helpful. In the context of IR, see Brown (1994).

92. Kant (2004), p. 92 (Ak. 4:340). Or as Norman Kemp Smith (2003) put it: "principles are never self-evident, and yet principles are indispensable. Such was Kant's unwavering conviction as regards the fundamental postulates alike of knowledge and of conduct" (36).

different men and women are all seeing the same world in roughly commensurate ways does not mean they are seeing that world *as it really is*.[93] The real world of things as they are outside of human perceptions of them—what Kant called *things-in-themselves* (akin perhaps, in another context, to what Alexander Wendt has called "rump materialism")—is largely beyond our reach. It is a fundamental limitation, he maintains, that must be accepted, with the hope that future generations will know more and the hope that personal freedom and happiness are possible even with what little is given to those living here and now. One may even discern with the passage of time a progressive trend; a "secret plan" of nature, cunning of history or a purpose to Providence.[94] But all of this remains, even so, within the bound of perceptual and rational faculties that imperfectly capture the world and that understand things "out there" by mediating them through sensory and logical faculties that change them, usually invisibly, occasionally profoundly.[95] One does one's best and places one's hopes in some kind of "transcendental escrow"—in God, as Rob Walker explained it, or one of God's "great secular substitutes": "Reason, History, the sovereign state, the sovereign individual [or] the universal class."[96]

Recognizing that the existence of such a transcendental escrow is a necessary aspect of reason—that reason necessitates "smuggling in" foundations that are absolute and otherworldly—was of the greatest importance to Adorno. The problem of the concept, its connection to the dialectical nature of enlightenment, and the way in which that dialectic had unfolded historically all stemmed from the challenge of remembering the limitations it places on human understanding. Reason depended on foundational values that lay beyond its own ambit, such that these values took on a patina of sanctity or

---

93. Kant (1996a), pp. 346–347 (Ak. A293/B349-A294/B350). On this debate in Kant, see Guyer (1987).

94. Kant (1996b) [1788], pp. 269–271 (*Critique of Practical Reason*, Ak. 5:162–163); see also Kant (1960) [1794], (*Religion within the Limits of Reason Alone*), bk. III; and 2001), ("Idea for a Universal History.") The discussion here is necessarily perfunctory, but see Habermas (1989), ch. 4, and Linklater (1990b), ch. 6. On progressivism in Kant, see Kant (2001) and Yovel (1980).

95. Kant (1996a): "For here we are dealing with a *natural* and unavoidable *illusion* that itself rests on subjective principles and foists them on us as objective ones...it is...a dialectic that attaches to human reason unpreventably and that, even after we have uncovered this deception, still will not stop hoodwinking and thrusting reason incessantly into momentary aberrations that always need to be removed" (pg. 350, Ak. A198/B354–55). Or as Adorno (2001) explains: "the content of Kantian philosophy, in so far as it has a negative content, lies precisely in the limits it sets to the absolute claims of the subject; these limits also imply a limit to what can be deduced from this philosophy, even though, on the other hand, it presents itself as a deductive system" (36).

96. Walker (1992), p. 20; see also Luoma-Aho (2009).

necessity. This, ultimately, was why the vocation of critique could not be discharged by one-off acts of critical debunking: replacing God's universe with Kant's moral law; replacing that, in turn, with Hegel's cunning of history, Fichte's German nation, Marx's universal class, and so on. Critique needed to be a continuous process, directed against thought itself.[97] Its failure to have understood this left it without the resources to check the regressive aspect of enlightenment reason; it simply reified, too, into its own hard-edged ideologies. "No universal history leads from savagery to humanitarianism," Adorno noted in what has become an oft-cited passage from the *Negative Dialectics*, "but there is one leading from the slingshot to the megaton bomb."[98] That problem is not limited to grand philosophical positions; all of IR's paradigms must come to grips with it as well. Does not IR-realism have ties to a notion of the nation with its roots in Hegel? Does not IR-liberalism assume existential positions on freedom and the will of the individual?

Yet the attempt to "put the concept of progress under the microscope... so as to strip it of its semblance of naturalness" revealed a further problem.[99] It might be that the dialectic of enlightenment reaches even here: that while the only history that exists leads from the slingshot to the H-bomb, it may also be "that the age of the bomb is the first in which we can envisage a condition from which violence has disappeared."[100] If reason suffers from a reliance on mythological or idealist moments, it nevertheless remains that no single or commanding position can be adopted to debunk them. One cannot cleanse thinking of its idealistic moments; one can only *chasten* those moments by bringing them into productive tension with others. One manages reifications by artfully counterbalancing them, one against another. In so doing, the world's buzzing and blooming vitality, complexity, and fecundity remain present to mind, even if theory cannot wholly accommodate it.

"Non-Identity" and Negative Dialectics

The aim of such counterbalancing is to continuously estrange concepts from the world they mean to describe: continually chastening reason by disrupting

---

97. Lukács (1971): "Reification...can be overcome only *by constant and constantly renewed efforts to disrupt the reified structure of existence by concretely relating to the concretely manifested contradictions of the total development, by becoming conscious of the immanent meanings of these contradictions for the total development*" (197, italics in original).

98. Adorno (1973), p. 320.

99. Adorno (2006), p. 139.

100. Adorno (2006), p. 159.

its identitarian tendencies and thus checking them. Not surprisingly, the name Adorno gave this process of estrangement derived from his concerns regarding identity thinking: *non-identity*. That is, Adorno wished to counter identitarian thinking by making the non-identity of concepts and things-in-themselves an a priori assumption. Because theorists can never be certain of what they know, or what it means—because our thoughts about the world are always at a remove from reality—theory must adopt a position of careful consideration and circumspection. Theorists are *positively* obliged to engage in a *negative* mode of thinking: to assume the insufficiency of their understanding.[101] Acknowledging the normative-partisan character of thought does not mean abandoning a position of theoretical coolness or detachment; rather, it means actively—even passionately, with all the tensions this compounding of sensibilities entails—committing oneself to that position.

Non-identity does *not* mean that there is no real world of actions, things, and events out there. Such claims turn quickly into nihilistic moral relativism, exactly the opposite of what such thought intends.[102] From the horrors of the twentieth century, it is only too apparent (with or without conceptual "proof") that violence and suffering are real. It is *viscerally* apparent. The question is whether that knowledge is best served by a process of conceptualization and reification or by attempts to combat those processes, thus preserving the dignity of individual beings and moments. For Adorno, the answer was clearly the latter: suffering was not to be classified or dealt with conceptually, but to remembered as a deep empathy for other fellow beings, a "felt absence," as Jay Bernstein has helpfully explained it, or "a normatively inflected awareness of dependence on sensuous particularity."[103] Only thus might it be preserved in its unreduced fullness and immediacy, without rationalizing, conceptual subterfuge. "The smallest trace of senseless suffering in the empirical world belies all the identitarian philosophy that would talk us out of that suffering... the physical moment tells our knowledge that suffering ought not to be, that things should be different."[104] Contrast that position

---

101. For an analogue in the sphere of international law, consider Koskenniemi's (2002) "new formalism"—even after universal legal principles are critiqued, Koskenniemi suggests, one still needs to find balance "between the Scylla of Empire and the Charybdis of fragmentation...the culture of formalism resists reduction to substantive policy, whether imperial or particular. It represents the possibility of the universal (as Kant well knew) but it does this by remaining 'empty,' a negative instead of a positive datum, and thus avoids the danger of imperialism" (504).

102. Habermas (1981).

103. Bernstein (2001), p. 331.

104. Adorno (1973), p. 203.

with Price's apology for conceptual theory, cited earlier; for Adorno, empathy must remain *outside* of reason so that it can *chasten* reason.

What does this mean for IR, in an era in which human destructive power has become all but absolute? One thing is certain: the ontological-epistemological-ethical problem set out here cannot be confined to any one paradigm or fact-value tradition. The problem of non-identity applies across the discipline, from neorealism to Marxism, from constructivism to quantitative analysis. All of its perspectives can be fashioned into credible and useful theoretical representations of the world. All also distort the world in potentially dangerous and unaccountable ways. Theorists cannot hide behind the claim that without concepts, all thought would be impossible. In itself, this claim is true. That granted, it does not change the fact that these same concepts distort the very things they purport to represent. We remain, Adorno holds, responsible for the things we claim to be true: our reliance on concepts is *our* problem, and there is no getting around or doing without them:

> The attempt to abolish concepts…to reduce them to mere tokens, abbreviations for the facts they subsume, devoid of any autonomy seems to me extremely narrow-minded. There is simply no thought without concepts…it is impossible to deny, simply in view of the immanent meaning of social knowledge, that the demand to eliminate concepts contains a chimerical and, one might almost say, a quixotic element.[105]

Theorists, on this account, cannot justify their uncritical treatment of those concepts, given their potential for harm, on the claim that without them "the genuinely unhypocritical relativist…[would] struggle for something to say and write."[106] Rather, theorists would need to remember that their ideas about the world are separate from the world itself; there will always be an unbreachable gap, one filled by narratives whose truth value will be only ambiguously discernible. So conceived, non-identity applies to all speculative and analytical thought: from the most prolix to the most parsimonious.

Yet—here recalling Kahn—practical theory *still has important work* to do in a world that is deeply interlinked and persistently diverse. Theorists seeking to make good on the ethos of the *animus habitandi* would still want to

---

105. Adorno (2000), p. 79.

106. Price and Reus-Smit (1998), p. 272. Compare to Adorno (1973): "Necessity compels philosophy to operate with concepts, but this necessity must not be turned into the virtue of their priority" (11). Also Marcuse (1964), pp. 105–107.

remain present to the reifying nature of thought and to the interplay of different worldviews and ideals. For Adorno, this suggested an adaptation of the symbiosis alluded to: nesting social science's traditional logics of identity within a larger dialectic. Such a dialectic would be *negative*, or *chastening*: it would not seek to create unity among divergent or incommensurate value positions, but to preserve them as disunited and incommensurate. "The name of dialectics says no more, to begin with, than that objects do not go into their concepts without leaving a remainder"—all those aspects, features, qualities, and unique properties that identitarian thinking elided through generalizing on the basis of outward similarity.[107] The aim of negative dialectics was to "indicate...the untruth of identity, the fact that the concept does not exhaust the thing conceived."[108]

> Such dialectics...does not tend to the identity in the difference between each object and its concept; instead, it is suspicious of all identity. Its logic is one of disintegration: of a disintegration of the prepared and objectified form of the concepts which the cognitive subject faces, primarily and directly.[109]

Put directly, negative dialectics sought to show how thought and reality were forever separate, how they could not be reconciled. It was "suspicious of identity"; that is, it assumed that *all* concepts, no matter how intuitively compelling, remained distinct from reality itself.[110]

Through negative dialectics, Adorno hoped to dispel the illusion that reason could be objective vis-à-vis the different historical, cultural, and subjective contingencies in which it is grounded. "Thoughts do not come flying along, but rather...crystallize in protracted subterranean processes, even if they emerge suddenly."[111] A useful analogy might be the experience of viewing

---

107. Adorno (1973), p. 5.

108. Adorno (1973), p. 5.

109. Adorno (1973), p. 145; Schoolman (1997), pp. 59–60. For earlier discussions of negative dialectics in IR, see Rengger (2001) and Roach (2007).

110. Adorno (1973): "A philosophy that...extinguishes the autarky of the concept, strips the blindfold from our eyes. That the concept is a concept even when dealing with things in being does not change the fact that on its part it is entwined with a non-conceptual whole. Its only insulation from that whole is its reification—that which establishes it as a concept....To change this direction of conceptuality, to give it a turn toward nonidentity, is the hinge of negative dialectics" (12).

111. Adorno et al. (1977), p. 82.

a print of one of Escher's famous optical illusions: like an optical illusion, concepts play tricks on one's mental faculties, creating false images in the mind. While one cannot unsee an optical illusion, neither is one forced to accept the patently false as true: one quickly learns to recognize such illusions. In a not-unlike manner, Adorno hopes that negative dialectics will condition theorists to look beyond the misleading certainty of their own concepts and thoughts: "disenchantment of the concept is the antidote of philosophy."[112] Or as Shannon Brincat put it, such a dialectics "exposes the unfinished process of the development of consciousness, reveals its incompleteness, and exposes the potentialities that are as yet unrealized but which are, potentially, realizable."[113]

This analogy, of course, has its limits: while one looks at an Escher print for only a moment before turning to something else, one's perceptions of the world as a whole are continuous and unceasing. Moreover, one knows an optical illusion to be false because individuals are firmly moored to commonsense spatiotemporal understandings, by which the impossibility of the illusion is made apparent. If all conceptual thought is suspect and non-identity the only (partial) means to combat it, it is clear that Adorno's critique is quite far-reaching and intellectually demanding. Concepts have no recourse to a firm real world on which they can draw; the reifications and false images of the mind can be dislodged only with other false images. There is no way to make the contradictions go away merely by averting one's eyes. "Empirical social research cannot evade the fact that all the given factors investigated, the subjective no less than the objective... are mediated through society."[114]

This points to another aspect of the *animus habitandi*. Since no form of thinking is complete unto itself, pointed critique must be wedded to collaborative sympathy: a "dialogical model of science," as Katzenstein and Sil have called it, that views scholars as a community, united in the inevitability of intersubjectivity (though not by common values).[115] Calling for the alienation of thought from truth, or concepts from things-in-themselves, is essentially asking the theorist to do the impossible: the reifying nature of thinking, the emotional toll of unflinching self-inspection, and perhaps even the rewards structure of a professionalized academy all militate against it. Habermas

---

112. Adorno (1973), p. 13.

113. Brincat (2009), p. 463.

114. Adorno et al. (1977), p. 84.

115. Katzenstein and Sil (2008), p. 125; also M. Polanyi (1962). The phrase "inevitability of intersubjectivity" is Jane Bennett's.

explained Adorno's position thus: "self-reflection, and precisely self-reflection, is a finite power, for it itself pertains to the objective context that penetrates it." This inherent fallibility, Habermas continued, "leads Adorno to plead for an 'addition of leniency'"—a firebreak against the tendency of theorists to view their own reflexivity with too much self-congratulation.[116] This is the spirit of the quotation from Bertolt Brecht with which this chapter opened: that they "who went under" in Europe's wars of ideology were carried away by the same reifying processes that infect all thought. It is only good fortune that separates those born "in dark times" from those born in happier ones, when "man is a helper to man." Theorists, like Brecht's survivors emerging from the flood, must each strive to help one another and to judge with forbearance.[117] If society is deeply administered and profoundly unfree, and if reification is encoded into the DNA of all concepts and theories, then it must be assumed to be so for *all* theorists, *all the way down*. There can be no "free-floating intellectuals" who possess the secret of truth, no elite-within-an-elite that can hold itself free from all taint of false consciousness.[118]

A Logical Impasse?

Given the difficulties it imposes on thought, non-identity poses serious barriers both to communication and to political action. Many, like Habermas, Seyla Benhabib, and Ira Katznelson—and as chapter 2 will discuss at length, IR theorists like Richard Wyn Jones, Andrew Linklater and Ken Booth—have argued that no systematic social science can proceed from it, that it leads to a philosophical and ethical dead end.[119] This is a complicated question,

---

116. Habermas (1985), p. 108.

117. Brecht (2003): "But you, when the time comes at last, and man is a helper to man, thinks of us with forbearance" (75). See also Neufeld (2001).

118. The term "free-floating intellectuals" is, of course, from Mannheim (1936). My use of the term here, however, borrows more from the pejorative appropriation of Mannheim than from the author himself. As Jay (1994) recalled, for Mannheim "free-floating intellectuals" "were not to be understood as floating amidst the parapets of an ivory tower. On the contrary, their participation in the world they hoped to understand was a precondition for a real contribution to that understanding" (179). Whether Mannheim achieved this is the substantive disagreement at issue here; on this point, see Adorno (1983), pp. 35–50.

119. Habermas (1984–87), Vol. I: "Horkheimer and Adorno face the following problem. On the one hand, they do not agree with Lukács' view that the seemingly complete rationalization of the world has its limit in the formal character of its own rationality....On the other hand, Horkheimer and Adorno radicalize Lukács' critique of reification. They do not consider the rationalization of the world to be only 'seemingly complete'; and thus they need a conceptual apparatus that will allow them nothing less than to denounce the whole as the untrue.

which—save for its immediate relevance for IR—the present work will not pursue. For his part, Adorno did not seem to think so: "it lies in the definition of negative dialectics that it will not come to rest in itself, as if it were total," he noted. "This is its form of hope."[120] Indeed, once sustainably chastened, IR might discover *new* kinds of purchase: using existing paradigms and fact-value traditions to construct a hybrid hermeneutic-deductive approach to international theory. This would mean turning such traditions backward on themselves: seeing them as highly parsimonious expressions of complex ideological or value positions, whose right to expression is neither to be denied nor to be co-opted, but simply let be, as they are.

Even if this position turns out to be unsustainable, however, the present attempt to develop it has value. Its failure would reinforce the claim that sustainable critique, however long it has been sought after by IR theorists of various stripes, is not to be found. What this would imply for the nexus between social science theory and ideology is sobering. It becomes even more so when one recalls how dependent highly rationalized societies are upon theoretical knowledge.

In at least one aspect, however, the dead-end nature of sustainable critique is not to be denied. Negative dialectics specifically seeks, as has been noted, *to slow down thinking*, given its inherent tendency to reify and the unforgiving material reality in which IR theorists work. Perhaps such considerations do lead to an impasse—or at least a self-imposed narrowing of scholarly opportunity. But if it is a narrowing that checks the potentially reckless appropriation of ideas by the careless and unprincipled, are such self-impositions so bad? "We can no longer believe with Hegel," wrote E. H. Carr in 1951, "in a metaphysical or divine reason inherent in reality and in the process of history. We can no longer believe that all the highest impulses in human nature derive from reason."[121] To chasten IR theory is to insist only that such skepticism be sustained with tenacity and persistence. It does not deny that 'unsustainable' forms of critique cannot have their uses in generating new forms of practical theory: consider the success constructivist IR enjoyed in the 1990s in finding opportunities—and not merely dangers—in the collapse of the Soviet Union,

---

They cannot achieve this." (377–78) See also Benhabib (1994), Chambers (2004), Habermas (1994), Katznelson (2003), and Wellmer (1976).

120. Adorno (1973), p. 406. See also Bennett (2001), Bernstein (2001), Zuidervaart (2007b), and the essays in D. Burke et al. (2007).

121. Carr (1951), p. 105.

122. Compare, for example, Wendt (1995) to Mearsheimer (1990). I treat Morgenthau at length in chapter 3.

or the important critique Morgenthau made in the postwar era of the fallacies of liberal legalism.[122] Only the product of such thought is not critique; it is simply more practical theory. No one would deny that practical theory matters, but it cannot on its own sustain IR's historic vocation.

Without question, sustainable critique involves an ethical choice: predicated on an *animus habitandi*, a will to dwell within and to abide. One of the goals of this chapter, and of this book, has been to persuade the reader to consider that choice. Is there not a pervasive blindness within academic and policy discourses to the effects of "blowback"?[123] Are not many present-day challenges the unforeseen reincarnations or lingering aftereffects of previous generations' policy decisions? It may be that Gabriel Almond and Walter Lippmann were correct: that representative democracy, in an age of instantaneous media reportage and highly centralized authority, cannot avoid the pressures that lead to shortsighted policy expedients, particularly in the realm of national security.[124] But that would suggest that academics, sheltered from such pressures, have the potential to supply a distinctive alternative voice. *If we can, is it not our obligation—our vocation—to do so?* If such theory ends in impasse, does not that impasse do important work, chastening understandings of events precisely at the point where partisan interests or personal desires are so often—and so self-servingly—held to converge with universal values?

Six decades after Hiroshima and Auschwitz and nine decades after Verdun, such far-reaching claims of vocation may smack of histrionics. The bipolar system of the Cold War evolved to contain its existential threats, however uncomfortably, and the contemporary global order may well do the same. But the depth of fear that the prospect of universal destruction has introduced into human existence; the ease with which it marries up to late-modern warmaking potential, both by states and by nonstates; and the suffering that comes of this are not so easily remedied. Nor is the moral callousness to which surviving in such a world gives rise. The ancients had only a precarious grip over the kind of practical reason that could bend nature to their will. Whatever fears that form of living engendered, it also imparted an existential *confidence* in which contemporary humanity cannot share: in the permanence of the world. "Generations rise and generations depart," it is written in Ecclesiastes, "yet the earth endures forever."[125] That confidence, precisely, is the faith that

---

123. Johnson (2000).

124. Lippmann (1922, 1925), Almond (1960) [1950], Holsti (1992), and Ruggie (1997).

125. Ecclesiastes 1:4.

the nexus of Comte, Bacon, and the technically intensive catastrophes of late modernity have taken away.

From there, the path to mass violence is so well known as to be almost banal: fear becomes despair; despair becomes desperation; desperation turns peremptory; peremptoriness generates resistance. Sometimes, the best thing is valiant, intellectually committed *in*action: *thinking speculatively and critically*, rather than *practically*. But a case for such thinking must be made: not as the betrayal of reason Kahn asserted it to be, but as an act of deep regard for a world whose complex interactions can never fully be known, for the unintended effects of force and policy, and for the fragility of individual and collective life. This, an expression of *animus habitandi*, is what sustainable critique aims for.

2

Sustainable Critique and Critical IR Theory: Against Emancipation

> *If you were to press me to follow the example of the*
> *Ancients and make a list of the cardinal virtues, I would*
> *probably respond cryptically by saying that I could think*
> *of nothing except for modesty. Or to put it another way,*
> *we must have a conscience, but may not insist on our own*
> *conscience.*
>
> —THEODOR W. ADORNO[1]

THE NOTION OF sustainable critique, as set out previously, derives from a sensibility with its roots in Frankfurt School social theory. It is not the only application of such theory to IR. Over some three decades, the scholars of the "Welsh school" of critical security studies (CSS)—among others, Andrew Linklater, Richard Wyn Jones, Ken Booth, and Steve Smith—have developed an innovative approach to normative IR theory that brings insights drawn from this same tradition, together with "English school" IR.[2] At the same time, a wider approach to critical IR theory (CIRT) has drawn heavily on the work of Jürgen Habermas, Max Horkheimer, Ulrich Beck, and others.[3] Yet despite distinct overlaps in foundational literature and scholarly sensibility, sustainable critique differs markedly from these earlier appropriations both in its normative commitments and in its understanding of the work of theory. The goal of this chapter is to set out these differences.

The main thrust of the argument can be briefly summarized: while CSS and CIRT use critique as a means, the present work holds it to be an end in itself. Sustainable critique mistrusts claims that, when thoroughly vetted and ontologically regrounded, oppression-free theories can be reliably distilled out

———————

1. Adorno (2001), pp. 169–170.

2. Key English school texts include Bull (1995), Manning (1962), Wight and Bull (1966), Linklater and Suganami (2006), and Buzan (2004).

3. A note here on the use of the modifier *critical* is apposite. Many critically inclined IR scholars adhere to a "large-C/small-c" distinction, with the former referring specifically to Frankfurt

of positive ethical principles. Recalling the discussion in the previous chapter, theorists like Robert Cox, Linklater, Booth, and Wyn Jones use critique *normatively*: as mode of conceptual debunking meant to clear the theoretical ground for a body of theory rooted in alternative notions of progress and emancipation. For its part, sustainable critique regards these alternative notions as comprising simply one more fact-value tradition: no less reliant upon reification than any other, and hence no less needful of chastening. It holds further that the burden of proof for any ostensibly *critical* theory—and all the more so for one cast in the historic vocation of IR—lies in showing that it can remain sufficiently reflexive to check the effects of those reifications and their potential to congeal into their own alternative future forms of oppression. This CSS and CIRT have not done. Chastened reason thus regards their appropriations of Frankfurt School social theory with much the same ambivalence that "classical" realists like Morgenthau regarded the innovations of neorealism: with appreciation for what is kindred and unease over what is elided.

To say this is not to deny the important inroads that CSS and CIRT have made in "disrupt[ing] some of the complacency of professors of International Relations."[4] Yet this success has come at a price. Critical theory in IR and critical security studies seem unable to move past these initial successes to preserve the necessary *self*-reflexivity that is the hallmark of Adorno's critique of reification. As Radmila Nakarada has argued more generally, contemporary critical IR theory remains of "uncertain reach"—too easily given to its own comfortable counterorthodoxies, too enamored of its own dissidence. "Contemporary global bifurcating processes overwhelm the ability to level insightful critique and to suggest directions for achieving a more humane world," Nakarada argued; as a result, critical IR theory has become entangled in "simplified Manichean matri[ces]."[5] Nakarada's argument, in effect, is that critical IR theory needs a critique of its

---

School social theory and the latter to "include approaches that are skeptical of the emancipatory project outlined by the Frankfurt school" Shapcott (2008, p. 329). This distinction cannot serve the present work: one of my key contentions is that the claim of a unitary "emancipatory project" within Frankfurt School social theory is *itself* mistaken. I shall thus distinguish between "sustainable critique" as the perspective advanced by this book, contrasting it in this chapter with established traditions and scholars that self-identify as "critical"—hence, critical IR theory (CIRT), critical security studies (CSS), and so on. For recent overviews of CIRT/CSS, see Rengger and Thirkell-White (2007); Booth (2005), ch. 1; C. Brown (1992), ch. 8; C.A.S.E. Collective (2006); Devetak (1996); Floyd (2007); George (1994), ch. 6; Jahn (1998); Shapcott (2008); Sterling-Folker (2006), ch. 6; and Williams and Krause (1997). The symposium on critical terrorism studies in *European Political Studies* 6 (2007) is also useful.

4. Wyn Jones (2001), p. 19.

5. Nakarada (2000), pp. 65 and 73.

own; that it lacks precisely the sustainable reflexivity that Adorno, Marcuse, and Horkheimer had come to regard as most urgent. Theorists must instead learn to "speak in several voices at the same time" to tease out thereby "new patterns of domination" emerging from changing, deeply contingent amalgams of history, power, emancipation, right, and freedom.[6] Anthony Burke agreed: "the critical project must think and conceive the *unthought*, and its limiting test ought not to be realism but responsibility."[7]

To use the distinction first made in the introduction, then, it is held that while CSS and CIRT have made their case as viable alternative forms of *practical theory*, they have failed to do so as *critique*. That is, they have failed to show how their alternative brands of emancipation (a positive value) might be squared with the Frankfurt School's commitment to full, sustainable reflexivity. The scholarly arc of "postpositivist" international theory—from the self-styled "dissidence" of Ashley and Walker to a social science via media—has shown how quickly postpositivist critique can rereify on the basis of new normative foundations.[8] *Dissidence*, it would seem, has been confused with *critique*. Yet the two are distinct: the latter speaks to relatively stable conditions of intellectual possibility, given the limits of thought, its reliance on reification, and the demands of practice; the former to what a dynamic marketplace of political values and movements will bear. Having shown that IR realism smuggles in notions of freedom, right, and the good life, CSS and CIRT posit values no less irreducible. It might be that, lacking historical associations with state violence, the latter values seem less dangerous than the former. But even if such claims could be verified historically, they would provide no assurances as to their future potential for harm. The process by which particular configurations of ideas become ideologically hegemonic is highly contingent. The past is not always prologue in any direct and clear sense.

On this account, CIRT and CSS are held to preserve only a truncated version of philosophical critique. This is not the first time that critical dialectics

---

6. Nakarada (2000), p. 70.

7. A. Burke (2007), p. 22. See also Mutimer (2009).

8. Sterling-Folker (2006): "The idea that we are free agents who create our own social institutions, and yet are constrained by the social structures that our very free agency creates, is a basic philosophical conundrum...but it was constructivism that was responsible for bringing it into the IR theoretical mainstream, and given its analytical interests and sources, constructivism has frequently been listed along other post-positivist approaches in the discipline....In practice, however, most constructivist IR scholars subscribe to positivism as well, arguing that traditional scientific methodologies can be consistent with the interpretivist foundations of constructivism" (pp. 117–118). The term *via media* is from Wendt (1999); *dissidence* is from Ashley and Walker (1990). See also Barder and Levine (2012).

have been so truncated. As Herbert Marcuse and W. G. Friedmann have both noted, the positivist turn of late-nineteenth-century social and legal theory made a similar move: appropriating the content of particular Hegelian concepts of the state, while stripping them of the historical and normative contingencies that Hegel hoped would protect them from ideological hypostatization.[9] This is, as Nicholas Rengger has noted, "at best a partial critical theory, and cannot live up to Adorno's hopes for it."[10] Or as the quote with which this chapter opens suggests, to insist on a place in theoretical pursuits for the dictates of *conscience* is not to be conflated with insisting on the dictates of *one's own conscience*.[11]

In retracing this truncation of critique and suggesting a way past it, I will proceed in four steps. In the first part of this chapter, the pathbreaking work of Linklater, Smith, Cox, and Booth are traced out from their origins in the 1980s to their marriage with Frankfurtian social theory in the Welsh school. Following this, the discussion broadens, considering "fourth debate" Habermasian thinking and critical pragmatism, as these have been taken up in IR more broadly. The next two sections use this discussion as a springboard to deepen an understanding of how Adornian thought understood the dangers of identitarian thinking and how his concepts of negative dialectics and non-identity might be operationalized within IR. The aim is to suggest a fuller and more sustainable notion of critique as a free-standing scholarly vocation in its own right. Building on the work of CSS and CIRT, it first develops the concept of the *constellation,* as this emerged in the writing of Max Weber and Theodor Adorno. It then uses Graham Allison's *Essence of Decision* to illustrate how such Weberian-Adornian constellations might be adapted to serve a sustainably critical research agenda.

A New Hope: Emancipation in Critical IR Theory

If mainstream IR and Frankfurt School theory share anything, it is grim inevitability. For Hans Morgenthau—more about this will be said in chapter 3—

---

9. Marcuse (1960); see also Friedmann (1967), pp. 164–176 and 253–274.

10. Rengger (2001), p. 102.

11. Booth (2007), for example, routinely conflates the two: "Reflexivity is critical theory's heartbeat. Critical theory, to be true to itself, must always be critical" (467). And yet *how* is it to be made so? Booth proceeds to dispose of some of the greatest moral questions of late modernity. Is there a possibility of real moral progress? Yes (pp. 124ff.). Was there dignity to be found in the Nazi death camps? Some, he answers, but very little (p. 104). Is Marx to blame for the excesses of Stalin? No (p. 49). Where, then, does reflexivity reside? While paying homage to Marcuse's "great refusal", Booth does precisely what Marcuse argued must *never* be done. "The critical theory of society," the latter argued, "possesses no concepts which could bridge the

this grimness took on a tragic quality: war among nations derived from the very Nietzschean qualities that made men and women properly *human*. Adorno, Horkheimer, and Marcuse had their own tragic sensibility; it is the basis of the chastened reason to which sustainable critique aspires and for which, it was argued, the *animus habitandi* militated.

By contrast, critical IR theory is a deeply optimistic enterprise. Andrew Linklater, who has for three decades pursued a far-reaching attempt to ground a critical reconstruction of IR, has called for theory "with an emancipatory intent."[12] Richard Wyn Jones has asserted that "the spirit and method of critical theory" support "positive visions of concrete utopias."[13] Ken Booth has looked to critical theory for "political and social progress," for "a world that progressively limits the power of regressive structures and processes" and that opens up new possibilities for "what it might mean to be human"—nothing less than "the philosophy, theory, and politics of inventing humanity."[14] Marc Lynch speaks of critical theory as delineating steps toward "a more just world order, a norms-based international society taking individuals rather than states as primary."[15]

The means for such theoretical opening up is ambitious: a far-reaching renegotiation of international theory, history, and politics. "Western theory and practice," noted Linklater, asserted a necessary opposition "between a sense of obligation to the state and a belief in obligations to humanity[.]"[16] Linklater proposed to close that gap. "A convincing philosophical reconciliation of the components of an apparently bifurcated moral and political experience" is possible, Linklater wrote in a powerful early formulation, and can have practical and operationalizable effects.[17] And later: "Any political theory which ignores the problems created by our double existence as men and citizens is no longer adequate to the conditions of modern political life; for it fails to attempt to harmonize all aspects of modern moral and political experience."[18] Mark Hoffman, in another highly influential early statement, explicitly drew on Marx's *Theses on Feuerbach*: "The point of International

gap between the present and its future; holding no promise and showing no success, it remains negative" (Marcuse [1964], p. 257).

12. Linklater (2007), pp. 178ff.

13. Wyn Jones (2005), p. 229.

14. Booth (2005), p. 263 and (2007), p. 112.

15. Lynch (2006a), p. 182.

16. Linklater (1990b), p. 15.

17. Linklater (1990b), p. 16.

18. Linklater (1990b), p. 36.

Relations theory is not simply to alter the way we look at the world, but to alter the world.... It must also offer us a significant choice, and a critical analysis of the quality and direction of life."[19] In a phrase that would be much bandied about, critical theory was touted as the "next stage in the development of International Relations theory."[20]

These statements were refinements of a proposition first put forward by Robert Cox: that "sophisticated theory"—by which Cox had meant critical theory since Gramsci—"reflects upon and transcends its own perspective." While "theory is always *for* someone and *for* some purpose," Cox argued, the critical theorist preserves *reflexivity:* she "stands apart from the prevailing order of the world and asks how that order came about."[21] From this insight, several lines of thought would develop. For Cox himself, reflexivity would be a means to develop more open-ended understandings of world order as historically and institutionally mediated, rather than conceptually given a priori.[22] For Ken Booth, it meant crafting targeted polemics, in the tradition of E. H. Carr's "utopian" wartime and postwar writings: attacking "the notorious euphemisms used by strategists to mask reality" and with them discourses that "privilege the security of the means as opposed to the security

---

19. Hoffman (1987), pp. 244–245. See also Cox (2008).

20. Hoffman (1987), p. 244. For responses, see Rengger (1988), Hoffman (1988), Lapid (1989b), and Linklater (1992).

21. Cox (1981), pp. 128–129; for recent restatements, see Cox (1995, 2008). See also Neufeld (1995), especially p. 42, and Linklater (1996), pp. 279–280.

22. Cox (1981), pp. 128–129. Cox does not intend his critical theory to address questions of theory and practice *as such*; he is interested in *particular* theories and practices. "Ontology," he wrote in 1992, "lies at the beginning of any enquiry. We cannot define a problem in global politics without presupposing a certain basic structure consisting of the significant kinds of entities involved and the form of significant relationships among them" (1996a, p. 144; see also 2001). This argument puts him into unexpected company; consider here his more recent discussions of "civilizations" (defined as "processes or tendencies" within a "historical dialectic [that] moves ever onward" [2000], p. 229) in world politics. "Used in the singular, [civilization] contains an implicit exclusionary, hierarchical meaning, distinguishing the civilized from the uncivilized or barbaric. Used in the plural, it acquires a pluralistic, inclusionary meaning—that there are different ways of becoming civilized" (1996b, p. 143). Can such fine distinctions – in this context, see also Katzenstein (2010) – resist political vulgarization? Huntington's civilizational model may be too divisive an example; consider instead William McNeill's *The Rise of the West.* Twenty-five years after its publication, McNeill (1992) reflected on its reception. While not written to lend transhistorical significance to "the temporary world experience of the United States," it nevertheless seemed in retrospect that "the warmth with which the book was received in the early 1960s did arise from this congruence" (xv–xvi). There remains a difference between a theorist's *intentions* and the *work that a particular theory does in the world*. Certainly, Cox is aware of this difference, but he does not see it as falling under the remit of critical IR. I think it should. See Cox (2000), p. 219, n. 6; also Schechter (2002), esp. pp. 12–17.

23. See Carr (1942, 1945, 1951). The term *utopian* is Carr's own; see his (2000), p. xix. Booth (1991a), pp. 313–14 and 320.

of ends."[23] "Words are all we have," Booth asserted in 1991, yet "our words do not work any more."[24] Positivism pretended to discover new words and concepts through ostensibly value-free political analyses, but in fact it prescribed them ex cathedra.[25] Critical IR theory would at least make its political and normative links explicit and find ways to keep them so. Another line of thinking can be discerned in Kimberly Hutchings's attempt to link critical Hegelianism and Foucauldian genealogy, with an eye to keeping the lines of appropriation open to public-scholarly scrutiny.[26] Still other lines seek to develop Habermasian communicative action (more on this later) or critically inflected pragmatism: learning, as Friedrichs and Kratochwil recently put it, "to act on reasonable bets."[27]

Such approaches presume that theorists know what emancipation is and that conceptual transparency will suffice to protect their understandings from unchecked reification. In the immediate post–Cold War era, such confidence could be discerned in debates over what do to with contestable terms like *security*: should it be regrounded, extended to cosmopolitan or nontraditional discourses and issue areas (environmentalism, refugee flows, global crime and prosperity), or alternatively withdrawn from discourse?[28] In more recent debates, the problem is no less contentious. Military interventions in Kosovo or Afghanistan are not disputed in terms of their humanitarian necessity, yet their dubious normative pedigree—acting without recourse to

---

24. Booth (1991a), pp. 313–314.

25. Booth (1991a), pp. 314 and 319: "Emancipation, theoretically, is security." Much hangs on the word *theoretically*. "Implicit in the preceding argument is the Kantian idea that we should treat people as ends and not means" (319). While a promising beginning, this is also (as Booth realizes) a *petitio principi*. Given that IR straddles "issues of peace and war, 'theories of the good life,' and 'theories of survival,' 'ethics of responsibility,' and 'ethics of conviction,'" it could not be otherwise (1991b, pp. 528–529). How does Booth propose that all of these questions be reconciled? By way of answer, he posits core values and then suggests ways to remake reality in their image. That is, to be sure, one of the vocations of theory. But it is *practical* theory, not *critical* theory, it does not explore the limits of thought in light of *both* the demands of practice *and* the limitations of right. Or to put this another way: positivism and IR realism are not of a piece; one can be (as chapter 1 argued Comte was) a utopian positivist.

26. Hutchings (1999): "Such honesty offers no guarantees of the persuasiveness of the position which is being argued for, but it does open up possibilities of recognition and validation which are closed off by normative claims which block the acknowledgment of their own conditioning and politics" (p. 184).

27. Friedrichs and Kratochwil (2009), p. 714. See also the essays in *Millennium* 31:3 (2002), *The Journal of International Relations and Development* 10:1 (2007), and *International Studies Review* 11 (2009).

28. On the former point, see Deudney (1990); S. Brown (1996), ch. 5; Levy (1995); and Matthews (1989). On the latter, Dalby (1997) is nonpareil.

the UN, using air power to reduce NATO casualties while greatly multiplying civilian deaths—cannot be overlooked. This is even more the case in light of the fact that such "legitimate but illegal" interventions seem in retrospect to have provided a pretext for U.S. unilateralism in Iraq.[29] The present discussion does not presume to adjudicate these claims. The point is the assumption among such scholars that such adjudication can, through a once-off application of critique, be placed on firm normative-ontological ground.[30] Critique, on such an account, would be a defined *moment* in thought, bounded on either end by practical theory building, rather than an ongoing, continuous interaction with practical reason.

Such approaches thus conceal a confidence in the power of discourse: the potential of thought to expose injustice, and the salutary effect of such exposition. Injustice does not inhere in discourse *as such*; rather, *particular* discourses enfold tendentious assumptions, which can be exposed and put right by periodic acts of critical debunking. This translates into three interlocking claims: the first of fact, the second of duty, and the third of consequence. Respectively, that discursive injustices can be put right; since they can be, they ought to be; and that when this is done, both the discipline and the world will be the better for it.[31] Critical IR theory is thus consciously and practically meliorist: it upholds, in Wyn Jones's moving formulation, "truth against the world" by keeping faith with a dream "of humanity triumphing over inhumanity, civilization over barbarity."[32]

Yet such declarations, and the theoretical ambitions that go with them, rest uneasily on the shoulders of the Frankfurt School tradition to which they lay claim. Horkheimer's widely cited essay "Traditional and Critical Theory" did state that the goal of "the new dialectical philosophy" was "man's emancipation from slavery."[33] But that was in 1936–37. As the previous chapter showed, such

---

29. See Beck (2005), Brown (2000), Cockayne and Malone (2006), Crawford (2003), Jabri (2005), Lynch (2006a), Shannon (2005), and the essays in *American Journal of International Law* (October 1999).

30. See Lynch (2006a), Jabri (2005), and Nakarada (2000).

31. Compare this to Smith (1995), who asks: What are the "self images" of IR as a discipline, and what are the "silences" in international theory that these self-images enfold? But Smith also acknowledges that "*all* self-images reflect normative concerns" (p. 30). There is, then, no breaking free, only knowing.

32. Wyn Jones (1999), p. 145. Linklater agreed, labeling "unconvincing" the claim that "we can neither specify the content of duties to humanity, nor envisage an international community responsible for their enactment" (1990b), p. 204.

33. Horkheimer (1986) [1937], p. 246.

brio did not survive the war.[34] Postwar Frankfurt scholarship was more than merely a critique of positivism; it had metamorphosed (or, some would say, metastasized) into a critique of *thought itself*. Practical reason and its dialectical, instrumentalizing quality *writ large* were what had come to concern these thinkers, not the political project to which a given body of theory lent itself, but the potential for domination that lay in *all* theory: left or right, dialectical or positivist.[35] "Critical International Relations theory must realize itself in the concrete emancipation of human beings," wrote Mark Neufeld.[36] But "concrete emancipation" means concretizing what freedom *is*; it must necessarily posit theory and the theorist as the arbiter of human values, placing them above the actual forms of life they encounter. How are critical IR theorists to reconcile such concretizations with the ethos of the *animus habitandi*?

Linklater's answer was an appeal to theoretical innovation. "Praxeological analysis" could fill the gap "to assist the development of new forms of authority and novel conceptions of citizenship which strike the appropriate balance between universality and difference."[37] But what is that "appropriate" balance, and how is it to be known? Linklater hoped that such judgments could be anchored to a postfoundationalist Habermasian logic of practice. The fault of Marxist sociology, Linklater noted, lay in a too-limited understanding of oppression that was focused only on questions of production, property, and class.[38] With the benefit of hindsight, this line of argument runs, contemporary social theory now knows that it must cast its net wider.

But—and this is the key point of disagreement between CSS and sustainable critique—contemporary social theory knows this only because humanity as a whole has survived the horrors that were mercilessly inflicted on a luckless many. Humanity learned, but too late to help those who "went under." Why should contemporary social theory, however sophisticated and well-meaning, be immune from its own myopias, as unimaginable to today's theorists as the

---

34. Honneth (2007): "it is open to argument whether both thinkers [i.e., Adorno and Horkheimer, DL] actually unwaveringly adhered to the approach of the *Dialectic of Enlightenment* until the end of their lives, but it is less disputable that neither remained willing to entertain any beliefs in an intramundane possibility for emancipation" (pp. 65–66).

35. Hence for Booth (2007) it is specifically "the earlier work of the Frankfurt school that is especially useful" to CSS; the later work is, as we shall see, held at arm's length (p. 41). This elision is repeated in Shapcott's (2008) recent survey: from Horkheimer's 1936 essay, he moves directly to Habermas.

36. Neufeld (1995), p. 124.

37. Linklater (1998), p. 44.

38. Linklater (1998): "Marxism failed as a critical theory because it believed that reconstructing property relations was tantamount to transforming political community" (p. 116).

horrors of two generations ago were to their forerunners? In what future catastrophes will this new social theory be implicated? Of course, it cannot be *proven in advance* that that such catastrophes or appropriations will take place. Yet the horrors of the twentieth century, and their persistence into the twenty-first, lead one to suspect that in late modernity the slope that leads from unchecked reification to scientifically authorized oppression might be especially slippery.

Suspecting this, contemporary theorists would presumably bear greater obligations to chastened self-examination than did their predecessors. To the extent that theorists know this and modify their practices accordingly, a progressive trend to knowledge of the praxeological sort might be discernible. But this would be a very different form of progress than that to which Linklater alludes. It would be *negatively dialectical*, in the sense described in chapter 1. That is, it would measure progress *not by the degree to which theoretical constructs increasingly resemble reality*, but rather to the extent that such constructs were able to do so *without becoming conflated with reality*. Progress, in negative dialectics, comes from theories that *sustain a sense of their own artificiality*, while preserving their power to meaningfully interpret a complex world.

Sustaining the obvious tension in these two positions was the shotgun wedding to which sustainable critique was said, in the introductory chapter, to aspire. It built on the sense of obligation expressed in Adorno, Horkheimer, and Marcuse: the task of attacking first-order social theory *at the moment of its creation in the mind of the theorist*. Only thus could theory keep faith with the recognition that thought had played in the age of purges, genocides, and engineered famines. It was an ethical choice, guided by what Adorno in *Negative Dialectics* called the new categorical imperative: "to rearrange [one's] thoughts and actions so that Auschwitz will not repeat itself, so that nothing similar will happen" again.[39] It is hard to see how this sensibility—that "wrong life cannot be lived rightly"—can be reconciled to Linklater's assertion that the Frankfurt School "did not abandon the position that the aim of social theory is the realization of the good life" and that a reliably "thin cosmopolitanism" can be constructed that will somehow be thick enough to create new forms of solidarity without that solidarity becoming oppressive.[40]

Indeed, one cannot avoid the sense that the already difficult idiom of postwar Frankfurt scholarship has been done a double disservice. To make its case,

---

39. Adorno (1973), p. 365.

40. Adorno (1974), p. 39; Linklater (1990a), p. 22; see also Price and Reus-Smit (1998), p. 262. On the good life, see Linklater (1998): "...forms of political community which release societalpotentials for achieving levels of universality and difference. Casting light on the prospects for advancement in this direction is one of the primary sociological aims of critical theory"

critical IR theory seems to have trivialized the core positions of these thinkers, only then to fault them for being trivial. Wyn Jones's characterization may
be taken as representative:

> Critical theory was intended to give a new, sophisticated voice to
> Marxist analysis, yet it found itself attacking the very intellectual tra-
> dition from which Marxism emerged.... Critical theory aimed at a
> relationship with emancipatory political practice, yet found itself in
> a position where all attempts at reforming society were dismissed as
> worse than futile. Critical theory aimed at rescuing the analysis of soci-
> ety from the aridity of traditional theory, yet it found itself arguing
> that all thought oriented toward society was irredeemably tainted and
> that the only thought that might retain any integrity was that oriented
> toward extrasocietal, extrahistorical remainders of the falsity of the real
> world.... Adorno and Horkheimer believed that redemption was an
> impossible dream.[41]

At best, Adorno, Horkheimer, and Marcuse were said to have staged a "retreat
from practice"; in less charitable characterizations, they were compared to
members of "a millennial religious cult...bearing witness to truth in a world
where all around them had succumbed to falsity and evil."[42]

(p. 181). By "thin cosmopolitanism," Linklater means a set of universal ideals and values thick
enough to "support the development of wider communities of discourse which make new
articulations of universality and particularity possible," yet not so thick as to congeal into
countervailing forms of oppression" (1998), p. 49; see also his 1999 and Frost (2009), pp. 11–19.

41. Wyn Jones (1999), pp. 50–51.

42. Respectively, Linklater (1990a), p. 24, and Wyn Jones (1999), p. 50; see also Booth (2007),
pp. 40–44 and ch. 3. Adorno and Horkheimer receive uneven treatment in these works. Wyn
Jones's reading of the epigrammatic notes that come at the end of the *Dialectic of Enlightenment*
provides an example. In response to one such epigram ("We owe the serum which a doctor
administers to the sick child to the attack on defenseless creatures"), Wyn Jones makes two
points: first, that "the serum does provide succor to the child; that is, the dark side of the epi-
sode is balanced by a positive outcome...the picture is not simply one of unrelieved horror"
and, second, that "an increasing awareness of animal suffering during the testing of products"
has led to technologies that reduce such testing. "Moral learning," he concludes, "has taken
place" (pp. 84–85). This misses the dialectical nature of such thinking. If modernity was an
unalloyed vista of either "unrelieved horror" or shimmering progress, then good and evil would
be easy to identify, and one would slowly vanquish the other. But Adorno and Horkheimer
assert it is not so. It is precisely *because* there is a dialectical quality to modernity that its darker
aspects are so easy to rationalize. To be sure, animals suffer less to produce serums than they
once did. But is this evidence of moral learning or a particular consumer-producer feedback
loop that has, *in this case*, yielded a happy result? Has "progress" has taken place? If so, can we

Such descriptions deeply misserve the complex positions they purport to represent.[43] Postwar Frankfurt School theory was, to be sure, at an impasse. But it was not—here recalling the discussion of Herman Kahn in the previous chapter—an impasse reducible either to a performative contradiction or to scholarly cravenness: the sort of thing one might overcome by fortuitous or bold reformulation. *Rather, it inhered in thought itself and thought's relationship with the world; it was to be dwelt in, not overcome.* Put differently, Adorno, Horkheimer, and Marcuse were not latter-day incarnations of Goethe's young Werther, choosing "despair or nihilistic rage" over active engagement in the world.[44] Rather, they were arguing for a *negative* moral transcendentalism, a combination of claims that cannot easily be made to sit at the same table.[45] "When philosophers... engage in conversation," Adorno wrote, "they should always try to lose the argument, but in such a way as to convict their opponent of untruth."[46] Since all (ostensibly) "emancipatory" theory must enfold textual and intellectual practices of domination, thought must become negative. This was, as political theorist Romand Coles has noted, a practice whose "very movements exemplify ethical engagement"—for only through such practices

---

say that the initial suffering was worthwhile in light of that happy result? To step down such a road—from observing a practice falling into desuetude to making a pronouncement of moral progress—Adorno and Horkheimer are arguing, *begins a process of thought that must inevitably instrumentalize suffering, regardless of whatever particular answer might be tendered.* That is the argument that Wyn Jones must meet. See Adorno and Horkheimer (2002), p. 185. A similar misreading, this time of Hannah Arendt, mars Booth (2007); see, for example, pp. 123–4, 200–201, and 261. Arendt's understanding of thinking and action are not philosophically absolute, but historically contingent, yet no account of this contingency is made. In Booth's treatment, Arendtian thought becomes oracular, as Straussian thought does at the hands of *engagé* neoconservatives. Critique is not to be directed merely at the *ends* of Enlightenment (following Kant, humanity's attempt to free itself from its self-imposed minority) but also at its *means* (*sapere aude!*). This is why Kant held that reason and ethics must be subjected to critique.

43. Linklater (1990a), pp. 24–25; George (1994), pp. 151–152; Wyn Jones (1999), ch. 2; Kubálková and Cruickshank (1985), pp. 206–208. See also Kołakowski (1978: III), ch. 10.

44. In one much-cited anecdote, Adorno is said to have stood at the edge of the Pacific Ocean and suggested placing a message in a bottle and casting it in the water. The anecdote was taken to imply that Adorno had despaired of being read and understood. See Wyn Jones (1995), pp. 306–307; Rengger and Thirkell-White (2007), p. 14; for accounts of this, see Lüdtke (1986) and Said (1994c), pp. 39–44.

45. Honneth (2007): "On the one hand, there are more and more who see in the *Dialectic of Enlightenment* a dangerous form of apocalyptic social critique; on the other hand, the attempt to treat the study in its entirety as a poetic work of art is gaining importance. In their opposing tendencies, however, both approaches converge in the intention to expel the *Dialectic of Enlightenment* from the realm of philosophically serious social critique" (pp. 50–51). See also Gross (1980); Bernstein (2001); Rose (1978), pp. 50–51; and Zuidervaart (2007b).

46. Adorno (1974), p. 70.

might reason treat seriously both its dialectical quality and its world-destroying potential.[47]

Having overlooked this, CSS and CIRT seem to have fallen into the very theory-practice dichotomy they ostensibly set out to problematize. The essence of reification lies in an acknowledgment that thought, albeit in complex, stochastic, and historically contingent ways, *becomes* practice. Adorno was pushing this logic as far as it could possibly go. Self-reflection—the very quality that Cox had argued made critical theory *critical*—was more than a machete with which to hack away at the scholarly-intellectual excesses of this paradigm or that image of thought. It had became "the true heir to what used to be called moral categories," the only way to preserve the problematic relationship that persists between ideas and things.[48] It was an act of deep care, an expression of the theorist's duty: first, do no harm.

Both Linklater and Wyn Jones (but not Booth) have since retreated from their dismissive initial evaluations of Adorno's work.[49] But that reconsideration has not, by and large, led to a sufficiently thorough reconsideration of Adornian ethics within either critical security studies or critical IR theory.[50] Wyn Jones hits the mark when recognizing that emancipation must serve as a "regulative ideal" for critical theory, rather than a concrete goal.[51] Yet the problem of identitarian thinking remains unconsidered: how are regulative ideals—ideal types, here given a Kantian gloss—to be kept from reifying? Were not concepts like realism's much-maligned "national interest" once *themselves* regulative ideals, meant to moderate the violence of interstate politics by subjecting them to particular standards of rationality?[52] This did not prevent their gradual concretization into a dangerous political ideology,

---

47. Coles (1997), p. 80. See also Heath-Kelly (2010) and Joseph (2011).

48. Adorno (2001), p. 169.

49. Linklater (2007), pp. 189–190; Wyn Jones (2005), pp. 220–223 and 231. But see Booth (2007): "the facts" disprove Adorno's claim "that poetry is impossible after Auschwitz" (p. 132). But Adorno, it will be recalled, withdrew this statement; see Bleiker (2009), p. 103; Thompson (2006), ch. 4; Jäger (2004), p. 187.

50. But see A. Burke (2007), Bleiker (2000), Brincat (2009), Rengger (2001), Roach (2007), Heine and Teschke (1996), Fluck (2010), Franklin (2005), and Rajaram (2002, 2006).

51. Wyn Jones (2005), p. 223. See also Pin-Fat (2010): "The ethics of universality lies in it never being fully possible: its grammatical (im)possibility" (p. 119).

52. A careful rereading of Meinecke's *Machiavellism* (1957) [1st German ed., 1924] might here prove rewarding. "*Raison d'état*," he notes in the opening pages of the work, "is the fundamental principle of national conduct, the state's first Law of Motion. It tells the statesman what he must do to preserve the health and strength of the State…the 'intelligence' of the State consists in arriving at a proper understanding of itself and its environment, and afterwards

a process owing, if Adorno is correct, to *their structure as concepts, not their particular content.* The systematic demolition of positivist IR's claims to value neutrality are to be welcomed, but precisely the same reservations would need to be leveled against the reconstruction of social theory that Linklater, Wyn Jones, and their colleagues propose to undertake.

Postnational Liberalism and Pragmatism

Such limitations are mirrored in attempts to read Habermasian "postfoundationalism" into IR. Appropriations of Habermas vary in extent and application. But the details are less important for the present discussion than the hope that his thought rekindled—as Neta Crawford put it, that Habermasian theory could "deliver insight and direction to students of international ethics, by suggesting a procedural program for addressing the urgent ethical dilemmas of world politics."[53]

Whether the immense canvas of Habermasian thinking can actually be applied to IR in a way that is both properly emancipatory *and* properly deontological depends very much on how one manages that appropriation.[54] To borrow Habermasian concepts ("public sphere," "system," "lifeworld") and convert them into empirical ideal types is certainly possible, but it is only half

---

in using this understanding to decide the principles which are to guide its behavior" (p. 1). Reason of state was thus a means to regulate and direct the violence endemic to world politics: such violence was to be subjected to particular "objective" criteria, rather than being left to princely whim. Yet as Meinecke himself realized after the Great War, the rise of mass politics had profoundly changed the game: "today the idea of *raison d'état*... is in the middle of a severe crisis. The natural basis of elemental passions which it possesses and which cannot...be subdued solely by its utilitarian middle ground, makes a more terrible impression today than ever before; and the civilizing achievements of the modern world tend rather to exaggerate it than restrict it. *All the ways in which the modern State has become enriched by successive influxes of liberal, democratic, national and social forces and ideas (and which hitherto we have tended to regard as pure enrichment and increase) have now shown their other face, and have brought raison d'état into contact with forces which it is no longer able of controlling*" (p. 423, emphasis added).

One might discern here an early recognition of the dialectical nature of reason: "the terrible antinomy between the ideals of rational morality and the actual processes and causal connections of history," which "we, the vanquished...see more clearly than the victor does" (p. 432). And indeed, Meinecke's solution approximates a chastening, negative dialectic. National interest and universal morals must be balanced against one another: each held by "the executive statesman...together in his heart, if he is not to let himself be overpowered by the daemon (which he is still not quite capable of shaking off completely)" (p. 433).

53. Crawford (1998), p. 121. Yet Crawford qualifies herself. "Paradoxically, realizing peace and justice in world politics is more likely if one gives up the urge to ground ethics in Enlightenment certainty."

54. Price and Reus-Smit (1998), Diez and Steans (2005), Hutchings (2005), Dallmayr (2001), Connolly (2001), Rengger (2001).

the equation.[55] One changes the terms of the game when one does this. "It is always possible, and often fashionable, to view philosophical doctrines in a non-philosophical perspective," warned Emil Fackenheim. "But this is always a risky procedure; for it involves dismissing the philosophy in question *as philosophy*."[56] Fackenheim was referring to scholars who read Kant's *Perpetual Peace* as a treatise in Eastonian political science. A comparable risk applies to patchwork appropriations of Habermasian thinking. In effect, it is suspected, these appropriations elide either the emancipatory aims of such thinking or its postfoundationalism.

It bears noting that Habermas himself—as distinct from his appropriations by IR theorists—has been consistently cautious on this point. While communicative action theory raises the possibility of reducing social and political domination, Habermas does not refute the grimness of Adorno and Horkheimer's *Dialectic of Enlightenment* or Marcuse's *One Dimensional Man*. To be sure, he takes issue with their negation of any possibility of escape, in particular, of Marcuse's "great refusal," and its simplistic appropriation by what used to be called the "new left."[57] But he does not presume to overcome or refute the dangers that attend "metaphysical" thinking. Rather, he aims to renounce ontology altogether; communicative action anchors political life in pragmatic speech acts and practices, rather than transcendent truth claims.[58]

---

55. For examples of this, see Risse (2000, 2002, 2004); Lynch (1999, 2000, 2002, 2003, 2005); Kantner (2006); Kantner and Liberatore (2006); van de Steeg (2002a, 2002b, 2006); Machill, Beiler, and Fischer (2006); and Eriksen (2005). Lynch in particular has explored normative tie-ins to his use of public sphere theory: exploring how Habermasian discourse ethics could inform the dialogue of "civilizations" (2000, 2005) or how it might help European or American theorists and policy makers combat overly reductionist assumptions in their own public discourses. (2003) But these approaches work at the margins; they suggest how knowledge of the Arab or Islamic world *as a public sphere* can facilitate conversation with other public spheres; the term *public sphere* becomes a stand in for "civilizational order" or "normative community." One must – as Lynch (2006b, pp. 51–68) begins to do – also address the risk that comes from reifying collective agents as parties *to* communicative action in the first place: the way in which particular collective identities (*huwiyya, qawmiyya, wataniyya, umma*, etc.) are or are not mobilized and to what end, and so on.

56. Fackenheim (1996), p. 35; see also Anievas (2005).

57. See the discussions at Habermas (1987), p. 113 and (1984), Vol. 1, pp. 366–399. On Marcuse, see the discussion in Habermas (2001), especially p. 162.

58. Habermas (1992): "Following the transition from the semantic to the pragmatic point of view, the question of the validity of a sentence no longer poses itself as a question about the objective relation of language to the world, detached from the process of communication.... Validity claims aim at being acknowledged intersubjectively by speaker and hearer; they can only be redeemed with reasons, that is, discursively, and the hearer reacts to them with rationally motivated "yes" or "no" positions.... For this reason, the comprehension of a speech act already points to the conditions for a possible agreement about what is said" (p. 74).

This is the (often overlooked) compliment that Habermasian deontology pays to its Adornian forbears. Domination-free public spheres, like Machiavelli's *stato*, cohere through the artful cantilevering of social-political relationships and require particular forms of civic *virtù*. The contrary beliefs of liberals and postmoderns are not debunked so much as they are decentered; pulled from the hard ground of metaphysics and replanted in dynamic social theory.[59] It is, in itself, a deeply chastened basis on which to understand political life.[60] The challenge facing those who would appropriate such thinking for IR is to do so in such a way that sustains precisely that chastened basis.

Retracing the steps of one such appropriation may help may illustrate the difficulties involved. Here again, Linklater's work can prove exemplary: Habermasian critical theory is woven in at two distinct points. First, Linklater uses Habermas as a means to counter the earlier Frankfurt School claim that all social knowledge is embodied ideology, borrowing here specifically from Habermas's early discussions of social science and hermeneutics. Although "at present there is no single movement or organization with the ability to promote universal moral principles in practice," Linklater suggests, "Habermas has shown how a contemporary critical theory can overcome the impasse which led Horkheimer and Adorno to abandon the emancipatory project."[61] Second, Linklater draws on Habermas's concept of communicative action to develop the praxeological framework onto which his progressivist historical-materialist narrative is fitted.[62]

Can Habermasian IR theory sustain these uses while preserving theoretical reflexivity? The answer is uncertain.[63] For communicative action to work, Linklater falls back on his initial animating assumption: that the universal-particular dichotomy that animates the European political tradition is a problem of *theory and practice*, rather than *ontology*. Or to put this another

---

59. On this point, Rorty (2006) provides a helpful synopsis. Habermas himself made this argument both in philosophical terms and programmatic ones; see respectively (1987) and (1981). See also Habermas and Derrida (2003).

60. Chambers (2004).

61. Linklater (1990a): "Habermas argues that the critical theorist ought to defend the ideal of the unity of the species, even if there is no guarantee that its unification will ever come about. Emerging global problems or crises may generate new historical subjects, but at present there is no single movement or organization with the ability to promote universal moral principles in practice. Nevertheless, by identifying the condition which may engender universalistic social movements, Habermas has shown how a contemporary critical theory can overcome the impasse which led Horkheimer and Adorno to abandon the emancipatory project" (pp. 26–7).

62. Linklater (1998), pp. 88–100 and 106.

63. Linklater (1998), pp. 213–220; Wyn Jones (1999), ch. 3.

way: that *underneath it all, we must all be more the same than we are different,* that there is a foundational universalism to the human community, and the cultivation of cosmopolitan practices and beliefs, on the one hand, and the critical deconstruction of particular interests, on the other, will clear a path to it. This may very well be so—but it may not. It assumes what most needs demonstrating: that, as Kimberly Hutchings put it, "there is such a thing as international society which both constitutes and is constituted by a variety of levels of political and economic order—[that] there is therefore no clear inside/outside distinction where nations and states are concerned."[64] This, as Linklater well knows, is precisely is what nationalism first emerged to defend and valorize: difference, in the face of ideological universalism.[65] Viewed through the prism of the "twenty years' crisis," German nationalism cannot but seem pathological. In Heinrich von Treitschke's and Carl von Clausewitz's writings, however, it was meant to be the political-ethical basis for mobilizing a cluster of religious, cultural, and linguistic traditions against forcible subordination: the leveling universalism of French revolutionary fervor.[66] Clausewitz and especially Treitschke bear the stigma of the excesses that would be committed in nationalism's name—and not entirely unjustly. But such excesses are not unique to nationalism. If a latent potential for criminality is to be the basis for ideological disqualification, then few social theories, or theorists, would pass muster.

Hence Habermas's caution on these very issues. Communicative action theory, it must be recalled, emerged not as an answer to the problem of freedom *as such,* but as a response to *particular* crises and forms of violence that existed within specific and already-constituted political lifeworlds.[67] To take

---

64. Hutchings (1999), p. 136. Or as Müller (2001) asks: "How, then, does understanding come into being in an international environment in which a shared lifework cannot be assumed? In view of the unmistakable fragmentation of the world, it is not hard to be skeptical about claims that a world culture is already developing and can be seen in globally shared truth criteria" (p. 169). To be sure, Müller has potentially compelling answers to this question, and these are not to be discounted. See also Müller (2004); Linklater and Suganami (2006).

65. Linklater (1998), pp. 51–55.

66. Compare Treitschke (1916), Vol. 1, pp. 23–24 and Vol. 2, pp. 577–578, to Linklater (1990b), p. 121. On Clausewitz, see the discussion in Lebow (2003), pp. 209–210.

67. This argument emerges in Habermas's early work: *The Structural Transformation of the Public Sphere* (1989; 1st German ed. 1962), *Toward a Rational Society* (1971), and *Legitimation Crisis* (1975). The problem is one of societies in which there is a disconnect between system and lifeworld, wherein a residual political-psychological demand for a particular culturally or historically contingent form of social or political freedom persists within a material order that no longer furnishes its conditions of possibility. The lifeworld is already an accomplished political fact; how could one protest the disappearance of something that had not "always already" been there? Communicative action can be "postmetaphysical" because it is nested within an

a further step, toward prescriptive theory encompassing "intersocietal, inter-state and intercivilizational interaction," is fateful; it is (as Eckersley points out) "to venture into waters that had been only partially charted."[68] Habermas knows that the constitution of a public sphere is predicated on foundational violence.[69] Once such violence is committed, it cannot be undone; one is obliged to proceed pragmatically with the world one has inherited, while committing oneself to doing better in the future. The project of communicative action—developing practices by which the work of *sustaining existing public spheres* is progressively emptied of violence—is a reasonable ethical response *only* in that context.

To turn such theory into a prescription for international politics may thus cross a dangerous line, for two reasons. First, it would seem to involve an ontological determination as to the nature of world society: suggesting that a *particular lifeworld* either is already, will become, or should be made coterminous with *the entire world*—that is, with the totality of all possible human events and experiences in all places and times. Can this be demonstrated with certainty? Failing such a determination, such thinking risks replicating the unchecked reifications of liberal developmentalist theories of the "stages of growth" variety, in which the history of one political community is rewritten prescriptively as a "modernization" blueprint for others, with its predictable social dislocations justified by appeal to deterministic visions of progress—clearly, a move with which Habermas would have no truck.[70]

---

established order; the metaphysical piper has already been paid. For a recent restatement of this position, see Habermas (2008): "Members of a local linguistic community experience everything they encounter in the world in the light of a habitual "grammatical" pre-understanding, not as neutral objects" (pp. 33–34).

68. Eckersley (2008), p. 349. Or as Hopgood (2009) put it: "our concern here is precisely with what we might call global civil society where...a lifeworld is absent" (p. 234). See also Wyn Jones (2005), Castiglione (2009), and Pensky (2005).

69. Habermas (1971): "only in an emancipated society, whose members' autonomy and responsibility had been realized, would communication have developed into the non-authoritarian and universally practiced dialogue from which...our ideal of true consensus are always implicitly derived. To this extent the truth of statements is based on anticipating the realization of the good life.... Only when philosophy discovers in the dialectical course of history the traces of violence that deform repeated attempts at dialogue and recurrently close off the path to unconstrained communication does it further the process whose suspension it otherwise legitimates: mankind's evolution to autonomy and responsibility" (pp. 314–315). On this point, see also Calhoun (1992), especially pp. 475–479; Apel (1990); and Bronner (2002), ch. 12.

70. As Adler and Crawford (2005) note: "A necessary condition for [Habermasian communicative action] processes to occur is the previous existence of a 'life-world' of shared understandings, meanings and discourse. But these are precisely the missing elements in conflicts

Second, as Janice Bially Mattern has demonstrated, it risks obscuring the inherently strategic nature of diplomatic speech, even when ostensibly put forward to convince rather than compel. Where argument, for Habermas, "is a way of 'wooing' willing interlocutors to agreement by illuminating the truth," diplomatic speech "cultivate[s] not attraction to truth but bias toward ideology."[71] Hence, "Linklater's ontological position is essentially a radicalization of the liberal nationalist argument," noted Kimberly Hutchings. While it "goes much further than liberal nationalism," it is no less a positive, foundationalist project.[72] It assumes a particular position within a contested field of argument: the degree to which territorial sovereignty is the central axis of political, social, and economic life. This is a central debate within IR; at bottom, it is irresolvable, save for by appeal to transcendently given normative considerations.[73] Such considerations involve the application of ideal types to real events, and so we are again back at the Adornian-reification problem.

In this, Linklaterian thinking is no different than any of the other practical traditions within IR theory that posit a complex moral-historical sensibility as the basis for present and future claims. But if so, then Habermas's pragmatism has been grafted onto IR by means of ontological-metaphysical truth claims as to the nature of the world. If this is so, in turn, then the entire justification for moving past the Adornian impasse collapses. With it goes Cox's much-vaunted distinction between traditional and problem-solving IR. All theory would be problem solving; it is only a matter of whether the theorist's

that pit states against each other" (p. 16). For a helpful survey of modernization theory, see Gilman (2003), ch. 5.

71. Bially Mattern (2005), p. 595.

72. Hutchings (1999), pp. 135–136. To that end, Hutchings (2007) has recently called for critical IR theory to consider the embedded notions of time and progress within its various traditions. Such an approach captures a *moment* of sustainable critique: the understanding that all narratives contain their implicit beginning and ending points, the timeline within which agents are constituted and in which they understand themselves to be acting.

73. Lose (2001): "Thus TCA [i.e., Habermas' Theory of Communicative Action] is built on a basic sociological argument: social integration in plural modern societies can only be achieved when social relations are organized 'according to the principle that the validity of every norm of political consequence be made dependent on a consensus arrived at in communication.' This is the core of Habermas' theory of social constructivism. It is founded on the fact that modern societies possess a normativity that is modern in the sense that it is self-referring and self-reflected, and therefore can be subjected to the demand for consensus and collective interpretation" (p. 187). This is *not* to claim that since "ideal speech acts" cannot be approximated in international politics, communicative action does not apply; on that point, see Haacke (2005), pp. 185–186; and Lose (2001), pp. 184–185.

commitments are present to thought.[74] If critical IR theory is to preserve its "human and generally hopeful account" of world politics, Nicholas Rengger noted, then it must acknowledge that "Adorno's problem...is real and has not yet been adequately dealt with."[75] Terms like *security* and *freedom* either *are* essentially contested (in which case they are contestable *by everyone* and *for everyone*) or they are not; they cannot be only at the time of this or that theorist's choosing. And anyway, as Bill McSweeney has noted, "All concepts of the social order are contested in the sense that they are inherently unstable models of order from which we...negotiate meaning."[76]

No less problematic are attempts to marry critique to pragmatism "to generate more just interpersonal and intersocietal relations," as Molly Cochran put it, by moderating "not the universal or particular *scope* of moral claims, but *the way they are put forward*."[77] The "weak foundations" on which social science rests cannot "yield non-contingent ethical claims." Hence, one must learn "to draw ethical conclusions, but to regard the conclusions found as nothing more than temporary resting places for ethical critique."[78] "Ontologies too," Cochran asserts, "should be held *weakly* and *contingently*."[79] In principle, no better summary of the aims of chastened reason could be made; not without reason does James Bohman state that "critical theory and pragmatism are...united in a particular democratic conception of practical social science."[80]

In practice, however, Cochran and Bohman are much more convincing in evincing the need than in actually meeting it. *How* are Cochran's ontologies to be preserved as "weak" in the mind of the theorist, given the nature of thought to reify? Does the "pragmatist emphasis on methodological pluralism" manage reification or give it more space to hide by keeping it out of view?[81] What chastens the combination of assumptions that frame Cochran's approach—the

---

74. Rengger (2001): "In other words, for...Adorno, the problem of nihilism constrains the problem of justice precisely by making an impossibility the sort of institutional-political recommendations that Linklater has made central to critical IR theory" (p. 102). See also Rengger (1999), ch. 4; Hutchings (1999), p. 78 and 82.

75. Rengger (2001), p. 103.

76. McSweeney (1999), p. 84; Buzan (1991), ch. 1; Smith (2005), pp. 27–28. See also Connolly (1983) and Gallie (1955–56).

77. Cochran (1999), pp. 3, 14 (emphasis in original).

78. Cochran (1999), pp. 16–17.

79. Cochran (1999), p. 204 (emphasis in original).

80. Bohman (2002), p. 501.

81. Bohman (2002), p. 502. On this point, see Horkheimer (2004), p. 565, and the discussion on analytical eclecticism in chapter 5.

commonsense judgments that underpin her strategy of "beginning from where we are?"[82] After all, both the discipline of IR and the larger political discourse within which it is nested supply many alternative accounts of "where we are"—as well as who "we" includes. Cochran does not *deny* these accounts so much as she avoids them; they lie, she explains, outside her argument's bailiwick.[83] If so, then how are her particular ontologies to be kept weak? What "outside" chastens them? There is certainly no disputing Cochran's claim that "normative IR theorists must face the questions feminists and others have been facing... now that the questioning of foundationalist epistemologies has been unleashed."[84] But if doing so requires sidestepping all the other core contentions that divide the various traditions of IR, the net effect is to replicate one of the processes by which foundationalist IR got to be that way: holding all variables still, save the one the theorist wishes to examine. Cochran would need something besides confessional statements of good will to keep her weak ontologies from reifying, as theirs did.

In this sense, Bohman's notion of theoretical multiperspectivalism goes further—and as shall become apparent in the forthcoming, such a conception of pragmatism could potentially resonate strongly with Adornian negative dialectics and its possible application to IR.[85] Yet one would still worry about the normative master concepts that guide his critique: the notions of democracy he wishes to advance and the domination he wishes to avoid. From where do they come? If Bohman's multiperspectivalism "does not... necessarily require theories, but may be simply a matter of excluded actors making vivid the biases and limitations of traditions that have collective authority," then what resources are left to critique them?[86] And what of those who suffer in silence?

The Adornian Alternative: Constellation and a Hermeneutic Turn

Conscious of how unchecked reification has found its way into CSS, CIRT, and critical pragmatism, sustainable critique moves in a different direction.

---

82. Cochran (1999), p. 277.

83. Cochran (1999), pp. 1–3.

84. Cochran (1999), p. 280.

85. Dewey's *The Public and Its Problems*, for example, could be a possible point of connection with Adorno's notion of the aesthetic. See his (1981) [1927]: "Men's conscious life of opinion and judgment often proceeds on a superficial and trivial plane. But their lives reach a deeper level. The function of art has always been to break through the crust of conventionalized and routine consciousness" (pp. 349–350).

86. Bohman (2002), p. 509.

If Adorno is correct, emancipation cannot be given up on: thinking would be impossible without it. But neither can it be positively theorized, pointed to with precision, or circled on a map. The dichotomy that many theorists active in CSS and CIRT seem to accept—that thought must either idealize the world and leave practices untouched or else be willing to take positive moral stands—is too narrow.[87] It is not enough to declare reflexivity as a scholarly watchword; one must also, as Adorno did, *rearrange one's thoughts* to allow for it. One does this by finding ways to pluralize mutually exclusive conceptions of emancipation and progress, without destroying their essential, exclusive, and incommensurate nature. One chastens not particular notions of freedom *in themselves*, but the truth claims that issue from them, motivated by an understanding of the limited purchase of thought and an abiding commitment to the *animus habitandi*: to dwelling within the irreducible complexity of the world. Unable to eliminate reification, one seeks means to manage or control it.

Adorno's notion of a *constellation* provides a means for operationalizing such a pluralization. Following Martin Jay and Richard Wyn Jones, Adorno's constellation denoted "a juxtaposed, rather than integrated cluster of changing elements that resist reduction to a common denominator, essential core, or generative first principle."[88] Applied to sustainable critique, the term describes arranging multiple perspectives around a particular event or cluster of events in world politics for the specific purpose of managing reification. The various paradigms of IR—those conjunctions of fact-value traditions and methodologies that produce disciplinary research programs—would be juxtaposed in hybrid and overlapping fashions around complex, uncertain events. The aim is to construct polyvocal and highly pluralist narratives. Individual paradigms

---

87. Hutchings (1999), ch. 7.

88. Cited here from Bernstein (1991), p. 8, but see Jay (1984a) and Roach (2007). Wyn Jones (2001), not surprisingly, adapts this to serve the aims of CSS and CIRT: in his understanding, constellations denote a juxtaposition "of rather distinctive approaches, all seeking to illuminate a central theme, that of emancipation" (p. 4). The goal is explicitly to galvanize "those forces that resonate to the progressive democratic impulse" and that "are apparently catatonic" in the face of contemporary outrages to human dignity and freedom. "The left," Wyn Jones laments, "has very little to offer" in the face of such outrages; he seeks a multiperspectival approach by which IR might help fill the breach (p. 19). The challenges facing such an approach have been discussed at length earlier; the key point here is that this usage quite consciously parts company with the main body of Adornian thought and from the aim of sustainable critique. "Emancipation," as Rengger (2001) explained, simply "was not one of Adorno's major concerns" (p. 102). A much earlier appropriation of the term *constellation* in IR also bears noting: Kindermann's "Munich school." For a brief discussion, see Dougherty and Pfaltzgraff (2001), pp. 80–81.

are understood to function like snapshots or sonar soundings: a means by which preexisting political-social-normative sensibilities are stretched and fitted onto a complex, indeterminate, vital world. They are nothing more than fixed perspectives or worldviews derived from both consciously and unconsciously formed ontological assumptions about the world, giving the observer a stable point of theoretical leverage over a world that resists reductive knowledge. While no single one—nor any collection of them—can ever reproduce the whole, the conjoint use of multiple such worldviews can immeasurably enrich theoretical understanding. First and most obviously, at the level of brute detail: each captures nuances that the others might overlook. But for a second, more profound reason as well: *the existence of many such worldviews helps remind the theorist of the limits of any single one.* The humility for which sustainable critique militates is given practical expression: the practice of constructing a constellation operationalizes the ethos of the *animus habitandi.*

In making sense of how constellations are understood to work, it may be helpful to recall Adorno's discussions of Max Weber, from whose interpretive sociology he adapted it. Consider the difficulty Weber faced, in a work like *The Protestant Work Ethic,* in trying to define something as enormous and multifaceted, as politically freighted and historically contingent as *capitalism.* "The attempt to give anything like a definition of it," Weber explained, "brings out certain difficulties which are in the very nature of this type of investigation"—it would close off the conversation before it could properly begin by reducing its elements to simplistic truisms.[89] For indeed—

> Such an historical concept...since it refers in its content to a phenomenon significant for its unique individuality, cannot be defined according to the formula *genus proximum, differentia specifica....* This is a necessary result of the nature of historical concepts which attempt for their methodological purposes not to grasp historical reality in abstract general formulae, but in concrete genetic sets of relations which are inevitably of a specifically unique and individual character.[90]

The concern Weber expresses here mirrors the problem of identitarian reason discussed by Adorno: the thirst to create workable generalities must not come at the cost of submerging context, individuality, and uniqueness. Yet simply rejecting conceptual definitions or ideal types tout court could not

---

89. Weber (1958b), p. 47. See also Brown (1994).

90. Weber (1958b), pp. 47–48. See also Mannheim (1952), pp. 134–146.

suffice; like Adorno and Herman Kahn, Weber recognized that one could not think without them. "In *all* cases, rational or irrational, sociological analysis both abstracts from reality and at the same time helps us to understand it," he explains. "Theoretical differentiation is possible…only in terms of ideal or pure types."[91]

Even so, concepts and ideal types remain structures of the mind, not facts in reality, hence the need to adopt research methods that allow them to be "gradually put together," to crystallize *postfacto*, as a kind of summing up. Constellations continuously reveal the concepts and theories they bring together as nodes embedded within dense, interactive nets of social meaning. By so juxtaposing them, they retain both their generative context and natural delimitations, checking their potential to identitarianism. "By themselves," Adorno explained, "constellations represent from without what the concept has cut away from within: the 'more' which the concept is equally desirous and incapable of being.… They attain, in thinking, what was necessarily excised from thinking."[92] The forgetting inherent in reification is thus checked at the source; *a critically reflexive moment might thus be rendered sustainable.*

So chastened, reification takes on a different, less threatening aspect. Understood to be inherent in all thinking, the work it does becomes simply part of the "underlaboring," both intellectual and physical, by which human beings make *the* world into *their* world, by which values, habits, and preferences are translated into the built and lived environment. Practical theory is once again that intellectual effort that codifies, organizes, and standardizes the practices that comprise that work. Critique, anchored in constellations of theories and events, continually retraces and chastens such theory, preventing both its own unchecked reification and that of the values, habits, or preferences it operationalizes. This is a sensibility that cuts equally at practical theory and at critique: like the scholars of the "third debate's" via media, it understands that an unrelievedly negative critique of practical reason would be as inimical to IR's historic vocation as its unreflective acceptance has been.[93] But it suspects—and has sought to demonstrate—that the challenge of balancing the two is greater than is generally supposed.

---

91. Weber (1978), p. 20. Indeed, such concepts work *precisely because* they abstract from reality: "the more sharply and precisely the ideal type has been constructed, thus the more abstract and unrealistic in this sense it is, the better it is able to perform its functions in formulating terminology, classifications, and hypotheses" (p. 21). And elsewhere: "An ideal-type…cannot be found empirically anywhere in reality. It is a *utopia*" (Weber [1949], p. 90, emphases in original).

92. Adorno (1973), p. 162.

93. Wendt (1999).

When viewed through the chastening framework of a constellation, critique could, perhaps, go beyond "making facile gestures difficult."[94] It could become a springboard for seeking out new voices and excluded perspectives. Through the multiple juxtaposition of many perspectives, the gaps between them stand out without placing any under erasure. The theorist would be encouraged to develop intuitions regarding the boundaries of a political discourse, for when she sees theories as operationalizations of fact and value, she might also begin to take note of all those positions for which there are no such operationalizations. Silences in theory would appear as the parallel of silences in political discourse: as voices not heard. The problem of identitarian thinking discussed in the last chapter might thereby be addressed, while avoiding its *bêtes noirs*: nihilism and scholasticism.

At the same time, constellations turn IR's long history of great debates and its broad array of methodological approaches into an asset. Each comes to represent a well-defined and carefully thought out research program, a tradition that gives expression to particular clusters of normative-political sensibility. Each, that is, considers international politics from its own distinctively positive position; it smuggles particular interests, identities, or parties into an analytical framework that interprets events in world politics. The proper move would be to reject any single method or model as enshrining some higher truth, while *embracing all methods as containing true reflections of particular combinations of interest and sensibility*. The expertise of the theorist lies in teasing multiple accounts out of complex and interconnected events, rather than forcing them into totalizing artificial syntheses. A constellation would surround events and problematics with voices that represent as many different parties to it as possible. All are—potentially, at least—importantly true, but none is privileged in that truth; rather, the key point is determining which positions, perspectives, or interests those particular methodologies represent, what interests they seek to advance. "Thought is abstract," noted philosopher of science Alfred North Whitehead in 1925, "and the intolerant use of abstraction is the major vice of the intellect."[95] This insight, adapted to the constraints of social science and the problems of late-modern world politics, expresses what the constellation aims at.

---

94. Foucault (1988), p. 155; cited here from Campbell (1998), p. 191.

95. Whitehead (1925), pp. 26–27. And later: "You cannot think without abstractions; accordingly it is of the utmost importance to be vigilant in critically revising your *modes* of abstraction" (pp. 85–86).

Such an approach to a text or to an event—one that seeks to expand discussion to include manifold possible understandings, rather than reduce it to singular moments of truth and falsity—embeds practical theory within a critical-hermeneutic tapestry, composed of elements drawn from a gamut of traditions and methods: positive and interpretive, nomothetic and intuitive.[96] Hermeneutics has a long tradition in world politics, and this is not the first attempt to bring it into contemporary IR.[97] But in keeping with the ethos of the *animus habitandi*, hermeneutics here serves a very particular function: a means of relating social-scientific knowledge to a political sphere with which such knowledge is radically incompatible, even if it is also deeply needed. It is what is left when the "transcendental escrow" described in the previous chapter is simply accepted as a necessary part of thinking. Rather than laboring in vain to do away with it, theory chastens itself in light of its inevitability.

The philosophical and political writings of Spinoza provide a useful point of entry into such a notion of hermeneutics. The proximity of Spinoza's political philosophy to Hobbes and Machiavelli has been widely discussed in the context of political realism, not least by Kenneth Waltz.[98] His rejection of religious dogma and his understanding of politics as an autonomous sphere of freely interacting entities share a common basis: a monistic worldview, in which God and human beings, nature and the universe are all, inseparably one, coexisting "on the same strip of territory."[99] To understand politics is to know of men "as they are" and not as this or that observer "would like them

96. This is admittedly a wide field. Dilthey (1972, 1989) is foundational; among contemporary theorists, see Bleicher (1980), Derrida (1978), Gadamer (1975), Giddens (1984), Habermas (1971, 1988), How (1995), Ricoeur (1981), Shapiro and Sica (1984), and Winch (1958). For a powerful critique, see Shklar (1998), ch. 5. This list, it is to be stressed, is not exhaustive.

97. See especially Yanow and Schwarz-Shea (2006); also, inter alia, Epp (1998); Galtung (1996); Hollis and Smith (1991), ch. 4; Kahn-Nisser (2011), Lebow (2003); Patomäki (2002); Rengger (2001); Shapcott (1994, 2004); and Wight (2006), ch. 7. Morgenthau (1972) also suggests a kind of hermeneutic; see chapter 3.

98. Waltz (2001) [1954] identifies him, for better or worse, with a "first image" approach. To be sure, Spinoza's *Political Treatise* can be read thus but only by ignoring, or at least doing considerable violence to, Spinoza's broader philosophical commitments. A monist, Spinoza would have chafed at the idea of "images" of world politics, as though one could freely and unproblematically choose the vantage point from which one observed the world. Such a conception would do violence to a world in which God and man, nature and matter, *natura naturans* and *natura naturata* are all one. Additional discussions of Spinoza in this context are numerous; a necessarily partial list includes Balibar (1998), ch. 3; Curley (1991, 1996); Den Uyl (1983), app. A; Haslam (2002), ch. 1; Israel (2001), part 2; Montag (1999); Montag and Stoltz (1997); McShea (1968), esp. chs. 4, 5, and 9; Prokhovnik (2004); Rosen (1972); Strauss (1997), esp. chs. 9–10; Van Gelderen and Skinner (2002), *passim*. I am indebted to Gadamer (1975), pp. 159–160, for this argument.

99. Connolly (2005), p. 22; paraphrasing from Spinoza's *Theological-Political Treatise*.

to be"—in the very same manner that to know of God is to understand the natural world, which is shaped and formed by the divine.[100] There are, on this account, no truths *of the world* that are not also *in the world*.

The defining moment for a Spinozist hermeneutics of world politics comes from his understanding of biblical interpretation. Making sense of the Bible, Spinoza affirms, is extremely difficult. Composed in an ancient tongue that was (and remains) only imperfectly understood, in a script that included neither vowels nor diacritical marks, and in a grammar that did not consistently denote tense or mood, even everyday meanings were hard to gather.[101] But this was not all. The text itself was held to be of sublime origin; how could ordinary reason penetrate it?[102] To be sure, Spinoza averred, "natural reason" could reduce to a minimum the text's uncertainties, but on its own, reason could never "explain everything in the Bible."[103] Simply by rendering its text tractable to thought, biblical exegesis was an inherently tendentious business.[104] The responsibility lay with readers, teachers, and believers to use the text as a guide to be interacted with, rather than as a means to enfold self-interest in a cloak of moral unassailability.

The challenge Spinoza identifies in making sense of biblical revelation parallels the difficulty, as noted previously, in making reason amenable to real-world politics. International relations—whether in the days of the Dutch republic or in our own—is hobbled by a sea of tendentious and partisan readings, which can find safe harbor among the welter of different languages, traditions, and cultures that participate in global events. As Richard Ned Lebow has observed, it is precisely this ambiguity that "provides an opening for those with political and intellectual agendas to try to capture [particular] texts to legitimize and advance their goals."[105] The same can be

---

100. Spinoza (1951) [1677], *Political Treatise*, ch. 1, p. 287.

101. Spinoza (1951), ch. 7, pp. 109–110. Spinoza gives the example of a citation from Genesis 21:12 made in the Epistle to the Hebrews 47:31, in which the author of the latter simply misreads the former. For more on this, see Levine (2011).

102. Spinoza (1951), ch. 7, p. 100; see also ch. 2.

103. Spinoza (1951), ch. 7, p. 113.

104. Yovel (1989): "according to Spinoza (following Machiavelli and Hobbes) the proper role of religion [is] political. It is subservient to the state and should foster its basic goals (security and liberty, in Spinoza's view) by educating people to a life of justice and solidarity; and these values can receive their content only from the civil government in its ordinary, secular legislation" (p. 198).

105. Lebow (2003), p. 51. And indeed, comparing the foregoing with Lebow's (2003, pp. 70–77) discussion of the interpretive difficulties involved in the contemporary reading of Thucydides is rewarding. The hermeneutic voice that Lebow is seeking—both by which to

said of the events *themselves*.[106] Spinoza himself affirms this: his method for interpreting the Bible, he states, "does not differ widely from the method of interpreting nature"—whether in its human or nonhuman aspects.[107]

Contemporary social science—and IR in particular—suffers from what Edward Luttwak has called a "learned repugnance" when it comes to matters of religion.[108] In that vein, drawing uon biblical hermeneutics may seem gratuitously exotic. But consider that modern hermeneutics emerges in the mid-1600s—in the same era that the Treaties of Westphalia are said to have established the norm of state sovereignty. This is not a coincidence. It has become something of a truism among liberal-inflected critiques of sovereignty that the latter has, from the moment of its birth, contained within it a clearly defined will to absolute domination; "the concept of sovereignty," Ruggie has noted, represented "merely the doctrinal counterpart of single-point perspective to the organization of political space."[109] While not without a certain validity, this view transfers a distinctly late-modern preoccupation with totalitarianism onto earlier generations, forgetting that sovereignty was a response to other problems, a different age. "Seeing like a state" has not always corresponded to the highly developed disciplinary and biopolitical mechanisms of surveillance that are today ubiquitous.[110] Princes were once *unable* to control the passions of their subjects. In the context of the wars of religion, that weakness, Dan Nexon has recently noted, had given rise to a political and humanitarian crisis "of sufficient magnitude to alter the European balance of power, both within and among even its most powerful political communities."[111]

---

reveal those moments in which IR theorists "mistake Enlightenment ideology for social reality" (62) and to clear the ground for a tragic vision of politics—is not absent from the western canon. As scholars of IR learn to identify the larger philosophical discourse from which the behaviorist and positivist traditions were drawn, the resources that were always already there simply become easier to see. Spinoza, with intellectual feet in the worlds of both western reason and biblical hermeneutics, is one such resource.

106. Barnett (2002), Campbell (1998, 2005), Mitzen (2006), Ringmar (1996), Weldes (1996), and Zehfuss (2005) also offer variants on this argument.

107. Spinoza (1951): "I may sum up the matter by saying that the method of interpreting scripture does not widely differ from the method of interpreting nature—in fact it is almost the same" (p. 99). See also Israel (2007), pp. xvi–xvii.

108. Here cited from Kubálková (2000), p. 676.

109. Ruggie (1993), p. 159; here cited from Bohman (2005), p. 62.

110. Scott (1998); Foucault (2004). On the limits of the premodern state, see Flathman (1993).

111. Nexon (2009), p. 3, and also Philpott (2001). This holds true even if, as Krasner (1999) notes, that norm was observed primarily in the breach.

So considered, sovereign noninterference could have emerged as a means to *defend and institutionalize political pluralism*, rather than as Ruggie's prototo-talitarian "single-point perspective."

Viewed thus, could not sovereignty be seen to do the same work in territorial circles that hermeneutics does in theological ones? The former delineates zones of rule so that different political entities can exist side by side. The latter does the same for believers trumpeting mutually exclusive readings of the same texts. Each, then, emerged as a compromise from the fury and destruction of the mid-1600s, "when Protestants and Catholics competed to see who could most brutally slaughter their religious opponents."[112] If, as many theorists of IR and IPE at present suspect, existing spheres of difference and right are being deterritorialized or are being reterritorialized in new ways—if, that is, contemporary scholars stand at the *end* of those processes whose beginning was Spinoza's point of departure, or in the midst of their dramatic transformation—then the value of such hermeneutics becomes apparent: a means to try on different conceptual characterizations on an as-if basis, without forgetting the reifications upon which any particular one relies.[113]

On this (quasi-Spinozist) account, IR is not a tool for distinguishing truth from falsehood; rather, it serves as an interpretive guide, helping the scholar retrace the ways in which particular political, cultural, and ideological sensibilities congeal into communities of interest. Theories lead scholars along the routes that such communities take when generating practical political agendas. They are less concerned with what is *real* in itself than with how inward values and assumptions give rise to real political effects. They remember that all knowledge is profoundly partial, subjective, and fragmentary and that concrete commitments "ground the researcher in his or her research community."[114] "Any social ontology is itself a horizon, a hermeneutical standpoint that enables and limits the possibilities of interpretation."[115] A constellation reminds the theorist that *different things are true for different people* and that noncontradiction is not an absolute value in the study of social and political things and kinds.[116] Reflexivity is not merely a means for

---

112. Scheuerman (2007a), pp. 65–66. See also Philpott (2001).

113. Here again, Ruggie (1993) is the *locus classicus*. See Hazbun (2008) for an up-to-date survey of this literature.

114. Jackson (2006), p. 278.

115. Patomäki (1996), p. 113. See also Latham (1997), intro.

116. Adorno calls this "clowning"; see (1973) p. 14. A longer discussion of this, in the context of aesthetics, can be found in Adorno (1997), pp. 118–136.

preserving openness within theoretical interpretation to other possibilities. It is the expression of a sacred duty: the means by which IR makes good on its historical vocation.

Concretizing the Constellation in IR: Allison's Essence of Decision

Such broadly philosophical discussions require concrete illustration to show what a negatively dialectical, constellar approach to IR might look like in practice. With that in mind, existing multiparadigmatic approaches provide a useful point of departure. Given both the clarity of its exposition and its canonical status, Graham Allison's *Essence of Decision* makes a convenient heuristic starting point. Allison's thesis is straightforward: important events in world politics must be analyzed from multiple perspectives. The nature of theory, Allison holds, is that in the process of placing real events into conceptual frameworks, the thing-in-itself—in this case, "the essence of decision"— is lost. As Allison quotes John Kennedy, the moment of sovereign decision "remains impenetrable" even to "the insider himself."[117] Theorists can never know the ultimate truth of political events, then, because no one does; there is no "horse's mouth" that can serve as theory's *fons et origo*. What remains are *views of events*, drawn out of a mixed, interconnected, deeply indeterminate world. Theories function as lenses by which to draw out and focus such views. The craft of the theorist lies in mapping narratives from these views, knowing, as it were, which lenses to choose, grinding them to suit the case at hand, and placing them at the correct focal depth. To that end, Allison deployed three overlapping paradigms (he called them "conceptual lenses") around his problem: a "rational actor" lens, an "organizational behavior" lens,

---

117. Allison and Zelikow (1999), p. x. Kennedy's actual comments bear noting in full. "The American Presidency, is a formidable, exposed, and somewhat mysterious institution. It is formidable because it represents the point of ultimate decision in the American political system. It is exposed because decision cannot take place in a vacuum: the Presidency is at the center of the play of pressure, interest and idea in the nation.... *And it is mysterious because the essence of ultimate decision remains impenetrable to the observer—often, indeed, to the decider himself*" (emphasis mine). Thus the "decider himself," on this account, is alienated from his own process of decision. Kennedy then went on to explain that this "mystery" was inherent to the functioning of modern society. "If the process of presidential decision is obscure, the necessity for it is all too plain. To govern, as wise men have said, is to choose. Lincoln observed that we cannot escape history. It is equally true that we cannot escape choice" (infra Sorensen [1963], p. xi). Recall here Adorno's (2006, p. 6) critique of late-modern administrative society: "even those on the commanding heights cannot enjoy their positions because even these have been whittled to the point where they are merely functions of their own function." *The president has no choice but to make choices.*

and a "governmental politics" lens. Each was selected to offset the other; the effect of all three was to illuminate the larger agenda that the author meant to set forth.[118]

Barring certain key constitutive differences—to which I will presently return—Allison is arguing for a simple constellation, intended to produce a chastening effect for both theorists and the consumers of theory. Each lens captures an important piece of a complex whole, while the presence of the other two affirms the inability of any one—or all of them together—to fully encompass that whole. "Because simplifications are necessary," Allison (here writing with Zelikow) avers, "competing simplifications are essential"; the work of scholarship must combine fact and interpretation.[119]

This shares certain resonances with the *animus habitandi*: the more certain one *feels*, the less one likely *knows*; certainty is born of simplicity, achieved by doing violence to a reality that is never, finally, knowable. By producing narratives that "are not flatly in conflict, but neither are they compatible," one actively intervenes to ensure that this awareness is not lost to reification's peculiar form of forgetting.[120] "No event," Allison asserted, "demonstrates more clearly than the [Cuban] missile crisis that with respect to nuclear war there is an awesome crack between *unlikelihood* and *impossibility*."[121] The enormity of that almost-event—one that would have meant the deaths of hundreds of millions—obliged him "to make persuasive an unhappy, troubling, but unavoidable fact about this world": that theory was in fact unequal to the challenges of the nuclear age, and there was a limit to the guidance that can be given to policy makers.[122]

Allison, then, wished to do more than produce useful knowledge. He wished to produce a *change of affect* among policy makers and academics, to produce a sense of humility and circumspection, the absence of which aggravated an already dangerous situation. A certain inexplicable confidence, he asserted, persisted among students of world politics:

118. Allison (1971): "Thus the models can be seen to complement each other. Model I [the rational actor model] fixes the broader context, the larger national patterns, and the shared images. Model II illuminates the organizational routines that produce the information, alternatives and action. Within the Model II context, Model III focuses in greater detail on the individual leaders of a government and the politics among them that determine major governmental choices" (p. 258).

119. Allison and Zelikow (1999), p. 8.

120. Hollis and Smith (1991), pp. 54–55.

121. Allison (1971), p. vii.

122. Allison (1971), p. vii.

> in the impossibility of nations stumbling—"irrationally"—into a
> nuclear exchange, in the manageability of nuclear crises, [and] in our
> understanding of the ingredients of crisis management.[123]

Allison's aim was to disabuse his readers of that overconfidence but to do so
carefully: not so completely that they might turn to nihilism or defeatism.
Like Herman Kahn, Allison recognized that he "could not stop the world
and get off." Yet like Adorno and Horkheimer, he realized that theory could
address the reality of late modern politics only by first affirming that it was
fundamentally unequal to it. "Professional analysts of foreign affairs (as well
as ordinary laymen) think about problems of foreign and military policy in
terms of largely implicit conceptual models that have significant consequences
for the content of their thought."[124] Making them aware of this was part of the
work.

By way of anticipating criticism, there are certainly important distinctions
between Allison's aims and means and those of sustainable critique. Using
the terms set up in the previous chapter, *Essence of Decision* is an analytical
response to reification par excellence: written for a select group of policy
makers, citizens, theorists, and writers, nested within a particular historical
moment. Allison's treatment of his various conceptual lenses is thus unapol-
ogetically ahistorical: they are offered as autonomous theoretical constructs,
outside the events they seek to understand. The historical framework goes
unexamined as well: the framework of the Cold War is accepted as a given
with which policy bureaucrats must make their peace. His aim is to have done
with the critical reflection as quickly as possible; duly chastened, we are to
return to the practical work of managing U.S. foreign policy. The ongoing
critical vocation developed in the present work thus goes much further than
does Allison's; its roots lie, I have suggested, in the defining features of late-
modern politics *itself*. Any constellation that would address *that* crisis would
need to be perched more widely, reach more deeply, and sustain itself across
time. It would suspect Allison's belief that a "reformed" theory could—once
debunked of its optimistic excesses—simply return to business as usual.

Yet the heuristic power of the comparison remains. The jump from
Allison's approach to a full-fledged constellar mosaic—in which established
paradigmatic research programs form the tesserae; in which a hermeneutic
of explanatory and interpretive logics are brought into sustained interaction;

---

123. Allison (1971), p. 259.

124. Allison (1971), pp. 3–4.

and in which a clear sense of vocation is constantly present—becomes less forbidding. It helps for two other reasons as well. First, it serves to demonstrate that the *practice* of sustainable critique—as distinct from arguments made here for its necessity—need not be impossibly philosophically rarefied; well-trained students of IR already have all the tools they need, and the accumulated insights that IR's existing stable of paradigms and research programs has produced need not be discarded. Second, it serves as a firebreak against the unrelieved negativity that, it is sometimes charged, follows from Adorno's practices of reflexivity. Sustainable critique is as attuned to the *possibilities* and *obligations* of practical reason—to what Adorno and Horkheimer called the promise of "freedom in society"—as to its inability to make good on them definitively or simply. The conclusion will return to these points at some length.

Toward Sustainable Critique: Concluding Thoughts

As distinct from CIRT and CSS, sustainable critique does not aim to provide seamless reconstructions of world politics or promise coherent, continuous discourses of world politics. Rather the opposite: it seeks to make individuals and polities aware of how deep skepticism must go in an era when crisis has become endemic to the human condition. It is a moral commitment that must be undertaken a priori, Weber's vocations of science and politics rendered *negative*.[125] Theory must be sundered from progress, if such a sundering is possible; doing so is not a retreat from responsibility, but acceptance of it. This, it is hoped, might keep faith with IR's vocation as a practical, knowledge-building enterprise. To be sure, the exposition here only begins the process of developing a properly constellar approach to IR. But it does suggest a direction toward which sustainable critique might move: built not only upon *concepts* but also on *aporias*. Following Tony Burke, these are events "that prevent...a metaphysical discourse from fulfilling its promised unity: not a contradiction which can be brought into a dialectic, smoothed over and resolved into the unity of the concept, but an untotalizable problem at the heart of the concept, disrupting its trajectory, emptying out its fullness, opening out its closure."[126]

Such a constellar project could still engage with the sorts of emancipation to which Habermasian thought has been put in projects like CSS and CIRT.

125. Barkawi (1998).

126. A. Burke (2007), p. 30.

However, it would do so at a different point: it would address Habermas's concerns regarding the impoverishing effects of elitist forms of expert knowledge on public culture and discourse and on the dangers these hold for societies in which freedom is mediated through public discourse.[127] Its goal would be not *emancipation*, but the *negation of false emancipations*. The IR theorist, on this account, is not a *creator* of public spheres (whether global, local, or deterritorialized), but a self-conscious, critical *participant* in them seeking to craft knowledge that can produce those necessary forms of reflection that have no place within their various forms of debate and discourse. Thus would it keep faith with the ethical impasse to which rational thought has come; thus would it answer Adorno's call for a "new categorical imperative" in which the prevention of human suffering is the sole and only positive principle. It would be *sustainably chastened*.

Fitting IR's paradigms into constellations, it is hoped, could help mark off the precarious line that sustainable critique must walk, if IR's historic vocation is to be upheld: helping keep the theorist's critical faculties sharp, while treading lightly when it comes to foundational claims of right and truth. "Having broken its pledge to be as one with reality," Adorno wrote, "philosophy is obliged ruthlessly to criticize itself."[128] Horkheimer concurred: "philosophy must not be turned into propaganda, even for the best possible purpose," and so did Marcuse.[129] The present era—in which philosophical, scholarly, and theoretical certainties are offered as political imperatives by both right and left—bears out the enduring challenge this poses.

Ken Booth, in his recent reworking of the critical security studies project, concludes his introduction to the subject with a quote from the *Communist Manifesto*: "all that is solid melts into air."[130] Booth means to suggest that realism must take responsibility for the catastrophes in which its thought is implicated. As it stands, the point is quite correct. But it is only half the story.

---

127. Habermas (1992): "What remains for philosophy, and what is within its capabilities, is to mediate interpretively between expert knowledge and an everyday practice in need of orientation....For the lifeworld must be defended against extreme alienation at the hands of the objectivating, the moralizing *and* the aestheticizing interventions of expert culture" (pp. 17–18). See also Passerin d'Entrèves and Benhabib (1996), esp. pp. 51–52.

128. Adorno (1973), p. 3.

129. Horkheimer (2004): "Is activism, then, especially political activism, the sole means of fulfillment, as just defined? I hesitate to say so. This age needs no added stimulus to action. Philosophy must not be turned into propaganda, even for the best possible purpose. The world has more than enough propaganda" (pp. 124–125). See also Marcuse (1964), p. 257. Though the culture industry was pervasive and dehumanizing, to dream of escape was reckless, futile.

130. Booth (2007), p. 36.

All that is airy—thought, speculation, deduction, and conceptualization—also congeals into matter, into policy and action. Thoughts become deeds; values harden into ideologies, institutions, and practices. Given that they do, critique must be inwardly, as well as externally, reflexive. To be effective, critique must return to the essential questions Kant raised: What can I know? For what can I hope? And most important of all: *What ought I do?*[131] In the context of scholarly IR, *to what policies, actions, interests, and ideologies will my reifications give aid and comfort if unchastened; not only those I intend or state but also those I do not—mindful of the complex, stochastic processes by which ideas find their way into the public sphere?* Thinking is part of the solution, but it is also part of the problem. Meeting the aims of IR is possible only if one can account for *both* aspects of reason's dialectic. Admittedly, doing so is difficult, more difficult than even the foregoing survey can fully explicate. But that difficulty only helps explain why sustainable critique has proven so elusive, despite a long consensus as to the need for it. It is to documenting this difficulty—IR's ongoing, but ultimately unsuccessful, attempt to wrestle the angel of reification and obtain the blessing of chastened reason—that the present work now turns.

---

131. Compare to Müller (2008) for fascinating connections between this project and the "cold war liberalism" of Shklar, Berlin, and others—a point to which chapter 5 will return.

3

The Realist Dilemma: Politics and the Limits of Theory

"After all, it is civilization that you are kicking against," said Vavasour.
"I do not understand what you mean by civilization," said Tancred.
"The progressive development of the faculties of man," said Vavasour.
"Yes, but what is progressive development," said Sidonia;
"and what are the faculties of man?"

—BENJAMIN DISRAELI[1]

FOLLOWING THE PATH set out in the introduction, chapters 3 through 5 change direction. It was argued in the opening pages of this book that all of the contemporary fact-value traditions in International Relations (IR) share a common sense of vocation. All, that is, emerged out of a desire to provide practical guidance for a world that, owing to a cluster of political, technological, and philosophical developments, had grown increasingly in need of such guidance. Yet the problem of reification—the discipline's ongoing failure to understand that problem to its true depth and to address it systematically— had prevented that "vocational" aspiration from being fully realized. While hardly unique to IR, the particular conditions within which world politics play out render this failure especially problematic; an additional measure of ethical reflexivity is needed. For IR to live up to its historic vocation, I have argued, its practical, problem-solving aspect needs a sustainably critical, chastening complement.

The previous two chapters made the case for sustainable critique in broadly theoretical terms: showing how reification was a necessary moment in conceptual theory that demanded explicit, ongoing methodological attention. The purpose of the present chapter and the subsequent two is to buttress this claim with case studies, drawn from the trenches of IR theory. I hope first to demonstrate how the problem of reification has escaped systematic consideration—despite a broad, intuitive understanding of the need. Second, I aim to show how that failure has frustrated IR's vocational ambitions. Given

---

1. Disraeli (1878), p. 148.

this pattern, I mean to show that theorists *ought* to consider sustainable critique—despite the counterintuitive and highly demanding forms of doublethink it requires.

With these ends in mind, the introduction of this book identified three dominant methodological turns (metaphysical, middle range, and third way) that have, in broad terms, characterized the various movements of IR theory across the past six decades. It also specified three dominant fact-value traditions within IR: realism, communitarianism, and individualism. These were summarized in tables 0.2 and 0.3, respectively. It is by parsing the former through the latter—as did table 0.4—that the major research paradigms in contemporary IR theory are understood to have emerged: classical realism from a broader realist tradition with a metaphysical methodology, functionalism from communitarianism and a metaphysical methodology, neofunctionalism from individualism and a middle-range methodology, and so on. Each paradigm is thus a unique combination of facts, values, and methods; both the particular reifications on which each one relies and the dangers such reifications pose if left unchecked are sui generis. Notwithstanding the broad patterns traced out in chapter 1, each paradigm must therefore be studied individually. Those studies provide the substance of this chapter and of chapters 4 and 5. I shall trace out the development of each paradigm with an eye to how it attempted to deal with the problem of reification and how—lacking a sustainably critical sensibility, grounded in negative dialectics and the ethos of the *animus habitandi*—it ultimately failed to do so.

The present chapter is comprised of three such case studies. Each focuses on a different paradigm within IR realism, that is, a different methodological parsing of the realist tradition, broadly considered. What I have called *metaphysical realism* is explored chiefly through the writings of Hans Morgenthau. *Middle-range realism* is studied through Waltzian structuralism. Finally, *third-way realism* is explored chiefly through the systemic constructivism of Alexander Wendt. In the closing pages of this chapter, I also briefly consider recent attempts to recast realism in a sustainably critical mode, chiefly through the work of Richard Ned Lebow and Michael C. Williams.

The general argument of this chapter may be briefly summarized as follows: certain philosophical affinities link realism to the critical line pursued in the previous two chapters. Both realism and Frankfurtian social theory are reactions to enlightenment reason: its pretensions to universal applicability and its related tendency to turn oppressive. There is, however, a central difference. Frankfurt School social theory would take a sharply antifoundationalist turn toward the negative dialectics of Adorno, Marcuse's great refusal, and the deontological social theory of Habermas. By contrast, realism has remained ambivalently tied to a particular, state-centered tradition, fusing elements of romanticism with realpolitik. While equally skeptical of enlightenment reason's universalist pretensions, this tradition countered not with deontology or antifoundationalism, but with an alternative positive absolute of its own: the national state. Where the enlightenment celebrated the universal and the cosmopolitan, the "*real*-state" sought to valorize and defend the unique, the particular, and the local.[2] Such states thus had a definite moral purpose, nested within a dynamic, dialectical understanding of the grand adversarial forces that had shaped European political life.[3] The difficulty of balancing the affirmation of that purpose against a particular, sustainable, and carefully targeted form of self-critique explains realism's ongoing, if ultimately unsatisfying, attempt to grapple with reification.

It must be stressed that the link between realism's positive and critical moments has been a matter of concern for IR theorists since the Second World War. Increasingly in the wake of that war, it had come to be understood that the same zeal with which national states pursued their particular interests helped catalyze both their potential for repression and those larger processes that were increasingly rendering traditional notions of power, security, and territory obsolete.[4] This gradual realization has placed particular tensions on postwar realism with which its key academic exponents are still grappling; that struggle, indeed, is what defines postwar realism as a coherent fact-value tradition. To serve one's own particular community, whether constituted along national or other lines, has increasingly come to mean either the embrace of a cosmopolitan world order or a universal social science whose

---

2. Herder provides a compelling example of this celebration of the particular. "In order to judge of a nation, we must live in their time, in their own country, must adopt their modes of thinking and feeling, must see how they lived, how they were educated, what scenes they looked upon, what were the objects of their affection.... All this too we must learn to think of not as strangers or enemies, but as friends and compatriots" (1833), Vol. I, pp. 27–28.

3. Treitschke (1916) [1897–1898]: "The extreme one-sidedness of the idea of nationality which has been formed during our century by countries big and small is nothing but the natural revulsion against the world-empire of Napoleon. The unhappy attempt to transform the multiplicity of European life into the arid uniformity of universal sovereignty has produced the exclusive sway of nationality as the dominant political idea" (Vol. I, p. 21). See also Vol. II, pp. 577–578; Reus-Smit (1999, 2011); and Halliday (1994), p. 2.

4. Herz (1957, 1959, 1968).

axioms underpin the interactions of (ostensibly) free, sovereign nation-states. Albeit for different reasons, both claims are deeply at odds with realism's commitment to the primacy of the political. Keeping all the pieces of that paradox present to mind is the challenge facing IR realism; to date, no paradigm has entirely succeeded. This is the theoretical niche to which sustainable critique must address itself.

With that in mind, this chapter begins with the work of Hans Morgenthau. In Morgenthau, one finds all of the elements for a sustainably critical approach to realism: a combination of both practical theory and reflexivity, a strong sense of the ethics and vocation of scholarship, and a deep commitment to what has been called—in his honor—the *animus habitandi*: the will to abide within a complex, dynamic world that resists reduction to simple concepts or explanations. Yet for Morgenthau, that chastened worldview remained bound up in a notion of reason that the experience of late modern politics had rendered untenable. Morgenthau simply failed to account for this—for the full measure of the "dialectic of enlightenment" problem described by Adorno and Horkheimer. Consequently, his practical theory could not adequately defend its reflexivity. It emerged looking not chastened, but anemic; he has addressed *specific* reifications but not the ongoing problem of reification *itself*. Morgenthau understood this, I shall argue, but only intuitively; it did not find systematic theoretical expression in his work. What remained was an unsatisfying combination of moral exhortation and political nostalgia—the space from which unchecked reification curdles into ideological backlash. Evidence of both are offered in the forthcoming.

Both the middle-range structuralism of Waltz and the third-way constructivism of Wendt—respectively, the attempt to recast realism either in terms of falsifiable counterfactuals or as a cultural outcome that can be altered through improved practices of discourse and the fostering of alternative social norms—emerged in the shadow of this backlash. Though clearly imbued with a sense of vocation, nothing like the sophistication of Morgenthau's approach to critique exists in either body of theory. This was not by chance. For these theorists, the problem of the *animus habitandi* was "merely" epistemological: a challenge to be overcome through bounded acts of critical debunking, rather than an ongoing process or an ethos to be embodied.

For Waltz, this debunking involved a two-step process. First, in a manner recalling Comte, metaphysics was to be excised from theory by grounding security competition not in "an assumed nature of man," but, as is well known, in the structure of a system.[5] That done, Waltz's next step was to embrace Karl

Popper's antihistoricism. There was a problem, however: Waltz realized that falsification—Popper's means for checking the reifications embedded in "scientific" propositions—was not fully compatible with IR, nor, indeed, had he provided clear propositions to test. Yet no explicit move to compensate with some other, enhanced form of reflexivity was made. Stripped of any means for the explicit interrogation of facts and values, the assumptions of neorealist theory took on the reality of fact: the tendency, as discussed in the introduction, of middle-range theory to conflate conceptual as-ifs with the reality they seek to describe. This was despite, as recent scholarship has shown, a clear normative sensibility within which Waltzian theory was anchored and to which Waltz himself appears to have been deeply committed.

Alexander Wendt, attempting to provide a synthesis of Waltz's practical theory and "third debate" critique, dealt with reflexivity a different fashion: by co-opting it into a narrative of historical progress. States were given a new, open-ended ontology as already-constituted social agents: as "people." By implication, Wendt held that what appeared to be *political* relations among states were in fact *social* ones, whose intersubjective, deliberative quality was obscured by a Hobbesian "culture of anarchy." This raised the possibility of "resocializing" the agents that took part in world politics. Just as individuals could, through discourse, create new communities of value and practice, so, too, could states. Critique—sustainable or otherwise—thus became a secondary problem: as practical theory evolved, the need for it would wither away.

Yet as Wendt well knew, his social theory of world politics had an ontological character of its own: a "rump materialism" in which it was nested and on which it relied. Specifically, Wendt replaced the primacy of the political with the primacy of the social. Whatever the virtues of such a move in practical terms, it simply debunked one reified conceptual metaphor to clear the ground for another. That done, international theory could on his account enter into its postcritical phase; no ongoing critical vocation was needed.[6]

This move left a welter of questions unsolved: how would deliberation among states be managed, such that it might avoid the classic problems of democratic participation and inclusion? Were not some differences essential, at least some of the time? Wendt has not been blind to these questions. His recent work has sought new images of thinking that move past traditional

---

5. Waltz (2001), p. 37. But see Crawford (2009).

6. Wendt (2001).

notions of conceptual thought and empirical observation, drawing particularly from quantum mechanics. Whether such a turn might sustainably manage—or overcome—the problem of reification remains to be seen; at all events, as now constituted and practiced, third-way realism has distinct and unaccounted-for normative commitments. If Wendtian constructivism is to avoid congealing into, or being taken up by, some new brand of postnational, cosmopolitan "repressive tolerance," its reflexivity will need the means to sustain itself.

As the closing section notes, the recent work of Lebow and Williams attempts just such a deeper and more sustainable reflexivity. As with the notion of critique advanced in the opening chapters of this book, one finds in Lebow both a deeply chastened understanding of the scholarly vocation and an attempt to sustain a constant interplay between social-scientific reductionism and philosophical hermeneutics. Similarly, adapting the "willful liberalism" of political theorist Richard Flathman to IR realism, Williams develops notions of skepticism and relationality that seek to mediate between a variety of forms of knowing and a deep sense of the limitations of thought. Yet where a constellation imagines a tradition that incorporates not merely realism but also other traditions drawn from liberalism and communitarianism, these approaches tend to equate the realist tradition with IR as such. Where is the "outside" for such theories; that is, what alternative bodies of normative commitment exist to remind us of the contingency of their paradigmatic assumptions? Absent this, how shall their core concepts be subjected to their own sort of chastening, negative critique?

The "Dutch Boy Syndrome": Morgenthau's Despairing Vocation

Recent years have witnessed a remarkable turnabout in the scholarly fortunes of Hans Morgenthau. While truncated characterizations of his core concepts—what Alan Gilbert called "forgetfulness about Morgenthau"—predominated well into the 1990s, both his practical theory and his reflexive-critical sensibilities are gaining new appreciation within the field.[7] On the practical side, this rediscovery has been led by a group increasingly known as the neoclassical realists: theorists emerging from the Waltzian tradition of

---

7. Gilbert (1999), pp. 66–69; see also Behr and Heath (2009). For influential (mis-)readings, see Mearsheimer (2004); Waltz (2001), pp. 34–39; Cox (1981); Doyle (1997); Tickner (1988); and Walt (1998). But note Armstrup (1978), Jervis (1984), and Söllner (1987).

balancing but seeking to work through its predictive inadequacies by cross-fertilizing it with systematic approaches to foreign policy.[8] Neoclassical realists vary in the degree to which they claim Morgenthau as a direct intellectual ancestor. Yet both the term itself and the related argument that theoretical parsimony must yield to a more holistic engagement with domestic politics point back to Morgenthau's understandings of power and interest.

A second group of theorists find in Morgenthau a compelling attempt to square the traditions and sensibilities of realism with a reflexive-emancipatory scholarly vocation.[9] Hence, Michael C. Williams detects in Morgenthau's body of writing a "sophisticated, self-conscious, and highly political interrogation of the relationship between power and politics"; William Scheuerman detects a "supple political ethics" weaving together readings of truth and power; and Ulrik Petersen argues that "Morgenthau's thought...paves the way for a critical intervention in contemporary debates about the relationship between identity and difference and the challenges this raises for ethical thought as it attempts to negotiate the inherent tension between the individual and its orders."[10] In particular, Murielle Cozette goes so far as to claim Morgenthau as IR realism's first serious critical theorist, committed to an "ethos of permanent criticism."[11]

In considering the depth and diversity of Morgenthau's published canon and the contested nature of his legacy, the present section makes three moves. First, I set out the metaphysical foundations of Morgenthau's approach to realism, in which both political action and academic theory are understood to

---

8. Rose (1998); Christensen and Snyder (1990), p. 138. Also Brooks (1997), Christensen (1996), Christensen and Snyder (1997), Friedberg (1988, 2000), Kitchen (2010), Lobell et al. (2009), Schweller (1998, 2006), Roth (2006), Snyder (1984, 1991), Taliaferro (2004), Wohlforth (1993), and Zakaria (1998). On anomalous predictions in defensive realism, see Vasquez and Elman (2003), Rosecrance and Stein (1993), Schroeder (1994), Wohlforth et al. (2007), and Brooks and Wohlforth (2008). Core texts in defensive realism include Waltz (1979), Van Evera (1999), Snyder (1991), and Posen (1984); see also Glaser (1994–95), Taliaferro (2000–01), and Frankel (1996), pp. xiii-xviii.

9. See the essays in Williams (2007) and Bell (2009), as well as Bain (2000), Barkawi (1998), Cozette (2008), Gismondi (2004), Jütersonke (2010), Lebow (2003, 2008), Molloy (2004), Murray (1996), Neacsu (2010), Petersen (1999), Pichler (1998), Pin-Fat (2005), Scheuerman (2007a, 2007b, 2008), Steele (2007), Williams (2004, 2005), Schuett (2007), Shilliam (2007), Tjalve (2008), Turner and Mazur (2009), and Wong (2000). See also recent reconsiderations of Reinhold Niebuhr and John Herz, which find similar themes, in Bacevich (2008 a, 2008b, 2008c), Booth and Wheeler (2008), Hacke and Puglierin (2007), Scheuerman (2009a), Stirk (2005), and the essays in the December 2008 (22:4) issue of *International Relations*.

10. Williams (2004), p. 634; Scheuerman (2007b), p. 526; and Petersen (1999), p. 84.

11. Cozette (2008), p. 27.

progress through a process of dialectical tension and synthesis. Morgenthau's approach to IR makes sense of world politics by translating visible events into transhistorical ideal types and master concepts. Once so translated, two things happen. First, the theorist gains access to a classical tradition of politics that can be interpreted to cast light on the problems of a particular genera- tion.[12] Second, the visible surface of day-to-day events can be understood— "however dimly... and tenuously"—in terms of deeper, interleaving tensions, which act on the institutions and conditions of a given moment.[13] This pro- vides a degree of insight as to how future events or possible policy options might unfold.

In effect, Morgenthau sets up a positive dialectic. Theory and ideas are con- stantly reinvigorated by the productive tension they exert on one another and with the material world by which they are constrained, though to which they are never wholly or simply reducible. Yet that progressivist notion, I suggest in the second part of this section, founders in the face of the challenges posed by late modernity. Morgenthau, I argue, understood this. However, his positive dialectics could not take systematic account of reason's regressive elements. The result was a sense of powerlessness and resentment that ultimately overwhelmed his otherwise chastened methodology. While understanding the need for sus- tainable critique, Morgenthau was ultimately unable to translate that need into concrete practices. Classical realism thus despite itself succumbed to the dia- lectic of enlightenment problem, as surveyed in the opening two chapters. The subsequent turns of realism as a tradition within IR, I argue, must be under- stood in light of that failure.

In the third part of this section, I explore how this failure continues to be felt in contemporary IR theory, through a reading of recent research undertaken by "neoclassical realist" Randall Schweller. I then explore how Morgenthau could have operationalized a sustainably critical notion of real- ism, first in an Adornian theoretical idiom and then in the framework of Arendtian thought to which his work shares explicit affinities.

---

12. Morgenthau (2004): "The problems of authority, the problems of the relations between the individual and the state, the purpose of the state, the common good, the issue of law *ver- sus* naked power, the problem of violence, the class problem, the distribution of wealth in political terms—all those problems are of a perennial nature. They have not been discovered or invented in the twentieth century. You can read any political writer—the prophets of the Old Testament or Indian political philosophers, not to speak of Confucius and the ancient Greeks—and you will find that they deal with essentially the same problems which baffle us today" (p. 15).

13. Morgenthau (1967a), p. 212.

Morgenthau's Positive Dialectics

In his 1972 *Science: Servant or Master*, Morgenthau gives an account of science quite similar to Adorno and Horkheimer's account of reason in the *Dialectic of Enlightenment*. Like Adorno and Horkheimer, Morgenthau is concerned with its regressive tendencies. Science is, on his account, the progress of conscious-ness toward ever-fuller reflexivity: "the attempt to make experience conscious in reason in a theoretically valid, systematic way."[14] This journey toward self-aware-ness, however, has been an unhappy one, for two reasons. First, "technology as applied science threatens to destroy man and his social and natural environ-ment through war and...social dislocation."[15] Second, "science has...destroyed that realm of inner freedom through which the individual could experience his autonomy by controlling, however precariously, the narrow conditions of his existence."[16] The "rationalized" man finds himself enslaved: "reduced to shak-ing his fists in impotent rage at those anonymous forces which control a goodly fraction of his life but which he cannot control."[17]

The broad strokes of this argument will by now be familiar: while reason had promised to forge a path to freedom, it had been waylaid from that path. Scientific knowledge had become merely an "instrument for acquiring, defending and dem-onstrating power."[18] In consequence, Morgenthau wrote in *Scientific Man versus Power Politics*, "rationalism ha[d] left man the poorer and ha[d] made the bur-den of life harder to bear."[19] Reason had fallen into full retreat; the resurgence in "astrology, prophecy, belief in miracles, occultism, political religions, sectarianism, all kinds of superstitions, and all the lower types of entertainment" was one conse-quence of this; a gradual decline into moral relativism among elites was another.[20]

Like Adorno—albeit never in his particular idiom—Morgenthau under-stood that concepts were never identical to the real-world things they pur-ported to describe.[21] Moreover, both saw dialectics as a means by which such

---

14. Morgenthau (1972), p. 1.

15. Morgenthau (1972), p. 3.

16. Morgenthau (1972), p. 3.

17. Morgenthau (1972), p. 4.

18. Morgenthau (1972), p.14; see also pp. 19 and 46.

19. Morgenthau (1946), p. 125; here cited from Scheuerman (2007b), p. 508.

20. See, respectively, Morgenthau (1946), p. 125; here infra Scheuerman (2007b), p. 508; and "Epistle to the Columbians" in Morgenthau (1960), here from Cozette (2008).

21. In his "Fragment of an Intellectual Autobiography," Morgenthau (1984) wrote of "the experience of disillusionment that is virtually coterminous with life itself, consciously lived."

non-identity could be constantly kept present to mind. Thinking, Morgenthau explained:

> exists in a tension between the darkness of not knowing and extinction from an excess of knowledge. That tension pushes thinking back and forth and thus creates its dynamic movement. The shock of not knowing drives human consciousness forward... and the will to live pulls it back from self-destruction toward the viable middle. In that middle, thinking comes to rest: the rest of creation[.][22]

Where the two accounts part company is in that final moment: Morgenthau's "rest of creation." The non-identity of ideas and things generated, for Morgenthau, understanding and the possibility of freedom. Progress began with the *méga thaumázein*—the great "shock of wonderment"— that ensued when "reason [found] itself in the face of the unforeseen and hence the unintelligible."[23] In preserving such wonderment and drawing inspiration from it, the intellect discovered its freedom and the scholar-theorist her vocation: Roy Bhaskar's dialectical "pulse of freedom," *avant la lettre*.[24]

For Adorno, by contrast, this was only half the story. Morgenthau's "shock of wonderment" produced not only enthusiasm but also *rage*: rage against things in the world for defying expectation and proving recalcitrant to control or rationalization.[25] Where for Morgenthau wonderment produced progress toward ideals and virtues, for Adorno it also inculcated a countermovement: reason's regressive and progressive moments were of a piece. *Pace* Morgenthau, Adorno held that thinking alone could not resolve this problem; space was needed for other forms of knowing that could check and balance them. In brief, where Adorno sought a *negative* dialectics, Morgenthau developed a *positive* one, taking his inspiration from

---

He continued: "Our aspirations, molding our expectations, take account of what we would like the empirical world to look like rather than what it actually is. Thus endlessly, empirical reality, denies the validity of our aspirations and expectations" (p. 16).

22. Morgenthau (1972), p. 58.

23. Morgenthau (1972), p. 25. For a deeper reading of the *méga thaumázein* in Morgenthau— though quite at odds with my mine—see Pin-Fat (2010).

24. Morgenthau (1972), pp. 24-5. Bhaskar (1993).

25. In Adornian parlance, this is "rage against the non-identical"; see Adorno (1973), pp. 22–24.

Weber's faith in a vocation of science that would somehow be redeemed by its completion.[26]

This image of the intellect as the agent of positive synthesis—and of the scholar-theorist who wields it—informs Morgenthau's sensibilities in every sphere. The desire for love and the will to dominate—crosscutting impulses whose interplay frames political life—issue from the existential loneliness of the human condition. We transcend that loneliness by internalizing it: by realizing that we are born alone and die alone.[27] The vocation of the public intellectual is defined by playing the tensions that make theoretical truths distinct from political ones.[28] The institutional manifestations of collective historical-cultural entities (states, nations, communities) strain against political contingency; in reconciling them, the foreign policy analyst discerns the "transcendent purpose that gives meaning to the day-to-day operations of [states'] foreign policy."[29] In each of these, there is a sense of vital interplay. When concepts harden or ossify into simple, monistic propositions, then regression—decay, decline, or decadence—cannot be far behind. The theorist's vocation is that of the demiurge, identifying those spaces in which thought has ossified and reinvigorating it. "This task...makes of the scholar indeed the 'supreme, genuine man.'"[30]

As such, theory is a form of political action. It does more than match or test causes and effects or the correspondence between concepts and real-world phenomena. If it is to be true to itself, therefore, political science must be more than merely a collection of "self-sufficient theoretical developments"; it must be carefully, self-consciously, *strategic*:

> While political science must thus come to terms with the problems of power, it must adapt its emphasis to the ever-changing circumstance of the times. When the times tend to depreciate the elements of power, it must stress its importance. When the times incline toward a monistic conception of power in the general scheme of things, it must show its

26. For Weber's influence on Morgenthau, see Barkawi (1998), Shilliam (2007), M. Smith (1986), Solomon (2010), Turner (2004, 2009), Turner and Mazur (2009), Williams (2005), and Morgenthau (1984), pp. 6–7, himself. On Weber in IR, see Mommsen (1984), Aron (1971), and Donnelly (2000).

27. Morgenthau (1962); also Schuett (2007), Solomon (2010), Petersen (1999), and Molloy (2004).

28. Morgenthau (1970): "the intellectual seeks truth; the politician, power"(p. 14).

29. Morgenthau (1960), p. 8, and (1976).

30. Morgenthau (1972), p. 72, here from Cozette (2008).

limitations. When the times conceive of power primarily in military terms, it must call attention to the variety of factors which go into the power equation and more particularly, to the subtle psychological relation of which the web of power is fashioned. When the reality of power is lost sight of over its moral and legal limitations, it must point to that reality. When law and morality are judged as nothing, it must assign them their rightful place.[31]

This sense of "rightful places" preexists the study of events and things: an a priori sensibility into which such study is fitted. Theory is predicated on an assessment of what the marketplace of ideas might need (a judgment of ethics) and what it will bear (a judgment of prudence).[32] When intellectuals fail to understand this as part of their vocation, whether by asserting ivory tower inviolability or contenting themselves with merely technocratic questions of fact in the absence of value, they betray that function.[33]

The Limits of Positive Dialectics: Reification, Despair, Backlash

This combination of dialectical reasoning and a directed sense of scholarly vocation may explain Morgenthau's appeal to students of critical theory seeking points of connection with the tradition of IR realism. Yet not all dialecticism leads to the same place—think here of the historicism of Ranke, Treitschke, and Meinecke.[34] Nor is the impulse to reflexivity, by itself, a guarantee of its realization. Theorists like Ned Lebow and Michael Williams are thus quite correct when they discern in Morgenthau a "tragic vision of politics" that connects, in its broad outlines, classical notions of *hubris* and *hamartia*, or a basis

---

31. Morgenthau (1966), p. 77, here from Lebow (2003).

32. See Rohde (2005) on Morgenthau as *"praeceptor Americae."* (p. 52). See also the 1948 edition of *Politics among Nations*: now "outside the enclosures of its continental citadel, taking on the whole of the political world as friend or foe," the United States had "become dangerous and vulnerable, feared and afraid" (p. 8).

33. Morgenthau (1970), pp. 16–17. See also (1967a): "In the never-ending conflict between the official doctrine, on the one hand, and truth and dissident prudential judgment on the other, dissent from the official doctrine is of necessity the 'aggressor.' ... Theories that are by their very existence committed to the avoidance of that task probe and expose nothing relevant and thus give by implication the sanction of truth and prudence to the official doctrine" (pp. 213–214). Russell (1991) is also helpful.

34. For example, Meinecke (1957, 1972).

for a "willful realism," in which theorists assert, and impose on themselves, a notion of their own limitations.[35] Yet there are limits to which this logic can be pressed and dangers that lie in the way. Although Morgenthau's critique of politics is a powerful tool when pointed outward—against, say, the ongoing folly of Vietnam—it lacks the tools to point such critique against itself.[36]

In Morgenthau's case, this lack of inward critique proves fateful. There is a crucial disconnect between the paradox of realism set out in the introduction and the Weberian notion of critique by which Morgenthau means to bridge it. The consequence is that Morgenthau comes to seem curiously at odds with himself: *unsparing* in his exhortations to scholars and theorists that they do their vocational duty and *despairing* given that the means he specifies for them to do so seem to him (correctly) to be insufficient to the task.[37] Left with nowhere to go, he redoubles these exhortations, deepening a sense of urgency and crisis, while providing no tools by which to either resolve or sustain it. With nowhere to go, it festers into backlash. One recalls the story of the little Dutch boy who tried to save his town by putting his finger in the dyke: as society moves into decline, Morgenthau sought to stop up the various cracks through which irrationalism was pouring into the public sphere. Unlike the children's story, however, the leaks were numerous, and new ones kept appearing. With only two thumbs, Morgenthau's theorist cannot stem the flood. Such a state of affairs cannot but take an emotional toll; the theorist will eventually be dragged into despair. Backlash cannot then be far behind.

Extending the analysis begun in the previous section can illustrate this breaking point. In *Science: Servant or Master*, it will be recalled, dialectics was the engine of progress. To this must now be added a sense of what Morgenthau held to be the task of thinking. Onto the "heroic" shoulders of the theorist, Morgenthau asserts, the nuclear era has placed a redoubled

---

35. Williams (2005); Lebow (2003).

36. Rafshoon (2001); See (2001).

37. Policy makers, too, as the discussion in Mazur (2004) reveals. In its closing essay, a "rediscovered" manuscript on Lincoln, Morgenthau explains his subject's greatness as a "combination of perfected potentialities" that "no other man known to history" possessed. Lincoln "can teach us...by dint of his greatness" (pp. 253–254). Or can he? In a debate on the possibility of being a good Christian and an effective politician, Morgenthau noted that the essence of politics was the instrumental use of others; this, he asserted, is fundamentally alien to the Judeo-Christian tradition. But was not Lincoln, one interlocutor pressed, able to reconcile these tensions? Indeed, Morgenthau replied, but Lincoln *"is a unique figure in history, completely atypical"* (p. 71, emphasis mine). As with his heroic theorist, Morgenthau wants to have it both ways: the prospect of achieving greatness is laid out, and then taken away, by the same intellectual action.

burden.[38] The American public sphere had grown stagnant.[39] The challenge to the theorist was to reimagine it: nothing less. From his essay "Death in the Nuclear Age":

> The possibility of nuclear death, by destroying the meaning of life and death, has reduced to absurd clichés the noble words of yesterday. To defend freedom and civilization is absurd when to defend them amounts to destroying them. To die with honor is absurd if nobody is left to honor the dead. The very conceptions of honor and shame require a society that knows what honor and shame mean.... It is this contrast between our consciousness and the objective conditions in which we live, the backwardness of our consciousness in view of the possibility of nuclear death, that threatens us with the actuality of nuclear death.[40]

Morgenthau, as is well known, had come to realize that nuclear weapons rendered "territorial" nation-states obsolete and a world state necessary.[41] With this, it must be recalled that Morgenthau held nation-states to be organic cultural-ethical units, not merely administrative ones. If the state has become emptied of meaning—whether owing to institutional ossification or technological superannuation—then anomie, decline, and nihilism cannot be far behind. In past eras, such developments had led civilizations to tragedy: over-extension and ultimately self-destruction. In itself this was nothing new, yet the modern era added the problem of nuclear weapons into the mix. Were the United States and the Soviet Union, by way of example, to reenact the deadly embrace of Athens and Sparta, it would not simply bring down Hellas. Armageddon in the nuclear age was global: potentially, at least, the very end of human civilization as such.[42]

It might be that a world state would open up new forms of community and belonging that could return to human life a kind of existential

---

38. On Morgenthau's heroic notion of scholarship, see Cozette (2008) and Russell (1991), esp. p. 134.

39. Hence Morgenthau (1960), pp. 5–6. Also Klusmeyer (2010).

40. Morgenthau (1961), p. 234, here in Craig (2003).

41. Craig (2003, 2007), Cozette (2008), Deudney (2007), Speer (1968), and Morgenthau, infra Mitrany (1966).

42. Morgenthau (1968).

balance.⁴³ Yet such a state, Morgenthau asserted, was not in the political offing: existing concepts and categories made it impossible to discuss even the idea of it without resort to the utopian or the politically marginal.⁴⁴ An impasse thus existed. Existing political discourses seemed to lead to catastrophe, and the conceptual foundations of new ones had not yet emerged. For theory to be relevant, it had to meet that impasse. Its ongoing failure to do so "threaten[s] us with the actuality of nuclear death."⁴⁵

Perhaps that impasse, in political terms, was real. Yet the cause of Morgenthau's despair lay elsewhere: in reification gone unchecked. He had let his conceptual tools get the better of him; in so doing, no solution *could* appear. The *méga thaumázein* and its grand battle with a world that was only indifferently responsive to human thought had ceased to be merely a poetic metaphor; it had *become* the world. Since that battle could no longer free humanity of unreason and grant security, and since Morgenthau had forgotten that these forces were essentially metaphorical, all seemed to him to be lost. Since his methods could admit no new grand concepts that might replace them or forge paths that might lead to such concepts, lost he would remain.

This was despite the fact that, as Daniel Deudney and Campbell Craig have recently noted, such concepts were clearly indicated by his own analysis. A world state of the sort Morgenthau came to hold was necessary would likely render many of the traditional concepts of sovereign political community obsolete.⁴⁶ "Barring an invasion of extraterrestrials or substantial colonization in outer space," Deudney writes, such a state would be an "inside" without an "outside."⁴⁷ If so, then the *lived experience* of citizenship in it perhaps exceeded the conceptual imaginaries that realism could bring to bear: neither analysis nor interpretation on the basis of age-old master concepts would do. By this logic, Morgenthau would need space to imagine new ones—the kind of space that sustainable critique aims to create. Since the space for such imagining is not systematically incorporated into his theory, his exhortations have nowhere to go: despair sets in, and his theoretical pronouncements take on an increasingly hectoring quality. The impasse of thinking and the danger of

---

43. See Russell (1991), pp. 132–4 on this point.

44. Morgenthau (1967b), ch. 29; Rice (2008), p. 285.

45. See Scheuerman (2007a), p. 77 and passim, McQueen (2012), esp. 237–9.

46. Craig (2007), Deudney (2007).

47. Deudney (2007), p. 41.

nuclear death become, for him, a *moral* failing: a *"refusal* to adapt thought and action to radically new conditions."[48] One might be led to think that churlishness on the part of theorists and citizens—rather than "the narrow conceptual vocabulary of realism" and the intellectually dampening effects of unchecked reification—is the cause of this impasse.[49]

From this forgetting and despair issues the "undeniable whiff of nostalgia" that many observers have detected in Morgenthau's thinking: a tendency to a conservatism that romanticizes older, premodern, or "premutilated" images of thought or life.[50] What is dangerous about such nostalgia is not the claim that there were things about the old days that should be valorized or are worth preserving. It is rather the danger that—facing the yawning challenge of the nuclear age and with ever fewer serviceable arrows in one's conceptual quiver—the despair for which such nostalgia is cover might tempt the theorist away from the aporias of late-modern politics and into some form or another of peremptory or ideological simplification. In *The Purpose of American Politics*, Morgenthau had written that crises of national purpose emerged when "the creative faculty [stood] baffled and paralyzed in contemplation of the unprecedented gulf that separate[d] the received ideas from the new experiences, despairing of the ability to bridge it."[51] When facing the utter terror of the nuclear age, with one's "creative faculty" similarly baffled, might not some theorists find the burden of Morgenthau's heroism too heavy to bear?[52] What resources does Morgenthau offer them by which to carry on?

---

48. Morgenthau (1961), p. 234, emphasis added.

49. Deudney (2007), p. 276. Herz's (2005) personal recollections also support this view. Morgenthau was, Herz wrote, "the great theorist of the modern European (and then European-American) state system from Westphalia to World War Two, with its more or less state power relations." Issues that might force a systematic rethinking of the global order (terrorism, environmental degradation, multinational corporations) simply "did not command his attention" (p. 27).

50. Scheuerman (2007a), pp. 66–68, (2007b), p. 518. Also Koskenniemi (2002), see pp. 437 and 471.

51. Morgenthau (1960), pp. 5–6.

52. Of Morgenthau's contemporaries, Karl Deutsch came closest to seeing this: "In Hans's case, his willingness to stand up for his values is very conspicuous in this country, but I do think that...if one treats politics as a pure analysis of power, it has to many of us a bit of the aspect of a...hard-boiled science. I would say that this does not happen in Hans Morgenthau's hands because he knows far too much history. It becomes more nearly that in the hands of such strategists as Herman Kahn. I am thinking of Heinrich Heine's poem of his dream in which a hangman walked behind him through the streets of Cologne, saying: 'I am the action behind your theories.' I hope that you, Hans, do not see the shadow of Herman Kahn behind you. I see him behind you sometimes, but I do not think that you want his shadow, because you have taught the importance of moderation and of good sense and of a sense of balance in these matters." In Charlesworth (1966), p. 233.

From Reification to Sustainable Critique: Morgenthau's Missed Opportunity

One need not look far to see how such a deadly cocktail of despair might play out in theory. Randall Schweller's recent *Unanswered Threats*—an attempt to broker a reengagement between IR theory and domestic policy—vividly demonstrates the loss of scholarly vocation to which it gives rise and the dangers of that loss. The empirical problem that concerns Schweller is "underbalancing," the ostensible tendency of liberal-parliamentary societies to defer mobilizing in the face of external threats and thus risk being bested by authoritarian or totalitarian regimes.[53] Realism, he asserts, has lost its necessary rhetorical edge:

> Realist theory, which surprisingly shares many of the geostrategic assumptions and views of the state that motivated the rise of fascism, cannot generate the political heat necessary to launch costly mobilization campaigns for offensive purposes; its structural balance-of-power logic is too arcane to be of much use to elites as a mobilizing ideology in an age of mass politics.[54]

Liberal-parliamentary states, Schweller fears, have a predilection for internal squabbling that places them at a mobilizing disadvantage vis-à-vis strongly centralized ones. The vocation of realist theory in such states, then, must be to remind citizens of the realities of power politics, and of their duties in light of those realities. Yet in just these states, he notes, realism suffers from a "large normative-prescriptive hole;" such theory cannot do the public-intellectual work required of it.[55] Differences in scholarly idiom notwithstanding, both the broad concerns Schweller evinces and his understanding of theory's vocation thus clearly mirror Morgenthau's own.[56] But where Morgenthau calls

---

53. I will not take up here whether "underbalancing" is *in fact* the problem Schweller suggests it is; for variants of that argument, see Friedberg (2000), Reiter and Stam (2002), Lake (1992) and Caverley (2010). For the present argument, this "empirical" question is less important than the normative one traced out in the foregoing: *what is at stake* in Schweller's argument? What is politics tacitly assumed to be? What dangers lie in such assumptions, and does Schweller perform the necessary due diligence in light of them? If not, what does that failure say about the larger problem of international theory following in the tradition of Morgenthau and classical realism?

54. Schweller (2006), p. 21

55. Schweller (2006), p. 21.

56. Schweller (2006), p. 110.

for a "heroic" redoubling of scholarly efforts to revitalize the public sphere, Schweller proposes a very different solution: realism, he asserts, must make its peace with the "decisionism" of Carl Schmitt and Wilfredo Pareto.[57] Governments must develop the means by which to reassert their dominance over civil society.

What Schweller's model stipulates, but does not consistently address, is the normative position embedded in his ostensibly "empirical" problem. If "strong and unified states" have an advantage over liberal-parliamentary ones when the time comes "to enact bold and costly policies, even when their nation's survival is at stake," then national interest is asserted to be analytically (and normatively?) prior to the will of the collective citizenry, working through established constitutional channels.[58] Liberal democracy is essentially security dysfunctional; citizens suffer from a tragic tendency to prefer fractional interests to the collective good of national security. Hence the reengagement with Schmitt's concept of the political: neither as an ideal type to be problematized nor as a critique of Weimar liberalism *but as the outline of a solution for a contemporary set of problems*, the challenges facing an unruly, pluralist superpower that may someday be forced to compete at a disadvantage with decidedly less pluralist peer competitors.

Schweller's turn to decisionism must not be overstated. Certainly, he is no apologist for fascism, which he denounces as "pseudo-science" and "'ideologized' power politics for mass consumption." Fascist leaders, on his account, threw "the realist baby out with the bathwater" and substituted "excessive and greedy" foreign policies in place of "sensible opportunities for expansion."[59] Even so, the upshot of his brief discussion—"more of a sketch than a finished portrait"—undercuts these provisos.[60] Fascist excesses are, on his account, historically contingent rather than arising from any necessary quality of thinking; they did not "have to have happened."[61] That argument may serve his broader claim that leaders of contemporary liberal-democratic states should take Schmitt and Pareto seriously; it does nothing to chasten the concept of national interest *itself*—the reification of which (as scholars like

---

57. Schweller (2006), pp. 117–125.

58. Schweller (2006), p. 130.

59. Schweller (2006), pp. 122 and 21, respectively.

60. Schweller (2006), p. 117.

61. Schweller (2006): "in practice, fascist leaders were...overconfident, reckless and too aggressive for their own good. I see no reason why this 'had to' have occurred, however" (p. 125).

Friedrich Meinecke, a contemporary of Schmitt, well knew) sat at the very core of fascism's "ideologized" worldview.[62] Reification is a function inherent to all thinking, regardless of any one author's intent; yet there is nothing endogenous to the approach Schweller sets out that might serve to check or chasten its dangerous potential.

Having lost sight of this, Schweller precisely illustrates how Morgenthau's positive dialectics, lacking a sustainably critical counterweight, remains vulnerable to reification. Master concepts like national security and freedom, ostensibly constructed to critique existing foreign policies, become progressively emptied of their critical content: conflated with real things and with only limited attention given to what may be at stake in that conflation. How will such "terrible simplifications" as *either* freedom *or* the nation—simplifications that concerned both Adorno and Morgenthau—be chastened? If Schweller fears that contemporary security challenges may make domestic freedom and international security unsustainable in tandem, then we would need to consider the possibility that the Schmittian lesson is the *opposite* of what he seems to suggest. Perhaps, to take a contemporary example, the United States lacks the means to effectively play the role of global hegemon while also sustaining its domestic freedoms. Perhaps that means attention must be paid to what makes those enemies so tenacious and those freedoms so tenuous. Simply naturalizing the existence of a particular cluster of threats seems likely to spur further cycles of repression and reaction not unlike those that engulfed and ultimately overwhelmed the Weimar state. Certainly, Schweller need not adhere to this argument, nor can one argue that it is overdetermined any more than was the rise of Hitler. Yet politics—as Schweller himself asserts—is a sphere of chance and contingency: overdetermination does not exhaust its horizons of possibility.

By chastening reason and creating a space for other sensibilities, a negatively dialectical Morgenthau would give the scholar-theorist both more room to work and a greater number of potential collaborators: from writers and humanists to everyday citizens. While such a move would deprive the theorist of the heroic status to which Morgenthau lays claim, it would also free her of sole responsibility for the salvation of freedom.

That such a self-chastening turn does not emerge in Morgenthau is surprising. Phrased in a different idiom, sustainable critique would do for social

---

62. See Meinecke (1957) [1924], p. 423ff. "Today the idea of *raison d'état*...is in the middle of a severe crisis."

science roughly what Hannah Arendt's notion of *natality* attempted for political philosophy:

> The miracle that saves the ... realm of human affairs ... is ultimately the fact of natality, in which the faculty of action is ontologically rooted. It is, in other words, the birth of new men and the new beginning, the action they are capable of by virtue of being born. Only the full experience of this capacity can bestow upon human affairs faith and hope.... It is this faith in and hope for the world that found perhaps its most succinct expression in the new words with which the Gospels announced their "glad tidings": "A child has been born unto us."[63]

Arendt's aim is to create a space for new concepts and understandings to emerge in classical notions of politics—even when all existing notions are superannuated and the world seems bent on its own ruin. This space, precisely, is what Morgenthau seems to lack, the source of his despair. Yet despite his well-known personal affection for Arendt and his great admiration for *The Human Condition*, nothing like this notion appears in his work.[64]

The resulting divergence in their views is marked. In *Science: Servant or Master*, Morgenthau imagines the theorist *suffering like Christ*: redeeming the world from the original sin of unreason, in a constant state of unfulfilled yearning.[65] Arendt's reading of Christianity could not be more different. It is not Christ's *martyrdom*, but his *birth* that contains the promise of the world's regeneration; not the endless attempt to *become* the divine, but merely to *bear witness* to its constantly renewing potential for the world. The former places the scholar-theorist between self-sacrifice and angry renunciation. The latter calls for humility, finding in it resources for hope, patience, and fellowship.[66]

63. Arendt (1958), p. 247. On Arendt and IR, see Owens (2007), Klusmeyer (2009), and Lang and Williams (2008).

64. On Morgenthau and the *Human Condition*, see Frei (2001), p. 113. On his and Arendt's personal friendship, see Morgenthau (1977), Person (2004), Stoessinger (2004), and Young-Bruehl (2004). Neacsu (2010) makes a similar point, albeit in a different idiom: that Morgenthau seeks a "re-enchantment" of politics through strong leadership, though the means to such a re-enchantment remain both underspecified in his work, and undercut by his other intellectual commitments. See pp. 161–74.

65. Morgenthau (1972): "by way of systematic theory, that is, science, [man] beholds in his own suffering the possibility of suffering altogether, as the Son of God possesses in His own suffering the reality of suffering altogether.... He will never equal God in the completeness of his consciousness, nor the Son of God in the completeness of his suffering. But in the fullness of the consciousness of his suffering, he becomes like God and is assured of his divine kinship" (pp. 68–69).

66. For a deeper comparative reading, see Klusmeyer (2009).

Because Morgenthau's dialectics move, as it were, only in one direction, his thinking cannot bend this way. A clearly progressive, humanistic, deeply caring sensibility poises itself to unchecked reification, "transform[ing] thinkers into mere digesters of human action."[67] Not without reason does Gismondi compare Morgenthau's understanding of human existence with "the fate of Tantalus, for whom the objects of desire were in view but always just out of reach,"[68] for even as the theorist's vocation is affirmed, its realization is placed just beyond reach.

Reification by "Ontological Smuggling": Waltz's Middle-Range Realism

Where Morgenthau's metaphysical realism translated the visible world of politics into the push and pull of dialectical forces—but in such a way as to reify those forces—middle-range realism makes a move analogous to that of Comte, surveyed in chapter 1. Metaphysical notions of essence are eschewed in favor of empirical realities and their visible interrelations. Not surprisingly, much of the ink spilled in the "third debate" between IR's positivist and post-positivist wings recalls similar arguments made in philosophy of science and social theory: from debates over Kuhnian "paradigmatism" to the German *positivismusstreit*.[69] The question is whether as-if assumptions made about world politics can remain chastened, given that such assumptions rely on something like Popper's notion of falsification to effect that chastening, and given that such falsification is ill-suited to the "social" sciences.

As much as possible, this section will take for granted, but not rehash, that line of third debate argument that attempts to expose the normative commitments embedded in Waltzian theory. These include criticisms regarding neo-realism's "Olympian detachment" in its search for "'value free' timeless laws,"[70]

67. Craig (2007), p. 211.

68. Gismondi (2004), p. 456; also Wong (2000), pp. 406–408. Tjalve (2008), esp. pp. 123–133, concludes differently: Morgenthau remained hopeful that "patriotic dissent" and strong leadership might yet revitalize the republic. My account does not dismiss this; as with Arendt (1958, pp. 323–325), Morgenthau held that the *potential* for a meaningful political existence still survived. That did not mean, however, that a space for such potential to be expressed *then existed* or *was likely to emerge.* How does one avoid the despair that may attend calling for a necessary thing that may never come to be? In Arendt, natality and friendship provide this "release valve." Nothing parallel is evident in Morgenthau.

69. Lakatos and Musgrave (1970), Adorno et al. (1977). Also Chernoff (2005, 2007), Elman and Elman (2003), Glynos and Howarth (2007), Hollis (1994), Hollis and Smith (1991), and Jackson (2010).

70. Alker and Biersteker (1984), p. 133.

its "Platonist preoccupation with form,"[71] and the observation that methodology can, if left unchecked, be conflated with ontology.[72] Similarly, Richard
Ashley's claim that in "leaving undisturbed, even confirming, our commonsense views of the world and ourselves," neorealism sought to "relieve... this
particular niche in the academic division of labor of responsibility for reflection on its own historicity" is accepted as essentially correct.[73]

That said, beyond evaluating its unsuccessful attempts at sustainable critique, no attempt to join in the pillorying of neorealism will be undertaken
here. For it might well be asked: *why would Waltz attempt a radical separation
of facts from values?* The answer lies in the impasse to which metaphysical realism had led: a problem Waltz had observed earlier than most. "There is, at
least in the United States, a certain uneasiness among teachers and students
of International Relations," he wrote in 1959.[74] That uneasiness rose from a
sense that the field was not equal to the challenges that faced it, producing
either "sterile systems of classification" or else displaying "erratic and naïve
judgment in the attempt to comprehend the movement of the real world."[75]
Morgenthau's political ethics filled its logical gaps by placing an enormous
burden on the heroic theorist and on theory as a form of political action.
Yet as Arendt noted—and as the earlier discussion of Schweller indicates—
there are tensions implicit in linking heroism (a form of political action) to
the contemplative life of the theorist (predicated on a withdrawal from such
action).[76] As the previous section noted, while Morgenthau the *thinker* has
been justly celebrated for having identified these tensions, Morgenthau's *theory* was less successful when it came to managing them.

Waltz's theory was, to be sure, no more successful on this front. That said,
what makes one set of unchecked reifications any worse than any other? "A
reflexive, critical science of international politics," Alexander Wendt noted,
"needs every kind of knowledge it can get."[77] If a *sustainably* critical view of
world politics is possible at all, it requires an affective disposition in which
all approaches are treated with a mixture of respect and suspicion. How else

---

71. Kratochwil (1993), p. 64.

72. Ruggie (1982), passim, and (1983), p. 285; also, see Alker and Biersteker (1984). Ruggie's
"tacit ontology" thesis at work can be seen in Schroeder (1994), pp. 147–148.

73. Ashley (1984), pp. 260–261.

74. Waltz (1959), p. 66. See also Halliday and Rosenberg (1998), p. 372, and Williams (2009).

75. Waltz (1959), pp. 66–67.

76. See Arendt (1958), pp. 15–17.

77. Wendt (1998), p. 117.

might the theorist preserve the mix of passion and detachment needed to patch together a constellar hermeneutic out of a variety of incompatible inter- pretive, critical, and positivist methodologies? With that in mind, none of the shortcomings of any particular approach or paradigm can be any more egregious than any other. From the standpoint of sustainable critique, then, there is something faintly disconcerting in the ease with which Waltz's reifi- cations have made him a *bête noir* for postpositivist IR, even as Morgenthau seems to be undergoing a rehabilitation, however much deserved.

This section makes two key arguments. First, the problem of reification as this comes up in Waltzian theory is retraced in some detail: the process by which neorealist epistemological counterfactuals come to be conflated, by Waltz himself, with real-world things or processes in international politics. Following this, the often-overlooked "caring" aspect of the Waltzian project is briefly considered by drawing primarily on recent discussions by Campbell Craig.

Consider, then, the following argument for a value-free approach to real- ism: if the specter of mass destruction had trumped all supposedly partisan agendas and brought the system of states into a kind of permanent and invol- untary political entente, then perhaps, it could be argued, the positivist-dialec- tical and fact-value divides had been bridged. If *anything* could have provided the "stability in fundamental maxims" that Comte held was "the first condi- tion of genuine social order," it would surely have been the horrors of a recent global war and the fear of its return in a nuclear-armed world.[78] It would not be a positive unity under the aegis of some shared cosmopolitan ideology, but a *negative unity*, based on the will neither to destroy nor to be destroyed, knit together by a set of baseline understandings about how the international system works. If the argument that the nuclear mushroom cloud imposes on all humanity a common fate holds true, then perhaps the fact-value distinc- tion can be, finally, got past.[79] Rather than a hazy set of realpolitik-*cum*-realist "principles" that each state would adapt to its own purposes, there might be a single, systemic logic for what had become a global political order in fact, if not in name or institutional structure.

This precisely is the context in which Waltzian neorealism should be understood. If the global military-political-economic order imposed a com- mon set of values and rules, then decisions and analyses might be reduced to rational calculations of value maximization; their "political" character could

---

78. Comte (1896), Vol. I, p. 16.

79. On this point, see Craig (2003).

be separated out,[80] not, it is to be stressed, because those values did not matter but rather because, in the shadow of nuclear destruction, consensus on them could be assumed. Here again the logic is Comtean: once consensus on core values is reached, critical speculation is made obsolete; it can be left to the side. Though direct consideration of nuclear questions does not play a major role in Kenneth Waltz's early theoretical work, it is with him that the attempt to make a neat division—between political *philosophy* and political *science*—finds its most thoroughgoing expression:

> The function of political philosophy is to help form, sharpen and critically ground the fundamental understandings that we all build up somehow in our minds. Partial theories then elaborate, complicate, and contribute immediate relevance. The first without the second can be sterile; the second without the first can easily produce either chaos or pseudo-scientific scholasticism.[81]

This is a radical break from classical realism, for it asserts that there is an extra-mundane conceptual unity to the world rather than a push and pull of dialectical opposites; moreover, one can understand the effects of this unity *on* politics by some language that is not *itself* political.

In one sense, this recalls the notion of an Adornian constellation: that International Relations cannot be viewed objectively because it is not really *there* in any definitive material sense. This, Waltz noted in 2001, was the consideration that had originally guided his three-image analysis in *Man, the State and War*:

> "Image" is an apt term both because one cannot "see" international politics directly, no matter how hard one looks, and because developing a theory requires one to depict a pertinent realm of activity. To say "image" also suggests that in order to explain international outcomes one has to filter some elements out of one's view in order to concentrate on the presumably fundamental ones.[82]

After all, foundational principles—as Waltz notes in his readings of Machiavelli—are always irrational, always exogenously given. They are *political* axioms; as such, they can never be proven in their own terms.[83]

---

80. On the "reduction to calculability," see Edkins (1999).

81. Waltz (1959), p. 67.

82. Waltz (2001), p. ix.

83. Waltz (2001), pp. 212–213.

The aim is to reground realism in such a way as to define its tragic elements out of existence. For Morgenthau, some combination of ontological anthropological and phenomenological assumptions—the desire for power and the limits of conceptual reason, both endemic to the human condition—was held to be the motor of political realism: it produced an autonomous realm known as "politics." For Waltz, that autonomy is simply established by fiat: "theory isolates one realm from others in order to deal with it intellectually."[84] The struggle that Morgenthau attributes to metaphysical forces is recast in structural terms, as deriving from the particular features of the international system. The overlap with Adornian thinking, though real, is thus limited in scope.

Waltz provides no explicit means to preserve a clear distinction between his as-if counterfactuals and the world they mean to describe, such that the two do not become conflated. It is clear that he wished to avoid making deep ontological claims about the real world—as to what states were or what the nature of "the political" might be. He expressed this desire repeatedly: laws and theories were merely "relations between variables."[85] Yet no mechanism— that is to say, sustainable critique—was specified to serve as the firebreak that would separate such "relations" from actual, worldly things and processes.

A disconnect thus emerged in his work. States, he affirmed, were likened in his model to economic firms but only, he asserted, for the purpose of creating a theoretical system to which the "real" world could be compared. The structure of a theory bore no necessary correspondence to reality: "theories do construct *a* reality, but no one can ever say that it is *the* reality" because "in reality, everything is related to everything else."[86] "A theory, though related to the world about which explanations are wanted, always remains distinct from that world. 'Reality' will be congruent neither with a theory nor with a model that may represent it."[87] It "is not a statement of everything which is important in international-political life, but rather a necessarily slender explanatory construct."[88] "Structures condition behaviors and outcomes," but

84. Waltz (2004), p. 175.

85. Waltz (1979), p. 1. See also Hoffmann (1958–59), pp. 357–358.

86. Waltz (1979), pp. 8–9. Also Waltz (1992, p. 22): "Theory is artifice. A theory is an intellectual construction by which we select facts and interpret them."

87. Waltz (1979), pp. 6–7. Or see Waltz (1997), pp. 913–914: "Theory, rather than being a mirror in which reality is reflected, is an instrument to be used in attempting to explain a circumscribed part of reality of whose true dimensions we can never be sure." More can be found in A. Kaplan (1964), chs. 9 and 10.

88. Waltz (1992), p. 32.

skilled political operators "transcend the limits of their instruments and break the constraints of systems that bind lesser performers."[89]

Here lies the disconnect: beneath all these declarations lies what appears to be a rather straightforward belief that the distinction between a naïve "pre-conceptual" picture of the world and a subsequent, but in some sense imaginary, "analytical" one can be preserved by simple declaration. The basis of this belief is not clear, but it is essential to the logic: a simple act of will must suffice to hold reification at bay. In Popperian thinking, it will be recalled, the notion of "crucial tests" and falsifiability played a central role in enforcing this distinction; it was a mechanism preventing theoretical constructs from becoming "metaphysicalized" truisms. But as Waltz well knew, such tests were not possible in the social sciences. "Because of the interdependence of theory and fact, we can find no Popperian crucial experiment, the negative results of which would send a theory crashing to the ground. The background knowledge against which to test a theory is as problematic as the theory itself."[90] If one cannot separate background knowledge from theory, one might well expect some other procedure to be incorporated into neorealism as a bar against forgetting the difference and conflating the two. One might, that is, expect some form of sustainable reflexivity to be woven into the theory. Yet nothing of the sort is developed.

The consequences of this omission are many, but one example will suffice. Consider Waltz's treatment of a rival structuralist theory, developed by Immanuel Wallerstein. Waltz, it will be recalled, organized his model of the international system around three key variables: anarchy, the functional similarity of the units in the system, and the distribution of resources within that system.[91] Were we to read Wallerstein as a predictive theorist, his model could be understood in analogous terms.[92] Sovereign states emerged from a global order in which "a single political system does not exist over all, or virtually all of the space."[93] Their interactions, as with Waltz, were primarily determined by the differential distribution of assets and capabilities: technology, manpower, investment capital, trade and primary goods, and the like.

---

89. Waltz (1986), pp. 343–344, here from Hollis and Smith (1991).

90. Waltz (1986), p. 334; also Molloy (2006); Waltz (1979), pp. 123–128; and Waever (2009).

91. Waltz (1979), pp. 88–99.

92. See Chase-Dunn and Sokolovsky (1983) and Doyle (1997), p. 486, for such readings.

93. Wallerstein (1974), p. 348.

But where Waltz assumed that learning and competition drove states to become more *similar*, Wallerstein suggested the opposite: that *differentiation*, according to economic roles, was the rule. Wealthy "core" states developed power-projection and rule-enforcement capabilities—blue-water navies, colonial armies and ministries, and so on—designed to protect and extend their profitable monopolies on high-value, capital-intensive functions. Poorer "peripheral" states developed into client regimes, whose competencies may be limited to supervising raw resource extraction and controlling social unrest. A middle group of states focused on various intermediary functions. Peripheral or semiperipheral states might *superficially* resemble core states in their institutional articulations, but the system actually causes them to become *less* isomorphic.

Waltz dealt with this by asserting a distinction of kind; Wallerstein's theory was *economic*, his was *political*:

> Wallerstein shows in many interesting ways how the world economic system affects national and international politics. But claiming that economics affects politics is no denial of the claim that politics affects economics and that some political outcomes have political causes.... An international-political theory serves primarily to explain international-political outcomes. It also tells us something about the foreign policies of states and about their economic and other interactions. But saying that…does not mean that one such theory can substitute for the other. In telling us something about living beings, chemistry does not replace biology.[94]

Waltz appears to have forgotten the distinction between his *analytical* categories and the *ontological* realities they describe.[95] In Waltzian theory, we

---

94. Waltz (1979), p. 39. Waltz also has another claim against Wallerstein: since his approach is broadly historical and constitutive, it is not properly *theory*. But as Wendt (1999, p. 87) has argued, does not this move overly gerrymander the term? "Constitutive theories are theories. They involve inferences from observable events to broader patterns, and inferences always involve a theoretical leap."

95. We may pass over the fact that Waltz's politics-economics distinction wrongly imputes to Wallerstein the position that economics is primary to politics. By an *economic* system, Wallerstein means only what Waltz means when he says an *anarchic* one: that there is no centralized system of command or compellance. "Capitalism," Wallerstein notes, "as an economic mode is based on the fact that the economic factors operate within an arena larger than that which any political entity can totally control" (p. 348). Political control predominates within states, which are nested within a larger anarchic world economy. Waltz says as much himself; it is the reason that he is able to apply theories of firms within economies to the world system so easily.

recall, all distinctions and correlations were analytical; in reality, "everything [was] related to everything else." On what basis, then, can Waltz differentiate between politics and economics? The analogy with chemistry and biology is apt: such definitions are of importance only to laboratory heads seeking to qualify for particular funding lines or for students debating where they should apply for graduate study: at the microcellular level, the happenings of the physical world simply *are*. In providing no explicit basis for specifying these distinctions, the door was open for structuralism to descend precisely into the same crass ideological reductionism that Popper so abhorred in "vulgar Marxist" and Hegelian readings of political economy and history: taking the contingencies of a particular era (late Victorian capitalism for Marx, the Prussian state for Hegel, postwar bipolarity for Waltz) and reading into them transcendent or universal principles that simply were not there.[96] Waltz tried to get around this problem by suggesting that his was a general theory of world politics and that specific foreign policy recommendations were not to be derived from it. He made, he asserted, no claim to explain "why state X made a certain move last Tuesday."[97] Critics, however, have been quick to point out that this distinction has been observed primarily in the breach.[98]

It may now be apparent why Ashley, Alker, Biersteker, and others suspected Waltz of having taken a side on the left-right ideological fault line that has divided political philosophy since the French Revolution. If Waltz was *not* arguing for the primacy of the nation-state, then one might have expected a kind of pluralistic openness to such theories. If he *was*, one would expect him to have made a clear ontological statement about *homo politicus*, as did Morgenthau. Neither was forthcoming. That neorealism, as Wendt and Friedheim put it, began to seem like a vector for smuggling normative values beneath the scholarly radar was therefore not entirely the fault of his critics.[99]

From this moment of reified forgetting, however, has grown a disciplinary metadiscourse that has eclipsed the vocational aspirations of Waltzian theory quite completely. In a recent survey, Campbell Craig has suggested that that Waltz's professions of value neutrality grew increasingly more performative as his professional stature grew and as he attempted to bring nuclear war into the

---

96. Popper (1966), p. 149.

97. Waltz (1979), p. 121. Also Halliday and Rosenberg (1998), p. 373; Wivel (2005); and Mearsheimer (2009).

98. Elman (1996), Wivel (2005), and Oren (2009).

99. Wendt and Friedheim (1995), p. 695.

purview of his systematic theory. The reality of nuclear war, "like a shadow, followed him wherever he went."[100] The end result, Craig asserted, was that Waltz had to make a choice. He chose bravely: "to favor an atheoretical program for great-power war avoidance over philosophical consistency."[101] Waltz's theories did not, then, come to points of impasse by chance or oversight. They reflected those moments when he *chose* to prefer his normative agenda—according to Hollis and Smith, to inform and influence policy makers and decision-making structures, with an eye to the collective good—over his analytical one.[102] With notable exceptions, this point has consistently eluded third debate critics of neorealism, for whom it has become "an apologia for the *status quo*" to be denounced rather than engaged.[103] Such arguments are not wrong so much as they are too simple. *All* reductive theory can be criticized for being reductionist, and occult motives for the particular variables they exclude can always be found if sought, just as, indeed, all antifoundationalist theory can be criticized for concealing within itself the seeds of some new foundationalism. Each aspect of the argument must be chastened by the other.

Epistemological Lowballing: Wendt's "Third Way"

Just such an alternative foundationalism is visible in the constructivism of Alexander Wendt. Coming out of the postpositivist debates of the 1990s, Wendt's *Social Theory of International Politics* wished to preserve the statist assumptions of neorealism but to reground them: to renegotiate the ontological basis of realism and hence the work it was able to do. Interstate relations were ideational-historical constructs; anarchy, Wendt proposed, could be understood as what states had made of it.[104] In replacing Waltz's states-as-economic-firms analogy with one of states as people,[105] Wendt meant to open up world politics to theories of intersubjectivity: interstate anarchy was

---

100. Craig (2003), p. 165.

101. Craig (2003), p. 165.

102. Hollis and Smith (1991) pick up on Waltz's concession in 1986 that "structural causes can be overcome" and "are *not* determining." If so, they argue, then neorealism must be (in Cox's terms) *for something*: to "influence the perceptions of those who take decisions on behalf of the state, give them an agenda to respond to and a set of constraints" and to "influence the way in which the decision-making processes operate within the state" (p. 117). The positive-normative distinction thus implodes.

103. Ashley (1984), p. 257. But see Hollis and Smith (1991), pp. 104–117.

104. Wendt (1992); see also (1999), pp. 8–22, 92–135.

105. "States are people too"; see Wendt (1999), pp. 215–243.

transformed from an immutable fact of political life into a cluster of contingent, open-ended cultures and practices. The aim was to create a space within which to theorize the possibility of new cultures and norms emerging among sovereign states: from a "Kantian" culture of friendship to perhaps even a world state.[106] Neorealists tended to view the end of the Cold War as either a source of new potential dangers or else an embarrassing theoretical anomaly to be ignored.[107] Wendt wished to tell a different tale.

Wendt's anthropomorphic view of states resembles, in a certain sense, Morgenthau's dialectical metaphysics—especially when viewed through his recent attempts to recast his rump materialist ontology through the "wave-particle duality" of quantum mechanics.[108] Where they differ is in the notion of critique they hold to be necessary for international theory to do its work. For Morgenthau, political life was held to be essentially resistant to conceptual theory; this resistance stemmed from their inherently divergent nature. For Wendt, the political is an outcome, the product of an antecedent set of social interactions among already-constituted agents: "ego" and "alter." Anarchy is thus radically less determinate than Morgenthau had supposed: "changing the practices" of the actors in an international system "will change the intersubjective knowledge that constitutes that system."[109] The aim of Wendtian theory is first to learn how those practices emerge and then to learn to shape or steer the process.[110] Critique is deferred to the margins: the means to ascertain what should be done with such knowledge, once it is obtained. Hence where Morgenthau's theory ends in precarious balances that must be sustained through heroic acts of thinking, Wendt quickly passes to what he calls a "postcritical" mode: theory is a means to "steer" world politics.[111]

Thus while Wendt attempts to recover some of the reflexivity that Waltz had carved out of Morgenthau's realism, he does so to very different ends.

---

106. Wendt (1992); also Wendt (1999), pp. 246–312 and 373–378; (2003).

107. Mearsheimer (1990), Allan and Goldmann (1995), and Lebow and Risse-Kappen (1995).

108. See Wendt (2006), pp. 191 and passim. In Wendt's earlier work, the degree to which such similarities exist may depend on how one reads his organicism. On this his critics are divided; compare Wendt (2004), Wight (2004), Neumann (2004), Jackson (2004), Doty (2000), Ross (2006), and Guzzini and Leander (2006). The closest parallels with Morgenthau can be found in the his early work, especially Morgenthau (1934).

109. Wendt (1992), p. 407; (1999), pp. 326–336.

110. Wendt (2001).

111. Wendt (2001), p. 212. And hence both the work and ethics of IR theorists can be transformed: "getting policymakers to accept responsibility for solving conflicts rather than simply managing or exploiting them" (1995, p. 81).

Political difference does not inhere in ontology for Wendt: agents exist a priori, but the nature of their interactions is indeterminate and radically open. Since difference has its origins in discourse, it can also be dissolved through discourse: by "talking about facts and values together."[112] Wendt may have loyalties to particular state forms and institutional arrangements—he states these—but it is the process of dialogue and interaction that does the key work of building them.[113] It is a pearl bought at great price: to assert the possibility of learning is to bring a particular brand of liberal corrigibility back into realism that is itself not innocent of political or ideological ramifications. *Social Theory of International Politics* was, Wendt himself has recently commented, "less a *via media* than an attempted synthesis of previously opposed positions"; an effort meant less to *sustain* unintelligible positions (as by, say, a constellation) than to *reconcile* them.[114]

Waltz, then, may have been smuggling in the autonomy of the political, but Wendt was doing some smuggling of his own: not merely the autonomy of the social, but a particular social telos. Lebow summed it up aptly: Wendtian theory was "another representative" of a genre that "posits the inevitable triumph of the Kantian world in the context of a world state."[115] The theory itself is neither wrong nor implausible; it simply posits a potential for discourse that is, at bottom, speculative and deeply contested. The limits of applying discourse theory and communicative action were discussed at length in chapter 2 in the context of applications of Habermasian theory to IR, and there is no need to return to them here. The key point is that they rely, at bottom, on an ontology that is neither politically innocent nor immune from the dangers of unchecked reification. Wendt has acknowledged that such ideas carry with them "ethical responsibilities" for theorists but never clearly spells out what these are or what practices they must engender.[116] The quote from Disraeli with which this chapter opened looms large: *what is progressive development? And what are the faculties of man?*

---

112. Wendt (2001), pp. 215–216.

113. Wendt (2000): "*Social Theory [of International Politics]* does reify the state, up to a point, and does so intentionally.... For all their faults, states are the only democratically-accountable institutions we have today to provide security and political order. Perhaps other, better institutions can one day be developed, but until then we would do well not to tear states down too quickly" (p. 174). See also Wendt (1999), pp. 370–378.

114. Wendt (2006), p. 182. An early version of this reconciliation can be found in Wendt (1987).

115. Lebow (2008), p. 97.

116. Wendt (2006), p. 217. On this point, see also Wendt (1998), pp. 111–112.

In Wendt's more recent theory, this precisely is what his quantum approach is meant to guard against: the particle-wave duality of quantum physics is meant to provide a basis by which different modes of explaining and understanding can coexist. "It would be absurd for the 'particle guys' to fight with the 'wave guys' about who has the truth, since the knowledge each offers is understood to be inherently partial, and so must be complemented with the other for a complete description."[117] True and certain, but does not *any* rehearsal of the hermeneutic circle—think of Hollis and Smith—produce this awareness?[118] The question is not "into what new idiom can I *again* retranslate my commonsense notion that agents and structures are reified abstractions" but rather "why, given the fact that everyone agrees that these reified abstractions *are* such, must we keep returning to them and 'redebunking' them?" For IR, the answer seems to be the specter of destruction: the peremptory desire for certainty, weighed against the knowledge of its impossibility. Committing to plurality *in the face of that* is the essential problem of sustainable critique, as is considering one's responsibility given that IR theorists are part of how the world constitutes itself. It cannot suffice to acknowledge that "we have ethical responsibilities" arising from this—but then to refrain from specifying what they are.[119] For sustainable critique, the beginning would come in recognizing that even Wendt's "complete description"—one that included both particle guys and wave guys—could be nothing of the kind. Rather than reinscribing social science into yet another dichotomy, it would seek to hold different approaches in dynamic, ongoing suspension: sustainable critique, built on the ethos of the *animus habitandi*.

Concluding Thoughts: Critical Realism and Sustainable Critique

While the weight of the field since Waltz has thus been behind the resolution of the tragic elements within realism, some theorists have recently begun reconsidering how positive and critical theory might be sustainably balanced against one another within realism. Noteworthy within these attempts are Lebow's recent *Tragic Vision of Politics* and Williams's "willful realism." Given the larger aims of this project, some brief mention of these approaches seems

---

117. Wendt (2006), p. 216.

118. Hollis and Smith (1991). See also Kessler (2007).

119. Wendt (2006), p. 217.

apposite. For reasons of space, however, this engagement is limited in scope, addressing itself specifically to the concepts in each designed to achieve effects akin to those to which sustainable critique aspires.

In chapter 2, it was suggested that the Adornian notions of negative dialectics and the constellation called for a constant playing off of the analytical-reductionist and interpretive moments of theory through a critical hermeneutic constellation. For his part, Lebow speaks of "tacking": using texts that "point away from themselves to ideas and feelings they cannot capture," moving "between the 'frolic in images' and bench science ... build[ing] unity in diversity and wisdom through uncertainty."[120] The aim is *sōphrosunē*: a way "to find a language appropriate to our time in which the lessons of tragedy can be expressed and speak meaningfully to us and our contemporaries."[121] Though phrased in a different idiom, no clearer call for chastened reason could be hoped for. Moreover, the intellectual process whereby Lebow understands that reflexivity gets lost—of *hubris* (pride) leading to *atē* (seduction), *hamartia* (missing the mark), and ultimately, *nemesis* (the wrath of the Gods)— certainly recalls, in more general terms, the process by which reification goes unchecked.[122] One need only imagine a mind being seduced by the beauty of its own concepts, lulled into conflating reality with those concepts, and reaping the whirlwind. Williams evinces a similar set of concerns: the tradition of IR realism is larger, more reflexive, and more diverse than present research practices admit. He wishes to recall a larger tradition that has been forgotten: "was there not another realism—within the existing 'tradition'—that could be brought into view by challenging contemporary claims about both the nature of Realism and the positions of classical thinkers within its tradition?"[123]

Lebow and Williams thus seek out and cultivate resources for a chastened mode of reflexivity. For Lebow, *tragedy*—a sustained confrontation "with our frailties and limits, and the disastrous consequences of trying to exceed them"— does this work.[124] Like the *animus habitandi*, it provides the impetus for seeking out a fuller, richer tradition of realism that can only be unlocked by bringing

---

120. Lebow (2003), pp. 52 and 389.

121. Lebow (2003), p. 366.

122. Lebow (2003): "The Frankfurt school embarked on a project that was a conscious parallel to the nineteenth-century evocation of tragedy and Greece; it drew on the German philosophical tradition, primarily Marx and Freud, to generate a space of critique" (p. 375). See also Williams (2005), p. 193 n.

123. Williams (2005), p. 4.

124. Lebow (2003), p. 20.

multiple forms of thinking and reading to bear against a common tradition or set of events. For Williams, this work is done by a combination of skepticism and relationality.[125] Though power politics is not rejected outright, Williams hopes to nest such notions in an ontological worldview with sufficient elasticity to keep their reifications present to mind: "a principled commitment to autonomy with the practical search for a modus vivendi and engagement between contrasting values and forms of life."[126] Both seek, like sustainable critique, a change of affect and sensibility, as well as a shift in scholarly approach.

Yet there are certain important differences. The *animus habitandi* derives from a particular quality held to inhere in *conceptual reason*: the obligations it imposes derive from their use of such reason. By contrast, Lebow's tragedy seems to hold a transhistorical status akin to the master concepts that guided Morgenthau. One thus wonders how Lebow would avoid the pitfalls discussed earlier in this chapter: the inability to turn them backward upon themselves that plagued Morgenthau. Recall that Adorno's critique of Kant lay not in the attempt to develop a systematic moral philosophy, but in the fact that the system he developed was a house built on sand; it required anchoring one's faith in a "transcendental escrow." Negative dialectics was needed precisely because that anchor, too, must be undone. *Any* anchor—Lebow's tragedy no less than any other—would have to be. Only thus could critique, like practical reason, also be sustained as a "treasure for all time."

A similar question can be directed to Williams. It is certainly true that "a willful realist tradition exists" within the texts and thinkers he has considered and that "coming to terms" with that tradition will produce both more nuanced insights and more sustained ethical engagements with the problems of world politics.[127] Yet it bears asking: does this go far enough? If it is true that these ethical positions were "always already there" and that willful realism (or for that matter, the *animus habitandi* or any other normative-critical impulse) merely *recovers* what had been forgotten (or read out) by previous generations, does it not bear asking *why* such forgetting takes place, and so easily, too? *Are there not dynamics in thinking that make such forgetting all but inevitable, if not actively checked?* If so, then simply exhorting theorists to do their duty is unlikely to go far enough to create sustainable reflexivity. Morgenthau had, as Williams and Lebow both note, fought that battle

---

125. Williams (2005), pp. 15–16.

126. Williams (2005), p. 208.

127. Williams (2005), p. 16.

and lost. If critical realism is to do better, it must learn from what its classical forebears *failed* to do, not merely what they *sought* to do.

Consider, in that vein, the possibility that critical realism does not go far enough. Lebow's notion of tragedy can serve here. "Thucydides was... not as pessimistic as many realist readings suggest," Lebow argues in *The Tragic Vision of Politics*. "Would he have invested decades in the research and writing of his history... if he had thought human beings and their societies were prisoners of circumstance and fate?"[128] Lebow's answer is, of course, negative: there would have been no reason to write the work in that case.

Or would there? Read Thucydides's belief in the timelessness of his writings with different inflection—a resigned, impassive, "tragic" one—and the motives one might attribute to his authorship of it change substantially. Since the earth's natural forces produce human life by dint of unalterable forces, that resigned rereading suggests, and since political life is a reflection of men's basic natures, empires will forever be lost to fecklessness and misjudgment. These losses will be unbearably tragic in two senses. First, they will claim many lives. Second, many of the lives lost will be squandered in the pursuit of ill-advised political adventures, wholly preventable if one possessed even a modicum of wisdom or introspection. So read, the eternal value of the *Peloponnesian Wars* lies not in its power to *instruct*, but to *console*: to bear witness to human folly and to remind the survivors of civilization's periodic calamities that, though their personal responsibility for such calamities may be great, the calamities *themselves* are merely a part of the human condition. Such a reading of Thucydides is here offered only provisionally, without a careful examination of the text: my aim here is only to probe the depth of Lebow's vision of tragedy by using it as a stress test for that vision. Let it therefore be stipulated to at present, solely for that purpose.

If viable, such a reading of Thucydides would seriously vitiate Lebow's position. Such consolations as Thucydides might hope to gain and pass on to future generations would rely on the certainty that the earth will outlast the follies of any one polity or civilization, that life will always go on, and that any one person's sufferings can always be shared, if not by one's own contemporaries, then in the eyes of that endless college of thinkers and doers who have come before us and those who shall survive us. Such was the consolation of philosophy in its premodern, prenuclear form: a way of "thinking oneself anew," when no single human mistake could destroy the world.[129]

---

128. Lebow (2003), p. 150.

129. Through Nietzsche, Dietz (2002) outlines such a reading: "By inventing an alternative world swept clean of horror, suffering and degradation, Thucydides... offers not only the

If Lebow is tempted into making Thucydides's consolation serve for the present day, he thus risks falling into his own kind of scholastic retreat from reality, for he would be ignoring the radical break that sets off late-modern material conditions from those of the ancients. After all, we have no such existential assurance as to the permanence of our world. That realization, indeed, was what had driven Morgenthau to take comfort in nostalgia: his realization that late-modern politics took place "under an empty sky from which the gods have departed."[130] It might seem, then, that Lebow's tragic vision cannot arrest the process of crisis and closure that hobbled Morgenthau. On the contrary: the ground would be prepared for yet another iteration of it. Here, the confluence of American global expansionism and radical evangelical Christianity seems to be a harbinger: the attempt to win back the favor of Morgenthau's "lost gods" by acts of Crusading passion rather than a sober determination to learn to live decently without them.

What Lebow needs is an "outside" to realism: a critical faculty for turning his master concepts back on themselves, to replace the political outside that is gradually disappearing—whether under the weight of the nuclear "new leviathan" or that of economic globalization. This would be an engagement with not merely one fact-value tradition, reconstructed along time and space, but several, *a constellation of many such traditions*, all working all at once, *affirming and negating both difference and cosmopolitanism at the same time*. Lebow certainly leads the reader in this direction. Moreover, his cultural theory of IR—which, for reasons of length, I have refrained from examining here—could be construed to provide many points of connection for it.[131] Yet active, conscious steps would need to be taken toward it. As this chapter noted in its opening pages, this is the very tension that has paralyzed realism for decades. It must be *actively* sustained.

Athenians but all of humanity a way of thinking themselves anew. It is thus 'a possession for all time.' It offers a path toward forgetting the evil of the day before" (p. 189).

130. Morgenthau (1967b), p. 249.

131. Lebow (2008); see in particular pp. 37–41.

4

Communitarian IR Theory: "The Common Socius of Us All"

The difference between living against a background of for-
eignness and one of intimacy means the difference between
a general habit of wariness and one of trust. One might call
it a social difference, for after all, the common socius *of us*
all is the great universe whose children we are.

—WILLIAM JAMES[1]

IR Liberalism: Two Traditions

In the next two chapters, the critical line developed in chapter 3 is turned to
IR liberalism: both the normative commitments on which its practical theory is posited and its abiding need for sustainable reflexivity. Like realism, IR
liberalism is an attempt to develop a body of practical international theory
to meet the challenges and opportunities of late-modern life. That similarity aside, however, both the nature of liberalism and its uncertain application to questions of world politics raise certain complexities when one seeks
to assess it in the context of IR's historic vocation. Notwithstanding recent
claims by Andrew Moravcsik, there is no single normative or conceptual tradition that unites the approaches collectively known within the discipline as
"liberal."[2] Hence, there can be no basis for a unitary discussion of the sort
undertaken in chapter 3. Rather, as Michael Doyle and Robert Keohane have

---

1. James (1996) [1909], p. 31.

2. Moravcsik (1997): "Liberal theory is analytically prior to both realism and institutionalism because it defines the conditions under which their assumptions hold" (p. 516). While
this position merits more extensive discussion than can be undertaken here, it will be persuasive only to the extent one accepts liberalism only as a set of tools for the analysis of civil
society—by which to explain the persistence of "Pareto inefficient" outcomes at the interstate level—and not as a normative set of assumptions about political life (p. 521). But then
it bears asking: given its obvious moral and ethical valences, why invoke the term *liberalism*
at all? Does it not invite confusion, especially in political communities prone to the belief
that liberal values are universal? See Long (1995), Jahn (2009, 2010), and Moravcsik (2010a,
2010b).

argued, liberal IR theory is "a family portrait of principles and institutions," from which theorists of world politics have selectively drawn.[3] As Onuf and Johnson have explained, "the liberal tradition reaches back to a time when no one drew a firm distinction between domestic and international affairs."[4] In consequence, no single institution or concept in IR liberalism can parallel the foundational status that the nation-state enjoys among IR realists.

The problem this poses to sustainable critique may be briefly summarized. The various paradigms of international theory are here understood as long-standing fact-value traditions, parsed through a variety of different methodological innovations as these have emerged over time. Sustainable critique, at least as conceived in the first two chapters, can work only once such traditions have been identified: in the present case, according to the way in which the liberal *socius* (to borrow a term from the epigram to this chapter) is made somehow analogous to the realist *polis*.[5] To sustainably critique such theory would be to check the reifications on which those translations rely: by problematizing them and yet also affirming their potential to do useful work within the confines of the values upon which they are predicated. For that, the family portrait of liberal IR theory must be resolved into distinct genealogical lines.

With that in mind, the present chapter and the next one argue that two distinct fact-value traditions have dominated liberal IR. The first is *communitarian*, in roughly the sense given this term by scholars like Charles Taylor and Amitai Etzioni, but originating in Ferdinand Tönnies's concept of *gemeinschaft*.[6] The second is *individualist*, used in a sense that parallels Tönnies's *gesellschaft* and as is captured in many contemporary understandings of global governance and world society.[7] These two traditions differ in their primary anthropological understandings of human political and social life, in their

---

3. Doyle (1997), p. 206; also Keohane (1990): "Liberalism does not purport to provide a complete account of international relations" (p. 175).

4. Onuf and Johnson (1995), p. 179.

5. For a recent example, see Altman and Wellman (2009).

6. This is a very broad literature, but key statements can be found in Etzioni (1993, 1995). See also Bellah et al. (1985), Galston (1991), Putnam (2000), and the "Responsive Communitarian Platform," the text of which appears at www.gwu.edu/~ccps/platformtext.html. Other IR theorists—on this point, see Morrice (2000)—anchor communitarianism in the high political theory tradition: see the essays in Avineiri and de-Shalit (1992) and, of course, the great community–great society dichotomy set up in Dewey (1981)[1927]. On *gemeinschaft*, the best source remains Tönnies (1957) [1887], ch. 1; see also Nisbet (1966), pp. 73–80 and 208–211; Heberle (1973); Parsons (1937), pp. 686–694; and Weber (1978), Vol. 1, pp. 40–43.

7. Tönnies (1957) [1887], see pp. 64ff.

normative commitments, and in what they hold to be the work of international theory.[8] Following a brief exposition of the two traditions, this chapter will focus on the former, and chapter 5 will take up the latter. The basic argument is that the two traditions coexist uneasily: each depends on the other to hold it in critical balance. When mapped onto problems of world politics, they are *each logically incompatible with one another and fundamentally unsatisfactory on their own*. The dichotomy they present is thus a persistent one: to be sustained, not resolved. To the extent that scholars in IR liberalism have realized this, they have moved closer to the sustainably critical ethos set out in the previous pages; none, however, has explicitly embraced it.[9]

---

8. I am certainly not the first to assert this division or similar divisions. For a compact discussion, see Morrice (2000), as well as Adler (2005), ch. 1; Brown (1992), chs. 2 and 3; Buzan (1993); Ellis (2009); Frost (1996), ch. 3; Cochran (1999); Kaiser (1972); Katzenstein (1975), ch. 2; Pin-Fat (2010); Rosamond (2000), pp. 43–45; Pentland (1973), introduction; Taylor (1968); Manning (1962), pp. 176–177; and Rengger (1992). A seminal version of this argument—addressed in chapter 2—is Linklater (1990b). Modelski's (1961) agraria-industria distinction also incorporates some of these themes, as does Jackson's (2002) reading of Brian Barry's economics-sociology divide in the social sciences and Joas's (2003) distinction between republican and utilitarian versions of liberal thinking.

A note here on nomenclature: the terms *gemeinschaft* and *gesellschaft* are usually translated as "community" and "society." To avoid untoward conflations with terms like *international community* or *global society*, which are frequently used without regard to the particular dichotomy outlined here, I have preferred *individualist* to *social*. The term *communitarian* poses a harder problem. Although the use I give the term here has wide representation in the literature (Adler [2005], Haas [1964], Taylor [1968], Katzenstein [1975]), *communitarianism* also variously denotes both a political sensibility (Etzioni [1995]) and a strand of republican thinking (Onuf [1998], Deudney [2007]). While apt to cause confusion, I have resisted changing the term; since an unacknowledged tension in Tönnies's primary understanding of this concept is, I am arguing, a key driver of reification in liberal IR circles, preserving a rapport with it seemed particularly important.

9. On this point, the communitarian-cosmopolitan distinction in republican international theory comes closest. For Nicholas Onuf (1998), communitarianism and cosmopolitanism are opposing poles of thought within an older, more variegated political legacy that is only partly preserved in contemporary IR. The former emphasizes local, particularist, and contingent aspects of the polity—those elements that, in the present argument, are construed to give the Jamesian *socius* its more intimate spaces—while cosmopolitanism speaks to shared values or identities, or natural laws, that exist "*as if . . .* outside of time and unaffected by contingency" (p. 89, emphasis in original).

How does this dichotomy find its way into contemporary liberal IR theory, and why would it be difficult to sustain? The answer—as the forthcoming argument will show—lies in Tönnies's account of *gesellschaft* as an historical emergence: it creates new conditions of intellectual possibility for values or identities to exist (or appear to exist) "outside of time." That is, Tönnies means to suggest a link between *concrete historical processes* (urbanization, the transformation to market economies, *embourgeoisement*, etc.) and the emergence of *new images or modes of thinking*; the ostensibly universal *ratio* championed by the enlightenment is, for him, a social-historical outcome. When viewed from within those concrete historical processes—and IR as a discipline is very much tied to them—the communitarian-cosmopolitan dichotomy that, in

Hence, before proceeding to the main substance of this chapter—case studies of metaphysical, middle-range, and third-way paradigms of communitarian IR liberalism, highlighting attempts by their promulgators to address the reifications upon which they rely—I will set out the distinction between individualism and communitarianism in greater detail. That done, the case studies undertaken here and in chapter 5 will echo those found in chapter 3. My aims are thus twofold: first, to show that (at least) two distinct traditions coexist under the broad banner of IR liberalism and, second, to show that, despite a general understanding of the problem of reification, each has failed to meet the challenge of theorizing or managing it adequately.

Between Community and Individual

Before turning to an in-depth discussion of liberal IR's communitarian strand, the distinction between it and individualism as sociological ideal types and their extrapolation into world politics must be fleshed out. Of the two, communitarian IR liberalism more closely resembles the realist traditions surveyed in chapter 3, and so it makes sense to begin there.[10] As with realism, the communitarian tradition holds that human beings "achieve fulfillment of their nature only in the context of social and political life"; moreover, one cannot assign logical or moral primacy to either the individual or the collective without doing considerable violence to the other.[11] Unlike IR realism, however, this claim is not tied to a tragic assumption of human nature or the autonomy of politics; neither must the key articulations of community emanate from a single sovereign center.[12] Rather, communitarians stress the particular qualities of the bonds themselves, which can emanate from multiple and overlapping sources. These bonds possess a kind of agency: symbolic, normative, and unifying powers.[13]

---

classical thought, was taken to be an enduring and essential feature of political life might now appear (correctly or otherwise) to be eminently resolvable. That is, the cosmopolitan position might appear to be superseded by the individualist one. On this account, the moral foundations of individualism and its corollaries for the study of social behavior *replace* the cosmopolitans' "natural laws." On this point, see chapter 5.

10. See Hartwich, Assmann, and Assmann (2004) for an interesting discussion of these resemblances.

11. Morrice (2000), p. 240; also Pentland (1973), pp. 29–39. Etzioni (1995) is also on point here: "Individuals are socially embedded rather than free standing. However...communities are composed of members, who at least in modern times, have varying degrees of individuality....Like hammer and nail, neither is more essential; they require one another" (p. 18).

12. For example, see Walzer's (1983, ch. 3) treatment of medieval Jewish communities.

13. Consider, for example, Manners's (2002) concept of "normative power": the unifying force of the EU lies not in the specific provisions of the *acquis communautaire*, but in the values it embodies.

Some sense of these powers is given in the quote from William James with which this chapter opened. At an intuitive level, James asserted, most human beings feel a common kinship with one another and with the "great universe whose children we are." No social, political, or moral doctrine follows unambiguously from that feeling. A hive of differentially interconnected physical and social spaces, the universe presents itself to individuals and groups as familiar and alien at turns. An individual's sense of belonging may derive not merely from those spaces that feel familiar, but to the *particular admixture* of familiarity and strangeness that particular communities sustain within and among themselves: public-private distinctions and the like. The process by which such feelings come into being, come to be shared on a consensual basis with others, and materialize into shared institutions is complicated and perhaps sui generis. Conceptual theory may be limited in the extent to which it can make sense of them. Nevertheless, the intuitive sense of a common *socius* is part of the human condition.

What follows from this is an act of faith: belief in a notion of commonweal that escapes reductive reason. Communities are in some attenuated sense living things, akin to coral reefs or to what the political theorist Jane Bennett calls an *assemblage*.[14] More than the sum of their parts and not wholly understandable in terms of an ordering center, their origins are something of a mystery, and their continued survival is more than a technical exercise that can be broken down into discrete acts of institutional lever pulling.[15] So understood, communities possess a kind of free-standing moral authority. Being fragile and difficult to cultivate and sustain, they require ongoing care and self-sacrifice; members are expected to be at least minimally public minded. A key role of practical theory, for communitarians, is thus to better understand and meet the challenges of preserving a vital sphere of public involvement. This includes defining community needs, apportioning duties fairly,

---

14. Bennett (2005): "An assemblage is, first, an ad hoc grouping, a collectivity whose origins are historical and circumstantial, though its contingent status says nothing about its efficacy, which can be quite strong. An assemblage is, second, a living, throbbing grouping whose coherence coexists with energies and countercultures that exceed and confound it. An assemblage is, third, a web with an uneven topography: some of the points at which the trajectories of actants cross each other are more heavily trafficked than others, and thus power is not equally distributed across the assemblage. An assemblage is, fourth, not governed by a central power: no one member has sufficient competence to fully determine the consequences of the activities of the assemblage. An assemblage, finally, is made up of many types of actants: humans and nonhumans; animals, vegetables, and minerals; nature, culture, and technology" (p. 445n2). Bennett is here building on the work of Gilles Deleuze.

15. Etzioni (1991): "Institutions, values, society and history can be guided but not controlled, let alone 'designed'" (p. 25).

educating citizens as to those duties, and designing spaces of public debate that are both accessible and responsive to citizens and stable enough to ensure that such engagement does not degenerate into factional stasis or mob rule.[16] Such tasks require mixing "local and contingent" political intuition with formal theoretical knowledge.[17]

Internation relations liberalism's second tradition is individualist. Here human beings are, as embodied individuals, the key a priori bearers of moral value.[18] The universe, on this understanding, is dual in nature: composed of moral forces on the one hand and material ones on the other. Uniquely, human beings combine the two. That is, they possess sparks of creativity and reason and a muscular real-world physical presence by which these can be made manifest. The public sphere is that arena in which those material manifestations of will play out. Individuals as both physical and moral agents are the atoms of social and political life. This atomism provides a stable ontology upon which one can begin to make reliable theoretical generalizations on the basis of interest, whether economic or political. This, in turn, raises the prospect of a public sphere that might, if it were sufficiently well designed, self-organize by means of judiciously counterbalancing some interests against others.[19] While this may be practically unachievable, it suggests an analytical ideal: "an approach to the analysis of social reality rather than…a doctrine of liberty."[20] That analytical ideal, however, has its own normative overtones. It suggests that the efficient functioning of public institutions does not (or ought not) rely on the moral virtues of individual citizens. Rather, there are external standards of value, grounded in a priori concepts of welfare or justice.

---

16. Bellah's "Social Science as Public Philosophy," in his (1985) is an apt example.

17. Onuf (1998), p. 109; also Deudney (2004), Lijphart (1969).

18. Beitz (1999), pp. 71–83.

19. Hence, for Beitz (1999), the construction of an "ideal theory" of global redistributive justice not for its own sake, nor as an exercise in moral perfectionism, but to supply "a set of criteria for the formulation and criticism of strategies of political action in the nonideal world" (p. 170). Or see those passages in the Federalist Papers that deal with faction and the role of faction in balancing mixed government, especially Nos. 9, 10, and 71. To wit: "a landed interest, a manufacturing interest, a mercantile interest, a moneyed interest, with many lesser interests, grow up of necessity in civilized nations, and divide them into different classes, actuated by different sentiments and views. The regulation of these various and interfering interests forms the principal task of modern legislation, and involves the spirit of party and faction in the necessary and ordinary operations of the government" (Hamilton et al. [2003]). Another version of this argument is found in Hirschman (1977).

20. Keohane (1990), p. 174. Or following Moravcsik (1997): "Liberal theory seeks to generalize about the social conditions under which the behavior of self-interested actors converges toward cooperation or conflict" (p. 517).

Progress is measured by the degree to which the efficient functioning of government in the service of those values is weaned from voluntarism and by the degree to which care of the commons is made a matter of administration, in the Saint-Simonian sense.[21] The analytical discourse thus suborns a normative one, which links theoretical reason to control and—somewhat counterintuitively—control to freedom.

Communitarian and individualist narratives form a dichotomy: each defines and opposes the other.[22] Communitarian thinking emphasizes the growth and cultivation of the public sphere, as that bundle of interconnections whose sum total—what Karl Deutsch called a sense of "we-feeling"—is always greater than the parts.[23] Theoretical innovation is understood in terms of reconceptualizing those relationships so that institutional arrangements can be made to better reflect individuals' beliefs and aspirations. Individualism, by contrast, seeks to shrink the public sphere to the greatest extent possible within a given material-social context, and theoretical innovation is understood in terms of political heuristics; "labor-saving devices" that increase the self-regulative capabilities of existing social, economic, or political orders and make the public sphere progressively less dependent on private virtue. The indifferent forces governing the universe are remade into the ally of humanity's enlightened fraction; practical theory enlists providence in the improvement of the human condition.[24]

Beneath these differences lies a deeper one, less well known to IR theory. The two are predicated on fundamentally different forms of thinking and knowing. The work of Ferdinand Tönnies, in particular on the primary sociological concepts of *gemeinschaft* and *gesellschaft*, helps to elucidate this difference. *Communitarian forms of life, Tönnies argued, do not admit of the atomism that forms the basis of individualist social forms and orders.* This social difference has philosophical and intellectual consequences: inter alia, it means less space for singular, individualized forms of consciousness or for logical-rational abstractions of the Cartesian *cogito ergo sum* variety. Indeed,

---

21. For this argument made in game-theoretic terms, see Schelling (1978); in institutionalist ones, see North and Thompson (1973) and North (1990).

22. Ellis (2009): "The most basic requirement for any putative international community is a unified society of states adhering to generally the same norms, rules, identities, and views of moral conduct. Without a common conception of the way society should be ordered and the goals to be achieved, there is no community as such; rather, there merely exists a society of states" (p. 4).

23. Deutsch (1957), pp. 36–37; also his (1954), ch. 2.

24. Viner (1972).

in language that recalls Adorno and Horkheimer—recall their discussion of Sade, surveyed in chapter 1—Tönnies goes so far as to suggest that reason is *destructive* of community. The dynamic interconnectivity of communitarian forms of life is naturally at odds with conceptual rigor: individuality, self-interest, deduction, and rationalization are all inimical to it. Such modes of thinking may seem timeless and perfectly natural to the contemporary theorist or citizen, Tönnies asserts, but they are historical, contextual, and deeply partisan, tied to the emergence of those forms of organization, production, and exchange typical to market societies and hence to *gesellschaft*. These ties have both intellectual and ideological consequences.

This claim requires some unpacking. Since markets employ cash exchange, rather than barter, gift, or labor exchange, they oblige specific intellectual tools: the ability to translate concrete particulars into universal, fungible abstractions like price and value. This ability, Tönnies held, paves the way for the universal abstractions of enlightenment philosophy, yet it also undermines those organic notions of community that may have existed previously. Just as money is transformed from a means of exchange into an end in itself, abstract notions of reason, justice, or truth become fungible with, and ultimately supersede, the real-world phenomena they emerged to help interpret. The ability to organize thought in instrumental-rationalist terms, then, lies in having internalized or naturalized—reified—the contingent workings of a particular social order within one's own reflective faculties.[25] As Tönnies explained it:

> [R]ational scientific and independent law was made possible only through the emancipation of individuals from all ties which bound them to the family, the land and the city and which held them to superstition, faith, traditions, habit, and duty. Such liberation meant the fall of the communal household... it meant the victory of egoism,

---

25. Here, Axelrod's ([1984], pp. 6–7) and Keohane's ([2005], pp. 74–75, 120–131) [1984]) discussions of self-interest are instructive. The assumption of self-interest, Axelrod notes, "allows an examination of the difficult case in which cooperation is not completely based upon a concern for others or upon the welfare of the group as a whole. It must, however, be stressed that this assumption is actually much less restrictive than it appears. If a sister is concerned for the welfare of her brother, the sister's self-interest can be thought of as including (among many other things) this concern for the welfare of the brother" (pp. 6–7). Axelrod is certainly correct: "enlightened self-interest" can sometimes produce the same systemic effects as altruism or empathy. But only sometimes; the two remain quite different. Consider an example: a child escapes death; his parents are relieved. Is that relief primarily selfish (release from the prospect of having to grieve for one's own child) or selfless (the avoidance of suffering by one who is loved unconditionally)? The distinction—between love of self and love of another, or at another "level of

impudence, falsehood and cunning, the ascendancy of greed for money, ambition, and lust for pleasure. *But it also brought the victory of the contemplative, clear and sober consciousness in which scholars and cultured men now dare to approach things human and divine. And this process can never be considered completed.*[26]

There is, to borrow from the institutionalist literature, a kind of epistemological-institutional lock-in at work here: established modes of thinking suborn certain forms of social reality and undermine others—even if those modes of thinking are themselves social artifacts.[27]

By way of anticipating objections, two provisos should be set out. First, I am not asserting that communitarian international theorists past or present consciously drew theoretical sustenance from Tönnies. That argument is largely beside the point. It is the *shape* of these concepts—the ways in which they both can and cannot describe political realities adequately, the ways in which the fact-value traditions to which they help give rise are parsed through methodologies to produce paradigms, and the ways in which those paradigms interact with one another and with events—that gives reification in liberal IR its distinctive shape. If the broad account of reification developed in the opening chapters holds, parallel lines of thought should reify in broadly similar ways, notwithstanding theorists' specific intentions or sources.

Second and related, given the historical trajectories of class conflict, German expansionism, and European colonialism, it might be tempting to dismiss Tönnies as denying premarket or nonmarket societies or social fractions—this or that class or estate, this or that "primitive" culture—the ability to think altogether. But to do so is actually to deepen precisely the reification that the foregoing discussion is meant to illuminate and chasten: conflating a particular, historically contingent form or image of thinking with thinking *as such*. Whether real people can or cannot engage in this or that form of

---

analysis," between Rousseau's *"volontaire generale"* and *"volontaire de tout"*—is profound; it is not (*pace* Axelrod) dissolved by the recognition that individuals have mixed motives.

26. Tönnies (1957), p. 202; emphasis added. Only the germ of this argument is given in Tönnies; for its full expression, see Simmel (2004) [1907]. See Arato (1974), pp. 152–153; Hopgood (2009), pp. 233–240.

27. Habermas (1984–87), Vol. 1: "As acting subjects switch to exchange-value orientations, their lifeworld shrinks to the format of the objective world; they assume toward themselves and others the objectivating attitude of success-oriented action and thereby make themselves into objects to be 'handled' by others. For the price of reifying interactions, however, they gain the freedom of strategic action oriented to their own success" (p. 359). On lock-in, see North (1990), pp. 23 n 7 and 92–93. On this point, see also Teschke (2003), ch. 2.

social organization or intellectual activity is beyond the present discussion. The point here is to discover what possibilities are conceivable within particular conceptual-theoretical schemes and why. To write liberal IR is to invoke a particular normative-ontological tradition—whether consciously or otherwise—whose depth is not generally appreciated. If liberal IR is to be made sustainably critical, those traditions must be fully unpacked.

Specifically, if conceptual knowledge *itself* is a partisan actor in the interpretation of reality, *then the very process of thinking conceptually* smuggles in normative commitments at a very deep level.[28] It is thus not merely that, as Richard van Wagenen noted, "the concept of community is elusive and slippery" and therefore its application to international politics is problematic, nor that, following Emanuel Adler, "the former [individualism] admits self-interest and the latter [communitarianism] denies it."[29] Conceptual thinking and communitarian sentiment contain basic incompatibilities—and divergent ideological affinities—at a very deep level. Holding them together is a challenge of some magnitude, yet it is only thus that each has a chance of sustainably managing reification. Meeting that challenge requires a finely calibrated sense of how specific social structures and intellectual constructs fit together, to what end, and of what is lost and gained. Such a sense—the basis of sustainable critique—would need to be carefully perched between the descriptive and the analytical. *The varying sensitivity displayed to the complexities of this challenge—in the context of different liberal IR paradigms—is what the next two chapters aim to unpack.*

In the context of IR liberalism's two traditions, the foregoing exposition suggests a kind of inchoate constellation that, as Peter Katzenstein noted in 1975, is already present.[30] In positing a mystical-affective center to society, communitarian approaches to IR contain a vital, organic core that is fundamentally resistant to conceptual decomposition. One can only describe such relations from the outside, whether by tracing out their interactions or by comparing them with established political forms. But there is a limit to the kinds of research programs such logic can sustain: the former risks obscurantist and/or romanticist mystification, the latter the historicist fallacy of defining the present in terms of the past. For its part, individualism risks defining

---

28. Recall here Adorno and Horkheimer (2002), as surveyed in chapter 1.

29. Respectively, van Wagenen (1965), p. 814; Adler and Barnett (1998), p. 31.

30. Katzenstein (1975): "Community and Society are interdependent. The story of the Tower of Babel illustrates that there can be no society...without a modicum of community...and...no community without a modicum of society" (p. 20).

precisely what is fundamentally *political* out of IR by reducing all interactions to processes of goal-seeking value maximization. The former was Ernst Haas's critique of "integrationist" approaches to IR that smuggled in, he argued, their own normative teleologies.[31] The latter has been the failure of individualist approaches, marked—as Robert Keohane aptly observed in 2002—by the tendency "to assume that the world is run by... 'rational and unheroic' members of the bourgeoisie."[32] If each gives rise to its own characteristic missteps, each also shines light on the missteps of the other. If so, then by studying the shape of these ideas and the way they either do or do not reduce the world to concepts and theories, clues can be found for creating the kind of constellation to which chapter 2 alluded. Keeping faith with the ethos of the *animus habitandi*—the will to dwell within the world, in its irreducible complexity—may lie in understanding how these ideas can be fitted together.

Plan of the Chapter

The remainder of this chapter will survey communitarian theory in its metaphysical, middle-range, and third-way articulations, respectively, through the paradigms of Mitranyan functionalism and the conceptual background against which it emerged, Deutschian transactionalism and cybernetics, and the communitarian constructivism of Emanuel Adler, Michael Barnett, Beverly Crawford, Vincent Pouliot, and others. The attempt to develop practical theory to further a unitary ethical-ontological position can be retraced through these works. Recognition of the need for sustainable critique—and at the same time, the absence of a means for realizing that need—emerges from these retracings as well.

In analyzing Mitrany, I begin by reconstructing the British Fabian tradition from which it drew and to which it responded. In that earlier tradition, the communitarian notions set out here were simply asserted: given as an act of faith. Where reification sneaked up on Morgenthau, Waltz, and Wendt, Mitrany was well aware of his normative commitments and actively engaged in their obfuscation. Keenly conscious of the ideological obstacles that marginalized communitarian sensibilities politically, his aim was to conceal those sensibilities by encasing them in pragmatic-functionalist language. In this, Mitrany was remarkably successful. Indeed, he may have been *too* successful: having

---

31. A compact version of this argument is made in Haas (1961); for a full explication, see (1964), especially parts 1 and 3, and Haas's 1968 introduction to *The Uniting of Europe*.

32. Keohane (2002), p. 272.

hidden his communitarian bona fides, functionalism had only the quality of its predictions to support it. When the latter proved flawed—a point chapter 5 will review at some length—the stage was set for Ernst Haas to appropriate functionalism and reground it on quite different normative foundations. In Mitrany's hands, reification became a political resource to be deployed: he would have us forget the communitarian faith on which functionalist ideas relied, so that they might gain traction in policy circles not amenable to airy concepts of a "great universe whose children we are." Yet that willed form of forgetting—exploiting reification rather than checking it—came at a price. Only some five decades later would functionalist theory again be in a position to address its communitarian roots squarely and argue for them.

In exploring middle-range communitarianism, I focus primarily on the work of Karl Deutsch. In line with Mitrany, Deutsch wished to assist those forces in world politics that, he held, pulled toward unity and openness. Yet where Mitrany hid his communitarian agenda, Deutsch sought to demystify it: to debunk *gemeinschaft*, uproot it from its metaphysical origins, and replant it in firm empirical ground. The many faces of Deutsch's work—from the study of "pluralistic security communities" to the "transactionalist" approach that aimed to explain their emergence—all play a role in this larger project. So did his attempt to recast political community in the new analytical idiom of cybernetics. Understood in cybernetic terms, peoples and nations were "communit[ies] of social communication habits."[33] "We-feeling" grew out of the habituated sharing of discrete bits of information. By studying how those bits were patterned and distributed, the emergence and collapse of communities could be understood; perhaps even new transnational ones could be engineered. The key was mastering the transformative effects of information, which both linked members of community from without *and* remade them from within.

Such mastery alone would not do away with the specter of political oppression. Indeed, given the way in which it conceptualized the relationship of individuals to collectivities, it could even provide a means by which to obscure and extend it: the problem of reification in its middle-range variant. This did occur to Deutsch, and he even perceived the broad outlines of the kind of ongoing, sustained reflexivity that would be needed to check it. Yet he offered no clear path by which to achieve it; no translation from the speculative to the practical is attempted. Three decades before "structuration" would make its way into "third (and fourth) debate" IR, Deutsch was attempting a conceptual third way of his own. That he would point to, but

---

33. Deutsch (1963), p. 177.

never undertake, the need for a sustainable reflexivity to make that third way work may prefigure similar such half-moves made later on.

Finally, third-way communitarianism is explored primarily through the work of Emanuel Adler. Adler stakes a median position between Mitrany's peremptory rejection of formal theory and Deutsch's fond embrace of it. Something like James's universal *socius* is asserted by fiat: both as a shared conceptual abstraction and as a set of material practices, Adler has argued, peace exists. Communitarian IR theory takes that existence as its point of empirical departure. True it is in pieces, which owe their fragmented existence to political contingency rather than to the a priori power of some or another grand idea. But if so, then practical theory finds its vocation in gathering up those pieces and deriving from them such lessons as are possible. Moreover, there is a commonsense understanding of the ideal of peace, which gives the empirical search for it a degree of cohesion—even if that ideal is, as Adler affirms, a "moving target" when viewed across eras or cultures.[34]

This nuanced stance should put third-way communitarianism in a space to sustainably critique itself. In practice, however, the same problem identified in the emancipatory critical theories surveyed in chapter 2 and in the constructivism of Price (chapter 1) and Wendt (chapter 3) reveal themselves here as well. What Adler offers first and foremost is a *vision*, but peace must ultimately be reduced to an operational *concept* if it is to be analyzed in the manner Adler proposes. As such, it is no less a positive basis for ideological reification than any other concept; that basis must be checked, even if the dynamism of the thing it aims to represent is recognized. To grow a conversation such that it includes more participants can be a kind of pluralism and hence a beginning, but it can also be a redistribution of the forces of oppression. How is the latter possibility to be kept in view, given the limits of conceptual theory when applied to politics? As with Deutsch, Adler is suggestive on this point; but such suggestions are only a beginning.

Metaphysical Communitarianism: Functionalism

The Fabian Impasse

The basic problem facing communitarians in the opening decades of the twentieth century was admirably summed up by G. D. H. Cole: "democracy face to face with hugeness."[35] An essential mismatch had emerged between high

---

34. Adler (2005), p. 208.

35. Cole (1950) [1941], pp. 90–97.

and low politics: between, that is, the institutions that governed economic and political life in advanced industrial states and the needs of individuals, families and, communities within them. "Democracy can work in the great States (and *a fortiori* between great States or over Europe or the world) only if each State is made up of a host of little democracies, and rests finally, not on isolated individuals but on groups small enough to express the spirit of neighborhood and personal acquaintance."[36] That mismatch had undermined the "vital associative life" that was held to be essential to a healthy social existence. Its social and political effects—from anomie to radicalism and world war— were captured in now-classic works like Karl Polanyi's *Great Transformation* and John Maynard Keynes's *Economic Consequences of the Peace.*[37]

In IR circles, the standard theoretical narrative is captured in E. H. Carr's *The Twenty Years' Crisis*, and its related socioeconomic ramifications were traced out in his related (but now much less widely read) *Conditions of Peace* and *Nationalism and After*.[38] Like Keynes and Polanyi, Carr's analysis provided a normative-anthropological diagnosis of the ills of late modernity. Older notions of the good life had become obsolete; newer notions had not yet emerged. As Carr explained:

> The old democracy, under which property-owners valued political rights as the prerogative and instrument of a ruling class, is dead. The new democracy, which seeks to make the masses conscious of their rights and of their responsibilities as a ruling class, has not yet been born. The crisis of contemporary democracy is that it is suspended between these two stages, enmeshed in the obsolete traditions of the first and therefore unable to break its way through to the second.[39]

Modern life needed a new sense of community, based on new mutual commitments to social welfare: a new conception of the good life. If Carr's analysis lacked the incisive synthesis of economics and social history captured in Polanyi or the prescience of Keynes (*Economic Consequences* was published

---

36. Cole (1950), p. 95.

37. Keynes (1919); Polanyi (2001) [1944].

38. Carr (1942, 1945); also Adler (2005), ch. 8. Earlier pieces of it may be found in Hobson's (1965) [1902] critique of imperialism, Angell's (1910) much-abused discussion of economic interdependence and its effects on sovereignty and power politics, and Keynes (1919).

39. Carr (1942), pp. 29–30.

in 1919, *Conditions of Peace* in 1942), both the overall gist and the prescriptive logic were the same:

> We must supplement political equality by a progressive advance towards social and economic equality; we must make the will of the ordinary citizen prevail against the organized forces of economic power; and we must draw the ordinary citizen more and more into the processes of administration.... None of these things is easy. But they may be found easier if we regard them...as ways of kindling in him a fresh sense of obligation—an obligation to make democracy work...because the antithesis of "we" and "they" will at last have been resolved.[40]

How was this transformation to be effected, in practical terms? It was one thing to assert that shifting political and economic relations had rendered existing institutions and values obsolete. It was quite another to build a critical mass of popular support around their restructuring. After all, H. G. Wells and Leonard Woolf had been making arguments of this sort for decades, to only limited effect.[41] So, too, had many others: the American historian Carl Becker, the progressivist Mary Parker Follett, the Weimar politician-industrialist Walther Rathenau, the pan-Europeanist Richard Coudenhove-Kalergi, the financier and self-taught political reformer Ivan Bloch, and the Catholic communitarians whose views were set out in the encyclicals *Rerum Novarum* and *Quadragesimo Anno*.[42]

Yet however ready postwar intellectual elites may have been to move past old notions of "we" and "they," mass political support for such sensibilities remained elusive.[43] Harold Engle aptly called this the "institutions-consensus dilemma." A sense of community or moral consensus, Engle asserted,

---

40. Carr (1942), p. 37. See also Cole (1950), Laski (1943), Keynes (1919), and Polanyi (2001) [1944], especially parts 1 and 3. For a brief survey on the diffusion of Keynesian ideas in the postwar international economic order, see Ikenberry (1993).

41. Woolf (1940); Wells (1901, 1919, 1933).

42. Becker (1944), Coudenhove-Kalergi (1926), Follett (1998) [1918], Rathenau (1921), Bloch (1899). For a survey of Catholic corporatism from the period, see Oakeshott (1939), ch. 2. On Mitrany, see Ashworth (1999), Navari (1995), and Long and Schmidt (2005). On Bloch, see Dawson (2002), de Wilde (1991), Welch (2000), and Clarke (1967).

43. H. G. Wells serves as a powerful example of the frustration this disconnect engendered. Though an ardent supporter of world government, Wells was perfectly aware of its practical-political impossibility: a dream to be worked toward, the labor of several lifetimes. When Wells speculates in the shorter term, his vision moves to the apocalyptic, as in his 1914 didactic novel, *The World Set Free*. The novel retrospectively narrates an imaginary history of a united

would need to precede any formal process of political union or reconfiguration among nation-states, if it was to proceed consensually. "Yet this 'sense of community' or 'moral consensus' [was] presumably *itself* the product of institutions, or of previous experience in international cooperation and organization."[44] Overcoming this "chicken and egg" impasse lay at the heart of the communitarian project.

The Mitranyan Breakthrough

Breaking that impasse was the signal contribution of David Mitrany's functionalist approach to world politics.[45] Mitrany's diagnosis does not differ materially from Carr's and even bears a distant resemblance to that of Adorno and Horkheimer. "Individuals and groups everywhere," he wrote in 1948, "are being integrated materially and emotionally within national units more close and intricate than ever before."[46] Yet at the same time, "these national units are being pressed by the logic of historical and social forces toward integration into a world society."[47] The result was a loss of political world: mass disorientation, mental stress, and emotional vulnerability. "Between the pursuit of a closed state and the call for a world community there is an impossible and intolerable contradiction," one that "subjects groups and individuals everywhere to

---

world community, built under the hand of enlightened scientists. Technology has freed human beings of want, scarcity, hatred, and fear. The key point in the story, however, is how humanity comes to be persuaded to take this path. A nuclear war breaks out, killing most of humanity and rendering its cities uninhabitable. With human civilization erased and society returned to a smaller, more human scale, men begin from scratch.

Why must Wells resort to such a catastrophe? Because, though a vocal advocate of world community, he was himself at a loss as to how that community might actually be realized. Even in his openly programmatic works, Wells speaks in rhapsodic tones of belief, akin to Comte's positivist religion of humanity, as "an intellectual rebirth," a species-wide awakening "to the new world that dawns about us." See Wells (2002) [1933], pp. 56 and 61; see also (1901), pp. 309ff. Thus, the nuclear fire of *World Set Free* allows him to skip nagging questions of process and revel in the dream. That Wells must resort to such tactics, even in his imagination— and this in a work that appeared in print *before* the horrors of the world wars even came to pass—is telling. Perhaps he is warning us, or perhaps he is, despite himself, seduced by the notion that with but a moment's pain, the course of humanity could be set right. On connections between Comte and Wells, see Wagar (2002), p. 13. On *The World Set Free*, see Schwenger (1986) and Willis (1995). On the connection between Comte, Wells, and the communitarian meliorism of E. H. Carr, see Berlin (1969), pp. xxviiff. and 91ff.

44. Engle (1957), pp. 5–6, emphasis added; see also Spinelli (1966), pp. 3–4.

45. Rosamond (2000), pp. 31–36.

46. Mitrany (1948), p. 72. Compare to Horkheimer (1950).

47. Mitrany (1948), p. 72.

a disrupting strain" that must be removed if healthy, stable forms of political community are to be restored.[48] Since "organic society could not flourish if human needs were not properly met," supranational coordinating institutions had to be devised.[49]

Mitrany, however, believed he had cracked the institutions-consensus dilemma. The trick was not to *create* consensus, but to *bypass* it, by moving purposefully behind the scenes to "weld together the common interests of all without interfering unduly with the particular ways of each."[50] Earlier advocates of political unification had got themselves caught up in the grandeur of the enterprises they proposed, giving rise to bombastic statements of political purpose and grand "constitutional convention" styles of diplomatic initiatives: castles built on sand. Functionalism took just the opposite approach: rather than entertaining grandiose formulations "for the gratification of visionaries," Mitrany proposed quietly seizing such opportunities as events saw fit to provide.[51] Decades of war had made a "desperate craving for peace" and "a tolerable normal life" effectively universal.[52] The various postwar programs for economic welfare and recovery were thus an opportunity: one could piggyback on the consensus such programs enjoyed to lay the institutional foundations for a postnational political order.

Mitrany's wartime writings use Roosevelt's New Deal as a model—seizing on despair over the economic depression of the 1930s to create new functions, roles, and powers for the federal government without rehashing old arguments about limited government or states' rights. "The New Deal was not a program, an ideology conceived and propagated as a theory before it had a chance to be practiced."[53] It was simply "an answer to the pleas and needs" of millions of men and women "in danger of being 'liquidated' by the depression"—compassion and pragmatism in equal parts.[54] Since no grand questions of constitutional theory were posed, no answers were needed:

---

48. Mitrany (1948), p. 72.

49. Ashworth (1999), p. 87.

50. Mitrany (1966), p. 68. Or see Lieber (1972): "Perhaps the key assumption here was that in…Western Europe there was no longer a distinctly political function, which was separate from economics, welfare or education, and which existed in the realm of foreign policy, defense, and constitution-making" (p. 43).

51. Mitrany (1966), p. 55.

52. Mitrany (1966), p. 56.

53. Mitrany (1975a), p. 160; also Mitrany (1946), pp. 9–10, 14, and 22; and Burley (1993).

54. Mitrany (1975a), p. 161.

"a great constitutional change has thus taken place without any changes in the Constitution."[55] By such actions, "the Federal Government has become a national government, and Washington for the first time really is the capital of the United States."[56]

In legal-constitutional terms, *how* such agencies came into being was less important for Mitrany than the *fact* of them—the effect they would inexorably exert, once they came into being. If the right institutional foundations were laid, then national frontiers would become meaningless, gradually overlaid "with a continuous growth of common activities and interests, as of common administrative agencies."[57] If this was a "constitutional revolution," it seemed an underhanded one. Mitrany, however, saw no need to apologize:

> Two characteristics of the moment suggest...the function of our time.
> The first is a blatant disregard for written rules and established rights,
> both within the nations as between them...the masses are demanding
> social action without regard to "rights" and the totalitarian dictators
> are playing the strong card of pragmatic socialism against constitu-
> tional democracy.[58]

As an approach to world politics, then, functionalism seems close to the position evinced by Herman Kahn in chapter 1: a sense of crisis, which breeds impatience, and a disdain for those who would split intellectual hairs. Not *thinking*, but *craftiness* is mandated by "the characteristics of the moment": doing what needed to be done.

The core assumption at work here is summed up by what Richard van Wagenen called the "benign spiral": new identities and loyalties would take root as functional integration gave rise to ever-thicker webs of social and political interaction.[59] Functionalism's supposed reliance on "noncontroversial" or "technical" issue areas—the use of "piecemeal international efforts in commonly recognized transnational problem areas which are readily adaptable to procedures shaped and accepted by modern man"—is thus a form of

55. Mitrany (1966), p. 57.

56. Mitrany (1975a), p.163.

57. Mitrany (1975a), p. 170.

58. Mitrany (1975a), pp. 106–107.

59. van Wagenen (1965), p. 813.

political sleight of hand.[60] Nothing is *really* apolitical; it is only a matter of what *appears* to be so and of using that appearance to best advantage.[61] If the common citizen failed to perceive what was at stake (or else did realize it and was willing to sell a share of her political patrimony for some of Mitrany's functionalist pottage), why not make use of that, as one would any other political resource? This was, Mitrany came close to admitting, a new kind of noble lie for a new political era, to be carried on the lips of modern-day philosopher-kings:

> Upon the political scientists falls...a special and urgent part in the diffusion of such a humanistic outlook. It is for them to rescue political theory from its slough of subservience, from being a mere handmaid supplying formal arguments to fit the policy of governments, as it did before to fit the policy of princes, and to make of it instead an instrument devoted *sine ira et studio* to the service of human progress.[62]

Again, Mitrany made no apologies. He was not to blame if all existing ideologies had dead-ended in repression. If triage was the order of the moment, one was obliged to deal with the fact directly, using such tools as were to be found.

Mitrany's impatience with questions of due process and political transparency extended to social-scientific "dogmatism" as well—that is, the expectation among theorists that, as an approach to world politics, functionalism must contain a coherent core of normative, empirical, or political assumptions or axioms. In his later writings, Mitrany denies any such foundations; first principles are derided as the hobgoblins of small minds. "If there be a truly a mortal sin in the profession of the social scientist," he wrote in the 1970s, "it is surely the sin of

---

60. Sewell (1966), p. 3. Or as Hirschman (1967) put it: "the only way in which we can bring our creative resources fully into play is by misjudging the nature of our task, by presenting it to ourselves as more routine, simple, undemanding of genuine creativity than it will turn out to be" (p. 13). I am indebted to Nye (1971) on this point.

61. Nye (1971) calls this the *law of inverse salience*: "the less important the task politically, either because of its technical nature or limited political impact, the greater the prospects for the growth of the organization's authority *vis-à-vis* the member states" (p. 23–4).

62. Mitrany (1933), pp. 175–176; also Mitrany (1948): "Social scientists must work in every field and by every means to further the idea and the emergence of a world community...the way to create a normal community is through the joint performance of a variety of common functions. We cannot have a world government before we have a world community, but we can begin to build up the parts of a world community before we get acceptance for a world government" (p. 84). See also the discussions in Haas (1964), p. 13; and Pentland (1973), ch. 3, esp. pp. 70–71.

dogmatism. Dogmatism, after all, is a denial of life."[63] But this assumes that one knows what "life" really is: a first principle, par excellence. Mitrany believed he possessed that knowledge and that others did not. Functionalist thinking, he asserted, concerned itself with the "relation of things"—a concern he held to be "the hallmark of a student, in the philosophical sense of the term."[64] Well and good, but what were those relations? Did not all dogmatisms begin with the claim of having characterized them in some superior fashion?

Mitrany's consistent theoretical disavowals put his subsequent readers— from Harold Engle and James Sewell to John Eastby and Lucian Ashworth—in a difficult situation when it comes to locating his writings within a constellation of interwar and postwar British thought.[65] His wartime writings, published largely in pamphlet form, contain few citations, while his later pronouncements as a functionalist éminence grise consistently disavow systematic pretensions, whether normative or intellectual: "I did not invent a doctrine," he would write of himself, "but...learnt a lesson." While functionalism was a "theory," Mitrany asserted that he meant by that only "an effort to make sense of one's experience...to locate and interpret the meaning of what one has lived."[66] Transcendent moral or conceptual authorities were studiously avoided: his arguments were tied to personal experiences (his life "as a journalist and student and (temporary) civil servant") and a finely honed intuitive sense—the "relation of things," which he took from L. T. Hobhouse and which served him as Mannheim's "free-floating intellectual" served E. H. Carr.[67] Once again, he saw no need to apologize. "Functional arrangements are spreading because they are necessary," Mitrany noted, not owing to their conceptual coherence or theoretical elegance.[68] "I confess myself greatly baffled by the rash of methodological efforts in pursuit of some 'scientific law' of international unity and disunity"; even the ideal "is almost alarming in its academic complacency."[69]

---

63. Mitrany (1975a), p. 16; see also (1971), pp. 541–542. Mitrany is quite liberal in his use of this label, which seems to serve as an all-purpose term of abuse. See, by way of example, (1933), pp. 20 and 62; and (1951), passim.

64. Mitrany (1975a), p. 37.

65. Engle (1957), Sewell (1966), Eastby (1985), Ashworth (1999), Pentland (1973), Navari (1995), de Wilde (1991), and Green (1969) also bear noting.

66. Mitrany, (1975a), pp. 45 and 47 n 1. In the second citation, Mitrany is quoting Alwin Gouldner. On loopholes in Mitrany's "methodologically naïve" approach, see Navari (1995), pp. 233–235; and Green (1969), p. 68.

67. On "free-floating intellectuals," see Mannheim (1936); for Mannheim's influence on Carr, see Jones (1998), ch. 6.

68. Mitrany (1971), p. 540.

69. Mitrany (1971): p. 542.

All of this, however, remains unconvincing. One does not purge one's thinking of dogma—for which read "unchecked reification"—merely by refusing to identify where one's own commitments lie. Indeed, the opposite: one gives those commitments greater space *to become* dogmas. In Mitrany's case, those commitments are not hard to identify: for on what authority, save that of his intuitive sense of the "relations among things," did he base his conclusion that functional arrangements would lay the foundations for new political forms of community? There was certainly little enough empirical evidence. Mitrany's claims regarding the New Deal derived from his time spent in the United States in the midst of Roosevelt's reforms.[70] Any claim as to their long-term effects on Americans' political sensibilities had to have been speculative: to gauge their long-term effects would require systematic data, gathered over several decades. As Mitrany himself admits, that data could not yet exist when he started developing functionalism in the early 1940s.[71]

Rather, functionalism relied on faith: faith in the ability of low politics to remake high politics by means of a natural unifying tendency that lay within the dynamics of human interrelations. Mitrany's critics would press this point. "There is probably a sound basis for [functionalism's] line of reasoning," Richard van Wagenen noted, "but it still represents only a belief."[72] Inis Claude went further:

> We do not even know how a nation comes into being, much less possess the key to contriving a we-group encompassing all of mankind.... There is an unmistakable tinge of brashness in the pretension to certainty that man can, in a magnificent spasm of resolve, catapult himself...into a situation of political unity capable of sustaining the essential instrumentalities of peace and order.[73]

In fact, Mitrany went even further. Unity was mankind's natural end and object. It was not merely that beneath the superannuated ideologies of

---

70. See Mitrany (1975a), pp. 25–27.

71. Mitrany (1975a, pp. 19–25) recollects that his first formal draft of something like the functionalist idea is in a Foreign Office memorandum written in 1941. The first edition of *A Working Peace System* was drafted in 1942 and appeared the following year. As late as 1946, Mitrany would acknowledge that the New Deal "is still in a formative stage"; elsewhere, "with the New Deal the home policy of America has literally been thrown into the melting pot, and the boiling is far from finished" (1946), pp. 1, 94.

72. Van Wagenen (1965), p. 813.

73. Claude (1964), p. 379. As did Sewell (1966): when did a fragile "web of agreements," untested by real political contest, create genuine political community? "How many small agreements make an agreement of genuine significance?" (p. 319).

previous eras lay a basic potential for cosmopolitan unity. It was that by strip-ping away those ideologies, the path was cleared to "remember" that unity. Though predating his mature functionalist theory by some years, his 1933 lec-tures, *The Progress of International Government*, expressed such faith clearly and in a voice that will now be familiar:

> we must begin by paying respect to, rather than ostracizing the habit of mind which looks upon humanity as a Whole, superior to any and every one of its sections and branches. "After all," said William James, "the common *socius* of us all is the great Universe, whose children we are....Not to demand intimate relations with the Universe, and not to wish them satisfactory, should be accounted signs of something wrong."[74]

Though often overlooked by his later readers, Mitrany never disavowed these early passages. Indeed, he would later reflect, the core of the functionalist approach was first set down in them.[75] Yet James, as noted before, resisted the simplistic reduction of such convictions into political programs. For all his denials, Mitrany seems to have done exactly this. Perhaps there was no other way to translate general sensibilities into workable political programs. But if so, all the more reason to sustainably critique them.

What, then, is to be made of the later Mitrany's denigration of dogmatism? Given both the marginal fate of earlier programs for "world improvement"—those surveyed earlier—and the fervent attacks to which "idealist" theories of world politics would be subjected after the war, some degree of evasiveness on this point is understandable.[76] Yet while Mitrany's denunciations ring true as general indictments of the excesses of behaviorism, they are ultimately unsat-isfying. Dogmatism is at bottom unchecked reification. It does not come from any *particular* ideology and cannot therefore be banished in a single rhetor-ical flourish, no matter how compelling. Intuitive political sensibilities ("the relation of things") cannot be communicated or acted upon on a mass scale without first being reified as concepts that can never fully convey them. This becomes dangerous when we forget the difference: when we hold to mental constructs as primary, even when they fly in the face of lived experience—the

---

74. Mitrany (1933), p. 175; emphasis as in original.

75. See Mitrany (1975a), pp. 18–19.

76. Though Morgenthau, as is well known, would come to be a supporter of Mitrany's, writing the introduction to his *Working Peace System*. See Mitrany (1966).

"denial of life" that Mitrany rightly denounced. But has he actually devised a means to check this denial, rather than merely denounce it? This much can be said: no such means is set out in the work. The need for sustainable critique and the ethos of the *animus habitandi* are paid stirring tribute, but no path to them is marked.

Lacking this, why would such views be any less disposed to dogmatism than what they sought to replace? Moreover, Mitrany would—and did—find himself unable to defend his communitarian principles from neofunctionalism's alternative normative agenda when his theoretical predictions came up short. Just as Morgenthau's theory seemed underspecified in the face of neorealism, functionalism's reliance on an intuitive notion of community would make it seem underspecified in comparison to neofunctionalism's reliance on individualist theories of rational interest.[77] Chapter 5 will return to this point.

The "Wise Android": Deutsch's Cybernetic Turn

Mitrany's legacy was thus a mixed bag: political acumen, communitarian faith, wisdom, and experience were used to advance a particular, highly contextual agenda. Yet questions of the sort that functionalism sought to address—the challenges that late modernity posed to world politics—were not limited to postwar Europe. Political communities were emerging or being attempted everywhere, from North America to Western Europe, from the United Arab Republic and the Mali Republic to the West Indies.[78] Could not these be studied and learned from? For that, however, theories of political unification would need a greater degree of systematicity and abstraction. This goal precisely was what drove "transactional" studies of global politics: the work of Karl Deutsch, Amitai Etzioni, the early work of Bruce Russett, and a host of others. "In our time and in the next thirty to fifty years," Deutsch noted in 1979, "humankind is and will be going through greater changes than ever

---

77. And like Morgenthau, Mitrany would turn to moral hectoring to fill the gap: "The political prospect looks like the slow inexorable march of a Greek tragedy.... The slowly matured virtues of modern virtues of civilization—the decencies and restraints of self-discipline, of inherited culture, of regard for common authority and the commands of religion—all these are now in disarray or decay, everywhere...the long liberal effort to stop small peoples and nations being dominated by the stronger has so far merely split the misuse of power into more numerous hands" (1975a), pp. 267–268.

78. Haas (1958, 1964), Deutsch (1954, 1957), Etzioni (2001) [1965], Foltz (1965), Russett (1963, 1967), Alker and Russett (1965), and Katzenstein (1975).

before. We need and we shall need more and better political steering than ever before if human civilization is going to survive."[79]

Deutsch's own research—to say nothing of that of his many students—attacked the problem of such steering through a wide range of interconnected research programs and methodologies, from historical case studies to formal modeling and large-N quantitative analyses.[80] For present purposes, however, three core sets of interlocking concerns are central: the detailed study of nationalism, the development of "pluralistic security communities," and a metatheoretical set of concerns regarding the development of new conceptual paradigms that brought these processes into sharper focus.[81] Each played a role in bringing rigor to the kinds of questions functionalist thinking had raised. Nationalism was analyzed in terms of discrete transactions, with an eye to understanding how these might be redirected to balance national particularism with transnational solidarity. International transactions were broken down and classified with an eye to their integrative content: "the internal changes within social groups or individual personalities which accompany the processes occurring between them."[82] Finally and perhaps most apropos for the present discussion, Deutsch sought to develop new epistemologies for making sense of collective identity and solidarity. "Many writers have transmitted to us generous visions of a future world-wide community of mankind. How to reach these goals in a world of stubborn facts, and how to develop a social science of nationalism and nationality capable of showing the probable consequences of decisions—these are goals toward which many steps have yet to be taken."[83]

Hence, where Deutsch's "pluralistic security communities" provide the point of departure for most contemporary reconsiderations of his international theory, of greater interest here is his *Nerves of Government*, first

---

79. Deutsch (1980), p. 23.

80. The best single volume reflecting the breadth of Deutsch's interests is his *festschrift* (Merritt and Russett [1981]). On formal modeling, see Deutsch et al. (1977). For examples of his approach to historical analysis, see Deutsch and Foltz (1963) and the opening sections of Deutsch (1954). For quantitative analyses, see the essays in Deutsch (1979), in particular parts 2 and 3, and Deutsch et al. (1967).

81. On nationalism, see Deutsch (1953); on security communities and transnationalism, see Deutsch (1954), Deutsch et al. (1957), and Deutsch et al. (1967); on cybernetics, see Deutsch (1963). For links between cybernetics and security communities, see his contributions to Jacob and Toscano (1964).

82. Deutsch (1954), p. 39n.

83. Deutsch (1953), p. 14.

published in 1963.[84] The book opens with a strong attack on the discipline. International Relations and political science were, Deutsch asserted, on the verge of a "philosophic crisis": it was "an age of re-examination of concepts, methods and interests, of search for new symbolic models and/or strategies in selecting their major targets for attack."[85] Empirical data were plentiful, but genuine insights were lacking.[86] Theory, he would note in 1971, was "passionate contemplation," the committed search for conceptual solutions to actual problems.[87] Yet for this, *thinking* was required, not merely the acquisition of more data to be run through existing models. "Progress in the effectiveness of symbols and symbol systems is thus basic progress in the technology of thinking, and in the development of human powers of insight and action."[88]

If such "action" was what humanity needed, *Nerves of Government* was Deutsch's attempt to provide the insight that could guide it. He began with a critical review of social science's dependence on conceptual analogies and metaphors. On the one hand, Deutsch noted, such metaphors were necessary conventions of thought. On the other, each gave rise to its own characteristic misprisions and oversights. By way of example, to think of society, as classical liberals did, in mechanistic terms of gears and mainsprings lent credence to a systematic search for regularity. Yet it also reified notions like the invisible hand among economists and the balance of power among students of world politics.[89] Similarly, organicist models of political community were useful in "directing men's attention to problems of interdependence and growth."[90] At the same time, such approaches often reified ethnocentrism dressed up as realpolitik: "the extolling of power by certain conservative writers, often in preference to its analysis."[91] It is not merely, Deutsch explains, that "no knowledge can be completely 'nonobjective' if it is to be applied"; it is also that those

---

84. On pluralistic and amalgamated security communities, see Deutsch et al. (1957), pp. 3–9. For contemporary reexaminations, see Adler (2005), Adler and Barnett (1998), and the following discussion.

85. Deutsch (1963), p. 4.

86. Deutsch (1960), p. 35.

87. Deutsch (1971), pp. 11–12.

88. Deutsch (1963), p. 10.

89. Deutsch (1963), pp. 26–30, 215. See also Haas (1953a, 1953b).

90. Deutsch (1963), p. 32.

91. Deutsch (1963), p. 111. Here recall Treitschke (1916) [1897–98]: "We may say that power is the vital principle of the State, as faith is that of the Church, and love that of the family" (Vol. 1, p. 23.)

borrowings are *themselves* historically contingent acts. "In this sense, knowledge is a physical process, or rather a configuration of physical processes" that include what we see and how we process it.[92] Knowledge and information *remake* those they touch. The conceptual shape of political science's existing metaphors and the political crisis facing both it and the larger world were therefore of a piece. Providing a breakthrough in the former could produce useful openings in the latter.

The foregoing reflections were thus not offered for their own sake. Deutsch's critique of past work was offered instrumentally to clear the ground for his own *cybernetic* model of political transaction, based on the work of Norbert Wiener.[93] Conceptually, cybernetics did for Deutsch's work something quite similar to what "structuration" theory would do for constructivist IR theory in the 1990s. It balanced agents and structures, contingent events, and combinations of value, belief, and preference.[94] Rather than foundering on the shoals of *either* the collective *or* the individual, Deutsch wished to conceptualize the in-between space: the patterns and flows that collectively comprised community. Understanding information flows created new vistas of imagination for the theorist and new political vistas as well. If indeed knowledge transformed agents even as it created structures, could not that realization provide a basis for systematically overcoming the "institutions-consensus dilemma" to which Mitranyan functionalism had also addressed itself, but on a much wider scale? But if this was a problem to be *overcome*—rather, say, than continually grappled with—it would seem to obviate the need for an ethos of sustainable critique.

---

92. Deutsch (1963), pp. 5 and 20.

93. Wiener (1948, 1950). "Let it be noted," wrote Wiener in 1950, "that the word 'governor' in a machine is merely the Latinized Greek word for steersman" (p. 9). See also Wiener (1948), p. 19. For a survey of cybernetics and its influence in the human and social sciences, see Heims (1991), Geyer and van der Zouwen (1994), and especially Alker (2011); on Wiener's collaboration with Deutsch and Wiener's influence, see Deutsch (1975) and Heims (1982).

94. Compare to Adler (2005): "within tightly coupled security communities, authority and legitimacy—the conditions under which states view each other as part of the community and give each other certain rights, obligations and duties—are contingent on their ability to abide by the cognitive normative structure of the cognitive region...cognitive structures—like games whose constitutive rules give meaning to the moves—constitute identities, interests and behavior, but are, in turn, also constituted by them" (p. 197). On Anthony Giddens's "structuration" theory and its application to different strands of constructivist IR, see Adler (1997), Dessler (1989), Gould (1998), and Wendt (1987). Connections between Deutsch and the early work of Giddens are made in Markovits and Oliver (1981), pp. 170–173.

In that vein, cybernetics understood states, individuals, groups, bureau-cracies, and ideological fractions as nodes embedded within complex net-works that selectively allowed in and parceled out both new information from outside and feedback among its parts. The overall structure of the network produced a certain kind of meaning or self-consciousness, while definable perspectives emerged from the location of particular nodes within the whole. As in classical communitarian thought, neither part nor whole existed outside of the other. Both the subjective content of the information and the objective structure of the network and its parts played a role:

> If we think of an ethnic or cultural community as a network of com-munication channels, and of a state or political system as a network of such channels and of chains of command, we can measure the "inte-gration" of individuals in a people by their ability to receive and trans-mit information on wide ranges of different topics with relatively little delay or loss of relevant detail.[95]

Where such theory differed from classical communitarianism was in Deutsch's attempt to break down James's "common *socius*" into quanta: into discrete bits of information ("patterned relationships among events") moving along a network. The unifying, holistic, and affective stuff that came with romantic-organismic models of nations and states—integrity and purpose, self-knowledge and self-love—would thus be preserved. Yet it was stripped of any mysterious, metaphysical claim of origin and hence (Deutsch hoped) of its potentially dangerous reifications. Identity emerged from the configu-ration of flows of information within a system and the conditioning of the nodes that received them. It was a remarkably bold and sophisticated attempt to recast communitarian thinking.

The aim was eminently practical. First, Deutsch wished to discover how a network's various states of openness and closure came about. Second, he wished to learn to control them, with an eye to the steering goals evinced ear-lier.[96] The ideal seemed to be a kind of intelligent self-organizing autonomy, balancing internal integrity and external openness: a sustainably harmonious

---

95. Deutsch (1963), p. 150.

96. That is, it is a "steering model" rather than a "drift model"; see Deutsch (1977).

social-political balance, a science of James's *socius*. The overall shape of that balance should by now be familiar:

> This line of thought might have some implications for the long-standing argument whether the coercive aspects of government may be expected to recede in the long run with the increase in wealth, education and perhaps in cultural and social integration, so that these aspects of the state might eventually "wither away," as envisaged by Marx and Engels, and more recently and vividly by H. G. Wells.... *The perennial vision of an eventual non-coercive world, so attractive to many early radicals and revolutionists... may not be impractical in principle.*[97]

The excessive rationalism of many formal theories, Deutsch noted, had gone too far in debunking communitarian values and sensibilities.[98] While excesses of nationalism or class identity may have produced catastrophic political consequences, it remained the case that collective identity was deeply woven into both human nature and political life. If this pointed to deep-seated atavistic tendencies in the human spirit or psyche, then all the more reason to learn to control them. "A generation haunted by the memory of atomic explosions and weary of crusades" would be forgiven for wanting to put such notions behind them and to abandon collective identity altogether.[99] But theorists did so only at their peril: "it may not be safe to disregard the individual and social insights of thousands of years, laid down in the great philosophic and religious traditions of mankind."[100]

Hence the vocational ambitions of cybernetic theory: "There is reason to suspect that many of the qualitative problems in social and political science may turn out to be problems of matching and complementarity in social communication."[101] If identity has a tendency to degenerate into chauvinism (a form of communicative self-closure), could not feedback loops be designed

---

97. Deutsch (1963), p. 124, emphasis added. On political evil and the self-closure of political systems, see Deutsch (1963), pp. 214–218; (1966), pp. xiii–xiv; and Alker (2011), pp. 361–364.

98. See, for example, Deutsch's (1963) discussion of game theory, pp. 57–59.

99. Deutsch (1963), p. 219. Recall Mitrany (1975): "Today we are in the early stages of a wholly new political society... the situation is new but the ideological ingredients are those laid down by democratic liberalism and Marxism, both products of the social transition of the nineteenth century... it is all a battle of ideologies drained of ideas: no concepts fresh to our time." (p. 27).

100. Deutsch (1963), p. 244; see also Charlesworth (1966), pp. 215–16.

101. Deutsch (1963), pp. 87–88.

that would facilitate openness to countervailing forces, like humility and reverence? If so, then developing the means to engineer such loops would be the work of cybernetic theory. Suppose that in moderation, a strong civic faith is a powerful firebreak against alienation and anomie, but that an excess of such faith can degenerate into Nuremberg rallylike displays of political self-worship or Stalinist cults of personality. Through cybernetics, communicative pathways that facilitate curiosity, openness to the other, or "grace" could be discovered and strengthened with an eye to keeping that civic faith in check.[102] A convergence between private desires and public goods might thus be generated. The careful construction of feedback loops would suit human needs, Deutsch suggests, in the same way that a key is made to suit the tumblers and notches of a lock. When correctly fashioned, the key fits within the lock easily and can be turned with a minimum of force. When the key sticks or the lock resists, it serves as a symptom of dysfunction or mismatch.[103]

Yet while Deutsch's practical theory clearly reflected a vocational approach to IR, and notions such as grace clearly reference the kind of chastened ethos to which sustainable critique aspires, there remained in Deutsch no sustainably reflexive component. Let it be stipulated that the kind of communitarianism to which Deutsch aspired could be, with sufficient conceptual refinement, achievable by the means he specified. There would still be no necessary connection between the tools he developed and those ends. Accepting that communicative openness provided a possible solution for the problem of political evil *in the longer term* did nothing to ensure that it could not be taken over by those with already-formed "evil" aims in the shorter one.[104] There would still be a period in which the cybernetic locksmiths were holding the political world in trust, just as with Mitrany. In his haste to address "charismatic" forms

---

102. For Deutsch (1963), *grace* was "treatment of the world beyond the self, or beyond any particular group or organization, as the potential source of aids or resources in goal-setting and learning" (p. 237). See also Alker (2011): a "life-affirming conception of growth" (p. 362). On this point, see also Deutsch's comments in Charlesworth (1966): "In operational and in normative terms, I prefer a system that has three properties, that is, it does not destroy the larger community, the larger system in which it exists; it can coexist with other systems on its own level; and it is solicitous of its components. This, of course, is a complicated way of saying that a nation-state should be a good citizen in the world, and it should be respectful of the personalities in the group or people which constitute it, but one can use stated empirical research methods to see whether a particular government professing to do such a thing, does it in fact." (p. 231)

103. Deutsch (1963), p. 148.

104. Though to be sure, the memory and image of totalitarianism was very much present for both Wiener and Deutsch. For Wiener, see his (1948), p. 38; and Heims (1982), pp. 307ff. For Deutsch, see (1963), pp. 101–105; and (1956), pp. 296–297.

of tyranny, Deutsch deferred treatment of those "rationalist" forms of tyranny to which cybernetics might easily lend itself.

Put another way, Deutsch had built his approach on a particular notion of power, which must itself be sustainably chastened. Recall that the engineering of feedback loops had not merely collective network effects (the creation of communal consciousness, memory, interests, etc.) but also effects at the level of the nodes—individual citizens—embedded in them. It was because information remade those it touched that networks could be engineered to serve public goods. But did this not risk becoming yet another form of violence or domination: a means of remaking the individual to serve the collective? Certainly, this would not be power in the first-dimensional sense that most concerned Deutsch, but following Steven Lukes or Michel Foucault—or, for that matter, Adorno, Horkheimer, and especially Herbert Marcuse—there remained modes of oppression that did not rely upon the direct imposition of force or influence by A onto B.[105] Deutsch did little to account for these. Having asserted the plasticity of individuals and polities, he may have held that such transformations were not especially violent and hence no accounting was needed.[106] But then, just as with Kenneth Waltz, one is faced with a case of conflating concepts with real-world things. What began as an episte-mological assumption—an alternative conceptualization of the individual-in-society for the purpose of framing his cybernetic approach—would become reified as ontology, as soon as the conceptual rubber of cybernetics met the road of policy making. Nothing endogenous to the theory checks the potential for harm that might come from this.

To his credit, Deutsch did come to realize this. A notion of reflexivity quite similar to that of sustainable critique appeared in the introduction that Deutsch wrote for the second edition of *Nerves of Government*, published in 1966. Cybernetics could not, Deutsch now noted, simply create new conceptual frameworks to attack old problems. The guidance of

---

105. Lukes (2005), Foucault (1979), and Marcuse (1964). On Deutsch's notion of power, see (1963), pp. 110–116; and (1968), chs. 3–4. See also Dahl (1957); Bachrach and Baratz (1962); Morgenthau (1967b), pp. 25–35; and Haugaard (2002). For a more recent discussion, see Adler (2005), pp. 193–195.

106. Deutsch (1963): "Since the network of the human mind behaves with some degree of plasticity, it can change many of its operating rules under the impact of experience. It can learn, not only superficially but fundamentally: with the aid of experience the human mind can change its own structure of preference, rejections and associations. And what seems true of the general plasticity of the individual human mind applies even more so to the plasticity of the channels that make up human cultures and social institutions and those particular individual habit patterns that go with them" (pp. 95–6).

wisdom was needed as well: that mode of thinking "which does not solve directly any given problem, but serves to decide what problems are worth solving."[107] To that end, "an ensemble of dialogues" was needed to direct the pursuit of knowledge, checking practical reason through ongoing self-examination:

> The pursuit of increased intellectual powers in terms of manipulative reason, wisdom and perceptive reason is most likely to occur within an *ensemble of dialogues*—internally, among parts of a single individual personality; societally, among small groups, large groups, and entire governments and nations; and silently, in terms of thought, research and evidence, among scientists and the external and internal universes of nature surrounding them.[108]

Certainly, this sounds promising, akin in many ways to the kind of constellation proposed in the earlier chapters. Yet beyond these few suggestive lines, Deutsch did not develop this notion of an "ensemble of dialogues," and the reader is left to wonder what precisely was meant by it. The implication seems to be that practical theory ("manipulative" and "perceptive" reason) and reflexivity ("wisdom") needed a kind of equipoise. Sustained self-interrogation through interlocking circles of discourse at a variety of social levels appeared to be the means to attain that equipoise. Yet Deutsch specifically refrains from weaving these insights into the theoretical approach he sets out.

This absence bears noting, for Deutsch's own thinking suggests a path to it. Broadening his notion of grace, as it emerged in the foregoing discussion,

---

107. Deutsch (1966), p. xv; see also (1971), pp. 16–17. Compare this to Deutsch (1963): "Perhaps we may yet come to recognize that the deep cleavage between the 'natural' and the 'social' sciences; between 'reason' and 'intuition' or 'reason' and 'wisdom'; between the search for truth and the search for goodness—perhaps we may come to recognize how much these cleavages were amplified and exaggerated in the thought of many good men between the times of Galileo and those of Einstein, by particular historical and social conditions in the Western world, and perhaps by the rather unwieldy intellectual equipment available during that period" (p. 34).

108. Deutsch (1966), p. xv, emphasis added. Methodologically, it must be said, Deutsch had long been deeply pluralist. Rejecting the idea that reductive social-scientific forms of knowledge and interpretive-humanistic ones could exist independently of one another, Deutsch decried the fact that "the community of students of political science" had long been divided along such lines. "These two groups are in danger of losing communication with one another" and this when preserving unity in the study of politics was "vitally important" (1960), p. 35; also Deutsch (1958, 1959, 1971). What is new here is the addition of wisdom as an external, moderating force, outside the model building of social science, to keep that project in tune with larger humanistic objectives; see Alker (2011), p. 364.

might have given added weight or substance to this striving for equipoise. In the foregoing, Deutsch seems to have conceived grace as a practical value: a design feature to be worked into feedback loops. It was, on this account, a means for the social engineer to attenuate inside-outside distinctions within such established feedback loops, so as to moderate the potential for political "closure," with its attendant dangers. If grace could be also turned *critically*, against the project of cybernetics itself—if, that is, an essential aspect of grace is knowledge on the part of the designer that *she, too,* must learn to look "beyond the self" for "aids or resources in goal-setting and learning"—that might give the ensemble of dialogues its own sustainable center of gravity.[109]

Could cybernetic theory, so reconceived, have retained both its normative and practical vectors? The reader is left to wonder. At all events, when compared to the detail with which the book develops its practical agenda, the short shrift given this belated turn to reflexivity is striking. However evocatively phrased, the need for sustainable critique is met neither simply by declaring that it exists nor by acknowledging the dangers that attend its absence. Yet Deutsch goes only that far.

Third-Way Communitarianism and the Primacy of Vision: Adler

Given the passion with which debates between "rational" and "reflectivist" methodology have been pursued in IR circles, it is surprising how naturally both the aims and methodology of Deutschian approaches map onto contemporary constructivism, in particular the communitarian work of Emanuel Adler, Michael Barnett, Beverly Crawford, and Vincent Pouliot, which claims both Deutsch's work on security communities and the earlier communitarian tradition as foundational.[110] These similarities, and the fact that Adler's work engages with the current state of the field, together mean that a brief exposition can suffice to develop these claims without recourse to a lengthy reconstruction of the historical-academic discourse of the sort taken in the previous two sections.

Three key points will be stressed. First, Adler is self-consciously engaged in a practical theory-and-knowledge building project, working through a

---

109. Deutsch (1963), p. 237.

110. Adler (2005), especially pp. 207–232; Adler and Barnett (1996, 1998); Adler et al. (2006). For recent monographs drawing on this approach, see Landau (2006) and Del Sarto (2006). On rationalism and reflectivism, see Keohane (1988).

normative tradition that explicitly traces its links both to Deutsch and to the Fabian tradition that animated Mitrany. Second, Adler takes a median position between Mitrany's suspicion of systematic theory and Deutsch, who as we have seen attempted to reduce communitarianism to patterns of empirical observables. Third, although Adler explicitly develops the links between his theoretical commitments and his normative ones, no *sustainably critical* perspective emerges within his brand of communitarian constructivism. Adlerian security communities are specifically designed to overlap and check other forms of political identity "out there" in the real world of politics, but they are not turned *inward*, against themselves. Adler certainly realizes that concepts of political identity cannot be "identical with themselves."[111] That said, his understandings of community are essentially continuations of what Deutsch called "we-feeling." As such, they provide no explicit means to preserve that non-identity.

These arguments can be taken one by one. First, as with Deutsch and Mitrany, this is practical theory with a distinctive normative-conceptual cast. The basis for international community lies latent within a certain human propensity for solidarity, but its outcome is far from assured. Adler is thus quite explicit in noting that theoretical action is also political action: one theorizes to identify and further desirable outcomes. "Merely to imagine security communities does not make them all-pervasive," he notes; their architects "must still compete with and fight against power-political practices and conflicting identities."[112] Moreover, it is practical theory in the service of a goal that has remained constant, from its Fabian conception, through the work of Deutsch, to the present.

At the end of the second millennium, peace, though still uncommon, does exist. It has a positive meaning, is ontologically real...and can be empirically described. The state of peace, as envisaged by E. H. Carr more than fifty years ago, given specific meaning by Karl Deutsch and Richard Van Wagenen more than forty years ago, and recently redefined by Emanuel Adler and Michael Barnett, is neither the antithesis of something else nor something that exists only in the future; rather, it is something very much like a *security community*.[113]

---

111. Bartelson (1998).

112. Adler (2005), p. 204.

113. Adler (2005), p. 208.

It is in this sense, then, that third-way constructivism, the cybernetic behaviorism of Deutsch, and the "methodologically naïve" but normatively communitarian functionalism of Mitrany find common ground "between a rationalist perspective that focuses on individuality and universality and an interpretive perspective that takes contextual knowledge, contingency and human interpretation to be the hallmarks of social reality."[114] They share a commitment to an understanding of political life that has a common end or telos—widening the circle of community by creating the conditions for shared identities to flourish. The key differences lie only in the methods used to characterize that telos and define the path toward it.[115] It is that vision—of a real peace that can be empirically described and pragmatically worked toward—that guides the project.

On the second point, Adler's work has remained circumspect when it comes to methodological reductionism. Consider his use of the term *we-feeling*, that core sensibility whose broad diffusion, in Deutsch's work, characterized a mature security community. Deutsch's move was to define key indicators for such feeling—through, for example, the formal study of nationalism—and on that basis to devise means to encourage their transnational dissemination.[116] Adler is less certain that this is possible. "Communitarian approaches," he noted in 2005, suffer not only "vagueness as to the nature, shape and extent of the communities under study" but are necessarily complicated by the fact that "people simultaneously participate in various overlapping communities whose boundaries are sometimes indistinct."[117] Hence, no play for anything like cybernetic reductionism is made here. Although Adler picks up on Deutsch's notion of we-feeling as the core sensibility that unites a mature security community, no effort is made to define that feeling in terms of primary analytical "atoms," akin to the discrete information flows in *Nerves of Government*.

Rather, we-feeling is discerned through intuitive observation of political practices: working anthropologically, so to speak, and not reductively. It is a move partway back to the Jamesian *socius* that prevailed in Mitrany's work: not

---

114. Adler (2005), p. 6. Or compare Mitrany's use of William James, as discussed earlier, to Adler's use of Mary Douglas: the idea that "Dirt…is matter out of place" (p. 187). Douglas's "dirt" is, in James's idiom "litter." On Mitrany as "methodologically naïve," see Navari (1995), p. 234.

115. Consider here Adler and Barnett's (1998) hypotheses that liberal ideas "are more prone to create a shared transnational civil culture" (pp. 40–1) and that "behind every innovative institution stand creative and farsighted political elites" (p. 43). If indeed "communicating and acting…are two sides of the same coin," when is that the case, and what does it mean? (2005, p. 219).

116. Hence Deutsch (1953); Deutsch and Foltz (1963).

117. Adler (2005), p. 6.

to be defined reductively, only described externally and glimpsed indirectly.[118] Such glimpses are obtained in two forms: through conveying a lived political experience in impressionistic terms or through specific practices or processes that are held to be indicative of shared political affinities or affects—norms, beliefs, or expectations.[119] Hence, a mature security community is mature because "the [individual] state's interests, and the identity of its people, can be exchangeable with those of the community."[120] This is attested to by the presence of institutions and practices: "community 'we-feeling'...is not only in people's heads, but it is also institutionalized in community practices"; these are "the material representation of the condition or state of peace."[121] It would be "pretentious or foolhardy" to believe that "*a* theory of community development or security communities" could be offered, given this.[122] There is no "contractual act of volition" but rather properties that are emergent "from a common culture."[123] "While we believe it is important to identify the causal variables at work in the development of a security community," Adler wrote with Barnett in 2000, "identity always works in relationship to and interacts with other social processes and variables."[124] Hence, one cannot avoid reifying

---

118. Adler and Barnett (1996): "The concept of community, which departs from the economism and rationalism that have dominated models of security politics and international relations...demands that we take both sociological theorizing and the profoundly social character of global politics seriously" (pp. 64–65).

119. Adler and Crawford (2006): "Based on concepts of pluralistic integration and exclusion, cooperative security is *comprehensive*, for it links classic security elements to economic, environmental, cultural, and human rights factors. It is also *indivisible*, in the sense that one state's security is inseparable from that of other states. Most important it is *cooperative*; that is, security is based on confidence and cooperation, the peaceful resolution of disputes and the work of mutually reinforcing multilateral institutions" (p. 9).

120. Adler and Barnett (1998), p. 48.

121. Adler and Crawford (2006), pp. 12–13. Or as Kupchan (2010) explains: "The normalization of cooperative practices informs a social reality that both parties deem to be noncompetitive, in turn enabling them to further let down their guard. In this sense, a self-fulfilling prophecy is at work. If both parties come to conceive of their relationship as noncompetitive and behave accordingly, then the relationship becomes effectively noncompetitive." (44–5)

122. Adler and Barnett (1998), p. 49. And as Adler and Crawford (2006) note: "A necessary condition for such processes to occur is the previous existence of a 'life-world' of shared understandings, meanings and discourse. But these are precisely the missing elements in conflicts that pit states against each other" (p. 16). Deutsch et al. (1957) said as much when they argued that "integration is a matter of fact, not of time" (p. 6).

123. Adler (2005), p. 197; see also Adler and Barnett (2000) and Buzan (1993). To be sure, one could then theorize the sources of that common culture in historical-philosophical terms. On this point—and with similar connections to Deutsch—see Senghaas (2002).

124. Adler and Barnett (2000), p. 324.

identity if one is to study it, but one must not forget that the reification is, after all, only that:

> While we believe...it is important to identify the causal variables at work in the development of a security community, to use counterfactual analysis to dispense with alternative hypotheses, and to be clear about what work identity is doing.... Identity always works in relationship to and interacts with other social processes and variables. Therefore...we are uneasy about the reification of the cultural-material dichotomy. This reification is important for any conversation with neo-liberalism or neo-realism, *but it unintentionally forces researchers to reproduce the very dichotomies that we find problematic.*[125]

This is the sensibility at work, too, in Adler's and Barnett's individual studies on Middle Eastern politics: in each, the emphasis is on doing justice to *both* a vigorously contested public sphere *and* a demanding structural environment that constrains even the most powerful players in profound and multifaceted ways.[126] It is also evident in his and Pouliot's understanding of international practices: on their account, the "gluons" that link and facilitate communication across the key dichotomies of social theory ("The material/meaningful, structural/agential, reflexive/background, and stability/change attributes of practice acquire concrete and workable theoretical and empirical meaning in the concept of *communities of practice*.")[127]

Careful though this approach is in not overstating what theory can do, the same caveat applies here as elsewhere: the problem of reification is not met merely by asserting that it exists. This is the third and last of the points set out: like Deutsch, Adler is aware of theory's reliance on reification. Yet that awareness does not translate into sustainably critical methods or practices: the dangers of reification running amok remain, despite being recognized and alluded to. Consider, by way of example, Adler's concept of "seminar diplomacy" as summarized here by Emily Landau: "a vehicle for social construction, and a framework within which...different strategic practices are applied."[128] The effect of interstate security dialogue, Landau convincingly demonstrates in her account of the Middle East Arms Control and Regional Security (ACRS)

---

125. Adler and Barnett (2000), pp. 324–325, emphasis added.

126. See the later essays in Adler (2005) and Barnett (1998, 2002).

127. Adler and Pouliot (2011b), pp. 10, 12 and 17 respectively, emphasis in original. See also Adler and Pouliot (2011a), pp. 3 and 14–19.

128. Landau (2006), p. 20. Also Adler and Barnett (1998), pp. 119–160.

talks, is that individual states are sometimes led to redefine their partial interests on the basis of joint understandings. "Seminar diplomacy can have important influences not only on the interests of the parties, but possibly on the definition of the strategic game itself."[129] There is no questioning this, only the ease with which such redefinitions can come to be translated into moral or political progress, taking for granted that mutual understanding and community building are a priori emancipatory. What if what is being "facilitated" through dialogue is cooperation among unpopular and domestically oppressive ruling elites? One would still be lowering transaction costs and transforming regional security practices, but the end result would not be a net decline in violence or oppression. One would simply be helping these regimes turn their resources inward—against homegrown opposition movements—by changing the equation of their external security and balancing costs. The IR theorist may well see this as progress if his or her view is confined strictly to international interactions.[130] But has that violence *disappeared* or has it merely *been forgotten*—by virtue of having moved into someone else's disciplinary bailiwick?[131]

Concluding Thoughts: From Communitarian to Individualist IR

Since its heyday in the work of Mitrany, communitarian approaches have remained a secondary tradition within IR theory. As Adler and Barnett have noted, while Deutsch's security communities approach to IR was widely cited,

---

129. Landau (2006), p. 20.

130. Hence, Adler (2005): "Peace, according to the positive definition put forward in the previous section, refers to *pluralistic*, rather than amalgamated communities. States that have integrated to the point where they constitute a new sovereign nation-state do not fulfill the ontological and epistemological conditions for peace *among* sovereign states" (p. 217). The problem may have been thus *redefined* in academic terms, but it has not thereby *disappeared*.

131. Landau makes a different argument in her analysis of Egypt's behavior in ACRS (see her [2001], pp. 22–27) but identifies the same critical upshot. The Israeli-Egyptian bilateral relationship unfolds, she notes, against the backdrop of Egypt's desire for regional preeminence within the Arab world. "Progress" in one set of relationships is translated into leverage in the other. For a longer *'durée'* variant of this argument, see Vucetic's (2011) account of the "Anglosphere": a security community comprised of the "Anglo-Saxon" states of Britain, the US, Canada, Australia and New Zealand. It is not merely, Vucetic points out, that the Anglosphere's notion of 'we-feeling' is predicated on a series of racialized social constructions, nor that these constructions inform the conjoint actions of its members. It is that it does so *even as the discursive structure of IR as a discipline conceals this racialism from view*. Since IR does not consistently take up race, the 'Anglosphere' appears artificially emancipatory when viewed through a communitarian lens. See pp. 4–8 and 148–53; also Vitalis (2005, 2010) and the essays on race and IR in *International Studies Perspectives* 9 (2008).

its concepts and methodologies were less widely taken up.[132] The same could well be said of his cybernetic model of politics. From the 1960s through the 1990s, individualist approaches held the dominant positions within liberal IR theory.

Chapter 5 will deal at some length with the reasons for this. The key point, however, emerges from the discussion with which this chapter opened: communitarian notions of solidarity—those arising from *gemeinschaft*—seem to resist conceptual reduction to some extent. If the work of theory is the creation of useful concepts or the understanding of wholes by their parts, communitarian thinking would seem to be at a distinct disadvantage. Deutsch, it is true, initially rejected such arguments: "no knowable object can be completely unique: if it were radically unique it could be neither observed nor recorded, nor could it be known."[133] Yet his later retreat to an "ensemble of dialogues" seems to suggest that he, too, had some doubts on this score. If community is a construct that must, in some ways, escape the sharp edges and definite lines of reductive thinking, then the case must be made for it in explicitly normative terms as *being worth knowing in its own right, notwithstanding the limitations that constrain the attempt.* Given, however, the tendency of such arguments to feed into ideological appropriations of their own, they require a sustainably reflexive approach to check their foundational reifications. Though they may play upon a notion of importance that derives first and foremost from a sense of moral vocation (rather than from, say, a sensibility that views the identification and filling of conceptual lacunae as an end in itself), such a vocation is not served if the resulting approaches create the foundations for new forms of political mystification. If theory is, as Piki Ish-Shalom has aptly put it, "a configuration of de-contested political concepts" around which instrumental reason congeals, then the content and object of that reason must remain a matter of central concern, as must the lines of its decontestation.[134] Such arguments must be *both* advanced in their own terms *and* actively critiqued.

---

132. Adler and Barnett (1998), pp. 8–9. But see the introduction of Deutsch (1966) – and more recently, Kupchan (2010), pp. 16–23 – for surveys of such research.

133. Deutsch (1963), p. 14.

134. Ish-Shalom (2006), p. 572. Or as Pentland (1973) noted three decades earlier: "For those…to whom integration means more than the preservation of peace among nations, the pluralists' minimal definition will seem inadequate. If the causes of war are traced…to deeper social and economic sources, or if welfare or social justice are held to be more important values than peace and security, then more demanding and dramatic forms of integration may be required" (p. 63).

In that sense at least, communitarianism imposes a degree of reflexivity, if not a wholly sustainable one, on the theorist. Since such theory is at a natural disadvantage in terms of rigor and parsimony, normative justifications have to be offered on its behalf. The opposite tendency precisely, as chapter 5 will show, pertains with regard to individualist approaches. Their commitment to individualism allows the creation of interlocking theories of personal and collective interest with far greater parsimony, specificity, and rigor. The discipline thus naturally rewards both these approaches and, by extension, the commitments on which they are predicated. Individualism's rise to dominance thus did not require a conscious ideological bias on the part of theorists; it emerged simply because the occult link between *gesellschaft* and conceptual thinking, discussed previously, was (and largely remains) insufficiently understood. The result is a tendency for communitarian theory to seem normative and for individualist theory to seem value-free. In fact, both are equally normative; what differs is the manner in which that normativity plays out. This argument will become clearer in the next chapter.

5

Individualist IR Theory: Disharmonious Cooperation

We need a conception of cooperation that is somewhat tart,
rather than syrupy-sweet.

—ROBERT KEOHANE[1]

International Relations Liberalism: From Communitarian to Individualist

To sustainably critique liberal IR, the previous chapter argued, coherent fact-value traditions within it had to be discerned. Drawing on Tönnies's ideal-types of *gemeinschaft* and *gesellschaft*, chapter 4 suggested two such traditions: the communitarian and the individualist. In the communitarian tradition, certain collective institutions were understood to have an irreducible political-moral character: a positive, unifying quality that gave the liberal *socius* a claim to moral legitimacy roughly akin to that which the state enjoyed in IR realism. By contrast, in the individualist tradition, moral authority rests in the natural rights of the individual, whose identity, preferences, and interests are logically prior to the state.[2] This chapter reviews the various methodological turns of individualist theory, with an eye to its ongoing attempts to deal with reification.

No less than any other fact-value tradition, individualist IR liberalism comes with its own heroic, teleological baggage, namely, that politics is either the institutionalized outcome of interactions among unitary, rational actors seeking to maximize their interests or else is best studied *as if* it were. The former summarizes the metaphysical basis for a theory of political right; the

---

1. Keohane (2005) [1984], p. 46.

2. Moravcsik (1997) puts this concisely: "The state is not an actor but a representative institution constantly subject to capture and recapture, construction and reconstruction by coalitions of social actors. Representative institutions and practices constitute the critical 'transmission belt' by which the preferences and social power of individuals and groups are translated into state policy.... Government policy is therefore constrained by the underlying identities, interest and power of individuals and groups ... who constantly pressure the central decision-makers to pursue policies consistent with their preferences" (p. 518).

latter, an epistemological principle for analyzing social order.³ Either way, such assumptions are no less normative than are those of communitarians; they seek to develop practical theory for particular ends.

Few contemporary IR theorists dispute the essentially artificial nature of atomistic models of social and political interaction. "Rationalist analysts of international politics," note Robert Keohane and Judith Goldstein, "have often recognized that the assumption of rationality, like that of egoism, 'is a theoretically useful simplification of reality rather than a true reflection of it.'"⁴ That admission is more easily made, however, than followed "all the way down." The reason lies in the occult link—traced out in chapter 4—between conceptual-rationalistic modes of thinking and the particular social and political forms that constitute late-modern life. "Society" has a genealogy that can be difficult for social scientists working in an individualist mode to see. "The very notion of rational choice," noted Walter Powell and Paul DiMaggio, "reflects modern secular rituals and myths that constitute and constrain legitimate action."⁵ In itself, such recognition—essentially a retreading of Max Weber's well-known "trackmen" metaphor—is welcome.⁶ If not on its own sufficient to sustainably critique individualist IR liberalism, acknowledging the artificiality of an analytical construct is surely an important first step. It suggests the line that such critique would need to take.

Plan of the Chapter

In broad terms, the structure of present chapter follows the same three-part case study format as the previous two. Metaphysical individualism is explored through the work of Ernst Haas, both his early neofunctionalist theory and his later attempts to develop progressivist theories of world politics through

---

3. Keohane (1990), p. 174.

4. Keohane and Goldstein (1993), p. 5, citing Keohane (2005) [1984], p. 108.

5. Powell and DiMaggio (1991), p. 10. Also Tversky and Kahneman (1986): "the modern theory of decision making under risk...was conceived as a normative model of an idealized decision maker, not as a description of the behavior of real people" (p. S251).

6. Weber's "trackmen" metaphor has become increasingly de rigeur among individualist theorists seeking to make common cause with constructivism; see Keohane and Goldstein (1993), Philpott (2001), and Legro (2005). Yet the question with such analogies is not merely what vistas they open up, but which they close off. "The essential problem is that the [railroad] metaphor takes for granted that the railway lines or tracks have already been laid; that is, that a social order is already in place" (Hall [1993], p. 48). See also Hobson (1998), Jackson (2002), Strong and Owen (2004).

concepts of social learning and the constructivist turn. Middle-range individualism is explored through the complex interdependence and liberal institutionalist paradigms of Robert Keohane and Joseph Nye. Finally, third-way individualism is explored through a variety of multiparadigmatic turns—a series of new approaches that seek to balance rationalism and reflectivism against one another. What these paradigms share, I shall argue, is a basic awareness of the problem of reification as it affects individualist IR theory. Despite that awareness, I shall claim, sustainable critique has been and will likely continue to prove elusive—even acknowledging the serious efforts and real innovations that have recently been made.

I begin with the work of Ernst Haas. In the 1950s and 1960s, Haas spearheaded the emergence of neofunctionalist integration theory: the attempt to reground Mitranyan functionalism in an open-ended individualist framework, avoiding what he held to be the "terminal concepts" of the communitarian tradition. His aims were twofold. First, he sought to break with those functionalist predictions that were at variance with the observed processes of European integration. Second, he wished to lay the foundations for a more wide-ranging, rigorous theory of political unification, beyond the European continent. However, Haas realized in the 1970s, those ambitions faced distinct challenges. There was an inherent tension in developing *theories* of political unification. Individualism imported its own set of terminal concepts. One was, after all, attempting to characterize and classify emergent political processes by means of concepts and categories drawn from past historical forms. These concepts and categories would necessarily have particular social, political, and normative genealogies of their own. While he wrote in a very different idiom, Haas's line of thinking here thus has certain affinities to the Adornian-Kantian critique of the concept set out in chapter 1, and it is through those affinities that his attempts at reflexivity will be explored.

With that in mind, Haas's work in the 1980s and 1990s turned toward theories of social learning. If concepts were generalized intellectual structures built out of past political forms, and if change was an inherent feature of late-modern life, then how societies evolved to absorb newness and change without generating political backlash bore studying. Observing the historical record, Haas believed he had discerned a pattern: liberal-nationalist states seemed especially capable in this regard. On the one hand, liberalism fostered openness, developing modes for routinizing social debate and contestation so that they did not boil over; on the other, nationalism ensured that societies involved in profound transformations would not sink into anomie or alienation. Change could thus be balanced against its more dangerous side effects.

In this observation lies an implicit recognition of the need for something like the doublethink that drives sustainable critique. That said, the attempt to relocate the locus of one's concepts does not change their reliance on reification. Predicated on a notion of universal progress to which his reflexivity did not wholly extend, this approach has its own quite serious potential for harm. While broadly aware of this, Haas wagered the risk to be worth the rewards. The present chapter does not dispute that judgment per se—all scholarship requires such wagers. Even so, it remains a normative judgment predicated on its own conceptual reifications; as such, it, too, must be brought under the aegis of sustainable critique.

The neoliberalism of Keohane and Nye picked up from the same conceptual impasse that had, in the 1970s, stymied neofunctionalism. But where Haas moved toward theories of social learning, Keohane and Nye worked in a different direction: avoiding grand theory and attempting to remain closer to the "ground" of world affairs. Specifically, Keohane and Nye wished to work empirically: what states *did*—as distinct from metaphysical discussions of what they *were*—formed the core of their approach. Their analysis suggested that realist notions of power and interest did not need to be replaced so much as complemented. Making sense of the broad sphere of world politics, they suggested, would be easier with multiple and overlapping logics of anarchy, rather than attempting to force all events and issues through a single unbending conceptual framework. In particular, they suggested, economic notions of interest seemed increasingly prevalent in particular contexts—even among states with enduring rivalries in other issue areas.

Significant in themselves, these observations suggested a further innovation. With the right combination of institutions, rules, and payoffs, could one not engineer conditions in which cooperative logics would hold sway across ever-wider swaths of interstate relations? Rather than relying on the altruism of states or leaders, who would somehow be persuaded to forgo private interests in the name of international public goods, could one not design institutions that appealed to those private interests? Could not cooperation be divorced—conceptually and practically—from attendant notions of altruism?

In taking that next step, however, Keohane and Nye's theory underwent a transformation, a variant of the same pattern of reification observed both in Waltz and in Deutsch. In prescribing on the basis of empirical observations, their ostensibly middle-range methodology had become, despite itself, an ontology. Keohane in particular has been consistently forthright in recognizing this problem and in evincing positions meant to grapple with it: in the 1980s, through adopting Lakatosian philosophy of science, and in the early 2000s, by proposing new normative regulative ideals, such as humility. Yet while evocatively stating the need for an ongoing reflexivity as a value in the abstract, Keohane has yet to undertake its operationalization in theory. Though a promising beginning, humility remains undeveloped in methodological terms.

By contrast, third-way multiparadigmatic approaches—initially promulgated by Jeffrey Legro and Andrew Moravcsik and developed more fully by Peter Katzenstein and Rudra Sil—move in precisely the opposite fashion. The methodological debates of IR, Katzenstein and Sil have argued, seem perpetually on the verge of scholasticism: spinning off into essentially irresolvable metaphysical debates. To avoid this, the diversity of its various elements needs to be actively fostered—if, that is, the field is to preserve its ability to speak helpfully to, and yet remain critical of, real-world policies and problems. To that end, they argue, theorists need to work in a mix of traditions, both rationalist and reflective, while simultaneously limiting the regional and temporal scope of their generalizations. The critical pragmatism surveyed briefly in chapter 2 plays an important role here as an "ideal-typical center," that is, as a means to balance among methods and avoid deep claims of ontology.[7]

At the level of concrete research practices, the negative-dialectical and constellar foundations of sustainable critique clearly resonate with the turn to multiple paradigms. Yet the manner in which its promulgators propose to effect the management of reification has serious shortcomings, albeit of a different sort. While reflexive *practices* are specified, the *values* they are meant to serve are left vague; a sense of vocation is evoked but left underspecified. One might, recalling the play *Six Characters in Search of an Author*, call this the Pirandello problem: multiple methodologies are put forward, but like Pirandello's characters, there is no clear unifying worldview (chastened or otherwise) to guide them, save an appeal to better theorizing: "blunt[ing] the sharpness of the present [paradigmatic] debates by recognizing the different kinds of insights each approach has to offer" and thereby "expanding the scope and quality of dialogue concerning practical problems in international life."[8] On this point, however, one must not generalize. One suspects that Katzenstein and Sil in particular might have more explicitly normative ends

7. Katzenstein and Sil (2008), p. 113.

8. Respectively, Sil (2000b), p. 354; Katzenstein and Sil (2008), p. 119.

in mind but are fearful of politicizing the academy. Fair enough, but recall the problem that stymied David Mitrany in chapter 4: without discussing those ends openly, how shall they be argued for and defended? Consider the work of these past three chapters: *every single one* of the paradigms reviewed had its beginnings as an eclectic alignment, a broad tapestry of methods and values, a "temporary resting place for inquiry."[9] *Every single one*, even so, found itself at pains to sustain the diversity from which it initially emerged, owing not to the fault of this or that theorist, but to reductionist dynamics immanent to thinking as such. Important theoretical innovations are being made here, which is all the more reason for a sustainably critical framework to check and chasten them.

Metaphysical Individualism: Ernst Haas and the Renewed March of Reason

As the previous chapter showed, a key move for the functionalism of David Mitrany had been to encode communitarian ideals into the reconstruction and welfare efforts that were being planned for postwar Europe. This was, it was noted, a rhetorically backhanded tactic: a virtue made of political neces- sity. The intellectual appeal that a united Europe held for many elites had not translated into a viable basis for consensual political action at the mass level. Indeed, by its own logic it could not have done: in classic chicken-and-egg terms, such support could emerge only once there was an institutional basis for it. To bridge this impasse, the European functionalist program took a page from Roosevelt's New Deal: piggybacking on the popular support for relief measures in the wake of upheaval and crisis as a 'carrier wave' onto which functionalist aims and methods could be encoded.

By the 1950s, the European political and institutional landscape had changed dramatically. Students and advocates of integration no longer needed as much rhetorical-political cover. Supranational integration having become a matter of declared policy, the next generation of integration theo- rists found themselves comfortably within the bounds of political consensus. "A [Walter] Hallstein and a Haas," Charles Pentland reflected in 1975, "each in his different style, expressed the same kind of assumptions and analyses."[10] He continued:

---

9. Katzenstein and Sil (2008), p. 115 (here quoting Molly Cochran).

10. Pentland (1975), p. 19. Hallstein was president of the Commission of the EEC from 1958 to 1967.

Academics moved easily...interviewing Eurocrats and absorbing the Community ethos. Eurocrats, in turn, read the resulting publications and found their behavior described, rationalized and even prescribed in a persuasive manner. The relation become so close that one neofunctionalist recently remarked on the "unnerving experience of hearing our special jargon spouted back at us by those whom we are studying."[11]

Success brought new problems, however. The community ethos to which Pentland alluded did not seem to have the shape or effects Mitrany had predicted. Mitrany had assumed an extant consensus among elites and technocrats. His notion to "weld together the common interests of all" without interfering unduly in the "ways of each" was meant to give those elites the political breathing room they needed so that this consensus could take root "via," as one sympathetic commentator then explained it, "the back door of operational integration."[12]

If Mitrany's account was correct, one would have expected to see elite-level altruism in the creation and workings of European institutions: a transnational community of apolitical experts, quietly collaborating on the basis of an a priori consensus. Yet in his 1958 study of European integration, Haas found differently:

> Perhaps the most salient conclusion we can draw from the [European] community-building experiment is the fact that major interest groups as well as politicians determine their support of, or opposition to, new central institutions and policies on the basis of a calculation of advantage.[13]

The new Europe, Haas argued, was not being built upon technocratic altruism. Functional integration had scored many successes, yet those successes seemed to be attributable to the self*ish*, not the self*less*. The true heroes of integration were savvy pragmatists, working "on the basis of a calculation of advantage."

---

11. Pentland (1975), p. 19; also Keohane and Nye (1975), pp. 400–401. Pentland is citing Schmitter (1970) p. 838.

12. Respectively, Mitrany (1966), p. 68; Kaiser (1972), p. 211.

13. Haas, (1958), p. xiv, also pp. 19–29.

This suggested that functionalist theory needed to be regrounded: pulled out of the communitarianism of Mitrany and William James and replanted in a more hard-nosed account of interest-group politics. In this section, I first explore how Haas attempted that regrounding—the basis of neofunctionalism—in the 1950s and 1960s. In the process of excising one set of reifications, however, Haas opened the door to another, a problem he would gradually come to realize. His attempts to deal with this—first by declaring neofunctionalism obsolescent and later by marrying progressivist accounts of social learning to the historical trajectory of liberal nationalism—are instructive for students seeking to develop a sustainably critical individualism in IR. In the process of attempting to meet the problems posed by neofunctionalism, Haas took a long, circular path that ultimately brought him back to Mitrany: both Mitrany's terminal concepts and their potential for unchecked reification. Spanning several decades of scholarship, this developmental arc will be explored at some length. It reveals the limitations of one-off acts of conceptual debunking, given the challenge reification poses to international theory.

Against Communitarianism: Neofunctionalism and Managed *Gesellschaft*

The individualist foundations of neofunctionalism were set out systematically in Haas's 1964 *Beyond the Nation State*. "Classical" functionalism, Haas asserted, "work[ed] with a terminal concept of immanent community much as Marxists use[d] the notion of the classless society."[14] As noted before, consensus among technocrats was assumed; all that was ostensibly lacking was a political backchannel by which that consensus could be translated into institutions and practices. Such backchannels had since become plentiful. Where, Haas now asked, were the cadres of functionalist technocrats working in lockstep? "Demonstrably, experts do not agree, and rival sets of organizational leaders see far from eye to eye."[15] What Haas observed, as he had noted in 1958, were "nationally constituted groups with specific interests and aims" who found in the new institutions of Europe opportunities to advance sectional and fractional interests.[16]

---

14. Haas (1964) p. 22.

15. Haas (1964), p. 32. See also Haas and Schmitter (1964).

16. Haas, (1958), p. xiv.

Functionalists' reliance on communitarian ideals, Haas then asserted, prevented them both from seeing this reality and from exploiting the opportunities it presented. For their part, Haas asserted, neofunctionalists would avoid specifying ideal future conditions and content themselves with the world as it was. The idiom he used to describe that world may now be familiar:

> The modern nation-state...is a *Gemeinschaft* that looks and acts much like the *Gesellschaft* we associate with our international system. Instead of being intimate and cozy, it functions like a large-scale bureaucratic organization. Its tasks may involve the maximization of the welfare of its citizens, but not necessarily in the sense of aggregating all their demands and hopes into a general consensus. International organizations and national states thus share many of the characteristics of a society; they differ in that the national state also enjoys the procedural dedication of its members, who identify with it vicariously. *Far from assuming any realization of the common good, we merely postulate the compatibility of the multi-group competitive national society with an agreement on the means of resolving internal conflict by peaceful methods.*[17]

What neofunctionalism "merely postulated" was—contra Mitrany—a notion of politics as the artful balancing of fractional interest, rather than the reconstitution of some lost sense of civic solidarity. This was a shot aimed directly at the heart of communitarianism: "managed *gesellschaft*," as Paul Taylor called it, or following John Ruggie, "embedded liberalism."[18] As Pentland explained:

> Neofunctionalism claims to have reconciled the classic functionalist concern with economics and welfare with a theory of political conflict and choice, and to have shown how integration can develop, not through an economically determined process but through the resolution of political conflicts among elites and interest groups. But the concept of political conflict derives from one of the dominant images of American political science—that of liberal, pluralistic interest-group politics played out against a backdrop of ideological consensus.[19]

---

17. Haas (1964) 39–40, emphasis added; also Taylor (1968) and Pentland (1973), p. 103. But see Sewell (1966), p. 49.

18. Taylor (1968, 1975, 1983); Ruggie (1982).

19. Pentland (1973), p. 110.

An essential, *metaphysical* disagreement as to the core stuff of political and social life was playing out here. (Paleo)-functionalism had, Haas suggested, "apparently misread the intent of the classical British liberals."[20] The first social fact of any relevance was the ability of individuals to identify and realize their own interest; only thus could "order... develop from chaos, the general good... from the compounding of ruthless egoism."[21] Theory must place actors "in history" and not "rely on some elusive general will to do the job for us."[22] Where Mitrany and Deutsch aimed to use low politics to reorder high politics, Haas and his colleagues rejected this dichotomy as false: the two were located, as Slaughter and Mattli have helpfully explained, along a continuum.[23] Neofunctionalism thus recast political integration in rationalist terms; "political actors" were, on this account, "*persuaded* to shift their loyalties, expectations and political activities toward a new and larger center, whose institutions possess or demand jurisdiction over the pre-existing national states."[24]

This conception overcame the need for the sort of high-handed, behind-the-scenes elements that figured so centrally in both Mitranyan functionalism and Deutsch's cybernetics. By discerning and balancing the interests of the various fractions of world society, Haas gave consensual, representative politics a new lease on life: eagle-eyed political entrepreneurs would identify opportunities in the new institutions of Europe and then sell them to national constituencies through a mixture of charisma and appeals to self-interest.[25] The expectation was for a spillover effect—linkages between issues would, as transnational interactions grew, create a demand for the expansion

---

20. Haas (1964), p. 32.

21. Haas (1964), p. 33.

22. Haas (1964), p. 464.

23. Slaughter and Mattli (2006), pp. 461–465.

24. Haas (1961), pp. 366–367, emphasis added. See also Haas (1958), pp. 13–14; (2004), pp. xiv–xv.

25. Haas (1964), pp. 97–103. Also Sewell (1966), pp. 255–264; Rosamond (2000), p. 61–68. The problem with this position, as Robert Cox (1969, p. 207) observed, was that it wound up reducing complex processes to Hegelian "world historical" explanations: the charismatic political entrepreneur as explanatory catchall. The failure of European integration was explained, and the failure of Latin American integration was predicted, on the basis of present or absent political exemplars. Hence, in Haas (1967): "Europe did not have a Bismarck in 1948 or 1950," and so its unification failed; "Latin America has no Bolivàr in 1967," and so it will fail (328). This would persist in Haas's thinking across the decades. From his 2004 discussion of EU expansion: "Not every politician west of the Oder is a Vaclav Havel" (p. lii).

of supranational governance and a withering away of the national state as the actor of consequence in world politics.[26]

No less than Mitrany, however, Haas's approach seemed to run afoul of actual political realities. In particular, many scholars at the time suggested, spillover had not taken place.[27] In the wake of French President Charles de Gaulle's ambivalent relationship to European unification, Haas realized that he had been blindsided by his own approach: a too-thin notion of political interest had obscured the communitarian aspect of politics.

> De Gaulle has proved us wrong.... Pragmatic interests, simply because they are pragmatic and not reinforced with deep ideological or philosophical commitment, are ephemeral. Just because they are weakly held they can be readily scrapped.[28]

An affective center remained part of any process of political integration. Nationalism was alive and well in Europe. "Efforts at building *gesellschaft* alone will not succeed," noted Ronn Kaiser in 1972. "What is required is changes in society which serve to build community at the same time."[29] Neofunctionalism was ill suited to guide this task.

While the empirical question of whether spillover occurred has recently engendered renewed debate and reexamination, this debate must not be allowed to eclipse an understanding of the conceptual limitations of neofunctionalism as it relates to sustainable critique.[30] Haas's notion of interest was predicated on an assumption of *gesellschaft*; whatever its criticism of

---

26. Haas (1958): "Sector integration...begets its own impetus toward extension to the entire economy even in the absence of specific group demands and their attendant ideologies" (p. 297). Also Hoffmann (1966), pp. 863 and 908–911; Hansen (1969); Rosamond (2000), pp. 59–68; Schmitter (1969); Slaughter and Mattli (2006); Haas (1967), p. 315, and (2004), p. xvff.; and Lindberg (1963), p. 10.

27. As Keohane and Nye (1975) put it: "Not only may spillover in some cases not occur at all; in others, the response can be negative" (p. 384).

28. Haas (1967), pp. 327–328.

29. Kaiser (1972), p. 225. See also Katzenstein (1975).

30. As Ruggie et al. (2005) recently put it, Haas may have been "wrong about being wrong" (p. 280). Also Niemann (1998), Rosamond (2005), Schmitter (2004), and Slaughter and Mattli (2006). Though this claim overlooks the fact that a compressed time scale was key to Haas's model—as Katzenstein (1971) has noted. For Deutsch and Mitrany, recasting national loyalties into supernational ones would be the work of decades and centuries; Haas was specifically aiming to do more in less time. To suggest that spillover works over that longer time scale, then, would seem to rehabilitate not *Haas*, but rather *Deutsch*.

communitarianism, it relied on terminal concepts of its own, which it had failed to chasten. That failure exacted a cost. Haas seemed to realize this as early as 1961, when he acknowledged that his model of political integration "fare[d] best in situations controlled by social groupings representing the rational interests of urban-industrial society, groups seeking to maximize their economic benefits and dividing along regionally homogeneous ideological-political lines."[31] That is, it fared best in those sectors of European society that most closely resembled an ideal-typical *gesellschaft*. Surely, this was not a coincidence.

But the mercurial foreign policy of de Gaulle drove the matter home. Haas, it will be recalled, had accused Mitrany of "misunderstanding" the classical liberal tradition. This was not so; Mitrany and his fellow communitarians—from Karl Polanyi and John Maynard Keynes to G. D. H. Cole—understood that tradition perfectly well. *They simply disagreed with Haas as to its ability to serve as a basis for long-term social, political, and economic stability in the postwar era.* After all, was not managed *gesellschaft* essentially similar to the transnational order wrought by Polanyi's "great transformation"?[32] That order had come to grief in 1914; if Haas and the neofunctionalists held that managed *gesellschaft* could serve as a basis for international order in the 1950s and 1960s, they had to address that earlier failure. Not having done so, the question became less empirical than metaphysical: one was making recommendations for future policy based on what one declared the good life to be.[33] Such declarations constitute commitments that need their own forms of chastening.

From Neofunctionalism to Liberal Nationalism: Taking Up the Gauntlet of Reflexivity

Haas's initial underestimation of the conceptual depth of the *gemeinschaft-gesellschaft* problem would not last long. By 1975, he characterized his earlier neofunctionalist theory as obsolete. The reason for that obsolescence, he explained, lay in an essential paradox within conceptual thinking that had earlier been elided. Though written in a very different idiom than that of

---

31. Haas (1961), p. 378; also the preface to Haas (1958).

32. Recall Polanyi (2001) [1944]: "The road to the free market was opened and kept open by an enormous increase in continuous, centrally organized and controlled interventionism....*Laissez-faire* was planned; planning was not" (pp. 146–147). See also Berman (2009).

33. Ruggie (1982), 393 and passim; see also Haas and Haas (2002).

Adorno and Horkheimer, and though it would lead in a very different direction, Haas's work on this point shares certain crossovers with the "dialectic of enlightenment" problem surveyed earlier.

To make sense of these connections, one must first understand in what particular way Haas held neofunctionalism to be obsolete. Certainly, he noted, neofunctionalist theory continued to generate useful knowledge: viable research programs, new hypotheses, and innovative standards of measure. Yet that flurry of activity concealed a deeper problem. However one might theorize political unification, one did so on the basis of concepts, which were themselves historical derivations. They thus concealed time-bound assumptions, which smuggled in normative-ontological assumptions about political order. The result was that "regional integration in Western Europe ha[d] disappointed everybody."[34] It had done so because "everybody" had imposed expectations onto that process, which had issued from reified—long forgotten, but still active—assumptions buried within their conceptual schematics. The result was a field that had fallen into rather patent self-contradiction:

> Theorists persist in believing that (a) Europe will still develop into a federation, (b) the member states will end up reasserting their sovereignty, and (c) the present pattern will continue indefinitely.[35]

To be clear, Haas was not arguing that conflicting empirical predictions were in themselves symptomatic of crisis. The argument was subtler. Neofunctionalism was attempting to discern order within an enormously complicated set of ongoing processes—processes into which (as Pentland had noted) the theory *itself* was feeding back. The question was whether, in these conditions, such theory could simultaneously preserve awareness of this complexity *and* develop concepts sufficiently capacious to bring order to it.[36] As early as 1970—with his realization that the term *integration* conflated "processes" with "conditions"—Haas had begun to suspect that it could not.[37] The field's self-contradiction was a symptom of that inability. "A different conceptualization" was needed, one that did not simply recycle nineteenth-century

---

34. Haas (1975b), p. 6.

35. Haas (1975b), p. 6.

36. Haas (1975b): "Integration theories…do not and cannot capture a pervasive condition that characterizes the entire earth and the whole range of international relations because they are inspired by a sense of orderly process and by the assumption that states manage to cope collectively according to the rationality of disjointed incrementalism" (p. 17).

37. See Haas (1970), Kaiser (1972), and Rosamond (2000), pp. 85–92.

modes, institutions, and orders back onto contemporary realities as reified ideal types.[38]

Essential to that different conceptualization was the notion of *turbulence*. A turbulent field, Haas noted, was "a policy space in which…confusion dominates discussion and negotiation. It can be sub-national, national, regional, inter-regional or global—or all at the same time."[39] Not only did integration theories fail to resolve the problem of turbulence but also they actually *exacerbated* it "because [such theories] provide certainty for *parts* of the field while further confusing an understanding of the *whole*."[40] Coming to terms with such turbulent fields was "emerging as the key political task in what remains of this century."[41] The extant network of supranational and intergovernmental institutions that made up European community was "a half-way house."[42] The challenge facing integration theory was to develop concepts that could describe its workings without obscuring the ongoing political processes that were remaking it: processes into which its own actions were feeding.

By now, such complicated forms of scholarly doublethink will be familiar; they recall the difficulty facing sustainable critique. Consider Haas's turbulence as an attempt to conceptualize the inconceivable: to move past one-off acts of conceptual debunking toward a kind of ongoing self-interrogation. Writing in 1981, Haas observed (rather like Deutsch had done, in *Nerves of Government*) that thinking was both a product of the world and a constituent part of it. How one conceived of a political regime (or for that matter, any other social or political institution) was "a function of how one [thought] about learning, about the growth of human consciousness, about social evolution."[43] Therefore, "we cannot know the reality 'out there' because our notion of what it contains changes with every twist of the scientific enterprise."[44] If ideas and things are mutually constitutive at the epistemological and ontological level simultaneously, then knowledge and power are mutually constitutive.

---

38. Haas (1975b), p. 17.

39. Haas (1975b), p. 18.

40. Haas (1975b), p. 18, emphasis in original. See also Haas (1975a): "Wholes are dangerous constructs because the feeling that they aptly cover the holes in our understanding may rest on a slipshod factual base and seek to combine without clear warrant the 'is' the 'ought to be,' and the 'may become'" (pp. 839–840).

41. Haas (1975b), p. 19.

42. Haas (1975b), p. 87.

43. Haas (1982), p. 207; also Ruggie (1975).

44. Haas (1982), p. 209.

At this point, Haas's venture in sustainable critique stood at a crossroads. He could either turn toward something like an Adornian negative dialectic or try to find an alternative positive basis on which to found social theory. He chose the latter:

> it is as unnecessary as it is misleading to juxtapose as rival explanations the following: science to politics, knowledge to power or interest, consensual knowledge to common interests. We do ourselves no good by pretending that scientists have the key for giving us peace and plenty; but we do no better in holding that politicians and capitalists, in defending their immediate interests with superior power, stop creative innovation dead in its tracks.... When knowledge becomes consensual, we ought to expect politicians to use it in helping them to define their interests; we should not suppose that knowledge is opposed to interest.[45]

Some forms of power-knowledge, Haas held, were better than others. The difference lay in *consensus*: "generally accepted understandings about cause-and-effect linkages about any set of phenomena considered important by society, provided only that the finality of the accepted chain of causation is subject to continuous testing and examination through adversary procedures."[46]Adorno, Horkheimer, and Marcuse would have deeply mistrusted this; it would have appeared to them an attempt to rehabilitate the Popperian notion that falsifiability could preserve the open society from its enemies.[47] How could one speak, they would have argued, of anything like freely given consensus in a world where personal sensibilities were subject to constant and unremitting manipulation? A "one-dimensional man" might accede to this or that social measure, but was not that achieved by radically impoverishing his social, moral, and emotional horizons?

Though Haas does not specifically address early Frankfurt School social theory, his essays on the indeterminacy of knowledge reveal some awareness of the position, at least in broad terms.[48] At all events, he rejects their

---

45. Haas (1990), pp. 11–12.

46. Haas (1990), p. 21.

47. Adorno et al. (1977).

48. Haas (1970, 1975a, 1982).

pessimism. Consensus, Haas seemed certain, could prevent knowledge from becoming domination.

> I make no claim that consensual knowledge is absolutely different from political ideology; on the contrary, the line between the two is often barely visible. Some will say that consensual knowledge is merely science-derived transideological and transcultural ideology. I would contest such a claim with only a mild amendment...that political choice infused with consensual knowledge is different from, and more pervasive than, choice informed exclusively by immediate calculations of material interest or by the availability of superior power.[49]

This was hardly a "mild" amendment: moral ideals could thus be asserted to exist; knowledge could thus uncover them; the historical arc of reason and history could be saved. Truth could still be truth, even if "what eventually becomes consensual may well [have] originate[d] as someone's ideology."[50]

This was parlous ground, and Haas knew it. If consensus was achieved through a process of reflection on the past and yet one's ability to reflect on that past was mediated through one's own present-day experiences, how was one not projecting one's own worldviews backward? Would not the past simply become prologue? How would one gain the perspective to distinguish between "consensus" and conditioning? The answer lay in science. "History has no purpose"; even so, "the language of modern science is creating a transideological and transcultural signification system" that has a progressive trajectory.[51] This held good even if the form of that convergence was visible only in retrospect; did not Hegel's owl of Minerva take flight only with the setting of the sun? It held, too, even if the scientific method was itself a mode of intellectual activity with a particular intellectual-historical provenance.[52]

---

49. Haas (1990), pp. 20–1.

50. Haas (1997), Vol. 1, p. 13: "Facts can be distinguished from values, but only in retrospect. Only after truth claims associated with a given research tradition have passed an appropriate reality test."

51. Haas (1990), p. 46. Compare Haas's argument here to Weber (1949), p. 58.

52. Haas (1990), pp. 46–49. Also (1997): "The hallmark of a modern culture is its ability to test its procedures of inquiry and to change them in order to achieve better practical results. *By that test, and by that test alone, Western science—including social science—is a superior form of rationality, because it is better in predictably achieving the practical purposes shared by all cultures.* If all cultures come to recognize the incommensurability of their traditional worldviews *and* decide by incremental steps that their inherited notions of causality lack something desirable, scientific knowing will become universal despite the critique of relativists" (Vol. 2, p. 416; first emphasis added).

It is important to acknowledge that while this embrace of science would close off the path to sustainable critique, Haas was not issuing a blunt-edged call for a return to positivism. Rather, his proposed path resembled the positive dialecticism of Morgenthau, with its ties to German idealism of the liberal-nationalist school. Haas was well aware of the problem expressed in the introduction by Weber's "Science as a Vocation" and developed at greater length in the closing pages of *The Protestant Ethic and the Spirit of Capitalism*: unchastened, instrumental reason led "to the loss of affect, the death of emotional ties among people, to [Weber's] Iron Cage."[53] He was aware, too, that reflexivity could be preserved only by a continuous process of chastening. The difference between Haas's approach and sustainable critique lay in *how* that chastening was to be effected: whose work it was and how deep it needed to go.

For sustainable critique, it will be recalled, such chastening was the work of individual theorists: an ethical commitment to the *animus habitandi*. For Haas, it was the work of collectives: of social or political orders, constituted in some ways and not in others. Specifically, Haas asserted in *Nationalism, Liberalism and Progress* (1997–2000), science was rendered sustainably reflexive when it was nested in *liberal-national political orders*. Reflexivity, Haas asserted, had a particular "elective affinity" for "the practice of pluralistic democracy and of liberal nationalism."[54] The workings of liberal nationalism, Haas argued, balanced rationalization against the emotional resources of nationalism: finding spaces for those marginalized by scientific progress while promoting society's progressive, consensual "re-rationalization."[55] "Liberal nationalism, more than any other, favors reason and progress."[56] Where Adorno had despaired of conceptual knowledge and turned it against itself, Haas sought a political structure that would institutionalize reflexivity, allowing reason to remain positive. Knowledge, on this view, could remain progressive in something like absolute terms. "Was Kant right after all, if for the

---

53. Haas (1997), Vol. 2, p. 4.

54. Haas (1997), Vol. 2, p. 415.

55. Haas (1997): "Rationalization and re-rationalization are facilitated by instrumental behavior, not by commitment to fixed principles, to an all-enveloping faith not shared by everyone, or in devotion to a mortal charismatic leader, fallible institution, or murky idea. Instrumental behavior also has a closer affinity to liberalism than any of the other ideologies we shall explore" (Vol. 2, p. 4).

56. Haas (1997), Vol. 1, p. 21. And later: "I treat nationalism as a form of rationality, an effort to impose coherence on societies undergoing change. I tailor the study of nationalism to exploring a core hypothesis: that there is a particular form of nationalism—liberal nationalism—that is likely to be the most successful in integrating societies that are undergoing change" (Vol. 1, p. 24).

wrong reasons?"[57] Haas's answer was a conditional yes: properly nested, liberal nationalism *produced* moral progress. "The enlightenment wins either way."[58]

What, then, was to be made of Haas's decades-long attempt to balance individualist and communitarian theory? That Haas recognized the need for something like sustainable critique is not to be doubted. Balancing nationalism and liberalism to produce progress seems exactly just such an attempt: Haas's preference for liberal nationalism is certainly not the result of simplistic post–Cold War triumphalism.[59] Yet his notion of progress, while carefully attenuated, seems to appeal to some kind of transhistorical universal, placed somewhere in the future. From there, how would one avoid making choices, or sacrifices, in the name of that future order—perhaps even suggesting that some should be sacrificed now, in the present, in the name of a such an order, and what it would be able to produce? If Haas turned out to be wrong—if liberal nationalism could not, in fact, sustain the balance he desired—what resources for self-critique or reflexivity would exist within the concepts he had produced? How would theorists check and chasten themselves?

Middle-Range Individualism: Keohane's Disharmonious Cooperation and "Humility"

As the previous section noted, the problems that had led Haas to pronounce neofunctionalism obsolescent in the 1970s were both empirical and metaphysical in nature. The empirical question centered on spillover: whether national states were set to be subsumed by supranational integration. The metaphysical questions centered around the problem of the concept and its ability to describe open-ended processes of political and institutional change.

Both concerns fed into neoliberalism as well: Keohane and Nye's complex interdependence project in the 1970s and Keohane's later work on liberal institutionalism. "World politics is changing," they noted in an influential early formulation, "but our conceptual paradigms have not kept pace."[60] While not seeking "to prove that states are obsolete," they noted, transnational relations "are an important part of world politics, and their importance has been increasing in the years since World War II."[61] A framework was

---

57. Haas (1997), Vol. 2, p. 454.

58. Haas (1997), Vol 2, p. 454.

59. See Haas (1997), Vol. 2, pp. 420–421.

60. Keohane and Nye (1971), p. 371.

61. Keohane and Nye (1971), p. 398.

needed for analyzing state behavior that relied on neither realist nor communitarian logic, that is, neither "assumptions about the 'public interest'" nor "the General Will."[62] In this section, I first trace out how Keohane and Nye developed such frameworks and then how they attempted—by their own admission, with limited success—to deal with the reifications on which those frameworks relied.

Complex Interdependence and the Middle-Range Turn

Writing in 1971, Stanley Hoffmann had aptly characterized the theoretical needs of the moment: "today we need neither stratospheric nor fragmentary theories, nor broad theoretical surveys, but studies in which the authors concentrate on important aspects of the international system, combining empirical treatment and theoretical analysis."[63] Rather than asserting a priori what states *were*, the logic went, theory must begin from they *did*. This suggested a positivist-empirical turn of the middle-range sort, akin to Waltz's "third image" turn in realism.[64] Keohane and Nye were attempting just such an analysis.

The common ground shared by the realist and liberal wings of the "neo-neo" convergence notwithstanding, there were key differences between Waltz's neorealism and what would come to be known as neoliberalism.[65] Where neorealists had posited a single logic of anarchy and explained variation in state behaviors through the distributions of material power, neoliberals were suggesting that multiple logics might both guide and explain behavior among states and that these logics varied from issue area to issue area. "Contemporary world politics," Keohane and Nye wrote in 1977, "is not a seamless web; it is a tapestry of diverse relationships. In such a world, one model cannot explain all situations."[66] And later: "our argument... is not that the traditional view of world politics is wrong. We believe that several approaches are needed, but to different degrees in different situations."[67]

---

62. Keohane (2005) [1984], p. 107.

63. In Nye (1971), p. v.

64. Keohane (1989), pp. 7–11; also (1986), p. 165 *et seq.* and Nye (1971), ch. 1.

65. On neorealism and neoliberalism, see Keohane (1986), Baldwin (1993), and Kegley (1995). The terms *neoliberalism* and *liberal institutionalism* will be used interchangeably; see Keohane (1989), pp. 7ff.

66. Keohane and Nye (1977), p. 4.

67. Keohane and Nye (1977), p. 242.

Since the particulars of Keohane's and Nye's brand of neoliberalism are well known, a brief summary can frame the present discussion. Power, in its traditional realist-materialist configuration, was decreasingly able to explain how relations unfolded among states; "the old concept of the national interest, tied to a notion of power as reasonably calculable and stable, is being dissolved, so to speak, from above, from the side, and from below."[68] Military superpowers increasingly found themselves at loggerheads with smaller rivals or even allies, who somehow held their own; tails were increasingly wagging dogs.[69] This did not mean, Keohane and Nye argued, that power in its traditional realist conception had utterly ceased to matter in world politics or that relations among states were at bottom any more amicable than they had been before. What it did seem to suggest was that certain classes of international interactions might be less sensitive to considerations of military power than were others. In those cases, they argued, principles of foreign policy drawn from realism's copybook might require reconsideration. Chief among these was the belief that only weak states profited by committing themselves to international institutions over the long term. In certain conditions, Keohane and Nye suggested, committing to rules or institutions could be to the advantage of the powerful as well as to the weak, even if the former suffered a disproportionate loss in their future freedom of action.[70] "The pursuit of flexibility can be self-defeating" when a fetish is made of it; "like Ulysses, it may be better, on occasion, to have oneself tied to the mast."[71]

At a broadly descriptive level, complex interdependence and Keohane's later work on liberal institutionalism proposed practical theoretical approaches for identifying such conditions and defining useful programs of action for them. At a further level of refinement, it suggested a positive-progressive agenda for international theory. Perhaps it would be possible to wean the relations of states progressively away from power politics by the intelligent design of rule-based institutions: to develop a golden mean between communitarianism's unrealizable dream of global harmony and the intolerable nightmare of unchecked anarchy. "Sophisticated students of institutions and rules have a good deal to teach us," Keohane wrote in 1984, for "they view institutions not

---

68. Hoffmann (1975), p. 203.

69. Keohane (1971); see also Hoffmann (1975) and Kaiser (1971).

70. Keohane and Nye (1977): "When military force is largely immobilized, strong states will find that linkage [i.e., between distributions of power and outcomes in world politics] is less effective. They may still attempt such links, but...their success will be problematic" (p. 31).

71. Keohane (2005) [1984], p. 17.

merely as formal organizations…but more broadly as 'recognized patterns of practice around which expectations converge.'"[72] Institutions would "not *override* self interest, but rather *affect calculations* of self-interest."[73] The quote with which this chapter opened expressed the spirit of this notion: it assumed cooperation among self-interested states seeking to advance their own sectional interests, rather than altruistic understandings of common goods. Such cooperation, Keohane noted, was "somewhat tart" rather than "syrupy-sweet," guided by individual self-interest rather than communitarian altruism.

In practice, the aim was to learn to produce international institutions and regimes that might be more than merely proxies for hegemonic power. If successful at doing so—if, following Keohane, such institutions provided information, increased credibility, and/or reduced uncertainty among their contracting parties—they might have *intrinsic* value, notwithstanding the calculus of interests that might have engendered their initial formulation.

For citizens of a superpower uneasily contemplating the prospect of its decline—facing the fallout of Vietnam, economic recession, and domestic malaise—the appeal of such "tart" cooperation is not hard to appreciate. It suggested a much-needed win-win scenario. Institutions would benefit the international community by lowering the cost of political transactions. But the superpower in the winter of its dominance benefited, too; with foresight and creativity, it could look forward to a posthegemonic 'soft landing', a stable order that might outlast its loss of strategic preponderance.[74] Informed by theories of hegemonic stability, realism had held that the decline of American power would set off a deluge of global conflict and war.[75] Such analyses, Keohane argued, defined the problem but offered no solution.[76] "Realism helps us determine the strength of the trap, but does not give us much assistance in seeking to escape.… We need to respond to the questions that realism

---

72. Keohane: 2005 [1984], p. 8. Keohane is citing Young (1980).

73. Keohane (2005) [1984], p. xi; emphasis added.

74. Keohane (2005) [1984], ch. 6; (1989), ch. 5; (1986), pp. 195–197; (2002), pp. 247–250.

75. See, for example, Gilpin (1981): sine waves of order and disorder, playing out across history, with a clear bottom line for American policy makers in the 1980s. "The tendency is for the economic costs of maintaining the status quo to rise faster than the economic capacity to support the status quo" (1981), p. 11. Because of this, "disequilibrium replaces equilibrium, and the world moves toward a new round of hegemonic conflict. It has always been thus and always will be, until men either destroy themselves or learn to develop an effective mechanism of peaceful change" (1981), p. 210.

76. Keohane (1986), p. 180.

poses but fails to answer: How can order be created out of anarchy *without* superordinate power; how can peaceful change occur?"[77]

Answering those questions would guide Keohane's subsequent theoretical embraces of game theory and rational choice in the 1980s and of the "ideas" literature of the 1990s.[78] Rational choice and game theory provided the foundations for understanding how particular structures of information sharing might combine with individual value maximization to produce beneficial effects around issue areas.[79] The ideas literature explored how those structures, once created, took on procedural-cultural flesh and sinew or guided policy makers when interests were unclear or contested.

Liberal Institutionalism's Unsustainable Reflexivity

Running through this research program is a clear normative agenda, which Keohane in particular has never denied.[80] While a deeply chastened affair— Keohane was deeply influenced by Judith Shklar's "liberalism of fear"—it defined particular normative aims and sought practical theoretical innovations by which to weave them into policy. The leaders of a declining power might thereby develop the skills to bequeath a benevolent, stable future to their posterity and the world.[81]

---

77. Keohane (1986) p. 199, emphasis in original; also 2005 [1984], pp. 67–78 and 245–246; and Nye (1990).

78. See, for example, Axelrod and Keohane (1986), Keohane and Ostrom (1995), and Keohane and Goldstein (1993). For a survey, see Katzenstein, Keohane, and Krasner (1998).

79. Keohane (2005) [1984], ch. 5. Katzenstein, Keohane, and Krasner (1998): "The initial inspiration for this line of argument came from new work in economics and from the renewed attention being paid to [prisoners' dilemma] games....Robert Axelrod suggested that PD could be resolved if the payoff matrix were not skewed too much in favor of the sucker's payoff, if games were iterated frequently and indefinitely, if the costs of monitoring others' behavior and of retaliating were sufficiently low, and if actors did not discount the future at too high a rate. Institutions could, it was argued, affect the values of those parameters, for instance, by nesting particular games in durable rules, providing information about other states' activities, and furnishing standards for evaluation whether cheating was taking place" (pp. 662–3). See Axelrod (1984), Oye (1986), and the discussion in Hollis and Smith (1991), pp. 130–135.

80. Keohane (2002): "My own liberalism, while resolutely anti-utopian, nevertheless offers normative as well as positive guidance for public policy" (p. 10). See also Keohane (1988), pp. 380–381; (2005) [1984], p. 12 and passim. See also Moravcsik (2003), pp. 162–163, and (2009).

81. Shklar (1957): "The inhibitions bred by our historical experience and by analytical honesty are overpowering. Moreover, the notion of political justice implies a moral imperative—and as such an end beyond what is known to exist. Unless we admit that the very notion is senseless, it demands at least an ounce of utopianism even to consider justice, and this utopianism, as we have amply seen, is absent today. All that our lack of confidence permits is to say that *it*

At bottom, a fear of domination is very much at work here. "No liberal"—
Keohane is here citing Shklar—"ever forgets that governments are coercive."[82]
Intramural debates over the workings of liberal institutionalism often eclipse
this: Keohane's "tart" vision of politics reflects a mistrust of utopianism that is
both deeply and self-consciously normative and deeply cosmopolitan.[83] When
viewed within the context of the Cold War, moreover, it reflects as much a
concern for freedom at home as it does for threats from abroad. In the context
of a long, bipolar standoff, leaders of liberal states with faltering economies
might face a rise in domestic opposition against the costs of superpower balancing. The temptation to meet this opposition by curtailing domestic freedoms—recall Schweller's embrace of Schmitt in chapter 3—would, in that
case, rear its ugly head. By reducing those threats, one might head off such
pressures before they went critical.

Keohane and Nye have thus consistently framed their practical theory
within a larger sense of IR's normative vocation. "Academic pens," they note,
"leave marks in the minds of statesmen, with profound results for policy";
sometimes they even materialize into "inappropriate or even disastrous
national policies."[84] Because of this, Keohane would later write, certain practices of reflexivity were obligatory: there was no unmediated interaction
between the observer and reality. "The choice for practitioners is not between
being influenced by theory or examining each case 'on its merits,'" he noted
in 1986; "it is rather between being aware of the theoretical basis for one's
interpretation and action, and being unaware of it."[85]

All of this assumes, however, that the given international order—the stability and continuity of which is liberal institutionalism's chief concern—actually
is as benevolent as Keohane and Nye believe it to be. Otherwise, one is simply

---

is better to believe in it than not—and that is hardly a theory of politics in the grand tradition"
(pp. 271–272, emphasis mine). See also Müller (2008). For Shklar's influence on Keohane, see
Keohane (2002), ch. 12, and (2004).

82. Keohane (2002), p. 282.

83. Keohane (2002): "Ironically, it is the privileged who often appeal to altruism—their own,
of course—as the guarantee against the abuse of power....Anyone my age has lived through
the disastrous failures of social systems, notably in Russia and China, based on the premise that
human nature can be remolded. The reality is that the worst people thrive under the cover of
such grand visions. In any event, the heterogeneity of the world's population makes it impossible to imagine any single ideology providing the basis for a coherent, value-based system of
global governance. The answer to global governance does not lie in revelation" (p. 257).

84. Keohane and Nye (1977), pp. 4–5, here paraphrasing Keynes's *General Theory of
Employment, Interest and Money*.

85. Keohane (1986), p. 4.

using institutionalism to prolong a given oppressive order by means of a variety of co-optations and rent-sharing agreements.[86] And indeed, following the terrorist attacks of September 2001, it was precisely this question that was begged.

In response, Keohane's ethical reflections took on both greater moral urgency and a more personal cast. Liberal IR theory, he had come to understand, had naturalized the methodological individualism on which its analyses were predicated:

> The attacks of September 11 reveal that all mainstream theories of world politics are relentlessly secular with respect to motivation. They ignore the impact of religion, despite the fact that world-shaking political movements have been so often fueled by religious fervor. None of them takes very seriously the human desire to dominate or to hate—both so strong in history and in classical realist thought. Most of them tend to assume that the world is run by those whom Joseph Schumpeter called "rational and unheroic" members of the bourgeoisie.[87]

For a discipline (and a paradigm) dominated by ritual professions of pessimism—Keohane's notion of cooperation, it will be recalled, specifically rejects "syrupy-sweet" altruism—the candor expressed here is remarkable. In the opening pages of this chapter, Keohane was cited affirming both the essential unreality of individualism and rationalism in world affairs and the need to keep that unrealism present to mind. "A decent respect for human life and the findings of social science," he had noted in 1984, "requires us to acknowledge that the assumption of pure maximizing rationality is not fully realistic."[88]

In effect, Keohane was now acknowledging that he had failed to take this earlier proviso sufficiently to heart. In reifying "tart" cooperation, neoliberals had *forgotten the centrality of the will to power in IR.* Such forgetting, he well knew, would have been unthinkable for a scholar like Shklar—or for any of the other theorists (Morgenthau, Herz, Deutsch) "who [had] experienced Nazism" personally: they "understood the fear of cruelty in their bones."[89] By contrast, those favored by fortune to have been born in happier places and times had

---

86. On this point, see Keohane, Moravcsik and Macedo (2009, 2011) and Gartzke and Naoi (2011)

87. Keohane (2002), p. 272.

88. Keohane, (2005) [1984], p. 108.

89. Keohane (2002), p. 283.

reified their own basic sense of well-being; since their political will was fungible with economic interests, so, too, was everyone else's. For such theorists—those whom bitter experience had not immunized against dreams of liberal eude-monism—concrete practices of self-chastening had to be developed. Lacking this, neoliberalism had turned "syrupy-sweet" despite itself. Only an extreme outside event—the terrorist attacks of September 2001, with the apparent paradox of well-educated individuals from prosperous families choosing self-immolation—could arouse neoliberals from their reified slumber.

Like Deutsch in chapter 4, Keohane both gestures to, and then does not systematically sketch out, how such a lacuna might be filled. Humility forms the basis of this suggestion; that is to be the bitter pill that would ensure the correct level of theoretical "tartness" overall:

> Over time...one's personal failure to solve certain problems or keep up with certain technical advances does induce humility. So does the broader recognition that one's own theory—in my case institutional theory—is only a partial approach to world politics, which needs to be combined with other perspectives.[90]

The ethos of the *animus habitandi* is clearly visible here. The affects, dispo-sitions, and experiences of individual theorists play a role in how theories emerge. Since theorists cannot know in advance how this will obscure their vision, such an approach would have to be complex and far-ranging. It would also need to check the professional demands of the scholarly enterprise. "Humility is probably not a positive attribute for a young scholar: one has to believe that one's own ideas are superior to conventional wisdom in certain areas, which requires...a certain arrogance."[91]

Yet having stated the need—and having admitted the costs of past mistakes—Keohane made no attempt to meet it. This neglect is marked. Keohane is one of the field's most influential methodologists and has defined, together with Gary King and Sidney Verba, one of political science's most widely accepted standards for theoretical rigor.[92] Who better to bring humil-ity into conformity with that high standard?[93] Yet nothing like it, or even a

---

90. Keohane (2002), pp. 9–10.

91. Keohane (2002), p. 9.

92. King, Keohane, and Verba (1994).

93. For an interesting attempt to begin such a consideration, see Tickner (2009).

path to it, is marked out. "Our task is to probe the deeper sources of action in world politics, and to speak truth to power—insofar as we can discern what the truth is."[94] Well and good, but as with Deutsch, such sensibilities are only the *beginnings* of sustainable critique. They are not met by bounded acts of conceptual self-examination, however beneficial such acts may be in themselves. They need *ongoing consideration.*

Third-Way Individualism: Multiple Paradigms and the "Pirandello Problem"

From the previous two case studies and those of chapters 3 and 4, a pattern has emerged: while the balance needed for sustainable critique has been appreciated in principle, making it work has proven difficult. For Haas, recognition that concepts were reifications led him to seek to transcend their limitations through social learning. The result was to rely on reifications of a different sort: a future-oriented notion of progress, rather than a backward-facing ideology of the state. Keohane and Nye took a different tack: in seeking to define states purely in terms of empirical observables, Keohane found that there was no way to prescribe on the basis of those observables without converting them into implicit ontologies—even when the dangers of doing so were wholly apparent. Realizing this, Keohane recently proposed an ethos of humility—akin to the *animus habitandi* proposed in the opening chapters of this book—but offered no clear guidelines as to how that humility was to be translated into the study of politics.

The marriage of third debate methodologies to the individualist fact-value tradition has raised its own prospects for a sustainably reflexive balance. Individualism's affinities to rationalist and behaviorist social science, on the one hand, and the affinities of constructivism to interpretive and reflexive approaches, on the other, make for a uniquely promising beginning. Impressive steps in this direction have, moreover, recently been made. An explicitly individualist first cut was made by Legro and Moravcsik in the late 1990s. A more deeply reflexive—though for that reason, also less distinctively individualist—effort has emerged more recently under the leadership of Katzenstein and Sil: analytical eclecticism (AE).[95] Each aims to sustain a

---

94. Keohane (2008), p. 709.

95. Katzenstein and Sil, it should be noted, quite consciously distance themselves from Legro and Moravcsik, and not without reason; that said, certain natural overlaps do suggest themselves. See Katzenstein and Sil (2008), p. 118.

concert of divergent theoretical voices "less ambitious than theoretical synthesis," as Sil put it, "but more significant than a juxtaposition of different approaches."[96] A growing body of literature is now attempting to delineate the outlines of such eclecticism, with an eye to facilitating "greater scope for communication and experimentation across research communities."[97]

Multiparadigmatic approaches share a key point of connection with sustainable critique. Both affirm the complexity of political life and wish theory to keep faith with that complexity. "One can find abundant support for any plausible conjecture about the causes of European integration," Moravcsik noted in 1998. Because this was so, "only by deriving competing hypotheses from general theories, multiplying observations, and paying attention to the quality of primary sources can we transcend such indeterminacy and bias."[98] Writing with Legro, Moravcsik went on to call for a "two-step" approach, by which "monocausal mania" is replaced with "multicausal, even multiparadigmatic syntheses."[99] "Each major international relations theory paradigm enjoys a comparative advantage in explaining a different input into the bargaining game," they note.[100] Perspectives must be chosen based not on what is *true*, but what is *useful*: "by examining what [a given theory] is able to exclude."[101] For Katzenstein and Sil, analytical eclecticism "should not be confused with theoretical synthesis, or the building of unified theory."[102] It is rather "focused on a given problem and assumes the continued existence of, and growing engagement between, competing research traditions."[103] As with sustainable critique, separateness and plurality are values in themselves, preserving what T. J. Pempel calls "an overarching ambiguity" that tries to

---

96. Sil (2004), p. 323. See also Sil and Doherty (2000).

97. Sil (2004), p. 324.

98. Moravcsik (1998), p. 11; cited here from Rosamond (2000), p. 19.

99. See Legro and Moravcsik (1999), p. 50; Feaver et al. (2000); and Legro and Moravcsik (2001). The key argument is that realism as an analytical paradigm has been so overstretched as to become meaningless. Their solution: reducing realism to a set of minimalist core assumptions is the necessary first step. Following this, they extend Putnam's (1988) and Christensen's (1996) "'two-stage' or 'two-step'" logic, which "assumes, *as any rationalist (or boundedly rational) theory of state behavior must*, that in world politics...preference and belief formation can be analytically separated from the strategic logic of interstate interaction" (p. 51, emphases mine). Another two-step method is proposed by Zürn and Checkel (2005).

100. Legro and Moravcsik (1999), p. 51.

101. Legro and Moravcsik (1999), p. 53.

102. Katzenstein and Sil (2008), p. 118.

103. Katzenstein and Sil (2008), p. 118.

keep faith with a world of emergent forms, alliances, structures, and regions to which established concepts are inherently unequal.[104]

Sustainable critique shares another point of common agreement with AE in particular: an explicit commitment to the discipline as a *vocation*. Both recognize IR as serving a function, or cluster of functions, within a larger society characterized by specific divisions of social and intellectual labor.[105] Merely bandying one methodology against another misserves that function: "scholarship should be about...the disciplined analysis of empirical puzzles"; IR should aim "to focus attention on a central question, and to engage that question fruitfully—that is, to follow the road of problem-driven rather than paradigm-driven research."[106]

Yet there is reason to question whether these approaches can sustain the polyvocality in practice to which they aspire in principle. The problem lies in a shared reliance on something like the critical pragmatism surveyed in chapter 2, ignoring the fact that—as was noted in that earlier discussion—such pragmatism may not furnish the kind of "negatively dialectic" self-critique that it both promises and holds to be essential.[107] The current multiparadigmatic turn posits its own foundational reifications, its own forms of unchecked forgetting. How shall they be chastened? An appreciation of the discipline's history would help here: existing research approaches, as the previous case studies have attempted to show, did not begin as hard, all-or-nothing scholarly orthodoxies. Their failure to sustainably critique themselves was a consequence not of conscious decision, but of failing to account for processes that affect *all* social and political theory. Lacking its own account of these same processes, how shall multiparadigmatic approaches do better?

These points can be addressed to AE and to Legro and Moravcsik in turn. Regarding AE's reliance on pragmatism, the position of Katzenstein and Sil bears close examination. It relies on the notion that

> *features of analyses in theories initially embedded in separate research traditions can be separated from their respective foundations, translated*

---

104. Pempel (2005), p. 1.

105. Katzenstein and Sil (2004, 2008); Sil (2004). Also Hemmer and Katzenstein (2002), p. 599 and Katzenstein (2010).

106. Respectively, Katzenstein and Okawara (2001–02), p. 154; and Katzenstein and Sil (2008), p. 110.

107. Cochran (1999), it will be recalled, spoke of "weak foundations" as a means to avoid "non-contingent ethical claims" (pp. 16–17); similarly, Katzenstein and Sil (2008) speak of "truth"

meaningfully, and recombined as a part of an original permutation of concepts, methods, analytics and empirics.[108]

Certainly—as the discussion of Graham Allison's *Essence of Decision* in chapter 2 showed—this is the case. Theories are "analytical tools or lenses with which to theorize about world politics"; they have a life separate from their generative logics or ontologies.[109] Were this not so, there could be no theory at all. Using multiparadigmatism to remain conscious of the limits of any one lens, moreover, can certainly help a deeply contested scholarly discipline improve "the quality and scope of dialogue among social scientists and the proximity of this dialogue to socially important normative and policy issues," while avoiding "recurrent debates over metatheoretical issues that defy resolution."[110]

That said, AE's particular reliance on pragmatism and problem-solving theory raises questions of its own.[111] Should "recurrent debates over metatheoretical issues" be *avoided* in the interest of problem solving or *chastened*? It is not merely a matter of understanding how political issues may best be studied; it is also a matter of why particular issues come to be known as "problems" and how. Otherwise, one is taking one's cues from a public sphere that

---

in the sense of being useful to policy makers as distinct from things that are true in themselves (p. 115). But as we have surveyed earlier, the assumption that these distinctions can be guarded against reification merely by declarative fiat bears questioning. On AE's and Legro and Moravcsik's common reliance on pragmatism, see Friedrichs and Kratochwil (2009).

108. Katzenstein and Sil (2008), pp. 111–112, italics in original.

109. Zürn and Checkel (2005), p. 1057.

110. Katzenstein and Sil (2008), pp. 113 and 120.

111. Katzenstein and Sil (2010, pp. 6–7) rely on Larry Laudan here. The key point is that, for Laudan, a theory's problem-solving qualities are independent of whether the "problem" to which it refers is factual or counterfactual; whether, that is, it solves an *actual problem of fact* or merely an inconsistency within a socially held—but "objectively" quite mistaken—consensus discourse. "*It is irrelevant whether the theory is true or false, well or poorly confirmed,*" hence "Ptolemy's theory of epicycles solved the problem of retrograde motion of the planets, regardless of whether we accept the truth of epicyclic astronomy" (Laudan [1977], pp. 22–23 and 24, emphasis in original). In politics, of course, traditions emerge from political, social, and cultural frameworks, which can include passions, fears, interests, or presuppositions of any sort or variety or even the possibility of radical evil. Laudan specifically avoids this issue: "we take science seriously precisely because it has promoted ends which we find cognitively important. More that that, it has become progressively more successful as time goes by. If you ask, 'Successful according to whom?'... the answer, of course, is... by our lights; progressive according to our standards" (1996, p. 138). But how wide does this "our" extend? Could it include students of "scientific" race theory, for example, given the "practical" solutions that twentieth-century political leaders have developed to address the problems they helped identify? See Laudan (1977), pp 13–15, 79–80, 104–105, 189–192, and esp. ch. 7; (1996), p. 85.

produces and refines particular clusters of questions without regard to the interests that are served or elided by that sphere's composition or discursive limits. This, precisely, was the reason that Dewey's formal, experimental theory found its chastening complement in his public-intellectual works and his writings on education: works like *The Public and Its Problems* and *How We Think*. Those works aimed to foster a responsive, engaged, and empowered public, populated by citizens able to evaluate claims both normatively and in terms of their logical validity.[112] Without this, would not pragmatism's experimental methodologies risk reproducing the excesses of positivism? Might not science again take on, as it had with Comte, a quasi-theological authority akin to that of revealed religion? As Max Horkheimer noted:

> In pragmatism, pluralistic as it may represent itself to be, everything becomes mere subject matter and thus ultimately the same, an element in the chain of means and effects. "Test every concept by the question 'what sensible difference to anybody will its truth make?' and you are in the best possible position for understanding what it means and for discussing its importance." Quite apart from the problems involved in the term "anybody," it follows from this rule that the behavior of people decides the meaning of a concept.... If the world should reach a point at which it ceases to care not only about... metaphysical entities but also about murders perpetrated behind closed frontiers or simply in the dark, one would have to conclude that the concepts of such murders have no meaning... since they do not make any "sensible difference to anybody."[113]

This mirrors a point that was made with reference to Haas's work: even an ostensibly deontological notion of progress may become dangerous when the terms of the political discourse that generated it are either forgotten or universalized, for then the essentially *political* nature of that discourse is elided. In its haste to meaningfully contribute to political discourses and to foster "the accommodation of scholars" with different perspectives, AE risks turning the

---

112. Kurki (2009): "The politics of pragmatism are rarely discussed in IR, but it should not be forgotten that pragmatism is not, nor did it claim to be, an apolitical PoS position. Pragmatist philosophers, from Dewey to Rorty, have always been open about their political predilections; they are liberal pluralists" (pp. 448–449).

113. Horkheimer (2004), p. 32. The quote within the quote is from James's *Problems of Philosophy*.

public sphere into a sort of "natural kind" that produces facts, values, and problems unproblematically.[114] Certainly, Katzenstein and Sil are aware of the problem; they specifically call for a balance between critical reflection and policy relevance, between "detachment and engagement."[115] But this begs more questions than it answers: what conceptual and critical work must be done to sustain that balance? What concessions will it oblige? How *specifically* are theorists meant to go about finding it? "The pragmatist's bet that we can set aside some of these questions long enough to present interesting research" must be weighed against the potential of that research to do real and immediate harm."[116] The question reverts back to "should" arguments; no single answer can satisfy all comers.

A more serious problem plagues Legro's and Moravcsik's earlier and more explicitly rationalist variant of multiparadigmatism. Their observation that "each major international relations theory paradigm enjoys a comparative advantage in explaining a different input into the bargaining game" is true enough, but is it not curious that the authors never seem to ask *why this is so*? Is it purely a coincidence? Or is it the case that particular theoretical narratives retain family affinities to particular constructions of ideas and interests or particular configurations of political or social life? When pressed by their critics, Legro and Moravcsik resolutely resist the reflexivity that would come of recognizing such affinities. What practical theory needs, they aver, is "a clear formulation" of its various constituent paradigms (realism, liberalism, etc.): what they are and what they are not. "Wouldn't anyone see this as desirable? Shouldn't everyone care?"[117] This misses the point; what everyone should care about are events in world politics: confluences of ideologies, theories, and material realities—precisely the richness that Moravcsik's earlier research on Europe so ably recovered. Insisting on clear formulations may begin the work of thinking through those confluences in some circumstances. In others, however, it may serve to obscure them by separating particular strands of theory from the historical and normative context of their emergence.

---

114. Sil (2004), p. 326.

115. Katzenstein and Sil (2010): "We are not suggesting here that all academic scholarship be reorganized so as to cater to the existing agendas of policymakers. Indeed, as Anne Norton cautions, problem-oriented scholarship can end up enlisting scholars in the unreflective service of those exercising power. In this it often reinforces acceptance of particular worldviews and uniform modes of inquiry at the expense of critical thinking in relation to existing policy agendas and practices" (p. 13).

116. Hurd, in Katzenstein and Sil (2010), p. 182.

117. Feaver et al. (2000), pp. 192–193.

For indeed, Legro and Moravcsik's argument quickly falls prey to its own reifications. In a 2001 essay, they complained that the unilateral interventionism evinced by Bush administration neoconservatives was intellectually flawed—*"faux* realism."[118] In itself, this characterization may well have been apt. Yet that brand of realism remained politically potent: the logical perfection of a foreign policy position—whether rooted in ersatz realism or the genuine article—is a matter of concern for scholars, not practitioners. It should hardly be a surprise that policy makers work instrumentally, *and indeed, eclectically*: divorcing theory from its generative ontological-normative framework and applying it in pragmatic fashion to advance values and agendas of their own. What Legro and Moravcsik might have said was that the faux realists were espousing the *wrong values*. True or false, that remains at bottom a *normative* question, not a scientific one.

The comparison between Legro and Moravcsik's multiparadigmatism and Katzenstein and Sil's AE demonstrates how very close the latter is to the sustainably reflexive ethos of the *animus habitandi*. Yet something more remains if AE is to make good on those aims. If, as AE seems to suggest, IR has a larger "problem-solving" vocation, there can be no truly "agnostic epistemological stance in which empirical puzzles drive the analysis within a broader perspective that is not committed a priori to the primacy of either agency or structure, materialism or idealism."[119] One can *play at such a position*, holding that in doing so, useful things will be learned. But then one is obliged to take on an equal burden in the direction of reflexivity: accentuating its conditional, as-if nature, reminding oneself that one is play acting. In all cases, the things theorists write and say are not separate from the world; *they are political ideas with agency in it*. Such new worlds as emerge—each with its own dissatisfactions, tensions, centers of hegemony, and nodes of resistance—will be reflections of the agency of those ideas, and their creators, in creative-destructive interaction with the world.[120] This is why, following Sil's earlier work, the "flexible rhetorics" and "cantilevered bridges" of so many attempts at theoretical synthesis

---

118. Legro and Moravcsik (2001).

119. Katzenstein and Okawara (2001–02), p.184.

120. Hence, for example, Checkel and Katzenstein's (2009) observation that European identity is politicized, that "there is no European one identity, just as there is no one Europe." Even for the privileged, "social barriers and identity issues…crop up as the 'Eurostars' must choose whom to marry, where to settle, how to raise their children, and when and where to start laying the foundations for their eventual retirement" (respectively, pp. 213 and 18). It appears that not all identities are fungible and that economic privilege is not a universal solvent even for those who have it to spare.

often produce such meager results. The "original foundational assumptions identified as research traditions" are so seldom "significantly relaxed" because they reflect reified normative-ontological commitments: commitments that are *felt and active*, even if they are not always consciously asserted.[121] Left unchecked, they will continue to produce the kind of myopia that can be so dangerous for students of IR. Shedding those commitments may require more than an act of will, however earnest.

If AE is to keep faith with its vocation, then, its promulgators must be willing to disclose *political* values, as well as its analytical ones, in light of the dialectic of enlightenment problem with which this book opened. The Pirandello problem must be addressed: the multiple paradigms of analytical eclecticism must find, and critique, the ethos they collectively represent. This is not merely a question of the tools one uses; it speaks to the world one hopes to build with them and the limitations of all such tools in light of such daunting tasks. Once upon a time, were not *all* research paradigms eclectic alignments of multiple, disjointed theories? Was not, that is, every theoretical innovation once the work of "scholars who consciously, selectively frame[d] their problems in new ways...because of a suspicion that existing modes of posing and addressing problems...[were] obscuring connections and complexities that need[ed] to be revealed"?[122] What became of such eclecticism, and how— without a clear statement of mission—shall these theorists avoid the fate of their predecessors?

In their 2008 essay, Katzenstein and Sil cite a contemporary critic complaining that "the standard IR article consists of pushing a huge rock of theory up a steep hill, in order to...smash a few pebbles of fact at the bottom."[123] The image is apt, but the argument is not new: Edward S. Corwin made it in 1929. In discussing the theoretical output of what was then called "the new political science," Corwin derided an immense theoretical "apparatus" that, while impressive in scale, seemed disappointing in its ability to generate insights.[124]

---

121. Sil (2000b), p. 372.

122. Sil (2004), p. 326.

123. Katzenstein and Sil (2008), p. 110.

124. Corwin (1929): "It would be quite impossible to exaggerate the impression left by the studies of this nature which the writer has seen, as to the competence of their authors; but as to the results obtained, the expression of enthusiasm may reasonably be more restrained. There was always an immense unlimbering of apparatus, an immense polishing of a technique already spotless; but it was all apparently for the sake of the game itself. The problems set were of no great evident moment, and the solutions provided either were inconclusive or merely substantiated what must have been the off-hand verdict of any rather intelligent and well-read observer" (pp. 588–589). See Somit and Tanenhaus (1967).

Methods, for Corwin, were "telic": they created knowledge useful in the service of an end and made sense only in light of those ends.[125] The field has since come full circle (perhaps more than once!), but the point has not changed. If AE is to move beyond restating the problem that Corwin first identified, it must marry its *methods* to an explicitly stated *ethos*. This means "thinking reification thoroughly."

That said, AE contains potentialities that elude sustainable critique. International Relations theory does not unfold in conditions of otherworldly repose. Theorists animated by the desire to be relevant to events as they unfold must be willing to suffer some sacrifice of philosophical precision. Analytical eclecticism can do this in a way that sustainable critique—with its explicit intention of *slowing down thinking*—cannot. The former's willingness to stake claims stands as a warning to the latter, lest sustainable critique *itself* devolve into scholasticism. It is not a simple question of right or wrong: each approach benefits from the other. To abandon practical reason in the face of real, apparent suffering owing to the absence of "a definitive consensus on methodological procedures or axiomatic principles" would be no less dangerous, no less irresponsible, than to dismiss the obligation of reflexivity on the basis that without reification "no thinking would be possible."[126] It is the space *between* those false dichotomies in which the vocation of IR theory remains possible.

Perhaps, then, a clear-eyed discussion of scholarly vocation is needed here. As the opening of this book asked, what is IR *for*? From what political moment is it coming and entering into? When does it serve policy makers, and when a cosmopolitan *sensus communis*? In contrast to earlier eras, modern-day governments and institutions possess substantial facilities for the creation of policy alternatives in-house; the world of international public policy has grown, benefiting in large part from the methodological innovations of academe. Do not, then, sufficient faculties for theoretically informed *action*—whether out of venality or generosity, whether out of interest or altruism—exist already? Is *clarity* more desperately needed from the academy, or *nuance*? For sustainable critique, the answer seems to be the latter. If so, then the passion for political action that is shared both by academics and by policy makers must be chastened. Action is policy makers' work. Chastening is ours. This is not to suggest

---

125. Corwin (1929): "The real destiny of political science is...criticism and education regarding the true ends of the state and how best they may be achieved" (p. 592).

126. Katzenstein and Sil (2008), p. 113.

that there cannot be contributions across the divide or that chastening is not its own form of action. It is only to suggest that our approaches come from different places within the larger orders in which we are all embedded. Here, AE and sustainable critique agree: *if academics give themselves over to the passion-induced blindness of politicians and activists, who shall do our work?*

6

Conclusion

TOWARD SUSTAINABLY CRITICAL INTERNATIONAL THEORY

Each century brought its portion of light and shadow, apathy and combat, truth and error, and its cortège of systems, new ideas, new illusions.... My gaze, bored and distracted, finally saw the present century arrive, and behind it the future ones. It came along agile, dexterous, vibrant, self-confident, a little diffuse, bold, knowledge-able, but in the end as miserable as the ones before, and so it passed.

—MACHADO DE ASSIS[1]

THE ARGUMENTS MADE in the foregoing chapters are more easily summa-rized than translated into a series of operational recommendations for future research. Both, however, are warranted. By way of summary, the key claim of the foregoing has been that the vocation of postwar International Relations (IR) needs some stable, sustainable practice of critique: a systematic way of reflecting both on the obligations and possibilities of thought and—no less importantly—on its limitations. Such practices are more easily described in the abstract than spelled out methodologically or integrated into existing approaches within IR. They require delicate, balanced calibration: broad enough to check the dangers stemming from practical theory's reliance on reification, yet not so broad as to destroy any possibility for such theory to meaningfully address real-world problems and concerns. Persistently diverse, fiercely contested, and increasingly interconnected, the late-modern world demands active stewardship and reflective administration. Given the dialectic of enlightenment problem set out in chapter 1, this means that theory's criti-cal and practical moments must be sustained at the same time.

---

1. Assis (1997), p. 20.

Sustainable critique is the name I have given to this difficult practice. In the opening chapters, both the nature of sustainable critique and the need for it were described in essentially philosophical terms; for this, I drew on the social theory of the postwar Frankfurt School. In later chapters, I explored the effects of its absence by means of case studies. Key theorists and paradigms within IR were surveyed, with an eye to both the various notions of reification at work within them and the means they proposed—or refrained from proposing—to meet their potential dangers. Though expressed in a variety of idioms and pursued with varying degrees of systematicity, a general awareness of reification was for all of these theorists an ongoing concern. Some, like Morgenthau and Deutsch, developed sophisticated understandings but left their methods underspecified. Others, like Wendt, and Katzenstein and Sil, developed innovative methodologies but placed them on restricted conceptual foundations, such that they were truncated in their reach.

Given the results of this survey, it bears asking: notwithstanding my claim for the need for sustainable critique, is it even *possible*? This question takes on particular urgency, given that I have chosen to rely on notions of reflexivity drawn from the unrelievedly negative work of Theodor Adorno. As earlier chapters have noted, social scientists and theorists from Jürgen Habermas and Seyla Benhabib to Ira Katznelson and Ken Booth have claimed that Adorno's work led to a scholarly-theoretical impasse. His war on conceptual theory, these scholars held, went too far; it scorched the ground of social science too completely.

It would be a mistake to dismiss this argument out of hand. Yet the coming pages aim to show that it is overblown. Certainly, the practice of sustainable critique erects distinct, enduring barriers to conceptual thinking. It does this *by design*. I have argued that, in an era of genocide and nuclear weapons, IR's reliance on reification is too dangerous to be to left to "the slow boring of hard wood": traditional scholarly processes of peer review and debate. Given the historical context in which they are working, theorists of world politics face particular, immediate, and highly demanding ethical obligations that must be met in real and immediate time. What I have called *slowing down thought* is meant to meet that obligation: the admittedly difficult form of theoretical doublethink that runs through sustainable critique. Rather than a unity of (social) science, sustainable critique has aimed to preserve what anthropologist Nadia Abu el-Haj has called *disunity* in the face of reason's tendency to elide the complexity and indeterminacy of social and political kinds.[2] I believe

---

2. Abu El-Haj (2001), pp. 277–278.

this sensibility can be translated into scholarly methods, and the following pages outline one possible attempt at doing so. Like the analytical eclecticism (AE) surveyed in chapter 5, it is multiparadigmatic. Unlike that approach, however, its parameters for paradigm selection are explicitly tied back to the ethos of the *animus habitandi*, as set out in chapter 1.

Whether that set of practices can strike the necessary balance between useful explanation and disruption—between positive theorizing and negative critique—remains open. The form of chastened reason proposed here could itself fall lure to some new, reductive synthesis. Or perhaps it will prove insufficient to address the challenges that face world politics in the coming decades. Yet even if either of these proves to be the case, the attempt would still be a fruitful one. It would reinforce the notion that there can be no redeeming IR—whether realist or idealist, scientific or sociological, positivist or postpositivist, emancipatory or postemancipatory—from the immediate claims of ideology and interest. What this would mean both for the academy and for the role of the public intellectual is a topic that exceeds the present discussion; but it would be profound.

One could characterize sustainable critique as a rearguard intellectual action. If all thinking is predicated upon reification, this would necessarily include critique itself: its own tendency toward exclusionary counterorthodoxies and ideologies. Viewing recent decades as a period of sustained political and philosophical crisis, the practices of sustainable critique called for here try to salvage those ideals that have historically animated IR, even as it fragments the conceptual tools most often used to realize them.

Chastened reason, admittedly, promises rather less than what drives most curious minds to develop new methods. It offers to do nothing better in any simple and practical sense, save to *chasten itself*. It aims to provide the theorist with tools that, when tied to practical theorizing, might help realize the vocation to which the discipline has historically aspired. Theorists might yet choose to disavow this vocation. Or they might choose to continue to conduct research in the same manner they always have— hoping against hope that ethicists within the academy and the norms of public and political discourse outside of it take up the gauntlet of moderating its potential to reification and ideological appropriation. *But for those who wish to take direct responsibility for the things they write and say, it may be the best that can be done: at least until such time as concepts and theories, subjects and objects, agents and structures no longer form the building blocks of systematic thinking or else the identity-difference divide is wholly excised from world politics.*

Central to this rearguard action has been accepting the ineluctability of reification. Sustainably critical IR is novel insofar as it strives to *manage* reification in an ongoing manner, not to undo it in one-off acts of critical debunking. It is for this reason that such effort has been devoted to defining reification and tracking awareness of it across IR. Since it is the engine by which ideas congeal into social and material facts, the attempt to think through it seemed necessary.

That work done, it may now be evident that effecting its management requires both a kind of normative advocacy and a form of rhetorical backhandedness. If all thinking relies on reification, and if one-off acts of conceptual debunking merely replace old reifications with new ones, then its management means aiming particular, carefully chosen, fact-value positions to either knock out others or to hold them multiply, such that no single one hardens into a new repressive orthodoxy. Such a move, in turn, requires the theorist to see the discipline's existing stable of research paradigms as rhetorical forms. When taken up by sustainable critique, IR paradigms have a dual value: they both tell stories in their own terms and counterbalance other stories, such that no single one can ever encompass the whole of a given event. In practice, this means cultivating a hermeneutic or curatorial (in the sense of a museum or exhibition curator) disposition that takes up a variety of affects as it weaves together stories of world politics: at turns dissident and credulous. This is the doublethink to which the introduction alluded; deeply chastened both by the need for theory and by its inadequacy, one must believe in it and yet not believe in it, at turns.

In the remainder of this conclusion, I try to sketch out—with some trepidation—concrete practices of sustainable critique, with an eye to integrating them into existing disciplinary methodologies and research practices. This will be done in three steps. First, the arguments of the opening chapters will be reprised and restated in terms that are intended to allow their theoretical operationalization and use. Second, that use will be illustrated in practical terms, by outlining a sustainably critical research project for future development. The Adorno- and Weber-inspired constellar logic of chapter 2 will be expanded and mapped out onto an enduring conflict: the "hundred years' war" over Israel and Palestine.[3] In the closing section, I will illustrate why such an approach is necessary by showing how existing modes of *both* practical reason and critique are unsustainable in light of the political crisis facing contemporary Middle Eastern politics. That is, I will try to show how they each

---

3. Gelvin (2005).

present unacceptable dangers and why sustainable critique, though difficult, is needed.

The "Hermeneutic Sphere": Toward a Sustainably Critical Research Program

Up to now, this study has focused primarily on what has been *missing* from IR research: the absence of sustainably critical practices in existing paradigms, despite intuitions about the danger of unchecked reification among their leading promulgators. The argument must now proceed from the opposite tack: sustainable critique must be fashioned into a workable research program. In that vein, the opening chapters of this work specified four interlocking elements held to be central to it: the critique of the concept, a historical understanding of the impasse of late modernity, a commitment to the ethical position of the *animus habitandi*, and the use of a negative dialectical turn. Each of these can be briefly summarized (see also table 6.1); following that, they can be set out in methodological terms:

Critique of the Concept. Sustainable critique recognizes the dangerous utility of concepts.[4] On the one hand, concepts allow theorists to sunder particular phenomena from the undifferentiated continuum of a real world in which there are no distinct causes or effects, in which—as Kenneth Waltz observed—"everything is related to everything else."[5] On the other hand, this sundering has a distinctly misleading effect: it makes "unlike things alike," "subsum[ing] the particular under the general, forc[ing] subjective and idiosyncratic identities into one unitary system of thought, one universal point of reference, one truth that silences all others."[6] Concepts thus tend to become conflated with the real-world things they originally aimed to describe. They become means rather than ends in themselves; reason tends toward instrumental domination. Moreover, the better concepts are in abstract analytical terms—the more useful they are and the more faithfully they mirror the things they intend to describe, the harder it becomes to guard against this deadly conflation. Following Adorno, this tendency to conflate concepts with things-in-themselves is known as *identitarian* or *identity thinking*.

---

4. This apt phrase—"the dangerous utility of concepts"—I take from Jane Bennett.

5. Waltz (1979), p. 8.

6. Respectively, Rose (1994), p. 157; Bleiker (2000), p. 140.

Table 6.1 Four Elements of Sustainable Critique

1. Critique of the Concept
2. Historical Analysis of Late Modernity
3. The *Animus Habitandi*
4. Negative Dialectics

Historical Analysis of Late Modernity. Sustainable critique acknowledges a complex dilemma facing conceptual thinking "after Auschwitz and Hiroshima." There have always been identitarian tendencies in thinking, but in the late-modern era, that process of instrumentalization and its potential for domination have taken on potentially world-destroying dimensions. Yet if conceptual reason poses one set of distinct dangers, eschewing such reason poses others no less grave. Despite their mutual exclusivity, then, neither the claim to abandon conceptual thinking nor to embrace it can be ignored. Hence the need for a new, sustainable entente between positive theory building and critique, if the vocation of IR is to be made good on.

The Animus Habitandi. However clear the connection between conceptual theory and the extreme violence of late-modern politics may be in principle, their actual interconnections in practice are diffuse and stochastic. In the face of immediate suffering or fear, human beings will, and should, seek to act in practical ways to ameliorate that suffering. Yet theorists can strive to do so from a perspective that avoids moral generalization or the application of first principles: they can *chasten their theory and the truth claims that issue from them.* This begins with the assumption of theory's inadequacy: that the full totality of the real world can *never* be captured by *any* combination of perspectives, ideas, or interconnections, no matter how thick.[7] An ethical position issues from this, which—in homage to Hans Morgenthau—I have called the *animus habitandi:* a will to abide, dwell within, and be chastened by a complex, diverse, and deeply interconnected world that escapes full comprehension. This is an a priori ethical commitment as much intuitive as intellectual. Believing that the world is more complex than theories and concepts make it appear—that, as Adorno put it, concepts and things-in-themselves are necessarily *non-identical*—one first resolves to study that world in ways that preserve and honor that complexity.

A Negative Dialectical Hermeneutic. The negative dialectical hermeneutic—the constellar approach described briefly in chapter 2—was

---

7. King, Keohane, and Verba (1994), p. 43.

proposed as a possible means by which that commitment might be translated into research. Applied to sustainable critique, the term *constellation* describes arranging multiple perspectives around a particular event or cluster of events in world politics for the specific purpose of managing reification. It uses the various paradigms of IR *instrumentally* to construct polyvocal, highly pluralist, and mutually balancing narratives that chasten one another.

Neither sustainable critique nor the constellar approach that follows from it qualifies as a theory of international politics in the traditional sense. Rather, sustainable critique is a practice, tied to a philosophical-normative sensibility: less "a theory *of* something" than "a way of theorizing about something."[8] Put more concretely, it is a way of redacting theoretical narratives in light of (1) the discipline's historic vocation, (2) the conceptual critique outlined here, and (3) the essentially contingent nature of politics. It aims to produce a change of scholarly affect: chastening both the theorist and the consumer of theory by balancing hope against despair, faith against skepticism.

With this in mind, the 'rogues' gallery' of reification set out in the introduction bears remembering. While a shared dynamic of reification united all the paradigms surveyed, there were contingencies that emerged from each, owing to the particular fact-value tradition from which they drew, the methods they employed, and the historical moment in which they emerged. Was human nature tragic in its asocial sociability, as many realists held? If so, how was that tragedy dealt with? For Morgenthau, it drove a progressive historical dialectic; for Waltz, it was absorbed into the third image, only to reappear incognito at key moments; for Wendt, it was to be dissolved through an emergent culture of global dialogue.

For communitarians and individualists, no assumption of tragedy was made. Yet, for communitarians, conceptual theory still had to find a way to conform to a reality that was stubbornly incompatible with it. Initially, this led David Mitrany to a denunciation of dogmatism in favor of an intuitive approach ultimately no less dogmatic. For Karl Deutsch and Emanuel Adler, it implied retooling the relationship between agents and structures, through concepts that would blur or remove their oppositional character. Deutsch deployed Norbert Wiener's cybernetic model to this end: Adler, structurationist, and third debate language theory. Yet despite differences in methods, the efforts themselves were essentially parallel in aim.

---

8. Olson and Groom (1991), p. 303.

For individualists, the assumption of individualism *itself* had to be reconciled to a political reality in which collectives remained a persistent feature and in which the administration of society complicated models based on unitary rational action. For Haas, scientific rationalization created certain opportunities and certain negative externalities, common to many societies across the globe. Since this was so, particular social and political structures could be developed to balance the former against the latter: nationalism and liberalism could be sustained in dynamic balance, with progress the result. For Keohane, this tension obliged a preanalytical ethical commitment to humility: his own understanding of the *animus habitandi*, however methodologically underspecified. Katzenstein and Sil, developing a pragmatically rooted analytical eclecticism, attempted to flesh out just such a kind of humility, though some doubt existed as to whether the problem-solving basis on which it rested could alone provide sufficient ethical-critical force to sustain it.

Although each of these paradigms was understood to have incorporated a commitment to some kind of ethical reflexivity or another, it was also argued that in no case was that reflexivity sufficient to the full challenge posed by unchecked reification. In emphasizing this, my aim was not to hold any particular approach up to ridicule: *all* theory involves reification, and as such no one is a priori worse or more dangerous than any other. Rather, I wished to illustrate the as-yet unmet need for sustainable critique. This was why, it was held, the Adornian-Weberian notion of negative dialectics involved deploying paradigms multiply, in constellations. Once it is accepted that all theories rely on reification, and once one learns to typologize those reifications, one discovers the power to redact one's theoretical understandings in light of that knowledge. One can select particular paradigms based on the reifications they suborn and set them against one another. Doing that might meet something like the notion of sustainable critique to which Weber and Adorno had alluded. In the process, moreover, it might produce the kind of change of affect previously called for. *When both theorists and consumers of theory are brought face-to-face with the reality that all theories produce undeniable claims of reason, while simultaneously doing violence to the real world they aim to disclose, their understanding of how knowledge works in politics would—it is to be hoped—be substantially, materially, and deeply altered.* It would, in a word, be *chastened.* This is the hope—however cautious and partial—that the practice of a negative dialectic opens up.

As a first-cut heuristic exercise, chapter 2 used Graham Allison's *Essence of Decision* to illustrate how such a chastening might be effected (figure 6.1). Allison, it will be recalled, did not choose his three analytical lenses—the

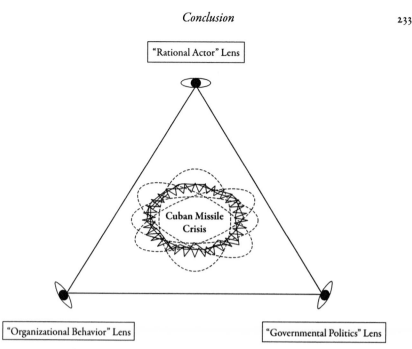

FIGURE 6.1 Allison's "Three Lens" Approach, Rendered as a Constellation *(Adapted from Allison: 1971)*

rational actor, organizational behavior, and governmental politics models—at random. Each drew on an existing paradigm, fashioning from it a complement, and a check, to the others. Americans lived in a world that teetered on the precipice of nuclear war, yet for Allison an inexplicable can-do optimism—faith in reason and interest—persisted among students of world politics and decision makers. That optimism, Allison suggested, was dangerous; it could lead to carelessness and thus needed chastening. His constellation of paradigms was the means to producing this chastening, his way of driving home "an unhappy, troubling, but unavoidable fact about this world," knowledge of which he believed to be essential to survival in the shadow of thermonuclear war.[9]

That chastening aim explains why Allison's narrative was so rich in ostensibly idiosyncratic details; one after another the various bureaucratic snafus, lazy oversights, and political foibles that marked the handling of the crisis were brought out and discussed.[10] Though certainly interesting in themselves, their value was not primarily anecdotal. They helped Allison illustrate his central

9. Allison (1971), p. vii.

10. See, for example, Allison (1971), pp. 127–132, 110–113, and 193–200.

point: although the dangers of the nuclear era might have far exceeded anything hitherto known, the limits of knowledge and the essentially contingent nature of politics remained basically unchanged. Kennedy's now well-known comment that the "essence of ultimate decision" remained impenetrable even "to the decider himself" recalls—albeit in a limited fashion—Adorno's nonidentity, learned from bitter experience.[11] Allison wished the reader to internalize that lesson, to emerge from it with a changed policy sensibility. It is not an easy lesson to internalize. Many deciders (and theorists) continue to resist it.

Even so, that lesson does not—as the closing pages of chapter 2 noted—go far enough for sustainable critique. While a useful illustration of a constellar sensibility, it remains only that. The difference lies in the notions of crisis at work in each. In *Essence of Decision*, the crisis in question was a bounded event; as if to dispel any doubt, the book's frontispiece featured a calendar with specific days—October 16–28, 1962—marked out in heavy type. For sustainable critique, by contrast, crisis is the condition of late-modern life *itself*. Its constellation must therefore be both wider and messier—able to accommodate a problem set in which the constitutive elements are themselves subject to debate and contestation. One's various lenses would need to be ground and set somewhat differently. Figure 6.2 suggests a notion of what such a constellation would look like, loosed from its Allisonian restraints.

In the coming section, the Israeli-Palestinian conflict is used to demonstrate how such a constellation might be constructed. It is a long-running conflict, with a history closely tied to the key flash points of late modernity: nationalism, genocide and ethnic cleansing, totalitarianism, and colonialism. In more immediate contexts, it touches on all of contemporary IR's hot buttons: resource and alliance politics; balancing and bandwagoning; the social construction of identity, culture, and politics; religion and secularism; terrorism and civilizational "clash"; nuclear proliferation; development, human security, and democratization; economic globalization as a vector for neocolonial forms of indirect rule; and so on. At the same time, it remains a conflict with a particular territorial and historical center of gravity. The thinking space of practical theory—the dispassionate, specialized work of seeking modalities by which a small, densely populated strip of territory might be shared by deeply divergent cultures—has important work to do here, which the obligation to reflexivity cannot be allowed to overshadow. It both counters the moral absolutism that is so much a part of how that conflict is sustained

---

11. Sorensen (1963), p. xi.

Note that events are not clearly marked off: they cluster together and obscure one another. The
perspectives are also differently located, as are the links among them. In some places there are gaps, in
others whole problem-sets are ignored by all perspectives, and in still others perspectives stand alone.
Finally, there is no dichotomy between observer and observed: subjects and objects, agents and
structures are all part of a single mass.

FIGURE 6.2 Real-World Constellations: A More Complex View

and combats the cynicism that often follows from claims of its intractability.[12]
To abandon such reason would thus be irresponsible. Even so, the essentially
contested nature of the conflict breeds distrust of it, for the complexity of the
conflict has been, and is, used in an equally tendentious fashion: as a kind of
"scholars' cant" by which to conceal or encode partisan positions. From here,
the temptation to withdraw back into moral simplicities suggests itself, but
this leads one back to precisely the impasse from which one started.

The challenge such a conflict poses to theory—even constellar theory—is
thus great. The conceptual common ground that binds the elements of Allison's
study together—the assumed historical framework, agreement on key figures
and moments—is absent here. No neutral narrative of key events, concepts, or
first principles can be admitted, for there is no consensus on them among the

12. See, for example, Miller (2010). The author, a staple figure in 1990s-era U.S. Middle East
diplomacy, has come to the conclusion that faith in Middle East peace is a "false religion." It
is not merely that such a conclusion dooms millions of people to war without end; it is that
Miller arrives at it by conflating a particular set of interests, priorities, and initiatives—what
Shlaim (1994) called the *Pax Americana*—with peace *as such*. Since the former failed, the latter
must be impossible. But it is not so, or at any rate one does not follow automatically from the
other. Demonstrating the space between them is *precisely* the work of sustainable critique.

actors themselves. Hence, one cannot easily assume a defined position outside of the conflict. Two other factors complicate this problem of perspective: first, this is not a bounded historical moment that has passed, but an ongoing set of processes creating new effects both locally and globally. Second, the Middle East conflict rests, for some, on transcendental (and indeed, chiliastic) foundations that undermine secular and synchronic notions of time, cause, and effect: divine intervention is explicitly appropriated by the various parties as a strategic resource. For all these reasons, there is no (small- or large-p) pragmatic basis available here that is not in some way exclusionary at the moment of its adoption. The event is essentially contested.[13]

Even so, a theoretical discussion must begin somewhere. Particular concepts, frameworks, and terms of reference are the means to delimit that "somewhere," even if they also introduce all the problems of reification discussed hitherto at length. For reflexivity to be sustainable, the artificiality of that somewhere must be kept present to mind. This, precisely, is where constellations composed of various different IR paradigms—think of the various viewpoints (represented as eyes) that dot figure 6.2—would come in. Each offers its own somewhere, its own internal logic for parsing out events and timelines. Each, when offered with others, also demonstrates that no single one is exclusive in its hold over the whole.

Sympathetic Knowledge

This usage changes the work that these paradigms do. They do more than "limit…the domain of analysis, identify…research puzzles, interpret…empirical observations, and specify…relevant causal mechanisms."[14] Each is a unique configuration of facts, values, and methods, reflecting particular normative agendas and sets of concerns. Understanding each paradigm thus—in terms of its reifications—means that the reality it discloses to the theorist becomes a subjective one: a view of how the world looks through the eyes of those who subscribe to those agendas and share those concerns. Each creates the condition of possibility for sympathetic understanding on the part of the theorist. Studying the world through paradigms, one reconstructs the worldviews that compose political discourse: one hears new voices, without having to discard one's own. Choosing as many paradigms "off the rack" as one can both allows the scholar to benefit from and speak to existing scholarship and reveals how particular

---

13. Connolly (1983); Gallie (1955–56).

14. Katzenstein and Sil (2010), p. 8.

clusters of perspective and interest translate across cultures, spaces, and times. Redacting them together gives a sense of how political discourse combines them, while also placing the reifications that each suborns in sharp relief.

Some will object at this point that sustainable critique merely moves reification to another moment of thought. Would not the redaction process itself—the act of choosing which paradigms are in or out, of "curating" one's multiparadigmatic 'exhibition'—become its own locus for unchecked reification? Here, the negative nature of this dialectic must be stressed. Understood in the context of the *animus habitandi*, the constellation gestures not to its *contents*, but to its *absences*: to the reality that is always larger than the narratives on display. While this awareness does not entirely undo the effects of exclusion, it does mitigate them substantially.

To make sense of this, some attention must be given to the particular kind of hermeneutics that negative dialectics enacts. Martin Hollis and Steve Smith's widely read *Explanation and Understanding in International Relations* can help. The pendulum swings of IR theory are there understood in terms of a hermeneutic circle.[15] "In all discussions of social life," they explain, "there are *always* and *inevitably* two stories to be told, one concentrating on Understanding, the other focusing on Explaining."[16] Each, they note, divides up the world in different ways and produces different kinds of knowledge. Yet each also has its own pitfalls and excesses. Against the links connecting explanatory logic and practical reason to oppression and domination, understanding has links to relativism and scholasticism.[17] Each compensates for the excesses of the other. As Dvora Yanow explains:

> Initial interpretation starts at whatever point is available or accessible, with whatever one's understanding is at that point in time. One makes a provisional interpretation of the text (or other focus of analysis) with the reflexive awareness that one's interpretation is likely to be incomplete and even possibly erroneous. One then engages the material in further study, at which point one revises one's initial, provisional interpretation. Additional analysis yields further revised interpretation; and so on.[18]

---

15. Hollis and Smith (1991), esp. ch. 9; also Yanow and Schwartz-Shea (2006), pp. 15–17.

16. Hollis and Smith (1991), p. 211; emphases and capitalization in original.

17. Hollis (1994): "All interpretations become defensible, but at the price that none is more justifiable than the rest. If this is indeed the upshot, the circle turns vicious and the hermeneutic imperative to understand from within leads to disaster" (p. 241).

18. Yanow and Schwartz-Shea: 2006, p. 16; also Olson and Groom (1991) and Holsti (1985).

Yanow's alternating process may explain why, when viewed across decades, the weight of theoretical fashion seems to swing between explanation and understanding: the pair form the limit parameters of a social science discourse that oscillates between them.[19] The progress of theory is, on this account, mapped through successive pendulum swings: layerings of deduction and induction, explanation and understanding, *verstand* and *verstehen*—and innovation and forgetting. Each creates its own kind of textual basis for the next layer: "further layers of understanding are added as each new insight revises prior interpretations in an ever-circular process of making meaning."[20]

If these theorists are correct, it means that the 'churn' of the hermeneutic circle is a continuously present third factor, driven in part by the shape of theories and in part by the way they map onto one another and reality. The churn *itself*, then, has a knowable history and trajectory, which helps produce the discipline's periodic moments of critical self-examination. The great debates of IR, on this account, constitute those latter moments.

If so, then tracking those moments, and the patterns that give rise to them, would become important. The very existence of such a churn implies that ideas have an internal coherence of their own; they can be alienated from the theorist, whose ability to discern this is determined, in part, by the particular admixture of explanation and understanding she employs. Theorists are in history, not above it.[21] If this is a cyclical process that repeats across time, then the potential for reflexivity is in some sense historically contingent, rather than wholly immanent to knowledge itself: a consequence of the particular historical-theoretical moment in which a theorist comes of age, quite apart from the content of those particular real-world problems that may motivate her work. "In the cultural [i.e., social] sciences especially," wrote Karl Mannheim in 1925, "we are convinced that not every question can be posed—let alone solved—in every historical situation." An "agitated wavelike rhythm" existed within intellectual currents, in part determining what was thinkable and knowable in particular social, cultural, and intellectual contexts.[22] Once realized, the theorist would presumably want to keep tabs on

---

19. Guilhot (2008).

20. Yanow and Schwartz-Shea (2006), p. 16.

21. Curtis and Koivisto (2010), Hamati-Ataya (2011b), Eagleton-Pierce (2011).

22. Mannheim (1952) [1925], p. 135. That said, Mannheim may have been rather more sanguine about the possibility of achieving through constellations "a synoptical orientation" (p. 136) of the entire field of social knowledge than is intended here. Thought for Mannheim had to transcend itself and relativize itself, though the degree to which his sociology of knowledge actually achieved this was fiercely debated. See Adorno (1983), pp. 35–50; Jay (1994); and Kettler and

it, on her place within that circle, and on ideas that might emerge, or fail to emerge, owing to such contingencies. Learning to track this rhythm would be a form of theoretical progress, too, though in a manner somewhat different than Mannheim conceived: in the *negative dialectical* form alluded to in the previous pages. Progress is attained *not when the space between concepts and things-in-themselves gets smaller in absolute terms* but rather *when awareness of that space—of non-identity—is better marked off*. That awareness is the space of sustainable critique: it is what protects such theory from the dangers of identitarian thinking.

In short, then, Hollis and Smith's hermeneutic circle creates the need for a third, reflexive axis. The *circle* would have to become a *sphere*.[23] If achieved, the movement of theory comes to be divorced from progress, at least in the teleological sense of getting closer to truth. When that happens, reification loses its sting. It remains imbricated in the process of knowing. But since that form of knowing is now unable to call together both a mutually exclusive worldview of "facts" and a transcendental-universal system of "values," it no longer presents the risks of domination that existed before. Reason is now chastened; reification is sustainably critiqued.

Steps toward such work have already been taken in what Roland Bleiker has called IR's "aesthetic turn."[24] Rather than reproducing, analyzing, or representing reality through simplified conceptual matrices, aesthetic IR aims to "engage the gap that inevitably opens up between a form of representation and the object it seeks to represent."[25] As Anca Pusca recently explained, the aim is to "challenge…all of our instincts as academics"; non-identity is preserved by interfering with our ability to unproblematically break down "text into concepts, logical flows and conclusions."[26] For Pusca, texts, meanings, images, and sensibilities are assembled into what Walter Benjamin called a *konvolut*, a

---

Meja (1995), ch. 5. On attempts to transcend "Mannheim's paradox," see Bluhm (1982) and Connolly (1967).

23. Following Habermas (1971): "The specific viewpoints from which, with transcendental necessity, we apprehend reality ground three categories of possible knowledge: information that expands our power of technical control; interpretations that make possible the orientation of action within common traditions; *and analyses that free consciousness from its dependence on hypostatized power*" (p. 313, emphasis mine).

24. Bleiker (2001, 2009). A number of journals have published special interviews on aesthetic theory, which together make for an excellent overview: see *Alternatives* 25:3 (2000), *Millennium* 30:3 (2001) and 34:3 (2006), and *Review of International Studies* 35:4 (2009). Another direction is taken by Jackson's (2006) notion of a "double hermeneutic."

25. Bleiker (2001), p. 512.

26. Pusca (2009), p. 241.

notion closely tied to Adorno's constellation. The aim is to foster "digressions and interpretations that although inspired by the text, often transgress it."[27]

Sustainable critique, however, retains a strong commitment to the tools that positive social science has helped create, once these are suitably chastened. In part, this is tactical: because of the rhetorical value such tools wield within political communities whose modes of governance and administration retain a strong liberal inflection. In part, however, it does so because it sees such administration as necessary, notwithstanding its evils, and as preferable to worse alternatives. The need to administer a large, diverse, and interconnected world does not disappear with the knowledge that this need cannot be met absolutely, notwithstanding the quandary this may place before theorists.

Moreover, as the previous chapters have shown, even the most ostensibly reductive social science paradigms at least *gesture* to some form of reflexivity, however philosophically thin or methodologically underspecified. This is potentially a point of connection and conversation with a larger community of academics and policy makers. In overlooking it, critically and aesthetically inflected IR risks making a fetish out of its own dissidence: perpetuating the sterility of methodological cum ideological great debates by overstating what such thinking can do. As Bleiker aptly notes, while "aesthetic approaches have begun an important process of broadening our understanding of world politics beyond a relatively narrow academic discipline," they do not—indeed, *cannot*—"supersede the need for rigorous social scientific inquiries."[28] With that in mind, sustainable critique aims *both* to make good on its own commitment to reflexivity *and* to provide a space for collaboration among theorists working across the discipline. It stands against reification without invoking a "unity of science," a common human destiny or history à la Hegel, or an "imagined community" of scholarly-normative consensus.

A Working Example: The Israeli-Palestinian Conflict and IR

The example raised earlier may illustrate the potential for such collaboration. Let a sample question be fashioned from the Israeli-Palestinian issue: why did the Oslo-Madrid process—the framework of negotiations between Israel and the states of the region begun in 1991 and in 1993 supplemented by direct

---

27. Pusca (2009), p. 241.

28. Bleiker (2009), p. 19.

talks between Israel and the Palestine Liberation Organization (PLO)—fail to result in a resolution of the Israeli-Palestinian conflict or a "normalization" (in Hebrew, *normalizatsiyya*; in Arabic, *tatbi'a*) of relations between Israel and its immediate neighbors?[29] Such a formulation casts the theorist, at least initially, in the role of one who must sort through various possible responses, rather than compose a simple answer. One assumes a large, complex picture in which many explanations are possible. One observes, too, that this messiness is itself a political resource. The conflict is essentially contested at nearly every point: explanations and understandings suborn, or are taken up by, political interests almost from the moment of their creation.

Two steps are required. The first step lies in building up the hitherto-neglected third axis of the hermeneutic sphere. In Adornian terms, this means identifying key ways in which identitarian thinking moves to conflate concepts and real-world things, in the context of a particular problem or issue area. The second step lies in developing a constellation of methodological paradigms that keep those various forms of non-identity in view, with an eye to producing the desired change of affect among theorists and readers of theory. These steps will be taken in turn (see also table 6.2).

Building up the Hermeneutic Third Axis

Building up the third axis of the hermeneutic circle means giving concrete meaning to non-identity: defining the particular ways in which a concept is distinct from the things it represents, understood within historical context. For the problem of Israeli-Palestinian politics, non-identity would need to be ordered along at least four different axes: relating to the conflict itself with itself, as a series of mutually exclusive national narratives; relating to the parties to it; relating to the larger system within which it is nested; and relating to the particular location of the scholar or theorist attempting to make sense of it.[30] Each of these may be taken in turn.

The non-identity of the conflict with itself speaks to the absence of a common neutral language to represent it conceptually. This absence is pervasive but is most readily illustrated through geography. There is no neutral name for the territory of Israel-Palestine itself, to say nothing of the various locales

---

29. For a sense of the term *normalization* as used in the present context see Mi'Ari (1999) and Scham (2000).

30. Singer (1961).

Table 6.2 Operationalizing Sustainable Critique

Step 1. Building Up a Critical Third Axis: Operationalizing Non-Identity
—Non-identity of the conflict with itself
—Non-identity of the parties
—Non-identity of the system
—Non-identity of the observer
Step 2. Constructing a Constellation: Paradigm Selection
—Structuralist Paradigm (Waltz, Mearsheimer, Walt)
—Historical Materialist Paradigm (McNeill, Wallerstein, Tilly)
—Deep Constructivist Paradigm (Hopf, Abdelal)
—Liberal-Pluralist Paradigm (Krasner, Narizny, Slaughter; Finnemore, Weldes)
—Emancipatory Paradigm (CIRT/CSS)

---

within it: the West Bank–Judea and Samaria, the Temple Mount–Dome of the Rock–Noble Sanctuary, and so forth. Nor can one refer unproblematically to the larger region to which it belongs: terms like "Middle East", too, are tendentious constructions.[31]

Such questions also have a genealogical-historical facet. What relationship have the contemporary Israeli towns of Kiryat Gat, Ashdod, or Ashkelon to those of Falujah, Isdud, or Majdal—the Arab communities that occupied the same locations prior to 1948?[32] What political resonances emerge when these names are placed alongside one another? What practices exactly are set in motion when those name changes are effected or when premodern Arab and Islamic appropriations of biblical sites are raised in response?[33] What account must be made for premodern appropriations with contemporary resonances, and how are contested spaces—like the urban spaces of the city of Jerusalem—physically cast and recast by each side, through different historical phases of the conflict?[34]

---

31. Bilgin (2004), Davison (1960), Ó Tuathail (1996), and Bonine, Gaspar, and Amanat (2011).

32. On this growing literature, see Slyomovics (1998) and the essays in Sa'di and Abu-Lughod (2007) and Tamari (1999). For maps of pre-1948 Palestine, see Khalidi (1992), Morris (2004), and Abu-Sitta (2004).

33. See, for example, Abu El-Haj (2001), Benvenisti (2000), Harkabi (1983), Ilias (2008), and Zerubavel (1995).

34. There is a wide variety of work on this: see, inter alia, Benvenisti (1995, 1996), Ben-Ari and Bilu (1997), Goddard (2010), Kimmerling (1983), Misselwitz and Rieniets (2006), Monk (2002), Newman (2000, 2001, 2002), Sasley (2010), and Yiftachel (2006).

One can go on, but the point is made. The key insight is that the discursive contestations described here parse out along a national divide: Israeli narratives or Palestinian ones. As such, they create mutually exclusive terrains. This discussion has been limited to geography, but similar points may be made with regard to historical narratives, the role of the social sciences, popular culture, and a variety of other questions.[35] In each case, the conflict cannot be said to be any one thing or list of things without stacking the political deck, yet in good "inside/outside" fashion, these practices of exclusion each help constitute one other.[36]

Non-identity is not limited to these questions. The national communities are themselves reifications, whose non-identity needs to be born in mind. Political collectives must be produced and reproduced at the everyday level from above and from below. Below lie everyday political-administrative processes: the functions and dysfunctions of institutions that reproduce the two communities. As an example, in Israel, certain administrative activities—granting citizenship rights, military service, the provision of educational services, marriage and burial rites—pit Israeli state interests against Jewish rituals that emerged in the Diaspora. In many of these spheres, Israeli personal law finds itself challenged by semiautonomous religious authorities, or else such law was never formulated.[37] This uneven legal-administrative landscape constitutes the limits and shape of the Israeli public sphere: not the power of states qua states, but of regimes, constitutional orders, or governing coalitions to build consensus

---

35. This is an enormous literature, and the following list is representative, rather than exhaustive: Said (1994b), Eyal (2006), Kramer (2001), Little (2002), Lockman (2010), MacFie (2000, 2002), McAlister (2001), Shohat (1989), Stein and Swedenburg (2005), and Tamari (2008). Within the context of IR, some of these issues are raised in Ahluwalia and Sullivan (2001), Halliday (2005), Isacoff (2002), and more broadly in Kratochwil (2006).

36. Kimmerling (2008), Bar-On (2008), and Rotberg (2006). The "inside/outside" dichotomy is from Walker (1992).

37. Hence, for example, there is no unified Israeli school system, nor is there an institution of civil marriage and divorce. This creates situations in which quasi-governmental institutions "compete" with one another: religious and secular schools may compete to become the default institutions of compulsory education for a particular ethnic immigrant community within Israel, for example, influencing voting and employment patterns. Alternatively, administrative bodies may compete: religious and secular courts, for example, may challenge one another's rights to preside over issues of divorce, child custody, and so forth. These examples, it is to be stressed, are merely suggestive; so, too, are the readings that follow. With regard to the Israeli context, see Arian (1989), Goldscheider (2002), Horowitz and Lissak (1989), Kemp et al. (2004), Khazzoom (2008), Kimmerling (1989), Kop and Litan (2002), Shafir and Peled (2002), Shapira (2004), Shenhav (2006), and Don-Yehiya and Liebman (1984). Widening this reading to include Palestine and the Arab world, the literature expands exponentially. Relevant works include Bellin (2004), Brand (1988), Brown (2003), Brynen (1995a, 1995b, 2000), Hammami (2000), Amal Jamal (2005), Amaney Jamal (2007), Kimmerling and Migdal

and political capital in the face of complex decisions that may challenge existing identities or interests. Though banal (in Michael Billig's sense of this term),
these are dynamic processes: they exist and have a knowable effect on how international politics is transacted, but they cannot easily be schematized.[38]

Above the national-level conflict is the international system in which it
is understood to be nested. Aspects of this nesting are captured in contemporary discussions on globalization in the Middle East: the intersection of
superpower interests, resource politics, capital flows, class identity and interest, and the like.[39] Others deal with the transnationalization of history and
memory: Jews and Arabs as "others" within a European culture that has done
violence to both, Israel and Jerusalem as symbolic ideals for settler societies
in the "new world," the loss of Palestine as a symptom of collective Arab or
Islamic political dysfunction in the modern era, the varied fate of Christians
and Jews within Islamic lands, Diaspora identities, and so forth.[40] In that context, Israel and Palestine become footballs: for the European Union, seeking to
expand its footprint as a unitary policy-making presence on the international
scene; for Diaspora Jews—and increasingly, Muslims and Arabs—seeking a
basis to create rallying points for mobilization within the countries of their
migration; for the United States, seeking to define a post–Cold War new
world order; for multinational corporations seeking new opportunities for
investment or labor and resource extraction.

(2003), Robinson (1997), Rubin (1999), Shain and Sussman (1998), and Shikaki (2002). Some
attention has been given to such questions in IR circles; see, for example, the relevant essays in
Adler (2005), as well as Del Sarto (2006), Landau (2006), Lynch (1999, 2006b, 2011), Sucharov
(2005), Telhami and Barnett (2002), and Waxman (2006).

38. Billig (1995); Brubaker (1996). A comparable example may be drawn from the challenges
facing Palestinian state makers. Gaza and the West Bank—assuming these to be the territories
on which at least a part of a future Palestinian state would be created—have inherited different
legal and institutional terrains owing to the legacy of their pre-1967 occupation. To impose a
uniform legal code over the Egyptian legal tradition prevailing in Gaza and the Jordanian one
in the West Bank would pit an ostensibly "national" government—on the one hand, a uniform
topography of administrative and personal law; on the other, its own set of sectional interests—against entrenched practices, traditions, and interests. For a brief survey of this issue, see
Robinson (1997).

39. On regional assessments at the crossing point of economics, politics, and globalization, see, inter alia, Ben Porat (2006), Drori (2000), Hazbun (2008), Nitzan and Bichler
(2002), Portugali (1993), Roy (2001, 2004), Samarah (2000), Ram (2008), and Silver (1990).
Dannreuther's (2010) historical-institutionalist approach is also of interest.

40. See, inter alia, Ajami (1992, 1999), Alcalay (1993), Anidjar (2003), Assmann (1997),
Boyarin and Boyarin (2002), Eyal (2006), Fromkin (1990), Gorenberg (2000), Grose (1983),
Lewis (1990, 2002), McAlister (2001), Oren (2007), Said (1994a, 1994b, 2000), Tuchman
(1984).

The fourth sort of non-identity speaks to that of the researcher, seeking to make sense of all this. On their own, the previous three forms of non-identity would actually serve to reproduce a particular, and extremely dangerous, positivist illusion: the ability of the theorist to stand outside of, and map out the interactions taking place within, a given set of complicated conflict processes. In fact, no such possibility exists. Some connections are obvious and apparent, but not all are. In this space, the aesthetic and imaginative element discussed previously comes to the fore.

Constructing the Constellation: An Analytical Table of Contents

The forms of non-identity just enumerated are to be sustained by exploiting the rhetorical effects of compounding paradigm on top of paradigm. Non-identity, it is hoped, would emerge gradually in the minds and sensibilities of theorists and their audiences from the dislocating effects of attempting to internalize incommensurable narratives surrounding the same event. Here again, Allison's *Essence of Decision* bears noting: on their own, his three lenses each illuminated different aspects of the Cuban Missile Crisis. However instructive these views were individually, the propounding of each one on top of the others produced a kind of cognitive dissonance. Allison channeled that dissonance, pointing his readers toward certain conclusions: the "unhappy facts" he wanted them to internalize about the limits of theory, their policy ramifications for the nuclear era, and the altered sensibility these realizations needed to generate. Neither direct exhortations nor any single one of his theoretical lenses produced these directly. They emerged in a roundabout way, as a kind of summing-up. A constellar approach to the Israeli-Palestinian conflict would work in a similar fashion.

Given the complexity of that conflict, there is a limit to which such an approach can be presented in a condensed fashion, as I now propose to do. However, a thumbnail sketch is possible—and will be undertaken here—conditional on the understanding that it is both incomplete and impressionistic. Recalling table 6.2, consider five narratives drawn from IR's major paradigms, devoted to answering the question: why did the Oslo-Madrid process—the series of bilateral and regional contacts initiated first in 1991 and then expanded in 1993—fail to generate a resolution of either the Israeli-Palestinian conflict or the wider regional one? Well-known paradigms can be selected for this: a structural "neo-neo" paradigm of the sort drawn from confluences between the work of Kenneth Waltz (chapter 3) and Robert Keohane (chapter 5), a historical-materialist paradigm that mirrors more closely classical IR realism and liberalism of the sort promulgated by Morgenthau (chapter 3) and the Mitranyan-Fabian tradition (chapter 4), a "deep constructivist" paradigm that deals with the constitutive tensions that produce political communities from the inside out (consider here the work of theorists like Ted Hopf and Rawi Abdelal), a "liberal-pluralist" paradigm that views foreign policy through the lens of fixed clusters of domestic interests (hence, work by Stephen Krasner and Kevin Narizny or Martha Finnemore and Jutta Weldes), and an "emancipatory" paradigm, building on the CSS/CIRT tradition surveyed in chapter 2. Each thumbnail sketch given here contains two distinct elements: it will speak to what particular narratives are able to illustrate and what they necessarily elide or reify.

From this combination of "one-two punches," it is hoped that a change of scholarly affect analogous to the one previously described might be produced vis-à-vis the Israeli-Palestinian conflict. That change of affect can be described as proceeding in three phases. First, a sense of dislocation is hoped for, stemming from the realization that all theoretical narratives *both* disclose a sense of the conflict that has an immediate ideological analogue within it *and* betray a larger reality that lies beyond comprehension. Second, from this sense of dislocation, a realization of finitude might follow: that while such narratives are inadequate, they are all any of us—thinkers, policy makers, human beings—have by which to make sense of the world. Third, from this sense of finitude, a sense of compassion and fellow feeling might come about. Human beings in Israel and Palestine both risk harm and do harm on the basis of reifications that—so it sometimes may seem—even a moment's reflection could expose as bankrupt. Yet no human life, no social or political existence, could be possible without such reifications; if they have brought some communities to grief and not others, could that not be mere chance? If the vocation of theory is to explode such reifications, is not their loss even so a real loss to those who have believed and struggled in their name? Would they not be so for us? And if that is the case, does not the process of exploding them require more than marshaling arguments of logic? Might it not first require an altered affective disposition? *If so, then to be caught between the hope and despair that these realizations engender, and to be chastened by that experience, would create the initial conditions of possibility for theorizing in a sustainably critical mode.*

The Structuralist Paradigm

The first account would be based on the kinds of 'neo-neo' structuralism that build off third-image approaches to world politics: the structure of the international system is understood as the primary determinant of political interaction, power is conceived of in largely material terms, and nation-states are the major actors of consequence.[41] When one examines the Oslo-Madrid process through such a lens, what insights does one gain?

In this context, third-image arguments are useful because they supply convenient before and after snapshots of a region or system that explain why particular states may have sought to change policies or alter alliance structures. How did the calculus of political power in the Middle East change following the collapse of the Soviet Union and the defeat of Iraq in 1991? How did it change again following the outbreak of Israeli-Palestinian violence in 2000, the 9/11 attacks in 2001, and the second U.S.-Iraq war in 2003? To what extent did balances of power reflect changing mixes of direct threat and interdependence, and to what extent were states obliged to adjust accordingly? Was there a metaphorical window of opportunity for a negotiated settlement that emerged from these changes, and, if so, did that window close or narrow at key moments? Is there a hard substrate of interests, economic or political, that belies the fulsome rhetoric of "peacemakers"? Does that hard substrate limit, shape, or belie more open-ended notions of interest as the product of social construction?

The usefulness of this paradigm granted, it also has its own need for sustainable critique. In particular, this relates to the tendency of theorists to conflate such snapshots with dynamic regional coalitions of political, economic, and military force. Certainly, such snapshots can help policy makers gauge the form and composition of diplomatic initiatives meant to produce diplomatic breakthroughs among rival parties and powers. Yet it also reifies those forces and the combination of powers and interests that sustain them. Peace—as Adler noted, in chapter 4—is not merely born of evenly matched political rivals who decide to "switch" rather than "fight": it is a state of amity among peoples, fractions, cultures, and classes. Although particular combinations of factors may combine to make particular diplomatic breakthroughs propitious, the nature of political possibility is that it cannot be reduced to lists of such factors. Peace cannot be conflated with an architectonic of power or a correlation of forces without losing its essence as a normative goal in the process.

A Historical-Materialist Paradigm

What is compelling about structuralism is also what most often raises the hackles of its critics: its ahistoricity, its assumption of universally shared and

---

41. Waltz (1979), Mearsheimer (2001), Van Evera (1999), and especially in the present context, Walt (1987).

understood concepts of power, or the uniform functioning of political institutions. Historical materialism calls all these assumptions into question: notions of power, institutions, and practices are traced as developmental patterns over the *longue durée*. Interests emerge from long processes of accumulation and consolidation: of power and capital, of strategic capabilities or administrative competencies. A variety of approaches attack political life from such perspectives: world-systems theory, military-historical approaches, and historical-institutionalist approaches.[42] These views interlock in complicated ways and produce rich narrative tapestries.

One brief example must suffice to illustrate both the discursive and critical potential of such paradigms. Israel gained its political independence in the wake of the Second World War: a small state, in an era of superpowers. In the state's early years, it enjoyed certain tactical and operational advantages that allowed it to punch above its geopolitical weight, including geographical compactness and relatively high levels of social solidarity and technical expertise among its citizens. Israel's armed forces parlayed these advantages into remarkable battlefield successes in 1967 and even 1973: exploiting rapid mobilization, short internal lines of communication, and commander initiative to the hilt.

Even prior to 1967, however, these advantages were understood to be temporary: the tide of history was against small states, and the ambitious modernization schemes many Arab states undertook were expected to gradually bear fruit. This created a strategic imperative: Israel's short-term tactical advantages had to be parlayed into a longer-term political entente.[43] This understanding took a new form in the 1990s. Although Nasserite modernization schemes proved ephemeral, Israel's combat doctrine faced considerable challenges: its doctrine of maneuver was bogged down by rapid urbanization throughout the region, by constabulary duties exacerbated in the first intifada, by the rise of both "smart" weaponry and asymmetric combat, and—though it is difficult to imagine now—by the specter of a loss of U.S. patronage with the collapse of the Soviet Union.[44] All the while, economic globalization and the retreat of the state created new forms of inequality, undermining the social solidarity key to a citizen military.[45]

42. See, respectively, Wallerstein (1974, 2004), Arrighi and Silver (1999); McNeill (1982), Gat (2006), Parker (1985), and Van Creveld (2007); Tilly (1992) and Spruyt (1994).

43. For a recent retracing of this understanding, see Shlaim (2000).

44. Inter alia, Heller (2000), Levite (1990), Van Creveld (2002), and Cohen et al. (1998).

45. On certain of these points, see Gal and Cohen (2000), Levy (2007), and Silver (1990).

This perception of grand, historical movement concealed its own dangers. It produced a deterministic sense of necessity in Israel: the Oslo-Madrid process seemed, in certain dovish political quarters, to be the Israeli nation's long-deferred rendezvous with destiny.[46] Had not all the political, social, and economic stars come into alignment to produce it? Was not failure, for all the reasons described before, simply unthinkable? On the one hand, such a sensibility helped dovish quarters of the Israeli polity force an alliance with the political center. On the other, the sense of ineluctability—that the *march of world-historical progress had allied itself to the Israeli left*—led many to ignore opposition in culturally dismissive, rather than politically forthright, terms. To oppose the particular notion of peace that was on offer was, increasingly, to be an ideological holdout—a reactionary anachronism that time would sweep away, rather than a political fraction with claims to be addressed. The result was a political deadlock: following Mark Heller, a "clash *within* civilizations."[47]

A "Deep Constructivist" Paradigm

Deep constructivism picks up precisely where the previous notion of historical materialism left off: with those paradigms that take broad-based national identity or communitarian discourses as primary.[48] In the present context, two versions of this paradigm would be apposite: first, a territorialized version of popular domestic resistance to, or sympathy for, diplomatic negotiations or territorial compromises whose symbolic value may challenge the organizing logic of a political community.[49] A second, deterritorialized version would propose more diffuse networks of identity and interest: confluences between particular factions in Israel or the Arab world with Diaspora communities or "loosely coupled" networks of "rooted cosmopolitans," as between the Israeli settler movement and American evangelical Christians.[50]

On this account, states may *deploy* national symbols, but they do not *own* them outright. States have certain bully pulpit advantages in national and international public spheres. Yet—particularly in an era when state structures

---

46. See, for example, Rabin (1996), Peres (1993, 1999), and Savir (1998).

47. Heller (2000, 2002).

48. For two approaches, see Hopf (2002) and Abdelal (2001). Teti (2007) is also of interest.

49. See, for example, Telhami and Barnett (2002) and Heller (2000).

50. On the latter point, see Gorenberg (2000), Martin (1999), Spector (2009), and the essays in Forbes and Kilde (2004). The terms *rooted cosmopolitanism* and *loose coupling* are from Tarrow (2005) and Tarrow and Della Porta (2005).

are in retreat, owing to globalization—those advantages are not decisive, and new venues for subverting them are constantly emerging.[51] In such contexts, states must, to paraphrase James Scott, develop new ways of seeing, or they risk losing control over national narratives.[52] In the process, history and memory become actively and more intensively mined at all levels: by states and by local and transnational communities of identity and interest.

On the one hand, such approaches offer the possibility of a national or collective culture with its own inherent sense of dignity and continuity: precisely those notions, as noted earlier, that gave early German forms of realpolitik its raison d'être in the face of an earlier brand of ideological universalism. Yet the tendency of such notions to fester into their own forms of hypernationalism, while obvious, still bears noting. The temptation to make a fetish of a particular form of life—Palestine prior to the *nakba*, the Judean hills in the days of the biblical Judges—given the chiliastic tendencies already latent within this conflict, makes this approach both necessary *and* highly dangerous.

A Liberal-Pluralist Paradigm

Deep constructivism retains a hidden assumption regarding the primacy of the political. Yet the existence of a given political order—recall James Mill's pungent characterization of British imperialism as a form of "outdoor relief" for second-tier aristocrats—creates social and economic opportunities for entrepreneurs of other sorts as well.[53] Viewing societies and social structures as reducible to the multiple and crosscutting interests of classes, parties, and interest groups, government appears on this view as kind of big tent, absorbing political pressures and disbursing resources and benefits in equal and opposite proportion. As in chapter 5, such scholarship studies the institutions of government as artifacts of past confluences of interest and emergent ones as means to discern how polyarchic constructions of individual rationality emerge and chart their course.[54]

---

51. Keck and Sikkink (1998); Tarrow (2005).

52. Scott (1998). On this point, consider recent attempts by Israel's Ministry of Public Diplomacy and Diaspora Affairs to create a grassroots Web-based movement to recast Israel's image "immediately" (i.e., without the mediation of the "traditional" mass media). http://masbirim.gov.il/eng/ (last accessed April 19, 2012).

53. Cited in Hobson (1902), p. 56; with regard to Israel-Palestine, see the fictional depiction in Koestler (1946), p. 58.

54. Krasner (1978), Schweller (2006), and Narizny (2007). Or one might employ constructivist approaches with a similar orientation, for example, Finnemore (1996), Weldes (1996), and Lynch (1999).

These assumptions inform a discussion of Israeli-Palestinian politics by exploring what happens in societies in which hegemonic ideologies have become severely eroded: where durable social and political structures persist only by virtue of a combination of habituated procedural consensus, institutional inertia, and sunk costs. Like deep constructivism, such an understanding assumes that both the Israeli state and the Palestinian leadership face challenges in mobilizing symbols and ideals. But deep constructivism sees the mantle for such struggle being taken up by committed groups of activists. Pluralism imagines, by contrast, a "fat middle" of rent-seeking classes, communities, individuals, fractions, or ethnicities, willing to barter political support for material benefit. The rituals of politics are adhered to in an instrumental fashion: they form the basic framework through which political goods are socially distributed. But the political stage is a bare one: such dramas and contests as exist are covers for a material tug-of-war. In addition to checking excessive reliance on discussions of identity politics, this approach also provides a way to explore unexpected convergences or alliances both domestically and across national lines.

Such an approach forthrightly defines political opportunities by identifying overlapping possibilities of political or economic rent sharing—for example, the U.S. free trade agreement with Israel and Jordan, which allowed firms in Israel to outsource low-skill labor and gave Jordanian manufacturers access to export markets and foreign direct investment.[55] Yet such approaches reify a vision of politics in which positional interests are wholly fungible with political loyalty, as though appeals to justice, equity, or history are irrelevant to politics.

An "Emancipatory" Paradigm

Building on the work of the critical IR theory surveyed in chapter 2, such paradigms view the Israeli-Palestinian conflict in terms of mutually incompatible emancipatory impulses.[56] The roots of the conflict lie in the desire of Jews and Arabs, Israelis and Palestinians, to be "free"—in whatever ways that may be taken to mean. Particular notions of freedom are understood to mutually exclude or undermine one another. Moreover, the process of producing freedom for some often involves the disenfranchisement

---

55. Work on this area is sparse, but see Kardoosh (2005), al Mdanat (2006), and Rosen (2004).

56. Booth (2007), Linklater (1990a, 1990b), and the essays in Roach (2008).

of others.[57] The dialectical nature of freedom, however, is an abstraction that is difficult to appreciate. This is true all the more, given the inability of many political actors—whether owing to the rapid social transformations of modernity or the philosophical aridity of mass politics—to think through what *freedom* can mean in terms not already superannuated by events.[58] Particular political demands—for a state of one's own, for sovereignty, personal freedom, self-determination—may themselves be parsed through the reified lingua franca of particular eras and traditions. If taken at face value, what do they produce? If not taken at face value, how can they be productively debated?

Though given to philosophical abstraction, such questions probe the limits of political possibility in concrete ways. To what extent can any negotiated solution between Israelis and Palestinians—whether achieved through one binational state or two national ones; whether achieved by direct negotiations or external imposition—produce the conditions for happiness? If no existing solution can, where must theorists look for new ideas? If a consensus understanding of the good life is held to be impossible to achieve within a given political time frame, or to sustain once reached, what does this mean? What remains?

Yet such approaches—as chapter 2 noted—can work backward, fostering their own potentially dangerous moments of reified forgetting. Calls for freedom have a totalizing quality: one must either be for them or against them, and identity frequently trumps argument.[59] Such calls can emerge as a form of peremptory intellectual backlash: impatience with the slow, one step forward, two steps back nature of conflict resolution. In the face of an intransigent political reality, one may naturally wish to stand up for simple truths. Yet those simple truths are so for a reason: because of the nuance they either conceal or erase.

The Constellar Production of Compassion

What work does such a confluence of paradigms do? In what way does it answer the call for sustainable critique? At one level, it produces a sense of deep unease: each argument negates the others' absolutist claims through successive

---

57. Ayyash (2010): "Every question asked and every answer delivered is transmitted through and in violence" (p. 117).

58. In the Israeli-Palestinian context, see Arendt (1978), especially pp. 164–177, and the essays in Said (2000).

59. In this context, see Monk (2002).

layers of complexity and nuance. A sense of respect is also engendered for a conflict that theory seldom appreciates to its full depth. Perhaps, too, by extension, it produces a sense of compassion for those swept up in that conflict and those who (inadvertently or otherwise) help perpetuate it. It will be understood to endure simply because it is *complicated*: because the degree of this complexity does not yield to any one set of insights or ideas and because that complexity catches every party to it unawares. By producing studies in which all arguments cancel each other out, what remains but a quiet, firm determination to demand compassion from all and to offer it to all?

That compassion matters. Without it, theory cannot meaningfully contribute to the region. Neither soft power, nor better PR, nor a new regional security architecture, nor new alliance structures can replace it. Positive social science can fill that notion of compassion with instrumental content once it exists, helping it mark off the realities it must face if it is not to spin out into the hopelessly utopian. But it cannot produce it. Sustainable critique might yet do better: helping to create it, sustain it, and moderate its translation into policy. It can point to the necessity for such compassion with unflinching firmness even as it acknowledges its own insufficiency in the face of it by showing how all simple narratives lead to impasse and how all ostensible shortcuts and expediencies are ultimately illusory. It comes to that position not *despite* the fact that it is academic, *but by virtue of that fact*. In the complex, highly technical context within which contemporary politics unfolds, academics have a unique role to play here. Unlike private citizens, academics have the time and the resources to acquire specialist knowledge. Unlike policy makers, they are not driven by the merciless pace of events. By virtue of being apart from the practice of politics, theory—passionate contemplation—can make a much-needed contribution to a marketplace of ideas that, without it, threatens to become ruthlessly zero-sum. This is the vocation of IR: academic contemplation's chastened, but unapologetic, contribution to political practice. It gives substantive content to Morgenthau's call—here recalling the discussion in the opening pages of this book—for international theory that is an "unpopular undertaking," but without rejecting policy relevance altogether; it marks out Stanley Hoffmann's "triple distance."

There is no question that such an approach complicates the work of the theorist considerably. Multiparadigmatic approaches demand multiple theoretical and analytical competencies. They are time and labor intensive. They require the additional work of redacting the whole into a chastened, sustainably critical metanarrative. Yet there are benefits as well: theory learns to speak not only in terms of its voices but also through its silences.[60] Once identified, those silences become the new spaces for developing additional perspectives and adumbrations. Sustainably balanced, practical and critical reason bring academic IR back to its historic aims and aspirations.

Politics without Compassion: More of the Same?

One cannot study recent events in the Middle East without a gnawing sense of despair. History seems to be repeating itself, with both regional and extraregional powers reiterating past mistakes. It is not that new perspectives are not heard or that new voices do not manage to break through into the public discourse. It is that the carrying capacity of that discourse, its shape and configuration, seems to ensure that while the *words* change, the *music* underneath them remains constant.[61] A constant percussion-beat of crisis and emergency impoverishes policy discourses by inducing haste, and a penumbra of dreams, beliefs, prejudices, and hopes creates a minefield of partisan sensibilities. Compassion and clearheadedness are either dismissed as self-indulgent or invoked in a tendentious manner.

Both dynamics have been surveyed in the previous chapters. The former, of course, was the position of Herman Kahn, as surveyed in chapter 1. The world presented certain dangers, Kahn explained. Much as we might wish to do so, "we cannot say 'stop the world, I want to get off'"; one either makes one's peace with "the unthinkable," or one denies one's duty to men and country.[62] The latter was the position of the CSS and CIRT traditions outlined in chapter 2: as though critique, or moral probity, were somehow the unique province of the political left; as though such critique had not metastasized into its own distinctive forms of horror many times before.

Both positions find their contemporary correlates in Middle Eastern policy discourses. In a region that seems set to go nuclear, comments by Uzi Arad—at one time a fellow in Kahn's Hudson Institute, later an intelligence official, and until recently National Security Adviser to Israeli Prime Minister Binyamin Netanyahu—carry a similar ring.

> I still remember Roosevelt and all the wise and enlightened types of the American security hierarchy in the period of Auschwitz, and I have retained the lesson. In Jewish history and fate there is a dimension of

---

60. Smith (1995).

61. Franklin (2005).

62. Kahn (1962), p. 23.

unfairness toward us. We have already been alone once, and even the good and the enlightened did not protect us. Accordingly, we must not be militant, but we must entrench our defense and security prowess and act with wisdom and restraint and caution and *sangfroid.* Never again.[63]

By "never again," Arad refers not merely to the Holocaust. He makes a connection between the Holocaust as a historical fact and a particular disposition to which its memory calls us: one of restraint, caution, wisdom, *sangfroid.* One cannot avoid, Arad notes, a sense of being back in the 1930s, with Israel taking the place of Czechoslovakia, Iran that of Germany, and the international community of diplomats falling over one another to obtain "peace in our time." With steely calm, Arad wishes to be clear:

> Never again will we be felled in mass numbers, never again will we be defenseless and never again will there be a situation in which those who harm us go unpunished.[64]

Arad is not the only Israeli politician to invoke the "Munich analogy" in the context of Israel's national security or nuclear policy, nor even its most senior one—particularly in the wake of comments by Iranian President Mahmoud Ahmadinejad.[65] Nor should such invocations be entirely reduced to either

---

63. Ari Shavit: "There Is No Palestinian Sadat, No Palestinian Mandela." *HaAretz,* July 11, 2009.

64. Shavit, "No Palestinian Sadat."

65. For discussions of the role of the Holocaust in Israel's nuclear strategy, Cohen (1998) remains the academic work of record; see also journalistic accounts in Hersh (1991) and Karpin (2006) and the impassioned discussion in the opening pages of Burg (2008). For coverage of Ahmadinejad's comments, see Ethan Bronner and Nazila Fathi, *New York Times,* June 11, 2006, Week in Review, p. 4; Nazila Fathi and Greg Myre, *New York Times,* October 27, 2005, p. 8a; Barbara Slavin, *USA Today,* December 15, 2005, p. 16a; Anne Bernard, *Boston Globe,* December 15, 2006, p. 1a; "Denying the Holocaust: Iran," *The Economist,* December 16, 2006; "Milking the Holocaust: Iran and Israel," *The Economist,* September 16, 2006. For statements linking these comments to the Holocaust by a variety of first- and second-tier Israeli and American officials, see *Jerusalem Post,* October 22, 2006, p. 1; April 3, 2006, p. 3; April 25, 2006, p. 1; December 15, 2006, p. 4; January 29, 2007, p. 4; *Los Angeles Times,* July 24, 2006, p. B11; *Fox News Online* July 29, 2007 (www.foxnews.com/story/0,2933,291078,00.html); and more recently, *HaAretz Online,* April 12, 2010 (www.haaretz.co.il/hasite/spages/1162479.html [Hebrew] and www.haaretz.co.il/hasite/spages/1162425.html [Hebrew]) and April 18 2012 (http://www.haaretz.co.il/news/education/1.1688910) [Hebrew]) Jeff Jacoby's comments in the *Boston Globe,* August 16, 2006, p. A9, are also of some interest here, as are Avi Dichter's comments, as Israeli Public Security Minister, to *The Economist:* "How Imminent or Real a Threat?" January 13, 2007; Niall Ferguson, *Los Angeles Times,* July 24, 2006, p. B11; and Fareed Zakaria, *Newsweek International Edition,* September 26, 2007.

deterrence signaling or to political opportunism. Arad's comments have the same ineluctable logic as did Kahn's: he imagines his country swallowed up in a mushroom cloud, a second holocaust.[66] Certainly, this is an unlikely outcome. But recognizing this only drives home Allison's "awesome crack between *unlikelihood* and *impossibility*," that same "unhappy, troubling, but unavoidable fact about this world" that in the nuclear era we ignore at our peril.[67] If IR dismisses such fears, it dismisses its own vocation.

Yet the ease with which Arad makes his connections—between Munich and Tehran—raises its own concerns. Do not these connections serve to deflect more immediate claims, closer to home: for territories held, or concessions not made, in other contexts or policy areas? Could not his steely calm blind him to the humanity of his enemies, and does that not pose its own dangers and myopias? "Peace in our time" is not always a chimera, just because it has been in certain circumstances and at certain moments. Just as with Kahn, to accept that his worldview coheres internally is not to suggest that it must be accepted uncritically. Any existing political state of affairs is the work of human beings; whatever collective action problems may bar its coordinated change, those difficulties are not tantamount to overriding laws of the natural world. Forgetting this can have baleful consequences, even if one's hopes must at times stretch to accommodate them. "The hope that earthly horror does not possess the last word is, to be sure, a non-scientific wish," Max Horkheimer once noted.[68]

Now consider such forms of critique as have been brought against such positions. Alastair Crooke's recent *Resistance: The Essence of the Islamic Revolution* provides a useful example. Like Arad, Crooke is a policy intellectual with a rich background in the field: former British intelligence, with stints advising senior European and American policy makers and in on-the-ground conflict mediation. But where Arad calls for *sangfroid* in the face of a world hostile to Jews and their state, Crooke makes a compelling case

66. Arad affirms this connection: "Kahn was a towering figure. He was a beacon of intelligence, knowledge and pioneering thought. He combined conceptual productivity, humor and informality. He attracted a group of devotees of whom I was one in the 1970s. But he also had bitter rivals who criticized him for even conceiving of the idea of a nuclear war. In the Cold War it was precisely those who talked about defense and survival who were considered nuclear hawks. The doves talked about 'mutual assured destruction,' which blocks any possibility of thinking about nuclear weapons. Like Kahn, I was one of the hawks. One of my projects was a paper for the Pentagon on planning a limited nuclear war in Central Europe." See Shavit, "No Palestinian Sadat."

67. Allison (1971), p. vii.

68. Jay (1973), p. xii.

for shifting the discourse on Islamic radicalism. Islamist resistance, Crooke argues, is nourished by many of the same values one finds on the American and European left. At stake are two dichotomous views of humanity:

> One view—the western one—privileges "individuality," and defines this "individuality" as the appropriate organizing principle around which society should be shaped. The other view—the Islamist vision—sees the human to be integral to a wider existence; intractably linked, and not separated, as "an individual," from others and the world that surrounds him or her; which sees the human as a multi-dimensional creature—larger than the sum of his or her desires and appetites, whose ability to access innate moral values, as the basis of his or her responsibility for the community, becomes the organizational principle for economics, society and politics.[69]

Elements in Crooke's reconstruction of this dichotomy are familiar. They are gleaned from Karl Polanyi and John Maynard Keynes, the poststructural tradition, Habermas, Adorno, and Horkheimer. Islamism is the political-philosophical expression of the Islamic world's attempt to defend itself against the depredations of a globally disembedded neoliberal order; against instrumental reason run rampant, against the reduction of human beings and the natural world "to specimen-objects for study, and to ever more narrowly focused and fragmented objects of enquiry."[70]

Yet to make his argument work, Crooke must reinscribe precisely the same reifications he ostensibly wishes to unmake: a west that is a unitary whole, alienated from itself and surviving parasitically on subaltern outsiders, and an Orient in which untrammeled authenticity still survives. It is the romantic's critique of the liberal enlightenment, the German right's critique of the German left, recast to fit the political dramatis personae of a world post-9/11 and 7/7.[71] Put another way, it is Edward Said's *Orientalism* writ backward: the "natural men" of the east can teach the soulless moderns.

---

69. Crooke (2009), pp. 29–30.

70. Crooke (2009), p. 145.

71. Crooke realizes this, but not all the way down. Two interlocking moves comprise this. In the first, Crooke acknowledges that he is engaged in a tendentious process of reification. He then pleads that this is an inevitable extension of thinking as such and proceeds to use his class categories as he will. "In using such general labels as 'Islamist' or the 'West,' any work can be held to be guilty of Edward Said's objections that there are no such categories.... These short cuts are acknowledged in advance; and any damage to meaning inflicted by their use, is regretted."

Notwithstanding its reductionism, Crooke's comparison rings true, just as Arad's does. But *why*? Crooke vilifies consumerism as though it were a conspiracy, rather than a stopgap measure meant to stanch a left-right fissure that had swallowed two entire generations in war. That is no excuse for oppressing Arabs and Muslims or installing client regimes to ensure the flow of oil. It may, however, explain why such policies might have been held to be necessary. Perhaps, in the nuclear era, Crooke's "human as a multi-dimensional creature" seemed to possess powers that could not be endured. What Islamists demand, by that logic, is a freedom that no one, in the wake of Auschwitz and Hiroshima, can responsibly possess. Crooke, one fears, does worse than overlook that position. He confers a veil of moral impeccability on those who *studiously* ignore it.

Reading Arad and Crooke together may thus drive one more to despair than to hope: as though the late-modern world can produce nothing but the same poisoned wine, served up in constantly changing bottles. It was this sense of despair that the quote with which this chapter opened sought to evoke: from Brazil's Machado de Assis. Though little known in the United States, Assis was among the most acute nineteenth-century observers of the hopes and fallacies of the modern age. His biting satire counseled chastened humility and probing, but also forgiving, self-examination: the same qualities that Adorno, writing seventy years later, would praise as the last surviving moral virtues of late modern life.[72] Sustainable critique finds its place there: it is that sensibility, applied to the problems, methods, and concerns of IR. It is a scholarly-research ethic for a world in which all practical theory is deeply imperfect and seems constantly to verge on oppression, yet where such theory remains all we have. If it can locate a space by which the tools of IR can be brought to bear against this dichotomy—to understand the realities they disclose, while also checking their reifications—it will have done its work well. At the very least, it will have showed the need for it.

That said, he notes, "What alternative is there? It is more accurate to state that there is no one *Shari'a*, and to distinguish all its variants; but if we do this on each occasion, and with each term, the ability to covey a message clearly and simply is impeded. Our objective here is focus down to the essence of the Islamist revolution, in order to convey the broader significance of what it portends to non-Muslims as well as Muslims. I have therefore continued to use these general terms, and ask the reader to understand that they do represent only generalizations" (pp. 33–34). Of course, Crooke does have alternatives: the constellation being one. And what do we do when Crooke then proceeds to disenfranchise all those in "the west" in equal-and-opposite fashion to those whom he critiques? Hence—ignoring both geography and demographics—Israel is for Crooke part of "the west": Islamist revolutionaries deny it a culture and history of its own, and Crooke simply follows suit.

72. For brief but suggestive discussion of the connections between Assis and Adorno, see López (2005).

Works Cited

Abdelal, Rawi: *National Purpose in the World Economy* (Ithaca, NY: Cornell University Press, 2001).

Abu El-Haj, Nadia: *Facts on the Ground: Archaeological Practice and Territorial Self-Fashioning in Israeli Society* (Chicago: University of Chicago Press, 2001).

Abu-Sitta, Salman H.: *Atlas of Palestine, 1948* (London: Palestine Land Society, 2004).

Adler, Emanuel: *Communitarian International Relations: The Epistemic Foundations of International Relations* (London: Routledge, 2005).

Adler, Emanuel: "Seizing the Middle Ground: Constructivism in World Politics." *European Journal of International Relations* 3:5 (1997), pp. 319–363.

Adler, Emanuel, and Michael Barnett: "Taking Identity and Our Critics Seriously." *Cooperation and Conflict* 35:3 (2000), pp. 321–329.

Adler, Emanuel, and Michael Barnett (eds.): *Security Communities* (Cambridge: Cambridge University Press, 1998).

Adler, Emanuel, and Michael Barnett: "Governing Anarchy: A Research Agenda for the Study of Security Communities." *Ethics and International Affairs* 10 (1996), pp. 63–98.

Adler, Emanuel, and Beverly Crawford: "Normative Power: The European Practice of Region-Building and the Case of the Euro-Mediterranean Partnership." In Emanuel Adler et al. (eds.): *The Convergence of Civilizations: Constructing a Mediterranean Region* (Toronto: University of Toronto Press, 2006), pp. 3–49.

Adler, Emanuel and Vincent Pouliot: "International Practices." *International Theory* 3:1 (2011), pp. 1–36. [2011a]

Adler, Emanuel and Vincent Pouliot (eds.) *International Practices* (Cambridge: Cambridge University Press, 2011). [2011b]

Adler, Emanuel, et al. (eds.): *The Convergence of Civilizations: Constructing a Mediterranean Region* (Toronto: University of Toronto Press, 2006).

Adorno, Theodor W.: "Society." *Salmagundi* 10–11 (1969–70), pp. 144–153.

Adorno, Theodor W.: *Negative Dialectics*, tr. E. B. Ashton (New York: Continuum, 1973).

Adorno, Theodor W.: *Minima Moralia* (London: Verso, 1974).

Adorno, Theodor W.: *Against Epistemology: A Metacritique* (Cambridge, MA: MIT Press, 1983).

Adorno, Theodor W.: *Prisms* (Cambridge, MA: MIT Press, 1983).

Adorno, Theodor W.: *The Culture Industry: Essays on Mass Culture* (London: Routledge, 1991).

Adorno, Theodor W.: *Aesthetic Theory*, tr. Robert Hullot-Kentor (Minneapolis: University of Minnesota Press, 1997).

Adorno, Theodor W.: *Introduction to Sociology* (Stanford, CA: Stanford University Press, 2000).

Adorno, Theodor W.: *Problems of Moral Philosophy* (Stanford, CA: Stanford University Press, 2001).

Adorno, Theodor W.: *Critical Models: Interventions and Catchphrases* (New York: Columbia University Press, 2005).

Adorno, Theodor W.: *History and Freedom* (London: Polity, 2006).

Adorno, Theodor W., et al.: *The Positivist Debate in German Sociology* (Portsmouth, NH: Heinemann, 1977).

Adorno, Theodor W., and Horkheimer, Max: *Dialectic of Enlightenment: Philosophical Fragments*, tr. Edmund Jephcott. (Stanford, CA: Stanford University Press, 2002).

Agamben, Giorgio: *Remnants of Auschwitz* (Brooklyn, NY: Zone, 2002).

Ahluwalia, Pal, and Michael Sullivan: "Beyond International Relations: Edward Said and the World." In Robert M. A. Crawford and Darryl S. L. Jarvis (eds.): *International Relations: Still an American Social Science?* (Albany, NY: State University of New York Press, 2001), pp. 349–67.

Ajami, Fouad: *The Arab Predicament* (Cambridge: Cambridge University Press, 1992).

Ajami, Fouad: *The Dream Palace of the Arabs* (New York: Vintage, 1999).

al Mdanat, Metri Fayez: *The Fiscal and Economic Impact of Qualifying Industrial Zones: The Case of Jordan* (Unpublished doctoral dissertation, Georg-August-Universität Göttingen, 2006): http://webdoc.sub.gwdg.de/diss/2007/al_mdanat_metri/al_mdanat_metri.pdf.

Albert, Mathias, and Tamar Kopp-Malek: "The Pragmatism of Global and European Governance: Emerging Forms of the Political 'Beyond Westphalia.'" *Millennium* 31:3 (2002), pp. 453–471.

Alcalay, Ammiel: *After Jews and Arabs: Remaking Levantine Culture* (Minneapolis: University of Minnesota Press, 1993).

Alker, Hayward, and Thomas J. Biersteker: "The Dialectics of World Order: Notes for a Future Archaeologist of International *Savoir Faire*." *International Studies Quarterly* 24:2 (1984), pp.121–142.

Alker, Hayward, and Bruce Russett: *World Politics in the General Assembly* (New Haven, CT: Yale University Press, 1965).

Alker, Hayward R.: "Political Community and Human Security." In Ken Booth (ed.): *Critical Security Studies and World Politics* (Boulder, CO: Lynne Rienner, 2005).

Alker, Hayward R.: "The Powers and Pathologies of Networks: Insights from the Political Cybernetics of Karl W. Deutsch and Norbert Wiener." *European Journal of International Relations* 17:2 (2011), pp. 351–378.

Allan, Pierre, and Kjell Goldmann: *The End of the Cold War: Evaluating Theories of International Relations* (London: Kluwer, 1995).

Allison, Graham: *Essence of Decision* (Boston: Little, Brown, 1971).

Allison, Graham, and Philip Zelikow: *Essence of Decision*, 2nd ed. (New York: Longman, 1999).

Almond, Gabriel A.: *The American People and Foreign Policy* (New York: Praeger, 1960).

Altman, Andrew, and Christopher Heath Wellman: *A Liberal Theory of International Justice* (New York: Oxford University Press, 2009).

Andersson, Hans E.: "What Activates an Identity? The Case of Norden." *International Relations* 24:1 (2010), pp. 46–64.

Angell, Norman: *The Great Illusion: A Study of the Relation of Military Power in Nations to Their Economic and Social Advantage* (New York: Putnam, 1910).

Anidjar, Gil: *The Jew, The Arab: A History of the Other* (Stanford, CA: Stanford University Press, 2003).

Anievas, Alexander: "Critical Dialogues: Habermasian Social Theory and International Relations." *Politics* 25:3 (2005), pp. 135–143.

Apel, Karl-Otto: "Is the Ethics of the Ideal Communication Community a Utopia? On the Relationship between Ethics, Utopia, and the Critique of Utopia." In Fred Dallmayr and Seyla Benhabib (eds.): *The Communicative Ethics Controversy* (Cambridge, MA: MIT Press, 1990), pp. 23–39.

Arato, Andrew: "The Neo-Idealist Defense of Subjectivity." *Telos* 21 (1974), pp. 108–161.

Arato, Andrew, and Paul Breines: *The Young Lukacs and the Origins of Western Marxism* (New York: Seabury, 1979).

Arendt, Hannah: *The Human Condition* (Chicago: University of Chicago Press, 1958).

Arendt, Hannah: *The Jew as Pariah: Jewish Identity and Politics in the Modern Age* (New York: Grove, 1978).

Arendt, Hannah: *Lectures on Kant's Political Philosophy* (Chicago: University of Chicago Press, 1989).

Arian, Asher: *Politics in Israel: The Second Generation* (Chatham, NJ: Chatham House, 1989).

Armstrup, Niels: "The 'Early' Morgenthau: A Comment on the Intellectual Origins of Realism." *Cooperation and Conflict* 13 (1978), pp. 163–175.

Aron, Raymond: "What Is a Theory of International Relations?" *Journal of International Affairs* 21 (1967), pp. 185–206.

Aron, Raymond: "Max Weber and Power Politics." In Otto Stammer (ed.): *Max Weber and Sociology Today* (New York: Harper Torchbooks, 1971), pp. 83–100.

Arquilla, John, and David Ronfeldt (eds.): *In Athena's Camp: Preparing for Conflict in the Information Age* (Santa Monica, CA: RAND, 1997).

Arrighi, Giovanni: *The Long Twentieth Century: Money, Power and the Origins of Our Times* (London: Verso, 1994).

Arrighi, Giovanni, and Beverly J. Silver (eds.): *Chaos and Governance in the Modern World System* (Minneapolis: University of Minnesota Press, 1999).

Ashley, Richard K.: "Political Realism and Human Interests." Symposium in Honor of Hans J. Morgenthau. *International Studies Quarterly* 25: 2 (1981), pp. 204–236.

Ashley, Richard K.: "The Poverty of Neorealism." *International Organization* 38:2 (1984), pp. 225–286.

Ashley, Richard K.: "Living on Border Lines: Man, Poststructuralism, and War." In James Der Derian and Michael J. Shapiro (eds.): *International/Intertextual Relations: Postmodern Readings of World Politics* (Lexington, MA: Lexington, 1989), pp. 261–321.

Ashley Richard K., and R. B. J. Walker: "Speaking the Language of Exile: Dissident Thought in International Relations." *International Studies Quarterly* 4 (1990), pp. 259–268.

Ashworth, Lucian M.: *Creating International Studies: Angell, Mitrany and the Liberal Tradition* (Aldershot, England: Ashworth, 1999).

Assmann, Jan: *Moses the Egyptian: The Memory of Egypt in Western Monotheism* (Cambridge, MA: Harvard University Press, 1997).

Avineiri, Shlomo, and Avner de-Shalit (eds.): *Communitarianism and Individualism* (New York: Oxford University Press, 1992).

Axelrod, Robert: *The Evolution of Cooperation* (New York: Basic Books, 1984).

Axelrod, Robert, and Robert O. Keohane: "Achieving Cooperation under Anarchy: Strategies and Institutions." In Kenneth W. Oye (ed.): *Cooperation under Anarchy* (Princeton, NJ: Princeton University Press, 1986), pp. 226–254.

Ayoob, Mohammed: *The Third World Security Predicament: State Making, Regional Conflict, and the International System* (Boulder, CO: Lynne Rienner, 1995).

Ayyash, Mark Muhannad: "Hamas and the Israeli State: A 'Violent Dialogue.'" *European Journal of International Relations* 16:1 (2010), pp. 103–123.

Bacevich, Andrew J.: "Introduction." In Reinhold Niebuhr: *The Irony of American History* (Chicago: University of Chicago Press, 2008). [2008a]

Bacevich, Andrew J.: *The Limits of Power: The End of American Exceptionalism.* (New York: Henry Holt, 2008). [2008b]

Bacevich, Andrew J.: "Prophets and *Poseurs*: Niebuhr and Our Times." *World Affairs* 170:3 (2008), pp. 24–37. [2008c]

Bachrach, Peter, and Morton S. Baratz: "Two Faces of Power." *American Political Science Review* 56:4 (1962), pp. 947–952.

Bacon, Francis: *New Organon and Related Writings*, ed. Fulton H. Anderson (Indianapolis : Bobbs-Merrill 1960),

Bain, William: "Deconfusing Morgenthau: Moral Inquiry and Classical Realism Reconsidered." *Review of International Studies* 26 (2000), pp. 445–465.

Baldwin, David: "The Concept of Security." *Review of International Studies* 23 (1997), pp. 5–26.

Baldwin, David A. (ed.): *Neorealism and Neoliberalism: The Contemporary Debate* (New York: Columbia University Press, 1993).

Balibar, Etienne: *Spinoza and Politics.* (London: Verso, 1998).

Barber, Benjamin: "The Politics of Political Science: 'Value-Free' Theory and the Wolin-Strauss Dust-Up of 1963." *American Political Science Review* 100:4 (2006), pp. 539–545.

Barber, Bernard: "All Economies are 'Embedded': The Career of a Concept and Beyond." *Social Research* 62:2 (1995), pp. 387–413.

Barder, Alexander and Daniel Levine: "'The World Is Too Much with Us': Reification and the Depoliticising of Via Media Constructivist IR." *Millennium* 40:3 (2012), pp. 585–604.

Barkawi, Tarak: "Strategy as a Vocation: Weber, Morgenthau and Modern Strategic Studies." *Review of International Studies* 24 (1998), pp. 159–184.

Barnett, Michael: "The Israeli Identity and the Peace Process: Re/creating the Un/Thinkable." In Michael Barnett and Shibley Telhami (eds.): *Identity and Foreign Policy in the Middle East* (Ithaca, NY: Cornell University Press, 2002), pp. 58–87.

Barnett, Michael, and Raymond Duvall: "Power in International Relations." *International Organization* 59 (2005), pp. 39–75.

Barnett, Michael, and Kathryn Sikkink: "From International Relations to Global Society." In Christian Reus-Smit and Duncan Snidal (eds.): *The Oxford Handbook of International Relations* (New York: Oxford University Press, 2008), pp. 62–83.

Barnett, Michael N.: *Dialogues in Arab Politics: Negotiations in Regional Order* (New York: Columbia University Press, 1998).

Bar-On, Dan: *The Others within Us: Constructing Jewish-Israeli Identity* (Cambridge: Cambridge University Press, 2008).

Bartelson, Jens: "Second Natures: Is the State Identical with Itself?" *European Journal of International Relations* 4:3 (1998), pp. 295–326.

Bauman, Zygmunt: *Modernity and the Holocaust* (Ithaca, NY: Cornell University Press, 1989).

Bauman, Zygmunt: *Globalization: The Human Consequences* (New York: Columbia University Press, 1998).

Bayliss, John, et al. (eds.): *The Globalization of World Politics: An Introduction to International Relations* (New York: Oxford University Press, 2008).

Beard, Charles: "Technology and the Creative Spirit in Political Science." *American Political Science Review* 21:1 (1927), pp. 1–11.

Beck, Ulrich: *The Reinvention of Politics* (Cambridge, England: Polity, 1997).

Beck, Ulrich: "Cosmopolitical Realism: On the Distinction between Cosmopolitanism in Philosophy and the Social Sciences." *Global Networks* 4 (2004), pp. 131–156.

Beck, Ulrich: "War Is Peace: On Post-National War." *Security Dialogue* 36 (2005), pp. 5–26.

Becker, Carl: *How New Will the Better World Be?* (New York: Knopf, 1944).

Behr, Hartmut, and Amelia Heath: "Misreading in IR Theory and Ideology Critique: Morgenthau, Waltz and Neo-Realism." *Review of International Studies* 35 (2009), pp. 327–349.

Beitz, Charles R.: *Political Theory and International Relations* (Princeton, NJ: Princeton University Press, 1999).

Bell, David A.: *The First Total War* (Boston: Houghton-Mifflin, 2007).

Bell, Duncan (ed.): *Political Thought and International Relations* (New York: Oxford University Press, 2009).

Bellah, Robert N., et al.: *Habits of the Heart: Individualism and Commitment in American Life* (Berkeley: University of California Press, 1985).

Bellin, Eva: "The Robustness of Authoritarianism in the Middle East: Exceptionalism in Comparative Perspective." *Comparative Politics* 36:2 (2004), pp. 139–157.

Ben-Ari, Eyal, and Yoram Bilu (eds.): *Grasping Land: Space and Place in Contemporary Israeli Discourse and Experience* (Albany: State University of New York, 1997).

Bender, Thomas: *The Intellect and Public Life: Essays on the Social History of Academic Intellectuals in the United States* (Baltimore: Johns Hopkins University Press, 1993).

Benhabib, Seyla: "The Critique of Instrumental Reason." In Slavoj Žižek (ed.): *Mapping Ideologies* (London: Verso, 1994).

Bennett, Jane: *The Enchantment of Modern Life: Attachments, Crossings, and Ethics* (Princeton, NJ: Princeton University Press, 2001).

Bennett, Jane: "The Agency of Assemblages and the North American Blackout." *Public Culture* 17:3 (2005), pp. 445–465.

Ben-Porat, Guy: *Global Liberalism, Local Populism: Peace and Conflict in Israel/Palestine and Northern Ireland* (Syracuse, NY: Syracuse University Press, 2006).

Benvenisti, Meron: *Intimate Enemies: Jews and Arabs in a Shared Land* (Berkeley: University of California Press, 1995).

Benvenisti, Meron: *City of Stone: The Hidden History of Jerusalem* (Berkeley: University of California Press, 1996).

Benvenisti, Meron: *Sacred Landscape: The Buried History of the Holy Land since 1948* (Berkeley: University of California Press, 2000).

Berger, Peter L., and Thomas Luckmann: *The Social Construction of Reality: A Treatise in the Sociology of Knowledge* (New York: Doubleday, 1967).

Berlin, Isaiah: *Four Essays on Liberty* (New York: Oxford University Press, 1969).

Berman, Marshall: *All That Is Solid Melts into Air: The Experience of Modernity* (London: Verso, 1982).

Berman, Sheri: "The Primacy of Economics versus the Primacy of Politics: Understanding the Ideological Dynamics of the Twentieth Century" *Perspectives on Politics* 7:3 (2009), pp. 561–78.

Bernstein, J. M.: *Adorno: Disenchantment and Ethics* (Cambridge: Cambridge University Press, 2001).

Bernstein, Richard: *The Restructuring of Social and Political Theory* (New York: Harcourt Brace Jovanovich, 1976).

Bernstein, Richard: *The New Constellation* (London: Polity, 1991).

Bernstein, Steven, et al.: "God Gave Physics the Easy Problems: Adapting Social Science to an Unpredictable World." *European Journal of International Relations* 6:1 (2000), pp. 43–76.

Bewes, Timothy: *Reification* (London: Verso, 2002).

Bhaskar, Roy: *Reclaiming Reality* (London: Verso, 1989).

Bhaskar, Roy: *Dialectic: The Pulse of Freedom* (London: Verso, 1993).

Bially Mattern, Janice: "Why 'Soft Power' Isn't So Soft: Representational Force and the Sociolinguistic Construction of Attraction in World Politics." *Millennium* 33:3 (2005), pp. 583–612.

Biddle, Stephen: *Military Power: Explaining Victory and Defeat in Modern Battle* (Princeton, NJ: Princeton University Press, 2004).

Bigo, Didier, and R. B. J. Walker: "Political Sociology and the Problem of the International." *Millennium* 35:3 (2007), pp. 725–739.

Bilgin, Pinar: "Whose 'Middle East'? Geopolitical Inventions and Practices of Security." *International Relations* 18:1 (2004), pp. 25–41.

Billig, Michael: *Banal Nationalism* (London: Sage, 1995).

Blaney, David L., and Naeem Inayatullah: *International Relations and the Problem of Difference* (London: Routledge, 2004).

Bleicher, Josef: *Contemporary Hermeneutics: Hermeneutics as Method, Philosophy and Critique* (London: Routledge, 1980).

Bleiker, Roland: *Popular Dissent, Human Agency and Global Politics* (Cambridge: Cambridge University Press, 2000).

Bleiker, Roland: "The Aesthetic Turn in International Political Theory." *Millennium* 30:3 (2001), pp. 509–533.

Bleiker, Roland: *Aesthetics and World Politics* (New York: Palgrave, 2009).

Bloch, Jean de [Ivan]: *The Future of War in Its Technical, Economic and Political Relations* (Boston: Ginn, 1899).

Bluhm, William T. (ed.): *The Paradigm Problem in Political Science* (Durham, NC: Carolina Academic, 1982).

Bohman, James: "How to Make a Social Science Practical: Pragmatism, Critical Social Science and Multiperspectival Theory." *Millennium* 31:3 (2002), pp. 499–524.

Bohman, James: "Toward a Critical Theory of Globalization: Democratic Practice and Multiperspectival Inquiry." In Max Pensky (ed.): *Globalizing Critical Theory* (New York: Rowman and Littlefield, 2005), pp. 48–71.

Bohman, James: "What Is to Be Done? The Science Question in International Relations." *International Theory* 1:3 (2009), pp. 488–498.

Bonine, Michael E., et al.: *Where Is the Middle East?* (Stanford, CA: Stanford University Press, 2011).

Booth, Ken: "Security and Emancipation." *Review of International Studies* 17 (1991), pp. 313–326. [1991a]

Booth, Ken: "Security in Anarchy: Utopian Realism." *International Affairs* 67:3 (1991), pp. 527–545. [1991b]

Booth, Ken (ed.): *Critical Security Studies and World Politics* (Boulder, CO: Lynne Rienner, 2005).

Booth, Ken: *Theory of World Security* (Cambridge: Cambridge University Press, 2007).

Booth, Ken, and Nicholas Wheeler: *The Security Dilemma* (New York: Palgrave-Macmillan, 2008).

Boyarin, Jonathan, and Daniel Boyarin: *The Powers of Diaspora: Two Essays on the Relevance of Jewish Culture* (Minneapolis: University of Minnesota Press, 2002).

Brady, Henry E., and David Collier (eds.): *Rethinking Social Inquiry* (Lanham, MD: Rowman and Littlefield, 2004).

Brand, Laurie: *Palestinians in the Arab World: Institution-Building and the Search for State* (New York: Columbia University Press, 1988).

Brecht, Bertolt: *Poetry and Prose* (New York: Continuum, 2003).

Brincat, Shannon: "Negativity and Open-Endedness in the Dialectic of World Politics" *Alternatives* 34 (2009), pp. 455–93.

Bronner, Stephen Eric: *Of Critical Theory and Its Theorists*, 2nd ed. (London: Routledge, 2002).

Brooks, Stephen G.: "Dueling Realisms." *International Organization* 51:3 (1997), pp. 445–477.

Brooks, Stephen G., and William Curti Wohlforth: *World out of Balance: International Relations and the Challenge of American Primacy* (Princeton, NJ: Princeton University Press, 2008).

Brown, Chris: *International Relations Theory: New Normative Approaches* (New York: Harvester Wheatsheaf, 1992).

Brown, Chris: "Turtles All the Way Down." *Millennium* 23:2 (1994), pp. 213–236.

Brown, Chris: "(Moral) Agency and International Society: Reflections on Norms, the UN, Southampton FC, the Gulf War and the Kosovo Campaign." Paper presented at the annual meeting of the International Studies Association, Los Angeles, March 2000.

Brown, Chris: "Situating Critical Realism." *Millennium* 35:2 (2007), pp. 409–416.

Brown, Chris: "The 'Twilight of International Morality'? Hans J. Morgenthau and Carl Schmitt on the *Jus Publicum Europaeum*." In Michael C. Williams (ed.): *Realism Reconsidered: The Legacy of Hans J. Morgenthau in International Relations* (New York: Oxford University Press, 2007), pp. 42–61.

Brown, Nathan J.: *Palestinian Politics after the Oslo Accords* (Berkeley: University of California Press, 2003).

Brown, Seyom: *International Relations in a Changing Global System*, 2nd ed. (Boulder, CO: Westview, 1996).

Brubaker, Rogers: *Nationalism Reframed*. (Cambridge: Cambridge University Press, 1996).

Brynen, Rex: "The Dynamics of Palestinian Elite Formation." *Journal of Palestine Studies* 24:3 (1995), pp. 31–43. [1995a]

Brynen, Rex: "The Neopatrimonial Dimension of Palestinian Politics." *Journal of Palestine Studies* 25:1 (1995), pp. 23–36. [1995b]

Brynen, Rex: *A Very Political Economy: Peacebuilding and Foreign Aid in the West Bank and Gaza* (Washington, DC: US Institute for Peace, 2000).

Brzezinski, Zbigniew: *Out of Control* (New York: Touchstone, 1993).

Bull, Hedley: "International Theory: The Case for a Classical Approach." *World Politics* 18:3 (1966), pp. 361–377.

Bull, Hedley: *The Anarchical Society* (New York: Columbia University Press, 1995).

Burg, Avraham: *The Holocaust is Over; We Must Rise from its Ashes* (New York: Palgrave Macmillan, 2008).

Burke, Anthony: *Beyond Security, Ethics and Violence: War against the Other* (London: Routledge, 2007).

Burke, Anthony: "Nuclear Reason: At the Limits of Strategy." *International Relations* 23:4 (2009), pp. 506–529.

Burke, Donald A., et al.: *Adorno and the Need in Thinking* (Toronto: University of Toronto Press, 2007).

Burley, Anne-Marie: "Regulating the World: Multilateralism, International Law, and the Projection of the New Deal Regulatory State." In John Gerard Ruggie (ed.): *Multilateralism Matters* (New York: Columbia University Press, 1993), pp. 125–56.

Butterfield, Herbert: *Christianity and History* (New York: Scriber's, 1950).

Buzan, Barry: *People, States and Fear* (Boulder, CO: Lynne Rienner, 1991).

Buzan, Barry: "From International System to International Society: Structural Realism and Regime Theory Meet the English School." *International Organization* 47:3 (1993), pp. 327–352.

Buzan, Barry: *From International to World Society?* (Cambridge: Cambridge University Press, 2004).

Buzan, Barry, and Richard Little: *International Systems in World History* (New York: Oxford University Press, 2000).

Buzan, Barry, and Ole Waever: *Regions and Powers: The Structure of International Security* (Cambridge: Cambridge University Press, 2003).

Calhoun, Craig (ed.): *Habermas and the Public Sphere* (Cambridge, MA: MIT Press, 1992).

Calhoun, Craig (ed.): *Dictionary of the Social Sciences* (New York: Oxford University Press, 2002).

Campbell, David: *Writing Security: United States Foreign Policy and the Politics of Identity*, 2nd ed. (Minneapolis: University of Minnesota Press, 1998).

Campbell, David: "Beyond Choice: The Onto-Politics of Critique." *International Relations* 19:1 (2005), pp. 127–134.

Carr, Edward Hallett: *Conditions of Peace* (New York: Macmillan, 1942).

Carr, Edward Hallett: *Nationalism and After* (New York: Macmillan, 1945).

Carr, Edward Hallett: *The New Society* (Boston: Beacon, 1951).

Carr, Edward Hallett: *The Twenty Years' Crisis* (New York: Harper Torchbooks, 1964).

Carr, Edward Hallett: "An Autobiography." In Michael Cox (ed.): *E. H. Carr: A Critical Appraisal* (London: Palgrave, 2000).

C.A.S.E. Collective: "Critical Approaches to Security in Europe: A Networked Manifesto." *Security Dialogue* 33 (2006), pp. 443–487.

Castells, Manuel: *The Rise of the Networked Society*, 2nd ed. (Boston: Blackwell, 2000).

Castiglione, Dario: "Political Identity in a Community of Strangers." In Jeffrey T. Checkel and Peter J. Katzenstein (eds.): *European Identity* (Cambridge: Cambridge University Press, 2009), pp. 29–51.

Caverley, Jonathan: "Power and Democratic Weakness: Neoconservatism and Neoclassical Realism." *Millennium* 38:3 (2010), pp. 593–614.

Chambers, Simone: "The Politics of Critical Theory." In Fred Rush (ed.): *The Cambridge Companion to Critical Theory* (Cambridge: Cambridge University Press, 2004).

Charlesworth, James C. (ed.): *A Design for Political Science: Scope, Objectives, and Methods* (Philadelphia: American Academy of Political and Social Science, 1966).

Chase-Dunn, Christopher, and Joan Sokolovsky: "Interstate Systems, World-Empires and the Capitalist World-Economy: A Response to Thompson." *International Studies Quarterly* 27:3 (1983), pp. 357–367.

Checkel, Jeffrey: "The Constructivist Turn in International Relations." *World Politics* 50:2 (1998), pp. 324–348.

Checkel, Jeffrey T., and Peter J. Katzenstein (eds.): *European Identity* (Cambridge: Cambridge University Press, 2009).

Chernoff, Fred: *The Power of International Theory* (London: Routledge, 2005).

Chernoff, Fred: *Theory and Metatheory in International Relations* (New York: Palgrave-Macmillan, 2007).

Chernoff, Fred: "Defending Foundations for International Relations Theory." *International Theory* 1:3 (2009), pp. 466–477.

Christensen, Thomas J.: *Useful Adversaries: Grand Strategy, Domestic Mobilization and Sino-American Conflict, 1947–1958* (Princeton, NJ: Princeton University Press, 1996).

Christensen, Thomas J., and Jack Snyder: "Chain Gangs and Passed Bucks: Predicting Alliance Patterns in Multipolarity." *International Organization* 44:2 (1990), pp. 137–168.

Christensen, Thomas J., and Jack Snyder: "Progressive Research on Degenerate Alliances." *American Political Science Review* 91:4 (1997), pp. 919–922.

Clarke, I. F.: "Forecasts of War in Fiction, 1803–1914." *Comparative Studies of History and Society* 10:1 (1967), pp. 1–25.

Claude, Inis L.: *Swords into Plowshares: The Problems and Progress of International Organization*, 3rd ed. (New York, Random House, 1964).

Clausewitz, Carl von: *On War*, tr. Michael Howard and Peter Paret (Princeton, NJ: Princeton University Press, 1984).

Cochran, Molly: *Normative Theory in International Relations: A Pragmatic Approach* (Cambridge: Cambridge University Press, 1999).

Cockayne, James, and David Malone: "Creeping Unilateralism: How Operation Provide Comfort and the No-Fly Zones in 1991 and 1992 Paved the Way for the Iraq Crisis of 2003." *Security Dialogue* 37 (2006), pp. 123–141.

Cohen, Avner: *Israel and the Bomb* (New York: Columbia University Press, 1998).

Cohen, Eliot, et al.: *Knives, Tanks and Missiles: Israel's Security Revolution* (Washington, DC: Washington Institute for Near East Policy, 1998).

Cole, G. D. H. *Essays in Social Theory* (London: Macmillan, 1950).

Coles, Romand: *Rethinking Generosity: Critical Theory and the Politics of* Caritas (Ithaca, NY: Cornell University Press, 1997).

Comte, Auguste: *The Positive Philosophy of August Comte*, 3 vols., tr. and abr., Harriet Martineau (London: George Bell & Sons, 1896).

Connolly, William E.: *Political Science & Ideology* (New York: Atherton, 1967).

Connolly, William E.: *Appearance and Reality in Politics* (Cambridge: Cambridge University Press, 1981).

Connolly, William E.: *The Terms of Political Discourse*, 2nd ed. (Princeton, NJ: Princeton University Press, 1983).

Connolly, William E.: *Identity/Difference: Democratic Negotiations of Political Paradox* (Ithaca, NY: Cornell University Press, 1991).

Connolly, William E.: "Cross-State Citizen Networks: A Response to Dallmayr." *Millennium* 30:2 (2001), pp. 349–355.

Connolly, William E. *Neuropolitics: Thinking, Culture, Speed* (Minneapolis: University of Minnesota Press, 2002).

Connolly, William E.: "Problem, Method, Faith." In Ian Shapiro, Rogers M. Smith, and Tarek E. Masoud (eds.): *Problems and Methods in the Study of Politics* (Cambridge: Cambridge University Press, 2004), pp. 332–49.

Connolly, William E.: *Pluralism* (Durham, NC: Duke University Press, 2005).

Corwin, Edward S.: "The Democratic Dogma and the Future of Political Science." *American Political Science Review* 23:3 (1929), pp. 569–592.

Coudenhove-Kalergi, Richard N.: *Pan-Europe* (New York: Knopf, 1926).

Cox, Michael (ed.): *E. H. Carr: A Critical Appraisal* (London: Palgrave, 2000).

Cox, Robert W.: "The Executive Head: An Essay on Leadership in International Organization." *International Organization* 23:2 (1969), pp. 205–230.

Cox, Robert W.: "Social Forces, States and World Orders: Beyond International Relations Theory." *Millennium* 10:2 (1981), pp. 126–155.

Cox, Robert W.: "Critical Political Economy." In Björn Hettne: *International Political Economy: Understanding Global Disorder* (London: Zed, 1995).

Cox, Robert W.: *Approaches to World Order* (Cambridge: Cambridge University Press, 1996) [1996a].

Cox, Robert W.: "Civilizations in World Political Economy." *New Political Economy* 1:2 (July, 1996), pp. 141–56. [1996b]

Cox, Robert W.: "Thinking about Civilizations." *Review of International Studies* 26 (2000), pp. 217–234.

Cox, Robert W.: "The Way Ahead: Toward a New Ontology of World Order." In Richard Wyn Jones (ed.): *Critical Theory and World Politics*. (Boulder, CO: Lynne Rienner, 2001).

Cox, Robert W.: "The Point Is Not Just to Explain the World, but to Change It." In Christian Reus-Smit and Duncan Snidal (eds.): *The Oxford Handbook of International Relations* (Oxford: Oxford University Press, 2008), pp. 84–93.

Cozette, Muriel: "Reclaiming the Critical Dimension of Realism: Hans J. Morgenthau on the Ethics of Scholarship." *Review of International Studies* 34 (2008), pp. 5–27.

Craig, Campbell: *The Glimmer of a New Leviathan: Total War in the Realism of Niebuhr, Morgenthau and Waltz* (New York: Columbia University Press, 2003).

Craig, Campbell: "Hans Morgenthau and the World State Revisited." In Michael C. Williams (ed.): *Realism Reconsidered: The Legacy of Hans J. Morgenthau in International Relations* (New York: Oxford University Press, 2007), pp. 195–215.

Crawford, Neta C.: "Postmodern Ethical Conditions and a Critical Response." *Ethics and International Affairs* 12:1 (1998), pp. 121–140.

Crawford, Neta C.: "The Slippery Slope to Preventative War." *Ethics and International Affairs* 17:1 (2003), pp. 30–36.

Crawford, Neta C.: "Human Nature and World Politics: Rethinking 'Man.'" *International Relations* 23:3 (2009), pp. 271–288.

Crawford, Robert M. A., and Darryl S. L. Jarvis (eds.): *International Relations: Still an American Social Science?* (Albany: State University of New York, 2001).

Crooke, Alastair: *Resistance: The Essence of the Islamist Revolution* (London: Pluto, 2009).

Cummings, Mary L.: "Ethical and Social Issues in the Design of Weapon Control Interfaces." *Technology and Society* (2003), pp. 14–18.

Cummings, Mary L.: "Automation and Accountability in Decision Support System Interface Design." *Journal of Technology Studies* 32:1 (2006), pp. 23–31.

Curley, Edwin: "A Good Man Is Hard to Find." *Proceedings and Addresses of the American Philosophical Association* 65:3 (1991), pp. 29–45.

Curley, Edwin: "Kissinger, Spinoza and Genghis Khan." In Don Garrett (ed.): *The Cambridge Companion to Spinoza* (Cambridge: Cambridge University Press, 1996).

Curtis, Simon, and Marjo Koivisto: "Towards a Second 'Second Debate'? Rethinking the Relationship between Science and History in International Theory." *International Relations* 24:4 (2010), pp. 433–455.

Dahl, Robert A: "The Concept of Power." *Behavioral Science* 2:3 (1957), pp. 201–215.

Dahl, Robert A., and Charles E. Lindblom: *Politics, Economics and Welfare: Planning and Politico-Economic Systems Resolved into Basic Social Processes* (New York: Harper & Brothers, 1953).

Dalby, Simon: "Contesting an Essential Concept: Reading the Dilemmas in Contemporary Security Discourse." In Keith Krause and Michael C. Williams: *Critical Security Studies* (Minneapolis: University of Minnesota Press, 1997).

Dallmayr, Fred: "Phenomenology and Critical Theory: Adorno." In Jay Bernstein (ed.): *The Frankfurt School: Critical Assessments, Vol. 3.* (London: Routledge, 1994).

Dallmayr, Fred: "Conversation across Boundaries: Political Theory and Global Diversity." *Millennium* 30:2 (2001), pp. 331–347.

Dannreuther, Roland: "Understanding the Middle East Peace Process: A Historical-Institutionalist Approach." *European Journal of International Relations* 17:2 (2010), pp. 187–208.

Davison, Roderic: "Where Is the Middle East?" *Foreign Affairs* 38:4 (1960), pp. 665–675.

Dawson, Grant: "Preventing a Great Moral Evil: Jean de Bloch's 'The Future of War' as Anti-Revolutionary Pacifism." *Journal of Contemporary History* 37:1 (2002), pp. 5–19.

de Assis, Joaquim Maria Machado: *The Posthumous Memoirs of Bras Cubas* (New York: Oxford University Press, 1997).

de Wilde, Jaap: *Saved from Oblivion: Interdependence Theory in the First Half of the Twentieth Century* (Aldershot, England: Dartmouth, 1991).

Dean, Mitchell: "*Nomos*: Word and Myth." In Louiza Odysseos and Fabio Petito: *The International Political Thought of Carl Schmitt* (London: Routledge, 2007).

Deibert, Ronald: "Harold Innis and the Empire of Speed." *Review of International Studies* 25 (1999), pp. 273–289.

Del Sarto, Raffaella A.: *Contested State Identities and Regional Security in the Euro-Mediterranean Area* (New York: Palgrave-Macmillan, 2006).

Den Uyl, Douglas J.: *Power, State and Freedom: An Interpretation of Spinoza's Political Philosophy* (Assen, Netherlands: Van Gorcum, 1983).

Denich, Bette: "Dismembering Yugoslavia: Nationalist Ideologies and the Symbolic Revival of Genocide." *American Ethnologist* 21:2 (1994), pp. 367–390.

Der Derian, James: *Antidiplomacy: Spies, Terror, Speed and War* (Boston: Blackwell, 1992).

Der Derian, James: *Virtuous War: Mapping the Military-Industrial-Media-Entertainment Network War* (Boulder, CO: Westview, 2001).

Derrida, Jacques: *Writing and Difference* (Chicago: University of Chicago Press, 1978).

Descartes, René: *Discourse on the Method and Meditations*, tr. Laurence J. Lafleur (New York: Library of Liberal Arts, 1960).

Dessler, David: "What's at Stake in the Agent-Structure Debate?" *International Organization* 43: 3 (1989), pp. 441–473.

Dessler, David: "Constructivism within a Positivist Social Science." *Review of International Studies* 25 (1999), pp. 123–137.

Deudney, Daniel H.: "The Case against Linking Environmental Degradation and National Security." *Millennium* 19:3 (1990), pp. 461–476.

Deudney, Daniel H.: "Publius before Kant: Federal-Republican Security and Democratic Peace." *European Journal of International Relations* 10:3 (2004), pp. 315–356.

Deudney, Daniel H.: *Bounding Power: Republican Security Theory from the Polis to the Global Village* (Princeton, NJ: Princeton University Press, 2007).

Deutsch, Karl W.: *Nationalism and Social Communication* (New York: Technology Press and Wiley, 1953).

Deutsch, Karl W.: *Political Community at the International Level: Problems of Definition and Measurement* (New York: Doubleday, 1954).

Deutsch, Karl W.: "Anatomy and Boundaries According to Communications Theory." In Roy G. Grinker: *Toward a Unified Theory of Human Behavior* (New York: Basic Books, 1956).

Deutsch, Karl W.: "Scientific and Humanistic Knowledge." In Harcourt Brown (ed.): *Science and the Creative Spirit* (Toronto: University of Toronto Press, 1958).

Deutsch, Karl W.: "The Limits of Common Sense." *Psychiatry* 22:2 (1959), pp. 105–113.

Deutsch, Karl W.: "Toward an Inventory of Basic Trends and Patterns in Comparative and International Politics." *American Political Science Review* 54:1 (1960), pp. 34–57.

Deutsch, Karl W.: *Nerves of Government* (Glencoe, IL: Free Press of Glencoe, 1963).

Deutsch, Karl W.: "Introduction." In *The Nerves of Government*, 2nd ed. (New York: Free Press, 1966).

Deutsch, Karl W.: *The Analysis of International Relations* (Englewood Cliffs, NJ: Prentice-Hall, 1968).

Deutsch, Karl W.: "On Political Theory and Political Action." *American Political Science Review* 65:1 (1971), pp. 11–27.

Deutsch, Karl W.: *Peace Research: The Needs, the Problems and the Prospects* (Middlebury, VT: Middlebury College, John Hamilton Fulton Memorial Lectureship in the Liberal Arts, 1972).

Deutsch, Karl W.: "Some Memories of Norbert Wiener: The Man and His Thoughts." *IEEE Transactions on Systems, Man and Cybernetics* (May, 1975), pp. 368–372.

Deutsch, Karl W.: "Toward Drift Models and Steering Models." In Karl W. Deutsch et al. (eds.): *Problems of World Modeling: Political and Social Implications* (Cambridge, MA: Ballinger, 1977), pp. 5–10.

Deutsch, Karl W.: *Tides among Nations.* (New York: Free Press, 1979).

Deutsch, Karl W.: "Political Research in the Changing World System." *International Political Science Review* 1:1 (1980), pp. 23–33.

Deutsch, Karl W., and William J. Foltz (eds.): *Nation-Building* (New York: Atherton, 1963).

Deutsch, Karl W., et al.: *Political Community and the North Atlantic Area.* (Princeton, NJ Princeton University Press, 1957).

Deutsch, Karl W., et al.: *France, Germany and the Western Alliance* (New York: Scribner's, 1967).

Deutsch, Karl W., et al. (eds.): *Problems of World Modeling: Political and Social Implications* (Cambridge, MA: Ballinger, 1977).

Devetak, Richard: "Critical Theory." In Scott Burchill and Andrew Linklater: *Theories of International Relations* (London: Macmillan, 1996).

Dewey, John: *The Public and Its Problems. The Later Works, 1925–53, Vol. 2* (Carbondale, IL: Southern Illinois University Press, 1981).

Diesing, Paul: *How Does Social Science Work? Reflections on Practice* (Pittsburgh, PA: University of Pittsburgh Press, 1991).

Dietz, Mary G.: *Turning Operations: Feminism, Arendt, and Politics.* (London: Routledge, 2002).

Diez, Thomas, and Jill Steans: "A Useful Dialogue? Habermas and International Relations." *Review of International Relations* 31 (2005), pp. 127–140.

Dilthey, Wilhelm: "The Rise of Hermeneutics." *New Literary History* 3:2 (1972), pp. 229–244.

Dilthey, Wilhelm: *Introduction to the Human Sciences.* (Princeton: Princeton University Press, 1989), tr. Rudolf A. Makkreel and Frithjof Rodi.

Disraeli, Benjamin: *Tancred; or, The New Crusade* (London: Longmans, Green, 1878).

Donnelly, Jack: *Realism and International Relations* (Cambridge: Cambridge University Press, 2000).

Don-Yehiya, Eliezer, and Charles Liebman: *Religion and Politics in Israel* (Bloomington: Indiana University Press, 1984).

Doty, Roxanne Lynn: "Desire All the Way Down." *Review of International Studies* 26 (2000), pp. 137–139.

Dougherty, James E., and Robert L. Pfaltzgraff Jr.: *Contending Theories of International Relations* (New York: Longman, 2001).

Doyle, Michael W.: *Ways of War and Peace* (New York: Norton, 1997).

Drori, Israel: *The Seam Line: Arab Workers and Jewish Managers in the Israeli Textile Industry* (Stanford, CA: Standard University Press, 2000).

Durkheim, Emile: *The Rules of Sociological Method* (New York: Free Press, 1964).

Duster, Troy: "Race and Reification in Science." *Science* 307 (2005), pp. 1050–1051.

Eagleton-Pierce, Matthew: "Advancing a Reflexive International Relations." *Millennium* 39:3 (2011), pp. 805–23.

Eastby, John H.: *Functionalism and Interdependence* (New York: University Press of America, 1985).

Eckersley, Robyn: "The Ethics of Critical Theory." In Duncan Snidal and Christian Reus-Smit (eds.): *The Oxford Handbook of International Relations* (New York: Oxford University Press, 2008), pp. 346–58.

Edgar, Andrew: "Reification." In William Outhwaite and Tom Bottomore (eds.): *The Blackwell Dictionary of Twentieth-Century Social Thought* (Oxford: Blackwell Reference, 1993), pp. 552–553.

Edkins, Jenny: *Poststructuralism and International Relations: Bringing the Political Back In* (Boulder, CO: Lynne Rienner, 1999).

Ellis, David C.: "On the Possibility of 'International Community.'" *International Studies Review* 11 (2009), pp. 1–26.

Elman, Colin: "Horses for Courses: Why Not Neorealist Theories of Foreign Policy?" *Security Studies* 6 (1996), pp. 7–53.

Elman, Colin, and Miriam Fendius Elman: "How Not to Be Lakatos Intolerant: Appraising Progress in IR Research." *International Studies Quarterly* 46 (2002), pp. 231–262.

Elman, Colin, and Miriam Fendius Elman (eds.): *Progress in International Relations Theory: Appraising the Field* (Cambridge, MA: MIT University Press, 2003).

Engle, Howard Edward: *A Critical Study of the Functionalist Approach to International Organization* (Unpublished Ph.D. Dissertation, Department of Public Law and Government, Columbia University, 1957).

Epp, Roger: "The English School on the Frontiers of International Society: A Hermeneutic Recollection." *Review of International Studies* 24:5 (1998), pp. 47–64.

Eriksen, Erik Oddvar: "An Emerging European Public Sphere." *European Journal of Social Theory* 8:3 (2005), pp. 341–363.

Etzioni, Amitai: *A Responsible Society: Collected Essays on Guiding Deliberate Social Change* (San Francisco, CA: Jossey-Bass, 1991).

Etzioni, Amitai: *The Spirit of Community: Rights, Responsibilities and the Communitarian Agenda* (New York: Crown, 1993).

Etzioni, Amitai (ed.): *New Communitarian Thinking: Persons, Values, Institutions, and Communities* (Charlottesville: University of Virginia Press, 1995).

Etzioni, Amitai: *Political Unification Revisited* (Lanham, MD: Lexington, 2001).

Evans, Gareth, and Yoriko Kawaguchi: *Eliminating Nuclear Threats: A Practical Agenda for Policymakers* (Canberra and Tokyo: International Commission on Nuclear Non-Proliferation, 2009).

Evans, Peter: *Embedded Autonomy: States and Industrial Transformation* (Princeton, NJ: Princeton University Press, 1995).

Eyal, Gil: *The Disenchantment of the Orient: Expertise in Arab Affairs and the Israeli State* (Stanford, CA: Stanford University Press, 2006).

Fackenheim, Emil: *The God Within: Kant, Schelling and Historicity.* (Toronto: University of Toronto Press, 1996).

Feaver, Peter D., et al.: "Brother, Can You Spare a Paradigm? (Or Was Anybody Ever a Realist?)." *International Security* 25:1 (2000), pp. 165–193.

Fierke, K. M.: *Changing Games, Changing Strategies.* (Manchester, England: Manchester University Press, 1998).

Finnemore, Martha: *National Interests in International Society* (Ithaca, NY: Cornell University Press, 1996).

Flathman, Richard E.: *Thomas Hobbes: Skepticism, Individuality, and Chastened Politics* (London: Sage, 1993).

Floyd, Rita: "Towards a Consequentialist Evaluation of Security: Bringing Together the Copenhagen and the Welsh Schools of Security Studies." *Review of International Studies* 33 (2007) pp. 327–350.

Fluck, Matthew: "Theory Truth, Values and the Value of Truth in Critical International Relations." *Millennium* 39:2 (2010), pp. 259–78.

Follett, Mary Parker: *The New State: Group Organization, the Solution of Popular Government* (University Park: Pennsylvania State University Press, 1998).

Foltz, William J.: *From French West Africa to the Mali Federation* (New Haven, CT: Yale University Press, 1965).

Forbes, Bruce David, and Jeanne Halgren Kilde (eds.): *Rapture, Revelation, and the End Times: Exploring the* Left Behind *Series* (New York: Palgrave-Macmillan, 2004).

Foucault, Michel: *Discipline and Punish* (New York: Vintage, 1979).

Foucault, Michel: *Politics, Philosophy, Culture: Interviews and Other Writings, 1977–1984*, ed. Lawrence D. Kritzman (London: Routledge, 1988).

Foucault, Michel: *"Society" Must be Defended* (London: Picador, 2004).

Fox, William T. R. (ed.): *Theoretical Aspects of International Relations* (Notre Dame, IN: University of Notre Dame Press, 1959).

Frankel, Benjamin (ed.): *Realism: Restatements and Renewal.* (London: Frank Cass, 1996).

Franklin, Marianne (ed.): *Resounding International Relations* (London: Palgrave-Macmillan, 2005).

Frei, Christoph: *Hans J. Morgenthau: An Intellectual Biography* (Baton Rouge: Louisiana State University Press, 2001).

Freund, Julien: *The Sociology of Max Weber* (New York: Pantheon, 1968).

Friedberg, Aaron L.: *The Weary Titan: Britain and the Experience of Relative Decline* (Princeton, NJ: Princeton University Press, 1988).

Friedberg, Aaron L.: *In the Shadow of the Garrison State: America's Anti-Statism and Its Cold War Grand Strategy* (Princeton, NJ: Princeton University Press, 2000).

Friedmann, W. [Wolfgang Gaston]: *Legal Theory*, 5th ed. (New York: Columbia University Press, 1967).

Friedrichs, Jörg, and Friedrich Kratochwil: "On Acting and Knowing: How Pragmatism Can Advance International Relations Research and Methodology." *International Organization* 63 (2009), pp. 701–731.

Fromkin, David: *A Peace to End All Peace: The Fall of the Ottoman Empire and the Creation of the Modern Middle East* (New York: Avon, 1990).

Frost, Mervyn: *Ethics in International Relations: A Constitutive Theory* (Cambridge: Cambridge University Press, 1996).

Frost, Mervyn: "A Road Not Taken: Ethics in IR at the Millennium." *Review of International Studies* 24 (1998), pp. 119–132.

Frost, Mervyn: "Common Practices in a Plural World: The Bases for a Theory of Practice." In Maria Lensu and Jan-Stefan Fritz (eds.): *Value Pluralism, Normative Theory, and International Relations* (London: Macmillan, 2000), pp. 1–23.

Frost, Mervyn: *Global Ethics: Anarchy, Freedom and International Relations* (London: Routledge, 2009).

Fukuyama, Francis: *The End of History and the Last Man* (New York: Free Press, 1992).

Gadamer, Hans-Georg: *Truth and Method* (New York: Continuum, 1975).

Gal, Reuven, and Stuart Cohen: "Israel: Still Waiting in the Wings." In Charles C. Moskos, et al. (eds.): *The Postmodern Military* (New York: Oxford University Press, 2000), pp. 224–41.

Gallie, W. B.: "Essentially Contested Concepts." *Proceedings of the Aristotelian Society* 56 (1955–56), pp. 167–198.

Galston William A.: *Liberal Purposes: Goods, Virtues and Diversity in the Liberal State* (Cambridge: Cambridge University Press, 1991).

Galtung, Johan: "Violence, Peace, and Peace Research." *Journal of Peace Research* 6:3 (1969), pp. 167–191.

Galtung, Johan: *Peace by Peaceful Means* (Thousand Oaks, CA: Sage, 1996).

Gartzke, Eric and Megumi Naoi: "Multilateralism and Democracy: A Dissent Regarding Keohane, Macedo, and Moravcsik." *International Organization* 65:3 (2011), pp. 589–98.

Gat, Azar: *War in Human Civilization* (New York: Oxford University Press, 2006).

Gazit, Shlomo: *Trapped Fools: Thirty Years of Israeli Policy in the Territories* (Portland, OR: Frank Cass, 2003).

Gelvin, James L.: *The Israel-Palestine Conflict: One Hundred Years of War* (Cambridge: Cambridge University Press, 2005).

George, Jim: *Discourses of Global Politics: A Critical (Re)introduction to International Relations* (Boulder, CO: Lynne Rienner, 1994).

Geyer, Felix, and Johannes van der Zouwen: "Norbert Wiener and the Social Sciences." *Kybernetes* 23:6–7 (1994), pp. 46–61.

Ghamari-Tabrizi, Sharon: *The Worlds of Herman Kahn* (Cambridge, MA: Harvard University Press, 2005).

Giddens, Anthony: *The Constitution of Society: Outline of a Theory of Structuration.* (Berkeley: University of California Press, 1984).

Gilbert, Alan: *Must Global Politics Constrain Democracy? Great-Power Realism, Democratic Peace, and Democratic Internationalism* (Princeton, NJ: Princeton University Press, 1999).

Gilman, Nils: *Mandarins of the Future: Modernization Theory in Cold War America* (Baltimore: Johns Hopkins University Press, 2003).

Gilpin, Robert: *War and Change in International Politics* (Cambridge: Cambridge University Press, 1981).

Gilpin, Robert: "The Richness of the Tradition of Political Realism." *International Organization* 38:2 (1984), pp. 287–304.

Gilpin, Robert: "No One Loves a Political Realist." *Security Studies* 5 (1996) pp. 3–26.

Gismondi, Mark: "Tragedy, Realism, and Postmodernity: *Kulturpessimismus* in the Theories of Max Weber, E. H. Carr, Hans J. Morgenthau, and Henry Kissinger." *Diplomacy and Statecraft* 15:3 (2004), pp. 435–464.

Glaser, Charles L.: "Realists as Optimists: Cooperation as Self-Help." *International Security* 19:3 (1994–95), pp. 50–90.

Glynos, Jason, and David Howarth: *Logics of Critical Explanation in Social and Political Theory* (London: Routledge, 2007).

Goddard, Stacie E.: *Indivisible Territory and the Politics of Legitimacy: Jerusalem and Northern Ireland* (Cambridge: Cambridge University Press, 2010).

Goldmann, Lucien: *Cultural Creation* (St. Louis, MO: Telos, 1976).

Goldscheider, Calvin: *Israel's Changing Society: Population, Ethnicity and Development* (Boulder, CO: Westview, 2002).

Gorenberg, Gershom: *The End of Days: Fundamentalism and the Struggle for the Temple Mount* (New York: Free Press, 2000).

Gould, Harry: "What *Is* at Stake in the Agent-Structure Debate?" In Vendulka Kubálková, et al. (eds): *International Relations in a Constructed World* (Armonk, NY: ME Sharpe, 1998), pp. 79–98.

Gray, Colin: "Nuclear Strategy: The Case for a Theory of Victory." *International Security* 4:1 (1979), pp. 54–87.

Green, Andrew Wilson: "Review Article: Mitrany Reread with the Help of Haas and Sewell." *Journal of Common Market Studies* 8 (1969), pp. 50–69.

Griffiths, Martin: *International Relations Theory for the Twenty-First Century* (London: Routledge, 2007).

Grose, Peter J.: *Israel in the Mind of America* (New York: Knopf, 1983).

Gross, David: "Lowenthal, Adorno, Barthes: Three Perspectives on Popular Culture." *Telos* 45 (1980), pp. 122–140.

Guilhot, Nicolas: "The Realist Gambit: Postwar American Political Science and the Birth of IR Theory." *International Political Sociology* 2 (2008), pp. 281–304.

Guilhot, Nicolas: "American Katechon: When Political Theology Became IR Theory." *Constellations* 17:2 (2010), pp. 224–53.

Guilhot, Nicolas (ed.): *The Invention of International Relations Theory: Realism, the Rockefeller Foundation, and the 1954 Conference on Theory* (New York: Columbia University Press, 2011).

Gunnell, John: "The Founding of the American Political Science Association: Discipline, Profession, Political Theory and Politics." *American Political Science Review* 100:4 (2006), pp. 479–486.

Guyer, Paul: *Kant and the Claims of Knowledge* (Cambridge: Cambridge University Press, 1987).

Guyer, Paul, and Allen W. Wood: "Introduction." In *Immanuel Kant: The Critique of Pure Reason*, tr. Paul Guyer and Allen W. Wood (Cambridge: Cambridge University Press, 1998), pp. 1–72

Guzzini, Stefano: "Structural Power: The Limits of Neorealist Power Analysis." *International Organization* 47:3 (1993), pp. 443–478.

Guzzini, Stefano: *Realism in International Relations and International Political Economy: The Continuing Story of a Death Foretold* (London: Routledge, 1998).

Guzzini, Stefano: "The Enduring Dilemmas of Realism in International Relations." *European Journal of International Relations* 10:4 (2004), pp. 533–568.

Guzzini, Stefano: "The Concept of Power: A Constructivist Analysis." *Millennium* 33:3 (2005), pp. 495–521.

Guzzini, Stefano, and Anna Leander (eds.): *Constructivism and International Relations: Alexander Wendt and His Critics* (London: Routledge, 2006).

Guzzini, Stefano, and Dietrich Jung (eds.): *Contemporary Peace Analysis and Copenhagen Research* (London: Routledge, 2004).

Haacke, Jürgen: "The Frankfurt School and International Relations: on the Centrality of Recognition." *Review of International Studies* 31 (2005), pp. 181–194.

Haas, Ernst B.: "The Balance of Power as a Guide to Policy-Making." *Journal of Politics* 15:3 (1953), pp. 370–389. [1953a]

Haas, Ernst B.: "The Balance of Power: Prescription, Concept, or Propaganda." *World Politics* 5:4 (1953), pp. 442–477. [1953b]

Haas, Ernst B.: *The Uniting of Europe* (London: Stevens & Sons, 1958).

Haas, Ernst B.: "International Integration: The European and the Universal Process." *International Organization* 15:3 (1961), pp. 366–392.

Haas, Ernst B.: *Beyond the Nation-State* (Stanford, CA: Stanford University Press, 1964).

Haas, Ernst B.: "*The Uniting of Europe* and the Uniting of Latin America." *Journal of Common Market Studies* 5 (1967), pp. 315–43.

Haas, Ernst B.: "The Study of Regional Integration: Reflections on the Joy and Anguish of Pretheorizing." *International Organization* 24:4 (1970), pp. 607–646.

Haas, Ernst B.: "Is There a Hole in the Whole? Knowledge, Technology, Interdependence and the Construction of International Regimes." *International Organization* 29:3 (1975), pp. 827–876. [1975a]

Haas, Ernst B.: *The Obsolescence of Regional Integration Theory* (Berkeley: Institute of International Studies, University of California, Berkeley, 1975). [1975b]

Haas, Ernst B.: "Words Can Hurt You: Or, Who Said What to Whom about Regimes." *International Organization* 36:2 (1982), pp. 207–243.

Haas, Ernst B.: *When Knowledge Is Power* (Berkeley: University of California Press, 1990).

Haas, Ernst B.: "Reason and Change in International Life: Justifying a Hypothesis." In Robert L. Rothstein (ed.): *The Evolution of Theory in International Relations* (Columbia: University of South Carolina Press, 1991), pp. 189–220.

Haas, Ernst B.: *Nationalism, Liberalism and Progress*, 2 vols. (Ithaca, NY: Cornell University Press, 1997).

Haas, Ernst B.: "Does Constructivism Subsume Neo-Functionalism?" In Thomas Christiansen, Knud Erik Jørgensen, and Antje Wiener (eds.): *The Social Construction of Europe* (London: Sage, 2001), pp. 22–31.

Haas, Ernst B.: "Introduction: Institutionalism or Constructivism?" In *The Uniting of Europe* (Notre Dame, IN: University of Notre Dame Press, 2004), pp. *xiii-*lvii.

Haas, Ernst B., et al.: *Scientists and World Order* (Berkeley: University of California Press, 1977).

Haas, Ernst B., and Peter Haas: "Pragmatic Constructivism and the Study of International Institutions." *Millennium* 31:3 (2002), pp. 573–601.

Haas, Ernst B., and Phillipe C. Schmitter: "Economics and Differential Patterns of Political Integration: Projections about Unity in Latin America." *International Organization* 18:4 (1964), pp. 705–737.

Haas, Ernst B., Mary Pat Williams, and Don Babai: *Scientists and World Order: The Uses of Technical Knowledge in International Organizations* (Berkeley: University of California Press, 1977).

Habermas, Jürgen: *Knowledge and Human Interests* (Boston: Beacon, 1971).

Habermas, Jürgen: *Legitimation Crisis* (Boston: Beacon, 1975).

Habermas, Jürgen: "The Dialectics of Rationalization: An Interview with Jürgen Habermas." *Telos* 49 (1981), pp. 5–32.

Habermas, Jürgen: *The Theory of Communicative Action*, 2 vols. (Boston: Beacon, 1984–87).

Habermas, Jürgen: *Philosophical-Political Profiles* (Cambridge, MA: MIT Press, 1985).

Habermas, Jürgen: *On the Logic of the Social Sciences* (Boston: Beacon, 1988).

Habermas, Jürgen: *Structural Transformation of the Public Sphere* (Cambridge, MA: MIT Press, 1989).

Habermas, Jürgen: *Postmetaphysical Thinking* (Cambridge, MA: MIT Press, 1992).

Habermas, Jürgen: "The Entwinement of Myth and Enlightenment: Re-Reading the *Dialectic of Enlightenment*." In Jay Bernstein (ed.): *The Frankfurt School: Critical Assessments, Vol. 3* (London: Routledge, 1994), pp. 35–50.

Habermas, Jürgen: *The Philosophical Discourse of Modernity: Twelve Lectures* (Cambridge, MA: MIT Press, 1997).

Habermas, Jürgen: *The Postnational Constellation: Political Essays* (Cambridge, MA: MIT Press, 2001).

Habermas, Jürgen: *Between Naturalism and Religion* (London: Polity, 2008).

Habermas, Jürgen, and Jacques Derrida: "February 15, or What Binds Europeans Together: A Plea for a Common Foreign Policy, Beginning in the Core of Europe." *Constellations* 10:3 (2003), pp. 292–297.

Hacke, Christian, and Jana Puglierin: "John H. Herz: Balancing Utopia and Reality." *International Relations* 21:3 (2007), pp. 367–382.

Hacking, Ian: "The Looping Effects of Human Kinds." In Dan Sperber, David Premack, and Ann James Premack (eds.): *Causal Cognition: A Multidisciplinary Debate* (Oxford: Clarendon, 1995), pp. 351–383.

Haidu, Peter: "The Dialectics of Unspeakability: Language, Silence and the Narratives of Desubjectification." In Saul Friedländer (ed.): *Probing the Limits of Representation: Nazism and the "Final Solution"* (Cambridge, MA: Harvard University Press, 1992), pp. 277–299.

Hall, John A.: "Ideas and the Social Sciences." In Robert O. Keohane and Judith Goldstein (eds.): *Ideas and Foreign Policy: Beliefs, Institutions and Political Change* (Ithaca, NY: Cornell University Press, 1993), pp. 31–54.

Halliday, Fred: *Rethinking International Relations* (Vancouver: University of British Columbia Press, 1994).

Halliday, Fred: *The Middle East in International Relations: Power, Politics and Ideology* (Cambridge: Cambridge University Press, 2005).

Halliday, Fred, and Justin Rosenberg: "Interview with Kenneth Waltz." *Review of International Studies* 24 (1998), pp. 371–386.

Hamati-Ataya, Inanna: "Contemporary 'Dissidence' in American IR: The New Structure of Anti-Mainstream Scholarship?" *International Studies Perspectives* 12 (2011), pp. 362–98. [2011a]

Hamati-Ataya, Inanna: "The 'Problem of Values' and International Relations Scholarship: From Applied Reflexivity to Reflexivism." *International Studies Review* 13 (2011), pp. 259–287. [2011b]

Hamilton, Alexander, James Madison, and John Jay: *The Federalist: with the Letters of "Brutus"* (Cambridge: Cambridge University Press, 2003).

Hammami, Rema: "Palestinian NGOs since Oslo: From NGO Politics to Social Movements?" *Middle East Report* 214 (2000), pp. 16–17, 27, and 48.

Handel, Michael I.: "Numbers Do Count: The Question of Quality versus Quantity." In Samuel J. Huntington (ed.): *The Strategic Imperative* (Cambridge, MA: Ballinger, 1982), pp. 193–228.

Hansen, Lene, and Ole Waever: *European Integration and National Identity: The Challenge of the Nordic States* (London: Routledge, 2002).

Hansen, Roger D.: "Regional Integration: A Reflection on a Decade of Theoretical Efforts." *World Politics* 21:2 (1969), pp. 242–271.

Hardin, Garrett: "The Tragedy of the Commons." *Science*, December 13, 1968, pp. 1243–1248.

Hardt, Michael, and Antonio Negri: *Multitude: War and Democracy in the Age of Empire* (Cambridge, MA: Harvard University Press, 2004).

Harkabi, Yehoshefat: *The Bar-Kokhba Syndrome: Risk and Realism in Israeli Politics* (Chappaqua, NY: Rossel, 1983).

Harrison, Neil E. (ed.): *Complexity in World Politics* (Albany: State University of New York Press, 2006).

Hartwich, Wolf-Daniel, Aleida Assmann, and Jan Assmann: "Afterword." In Jacob Taubes: *The Political Theology of Paul* (Stanford, CA: Stanford University Press, 2004), pp. 115–42.

Harvey, David: *The Condition of Postmodernity* (Boston: Blackwell, 1990).

Haslam, Jonathan: *The Vices of Integrity: E. H. Carr, 1892–1982* (London: Verso, 1999).

Haslam, Jonathan: *No Virtue Like Necessity: Realist Thought in International Relations since Machiavelli* (New Haven, CT: Yale University Press, 2002).

Haugaard, Mark (ed.): *Power: A Reader* (Manchester, England: University of Manchester Press, 2002).

Hayek, Friedrich A. von: *The Road to Serfdom* (Chicago: University of Chicago Press, 1944).

Hazbun, Waleed: *Beaches, Ruins, Resorts: The Politics of Tourism in the Arab World* (Minneapolis: University of Minnesota Press, 2008).

Heath-Kelley, Charlotte: "Critical Terrorism Studies, Critical Theory and the 'Naturalistic Fallacy.'" *Security Dialogue* 41:3 (2010), pp. 235–54.

Heaphy, Brian: *Late Modernity and Social Change: Reconstructing Social and Personal Life* (London: Routledge, 2007).

Heberle, Rudolf: "The Sociological System of Ferdinand Tönnies: An Introduction." In Werner J. Cahnman (ed.): *Ferdinand Tönnies: A New Evaluation* (Leiden, Netherlands: E. J. Brill, 1973), pp. 47–69.

Hegel, G. W. F.: *Philosophy of Right*, tr. S.W. Dyde (Amherst, MA: Prometheus, 1996).

Heilbroner, Robert L.: *The Worldly Philosophers* (New York: Simon and Schuster, 1953).

Heims, Steve J. *John von Neumann and Norbert Wiener: From Mathematics to the Technologies of Life and Death* (Cambridge, MA: MIT Press, 1982).

Heims, Steve J.: *The Cybernetics Group* (Cambridge, MA: MIT Press, 1991).

Heine, Christian, and Benno Teschke: "Sleeping Beauty and the Dialectical Awakening: On the Potential of Dialectic for International Relations." *Millennium* 25:2 (1996), pp. 399–423.

Heller, Mark: *Continuity and Change in Israeli Security Policy* (Oxford: International Institute for Strategic Studies, 2000).

Heller, Mark: "September 11: The Clash within Civilizations." *Strategic Assessment* 4:4 (2002); http://www.inss.org.il/publications.php?cat=21&incat=&read=694, last accessed 19 April 2012. (NP)

Hellmann, Gunther (ed.): "Forum: Pragmatism and International Relations." *International Studies Review* 11 (2009), pp. 638–662.

Hemmer, Christopher, and Katzenstein, Peter J.: "Why Is There No NATO in Asia? Collective Identity, Regionalism, and the Origins of Multilateralism." *International Organization* 56:3 (2002), pp. 575–607.

Herder, Johann Gottfried von: *The Spirit of Hebrew Poetry*, 2 vols., tr. James Marsh (Burlington, VT: E. Smith, 1833).

Herrmann, Margaret G.: "One Field, Many Perspectives: Shifting from Debate to Dialogue." In Donald J. Puchala (ed.): *Visions of International Relations: Assessing an Academic Field* (Columbia: University of South Carolina Press, 2002), pp. 16–41.

Hersh, Seymour: *The Samson Option* (New York: Random House, 1991).

Herz, John: "Letter to the Morgenthau Conference." In Christian Hacke et al. (eds.): *The Heritage, Challenge and Future of Realism: In Memoriam, Hans J. Morgenthau (1904–1980)* (Göttingen: V & R Unipress, 2005), pp. 23–28.

Herz, John H.: "The Rise and Demise of the Territorial State." *World Politics* 9:4 (1957), pp. 473–493.

Herz, John H.: *International Politics in the Atomic Age* (New York: Columbia University Press, 1959).

Herz, John H.: "The Territorial State Revisited: Reflections on the Future of the Nation-State." *Polity* 1:1 (1968), pp. 11–34.

Hinsley, F. H.: *Power and the Pursuit of Peace* (Cambridge: Cambridge University Press, 1967).

Hirschman, Albert O.: "The Principle of the Hiding Hand." *The Public Interest* 6 (1967), pp. 10–23.

Hirschman, Albert O.: *The Passions and the Interests* (Princeton, NJ: Princeton University Press, 1977).

Hobhouse, L. T.: "The Law of the Three Stages." In *Sociology and Philosophy*, ed. Morris Ginsberg (Cambridge, MA: Harvard University Press, 1967), pp. 59–79.

Hobson, J. A.: *Imperialism: A Study* (New York: James Pott, 1902).

Hobson, John M.: "The Historical Sociology of the State and the State of Historical Sociology in International Relations." *Review of International Political Economy* 5:2 (1998), pp. 284–320.

Hoffman, Mark: "Critical Theory and the Inter-Paradigm Debate." *Millennium* 16:2 (1987), pp. 231–249.

Hoffman, Mark: "Conversations on Critical International Relations Theory." *Millennium* 17:1 (1988), pp. 91–95.

Hoffmann, Stanley H.: "International Relations: The Long Road to Theory." *World Politics* 11 (1958–59), pp. 346–377.

Hoffmann, Stanley H.: "Obstinate or Obsolete? The Fate of the Nation-State and the Case of Western Europe." *Daedalus* 95:3 (1966), pp. 862–915.

Hoffmann, Stanley H.: "Notes on the Elusiveness of Modern Power." *International Journal* 30 (1975), pp. 183–206.

Hoffmann, Stanley H.: "An American Social Science: International Relations," *Daedalus* 106 (1977), p. 51.

Holborn, Hajo: "The History of Ideas." *American Historical Review* 73:3 (1968), pp. 683–695.

Holden, Gerard: "Who Contextualizes the Contextualizers? Disciplinary History and the Discourse about IR Discourse." *Review of International Studies* 28:2 (2002), pp. 253–270.

Hollis, Martin: *The Philosophy of Social Science* (Cambridge: Cambridge University Press, 1994).

Hollis, Martin, and Steve Smith: *Explaining and Understanding International Relations* (Oxford: Clarendon, 1991).

Holsti, K. J.: *The Dividing Discipline* (Boston: Allen and Unwin, 1985).

Holsti, Ole R.: "Public Opinion and Foreign Policy: Challenges to the Almond-Lippmann Consensus Mershon Series: Research Programs and Debates." *International Studies Quarterly* 36 (1992), pp. 439–466.

Honig, Bonnie: *Political Theory and the Displacement of Politics* (Ithaca, NY: Cornell University Press, 1993).

Honig, Jan Willem: "Totalitarianism and Realism: Hans Morgenthau's German Years." *Security Studies* 5:2 (1995–96), pp. 283–313.

Honneth, Axel: *Disrespect: The Normative Foundations of Critical Theory* (Cambridge: Polity, 2007).

Honneth, Axel: *Reification: A New Look at an Old Idea* (New York: Oxford University Press, 2008).

Hook, Sidney, et al. "Western Values and Total War." *Commentary* (October 1961) pp. 277–304.

Hopf, Ted: *Social Construction of International Politics* (Ithaca, NY: Cornell University Press, 2002).

Hopgood, Stephen: "Moral Authority, Modernity and the Politics of the Sacred." *European Journal of International Relations* 15:2 (2009), pp. 229–255.

Horkheimer, Max: "The Lessons of Fascism." In Hadley Cantril (ed.): *Tensions That Cause Wars* (Urbana: University of Illinois Press, 1950).

Horkheimer, Max: *Critical Theory: Selected Essays* (New York: Continuum, 1986).

Horkheimer, Max: *The Eclipse of Reason* (New York: Continuum, 2004).

Horowitz, Dan, and Moshe Lissak: *Trouble in Utopia: The Overburdened Polity of Israel* (Albany: State University of New York Press, 1989).

Hostettler, Nick, and Alan Norrie: "Are Critical Realist Ethics Foundationalist?" In Justin Cruickshank (ed.): *Critical Realism: The Difference That It Makes.* (London: Routledge, 2003), pp. 30–54.

How, Alan: *The Habermas-Gadamer Debate and the Nature of the Social* (Aldershot, England: Avebury, 1995).

Hullot-Kentor, Robert (ed.): *Things Beyond Resemblance* (New York: Columbia University Press, 2006).

Hurd, Elizabeth Shakman: *The Politics of Secularism in International Relations* (Princeton, NJ: Princeton University Press, 2008).

Hutchings, Kimberly: "Speaking and Hearing: Habermasian Discourse Ethics, Feminism and IR." *Review of International Studies* 31 (2005), pp. 155–65.

Hutchings, Kimberly: *Kant, Critique and Politics* (London: Routledge, 1996).

Hutchings, Kimberly: *International Political Theory: Rethinking Ethics in a Global Era* (Thousand Oaks, CA: Sage, 1999).

Hutchings, Kimberly: "The Nature of Critique in Critical International Relations Theory." In Richard Wyn Jones (ed.): *Critical Theory and World Politics* (Boulder, CO: Lynne Rienner, 2001), pp. 45–61.

Hutchings, Kimberly: "Happy Anniversary! Time and Critique in International Relations Theory." *Review of International Studies* 33 (2007), pp. 71–89.

Huysmans, Jef: "Security! What Do You Mean? From Concept to Thick Signifier." *European Journal of International Relations* 4:2 (1998), pp. 226–255.

Huysmans, Jef: "Know Your Schmitt: A Godfather of Truth and the Specter of Nazism." *Review of International Studies* 25 (1999), pp. 323–328.

Huysmans, Jef: "The Jargon of Exception: On Schmitt, Agamben and the Absence of Political Society." *International Political Sociology* 2 (2008), pp. 165–183.

Ikenberry, G. John: "Creating Yesterday's New World Order: Keynesian 'New Thinking' and the Anglo-American Post-War Settlement." In Judith Goldstein and Robert O. Keohane (eds.): *Ideas and Foreign Policy: Beliefs, Institutions and Political Change* (Ithaca, NY: Cornell University Press, 1993), pp. 57–86.

Ilias, M. H.: *Space, Memory and Jewish National Identity* (New Delhi: New Century, 2008).

Isacoff, Jonathan B.: "On the Historical Imagination of International Relations: The Case for a 'Deweyan Reconstruction.'" *Millennium* 31:3 (2002), pp. 603–626.

Ish-Shalom, Piki: "Theory as a Hermeneutical Mechanism: The Democratic-Peace Thesis and the Politics of Democratization." *European Journal of International Relations* 12:4 (2006), pp. 565–598.

Ish-Shalom, Piki: "Theorizing Politics, Politicizing Theory and the Responsibility That Runs Between." *Perspectives on Politics* 7 (2009), pp. 303–316.

Israel, Jonathan I.: *Radical Enlightenment: Philosophy and the Making of Modernity, 1650–1750* (New York: Oxford University Press, 2001).

Israel, Jonathan I.: "Introduction." In Baruch de Spinoza: *Theological-Political Treatise* (Cambridge: Cambridge University Press, 2007).

Jabri, Vivienne: "Critical Thought and Political Agency in Time of War." *International Relations* 19 (2005), pp. 70–78.

Jackson, Patrick Thaddeus: "Rethinking Weber: Towards a Non-Individualist Sociology of World Politics." *International Review of Sociology* 12:3 (2002), pp. 439–468.

Jackson, Patrick Thaddeus: "Hegel's House, or 'People Are States Too.'" *Review of International Studies* 30 (2004), pp. 281–287.

Jackson, Patrick Thaddeus: "Making Sense of Making Sense: Configurational Analysis and the Double Hermeneutic." In Dvora Yanow and Peregrine Schwartz-Shea (eds.): *Interpretation and Method* (Armonk, NY: M. E. Sharpe, 2006).

Jackson, Patrick Thaddeus: "Foregrounding Ontology: Dualism, Monism and IR Theory." *Review of International Studies* 34 (2008), pp. 129–153.

Jackson, Patrick Thaddeus: "A Faulty Solution to a False(ly Characterized) Problem: A Comment on Monteiro and Ruby." *International Theory* 1:3 (2009), pp. 455–465.

Jackson, Patrick Thaddeus: *The Conduct of Inquiry in International Relations* (London: Routledge, 2010).

Jackson, Patrick Thaddeus, and Stuart J. Kaufman: "Security Scholars for a Sensible Foreign Policy: A Study in Weberian Activism." *Perspectives on Politics* 5:1 (2007), pp. 95–103.

Jackson, Patrick Thaddeus, and Daniel H. Nexon: "Paradigmatic Faults in International-Relations Theory." *International Studies Quarterly* 53:4 (2009), pp. 907–930.

Jacob, Philip E., and James V. Toscano (eds.): *The Integration of Political Communities* (Philadelphia: Lippincott, 1964).

Jäger, Lorenz: *Adorno: A Political Biography* (New Haven, CT: Yale University Press, 2004).

Jahn, Beate: "One Step Forward, Two Steps Back: Critical Theory as the Latest Version of Liberal Idealism." *Millennium* 27:3 (1998), pp. 613–641.

Jahn, Beate: "Liberal Internationalism: From Ideology to Empirical Theory—And Back Again." *International Theory* 1:3 (2009), pp. 409–438.

Jahn, Beate: "Universal Languages? A Reply to Moravcsik." *International Theory* 2:1 (2010), pp. 140–156.

Jamal, Amal: *The Palestinian National Movement: Politics of Contention, 1967–2005* (Bloomington: Indiana University Press, 2005).

Jamal, Amaney: *Barriers to Democracy: The Other Side of Social Capital in Palestine and the Arab World* (Princeton, NJ: Princeton University Press, 2007).

James, William: *A Pluralistic Universe* (Lincoln: University of Nebraska Press, 1996).

Jarvis, Darryl S. L.: *International Relations and the Challenge of Postmodernism* (Columbia: University of South Carolina Press, 2000).

Jaspers, Karl: *On Max Weber* (New York: Paragon House, 1989).

Jay, Martin: *The Dialectical Imagination: A History of the Frankfurt School and the Institute of Social Research, 1923–1950* (Boston: Little, Brown, 1973).

Jay, Martin: *Adorno* (Cambridge, MA: Harvard University Press, 1984). [1984a]

Jay, Martin: "Adorno in America." *New German Critique* 31 (1984), pp. 157–182. [1984b]

Jay, Martin: "The Frankfurt School's Critique of Karl Mannheim and the Sociology of Knowledge." In Jay Bernstein (ed.): *The Frankfurt School: Critical Essays, Vol. 1* (London: Routledge, 1994).

Jay, Martin: *The Dialectical Imagination: A History of the Frankfurt School and the Institute of Social Research, 1923–1950*, 2nd ed. (Berkeley: University of California Press, 1996)

Jenemann, David: *Adorno in America* (Minneapolis: University of Minnesota Press, 2007).

Jervis, Robert: "Hans Morgenthau, Realism and the Scientific Study of World Politics." *Social Research* 61:4 (1984), pp. 853–876.

Jervis, Robert: *System Effects: Complexity in Political and Social Life* (Princeton, NJ: Princeton University Press, 1997).

Joas, Hans: *War and Modernity* (Cambridge: Polity, 2003).

Johnson, Chalmers: *Blowback: The Costs and Consequences of America's Empire* (New York: Metropolitan, 2000).

Jones, Charles: *E. H. Carr and International Relations: A Duty to Lie* (Cambridge: Cambridge University Press, 1998).

Joseph, Jonathan: "Terrorism as a Social Relation within Capitalism: Theoretical and Emancipatory Implications." *Critical Studies on Terrorism* 4:1 (2011), pp. 23–37.

Joseph, Jonathan and Colin Wight (eds.): *Scientific Realism and International Relations* (London: Palgrave, 2010).

Judt, Tony: *Postwar: A History of Europe since 1945* (New York: Penguin, 2005).

Jütersonke, Oliver: *Morgenthau, Law and Realism* (Cambridge: Cambridge University Press, 2010).

Kahler, Miles: "Inventing International Relations: International Relations Theory after 1945." In Michael Doyle and G. John Ikenberry: *New Thinking in International Relations Theory* (Boulder, CO: Westview, 1997).

Kahn, Herman: *On Thermonuclear War* (Princeton, NJ: Princeton University Press, 1961).

Kahn, Herman: *Thinking about the Unthinkable* (New York: Horizon, 1962).

Kahn, Herman: *Thinking about the Unthinkable in the 1980s* (New York: Simon and Schuster, 1984).

Kahn-Nisser, Sara: "Toward a Unity of Ethics and Practice: Interpreting Inclusion and Diversity." *International Studies Review* 13 (2011), pp. 387–410.

Kaiser, Karl: "Transnational Politics: Toward a Theory of Multinational Polities." *International Organization* 25:4 (1971), pp. 790–817.

Kaiser, Ronn D.: "Toward the Copernican Phase of Regional Integration Theory." *Journal of Common Market Studies* 10:3 (1972), pp. 207–252.

Kaldor, Mary: *New and Old Wars*, 2nd ed. (Stanford, CA: Stanford University Press, 2007).

Kant, Immanuel: *Religion within the Limits of Reason Alone.* (New York: Harper Torchbooks, 1960).

Kant, Immanuel: *On History*, ed. Lewis White Beck (Upper Saddle River, NJ: Prentice-Hall, 2001).

Kant, Immanuel: *Critique of Pure Reason*, tr. Werner S. Pluhar (Indianapolis, IN: Hackett, 1996). [1996a]

Kant, Immanuel: *Practical Philosophy*, ed. Mary Gregor (Cambridge: Cambridge University Press, 1996). [1996b]

Kant, Immanuel: *Prolegomena to Any Future Metaphysics*, ed. Gary Hatfield (Cambridge: Cambridge University Press, 2004).

Kantner, Cathleen: "Collective Identity as Shared Ethical Self-Understanding: The Case of the Emerging European Identity." *European Journal of Social Theory* 9:4 (2006), pp. 501–523.

Kantner, Cathleen, and Angela Liberatore: "Security and Democracy in the European Union: An Introductory Framework." *European Security* 15:4 (2006), 363–383.

Kaplan, Abraham: *The Conduct of Inquiry: Methodology for Behavioral Science* (New York: Chandler, 1964).

Kaplan, Morton A.: "The Next Great Debate: Traditionalism vs. Science in International Relations." *World Politics* 19:1 (1966), pp. 1–20.

Kardoosh, Marwan A.: *Qualifying Industrial Zones and Sustainable Development in Jordan* (Amman: Jordanian Center for Public Policy Research and Dialogue, 2005). www.jcpprd.org/En/researchdetail.php?Researchid=4.

Karpin, Michael: *The Bomb in the Basement: How Israel Went Nuclear and What It Means for the World* (New York: Simon and Schuster, 2006).

Katzenstein, Peter J.: "Hare and Tortoise: The Race toward Integration." *International Organization* 25:2 (1971), pp. 290–295.

Katzenstein, Peter J.: *Disjoined Partners: Austria and Germany since 1815* (Berkeley: University of California Press, 1975).

Katzenstein, Peter J.: "Regionalism and Asia." *New Political Economy* 5:3 (2000), pp. 353–368.

Katzenstein, Peter J.: "Small States and Small States Revisited." *New Political Economy* 8:1 (2003), pp. 9–30.

Katzenstein, Peter J.: *A World of Regions: Asia and Europe in the American Imperium* (Ithaca, NY: Cornell University Press, 2005).

Katzenstein, Peter J.: *Rethinking Japanese Security: Internal and External Dimensions* (London: Routledge, 2008).

Katzenstein, Peter J.: "'Walls' between 'Those People?' Contrasting Perspectives on World Politics." *Perspectives on Politics* 8:1 (2010), pp. 11–25.

Katzenstein, Peter J., Robert O. Keohane, and Stephen D. Krasner: "International Organization and the Study of World Politics." *International Organization* 52:4 (1998), pp. 645–685.

Katzenstein, Peter J., and Nobuo Okawara: "Japan, Asian-Pacific Security, and the Case for Analytical Eclecticism." *International Security* 26:3 (2001–02), pp. 153–185.

Katzenstein, Peter J., and Rudra Sil: "Rethinking Asian Security: A Case for Analytical Eclecticism." In J. J. Suh, Peter J. Katzenstein, and Allen Carlson (eds.): *Rethinking Security in East Asia: Identity, Power, and Efficiency* (Stanford, CA: Stanford University Press, 2004), pp. 1–33.

Katzenstein, Peter J., and Rudra Sil: "Eclectic Theorizing in the Study and Practice of International Relations." In Christian Reus-Smit and Duncan Snidal (eds.): *The Oxford Handbook of International Relations* (New York: Oxford University Press, 2008), pp. 109–130.

Katzenstein, Peter J., and Rudra Sil: *Beyond Paradigms: Analytic Eclecticism in the Study of World Politics* (New York: Palgrave, 2010).

Katznelson, Ira: *Desolation and Enlightenment: Political Knowledge after Total War, Totalitarianism and the Holocaust* (New York: Columbia University Press, 2003).

Keck, Margaret, and Kathryn Sikkink: *Activists without Borders: Advocacy Networks in International Politics* (Ithaca, NY: Cornell University Press, 1998).

Kegley, Charles W. (ed.): *Controversies in International Relations Theory: Realism and the Neoliberal Challenge* (New York: St. Martin's, 1995).

Kemp, Adriana, et al. (eds.): *Israelis in Conflict: Hegemonies, Identities and Challenges* (Portland, OR: Sussex Academic, 2004).

Keohane, Robert O.: "The Big Influence of Small Allies." *Foreign Policy* 2 (1971), pp. 161–182.

Keohane, Robert O.: *After Hegemony* (Princeton, NJ: Princeton University Press, 2005 [1984]).

Keohane, Robert O. (ed.): *Neorealism and its Critics* (New York: Columbia University Press, 1986).

Keohane, Robert O.: "International Institutions: Two Approaches." *International Studies Quarterly* 32:4 (1988), pp. 379–396.

Keohane, Robert O.: "International Institutionalism: A Perspective on World Politics." In *International Institutions and State Power* (Boulder, CO: Westview, 1989), pp. 1–20. [1989a]

Keohane, Robert O.: *International Institutions and State Power* (Boulder, CO: Westview, 1989). [1989b]

Keohane, Robert O.: "Theory of World Politics: Structural Realism and Beyond." In *International Institutions and State Power* (Boulder, CO: Westview, 1989). [1989c]

Keohane, Robert O.: "International Liberalism Reconsidered." In John Dunn (ed.): *The Economic Limits to Modern Politics* (Cambridge: Cambridge University Press, 1990).

Keohane, Robert O.: *Power and Governance in a Partially Globalized World* (London: Routledge, 2002).

Keohane, Robert O.: "Theory and International Institutions." Interview with Harry Kriesler: *Conversations with History* (Institute of International Studies, University of California, Berkeley, March 9, 2004). http://globetrotter.berkeley.edu/people4/Keohane/keohane-con0.html.

Keohane, Robert O.: "Big Questions in the Study of World Politics." In Duncan Snidal and Christian Reus-Smit: *The Oxford Handbook of International Relations* (New York: Oxford University Press, 2008), pp. 708–715.

Keohane, Robert O.: "Political Science as a Vocation." *PS: Political Science and Politics* 42 (2009), pp. 359–363.

Keohane, Robert O., and Judith Goldstein: *Ideas and Foreign Policy: Beliefs, Institutions and Political Change* (Ithaca, NY: Cornell University Press, 1993).

Keohane, Robert O., Stephen Macedo, and Andrew Moravcsik: "Democracy-Enhancing Multilateralism." *International Organization* 63:1 (2009), pp. 589–98.

Keohane, Robert O., Stephen Macedo, and Andrew Moravcsik: "Constitutional Democracy and World Politics: A Response to Gartzke and Naoi." *International Organization* 65:3 (2011), pp. 599–604.

Keohane, Robert O., and Joseph S. Nye (eds.): *Transnational Relations and World Politics* (Cambridge, MA: Harvard University Press, 1971).

Keohane, Robert O., and Joseph S. Nye: "International Interdependence and Integration." In Fred I. Greenstein and Nelson W. Polsby (eds.): *International Politics* (Reading, MA: Addison-Wesley, 1975), pp. 363–414.

Keohane, Robert O., and Joseph S. Nye: *Power and Interdependence* (Boston: Little, Brown, 1977).

Keohane, Robert O., and Joseph S. Nye: "The Club Model of Multilateral Cooperation and Problems of Democratic Legitimacy." In Robert O. Keohane (ed.): *Power and Governance in a Partially Globalized World* (London: Routledge, 2002), pp. 219–44.

Keohane, Robert O., and Elinor Ostrom (eds.): *Local Commons and Global Interdependence* (Thousand Oaks, CA: Sage, 1995).

Kessler, Oliver: "From Agents and Structures to Minds and Bodies: of Supervenience, Quantum and the Linguistic Turn." *Journal of International Relations and Development* 10 (2007), pp. 243–71.

Kettler, David, and Volker Meja: *Karl Mannheim and the Crisis of Liberalism* (New Brunswick, NJ: Transaction, 1995).

Keynes, John Maynard: *Economic Consequences of the Peace* (New York: Harper, 1919).

Khalidi, Walid (ed.): *All That Remains: The Palestinian Villages Occupied and Depopulated by Israel in 1948* (Washington, DC: Institute for Palestine Studies, 1992).

Khazzoom, Aziza: *Shifting Ethnic Boundaries and Inequality in Israel* (Stanford, CA: Stanford University Press, 2008).

Kiernan, Ben: *Blood and Soil: A World History of Genocide and Extermination* (New Haven, CT: Yale University Press, 2007).

Kimmerling, Baruch: *Zionism and Territory: The Socio-Territorial Dimensions of Zionist Politics* (Berkeley, CA: Institute of International Studies, 1983).

Kimmerling, Baruch: *The Israeli State and Society: Boundaries and Frontiers* (Albany: State University of New York Press, 1989).

Kimmerling, Baruch: *Clash of Identities: Explorations in Israeli and Palestinian Societies* (New York: Columbia University Press, 2008).

Kimmerling, Baruch, and Joel S. Migdal: *The Palestinian People: A History* (Cambridge, MA: Harvard University Press, 2003).

King, Gary, et al.: *Designing Social Inquiry: Scientific Inference in Qualitative Research* (Princeton, NJ: Princeton University Press, 1994).

Kitchen, Nicholas: "Systemic Pressures and Domestic Ideas: A Neoclassical Realist Model of Grand Strategy Formation." *Review of International Studies* 36 (2010), pp. 117–143.

Kitcher, Patricia: "Introduction." In Immanuel Kant: *Critique of Pure Reason*, tr. Werner Pluhar (Indianapolis, IN: Hackett, 1996).

Klusmeyer, Douglas: "Beyond Tragedy: Hannah Arendt and Hans Morgenthau on Responsibility, Evil and Political Ethics." *International Studies Review* 11 (2009), pp. 332–351.

Klusmeyer, Douglas: "Hans Morgenthau on Republicanism." *International Relations* 24:4 (2010), pp. 389–413.

Knorr, Klaus, and James Rosenau (eds.): *Contending Theories of International Relations* (Princeton, NJ: Princeton University Press, 1969).

Knowlton, James, and Truett Cates: *Forever in the Shadow of Hitler? Original Documents of the* Historikerstreit, *the Controversy Concerning the Singularity of the Holocaust* (Atlantic Highlands, NJ: Humanities Press, 1993).

Knutsen, Torbjorn L: *History of International Relations* (Manchester, England: Manchester University Press, 1997).

Koestler, Arthur: *Darkness at Noon*, tr. Daphne Hardy (New York: Modern Library, 1941).

Koestler, Arthur: *Thieves in the Night* (New York: Macmillan, 1946).

Kołakowski, Leszek: *Main Currents of Marxism*, 3 vols. (Oxford: Clarendon, 1978).

Kop, Yaakov, and Robert E. Litan: *Sticking Together: The Israeli Experiment in Pluralism* (Washington, DC: Brookings, 2002).

Kornprobst, Markus: "International Relations as a Rhetorical Discipline: Toward (Re)newing Horizons." *International Studies Review* 11:1 (2009), pp. 87–108.

Koskenniemi, Martti: *The Gentle Civilizer of Nations* (Cambridge: Cambridge University Press, 2002).

Koskenniemi, Martti: "Miserable Comforters: International Relations and New Natural Law." *European Journal of International Relations* 15:3 (2009), pp. 395–422.

Kramer: Martin: *Ivory Towers on Sand: The Failure of Middle Eastern Studies in America* (Washington, DC: Washington Institute for Near East Policy, 2001).

Krasner, Stephen D.: *Defending the National Interest: Raw Materials and US Foreign Policy* (Princeton, NJ: Princeton University Press, 1978).

Krasner, Stephen D.: "Structural Causes and Regime Consequences: Regimes as Intervening Variables." In *International Regimes* (Ithaca, NY: Cornell University Press, 1983), pp. 1–21.

Krasner, Stephen D.: *Sovereignty: Organized Hypocrisy* (Princeton, NJ: Princeton University Press, 1999).

Kratochwil, Friedrich: *Rules, Norms and Decisions: On the Conditions of Practical and Legal Reasoning in International Relations and Domestic Affairs* (Cambridge: Cambridge University Press, 1991).

Kratochwil, Friedrich: "The Embarrassment of Changes: Neo-Realism as the Science of Realpolitik without Politics." *Review of International Studies* 19:1 (1993), pp. 63–80.

Kratochwil, Friedrich: "History, Action and Identity: Revisiting the 'Second' Great Debate and Assessing Its Importance for Social Theory." *European Journal of International Relations* 12:1 (2006), pp. 5–29.

Kratochwil, Friedrich: "Of False Promises and Good Bets: A Plea for a Pragmatic Approach to Theory Building." *Journal of International Relations and Development* 10:1 (2007), pp. 1–15.

Kubálková, Vendulka: "Towards an International Political Theology." *Millennium* 29:3 (2000), pp. 675–704.

Kubálková, Vendulka, and A. A. Cruickshank: *Marxism and International Relations* (Oxford: Oxford University Press, 1985).

Kuhn, Thomas: *The Structure of Scientific Revolutions*, 3rd ed. (Chicago: University of Chicago Press, 1996).

Kupchan, Charles: *How Enemies Become Friends* (Princeton: Princeton University Press, 2010).

Kurki, Milja: *Causation in International Relations: Reclaiming Causal Analysis* (Cambridge: Cambridge University Press, 2008).

Kurki, Milja: "The Politics of the Philosophy of Science." *International Theory* 1:3 (2009), pp. 440–454.

Lakatos, Imre, and Alan Musgrave (eds.): *Criticism and the Growth of Knowledge* (Cambridge: Cambridge University Press, 1970).

Lake, David: "Powerful Pacifists: Democratic States and War." *American Political Science Review* 86:1 (1992), pp. 24–37.

Lake, David: "Why 'Isms' Are Evil: Theory, Epistemology, and Academic Sects as Impediments to Understanding and Progress." *International Studies Quarterly* 55 (2011), pp. 465–480.

Landau, Emily B.: *Egypt and Israel in ACRS: Bilateral Concerns in a Regional Arms Control Process* (Tel Aviv: Jaffee Center for Strategic Studies, 2001).

Landau, Emily B.: *Arms Control in the Middle East: Cooperative Security Dialogue and Regional Constraints* (Portland, OR: Sussex Academic, 2006).

Lang, Anthony F., and John Williams: *Arendt and International Relations: Readings across the Lines* (London: Palgrave-Macmillan, 2008).

Lapid, Yosef: "*Quo Vadis* International Relations? Further Reflections on the 'Next Stage' of International Theory." *Millennium* 18:1 (1989), pp. 77–88. [1989a]

Lapid, Yosef: "The Third Debate: On the Prospects of International Theory in a Post-Positivist Era." *International Studies Quarterly* 33:3 (1989), pp. 235–254. [1989b]

Laski, Harold J.: *Reflections on the Revolution of Our Time* (New York: Viking, 1943).

Lasswell, Harold: "The Garrison State." *American Journal of Sociology* 46:4 (1941), pp. 455–468.

Latham, Andrew: "Warfare Transformed: A Braudellian Perspective on the 'Revolution in Military Affairs.'" *European Journal of International Relations* 8:2 (2002), pp. 231–266.

Latham, Robert: *The Liberal Moment: Modernity, Security, and the Making of Postwar International Order* (New York: Columbia University Press, 1997).

Laudan, Larry: *Progress and Its Problems* (Berkelely: University of California Press, 1977).

Laudan, Larry: *Beyond Positivism and Relativism* (Boulder, CO: Westview, 1996).

Lazarsfeld, Paul F.: "Remarks on Traditional and Critical Communications Research." *Studies in Philosophy and Social Science* 9:1 (1941), pp. 2–16.

Lebow, Richard Ned: *The Tragic Vision of Politics: Ethics, Interests, Orders* (Cambridge: Cambridge University Press, 2003).

Lebow, Richard Ned: *A Cultural Theory of International Relations* (Cambridge: Cambridge University Press, 2008).

Lebow, Richard Ned: "The Ancient Greeks and Modern Realism: Ethics, Persuasion and Power." In Duncan Bell (ed.): *Political Thought and International Relations* (New York: Oxford University Press, 2009), pp. 26–40.

Lebow, Richard Ned: *Why Nations Fight* (Cambridge: Cambridge University Press, 2010).

Lebow, Richard Ned: "Review Essay: Philosophy and International Relations." *International Affairs* 87:5 (2011), pp. 1219–1228.

Lebow, Richard Ned, and Thomas Risse-Kappen: *International Relations Theory and the End of the Cold War* (New York: Columbia University Press, 1995).

Legro, Jeffrey D.: *Rethinking the World: Great Power Strategies and International Order* (Ithaca, NY: Cornell University Press, 2005).

Legro, Jeffrey W., and Andrew Moravcsik: "Is Anybody Still a Realist?" *International Security* 24 (1999), 5–55.

Legro, Jeffrey W., and Andrew Moravcsik: "*Faux* Realism: Spin versus Substance in the Bush Foreign Policy Doctrine." *Foreign Policy* 125 (2001), pp. 80–82.

Levi, Primo: *The Drowned and the Saved* (New York: Vintage, 1988).

Levine, Daniel J.: "International Theory and the Problem of Sustainable Critique: An Adornian-Biblical Parable," *Borderlands* 10:1 (2011), 1–41.

Levite, Ariel: *Offense and Defense in Israeli Military Doctrine* (Boulder, CO: Westview, 1990).

Levy, Marc A.: "Is the Environment a National Security Issue?" *International Security* 20:2 (1995), pp. 35–62.

Levy, Marion J. Jr.: "Does It Matter if He's Naked? Bawled the Child." In Klaus Knorr and James Rosenau (eds.): *Contending Theories of International Relations* (Princeton, NJ: Princeton University Press, 1969).

Levy, Yagil: *Israel's Militarist Materialism* (Lanham, MD: Lexington, 2007).

Lewis, Bernard: "The Roots of Muslim Rage." *Atlantic Monthly* 266:3 (1990), pp. 47–60.

Lewis, Bernard: "What Went Wrong?" *Atlantic Monthly* 289:1 (2002) pp. 43–45.

Lieber, Robert J.: *Theory and World Politics* (Cambridge, MA: Winthrop, 1972).

Lijphart, Arend: "Consociational Democracy." *World Politics* 21:2 (1969), pp. 207–225.

Lijphart, Arend: "The Structure of the Theoretical Revolution in International Affairs." *International Studies Quarterly* 18:4 (1974), pp. 141–174.

Lindberg, Leon: *The Political Dynamics of European Integration* (Stanford, CA: Stanford University Press, 1963).

Linklater, Andrew: *Beyond Realism and Marxism: Critical Theory and International Relations* (New York: St. Martin's Press, 1990). [1990a]

Linklater, Andrew: *Men and Citizens in International Relations*, 2nd ed. (London: Macmillan, 1990). [1990b]

Linklater, Andrew: "The Question of the Next State in International Relations Theory: A Critical-Theoretical Point of View." *Millennium* 21:1 (1992), pp. 77–98.

Linklater, Andrew: "The Achievements of Critical Theory." In Steve Smith, Ken Booth, and Marysia Zalewski (eds.): *International Theory: Positivism and Beyond* (Cambridge: Cambridge University Press, 1996), pp. 11–44..

Linklater, Andrew: *The Transformation of Political Community: Ethical Foundations of the Post-Westphalian Era* (Boston: Blackwell, 1998).

Linklater, Andrew: "Transforming Political Community: A Reply to My Critics." *Review of International Studies* 25 (1999), pp. 165–75.

Linklater, Andrew: "The Changing Contours of Critical International Relations Theory." In Richard Wyn-Jones (ed.): *Critical Theory and World Politics* (Boulder, CO: Lynne Rienner, 2001), pp. 45–61.

Linklater, Andrew: *Critical Theory and World Politics: Citizenship, Sovereignty, and World Politics* (London: Routledge, 2007).

Linklater, Andrew, and Hidemi Suganami: *The English School of International Relations: A Contemporary Reassessment* (Cambridge: Cambridge University Press, 2006).

Lippmann, Walter: *Public Opinion* (New York, Macmillan, 1922).

Lippmann, Walter: *The Phantom Public* (New York: Harcourt, 1925).

Little, Douglas: *American Orientalism: The United States and the Middle East since 1945* (Chapel Hill: North Carolina University Press, 2002).

Lobell, Steven E., et al. (eds.): *Neoclassical Realism, the State and Foreign Policy* (Cambridge: Cambridge University Press, 2009).

Lockman, Zachary: *Contending Visions of the Middle East: The History and Politics of Orientalism* (Cambridge: Cambridge University Press, 2010).

Long, David: "The Harvard School of Liberal International Theory: A Case for Closure." *Millennium* 24:3 (1995), pp. 489–505.

Long, David, and Brian C. Schmidt (eds.): *Imperialism and Internationalism in the Discipline of International Relations* (Albany: State University of New York Press, 2005).

López, Silvia L.: "Peripheral Glances: Adorno's *Aesthetic Theory* in Brazil." In Max Pensky (ed.): *Globalizing Critical Theory* (New York: Rowman and Littlefield, 2005), pp. 241–253.

Lose, Lars G.: "Communicative Action and the World of Diplomacy." In Karin Fierke and Knud Erik Jørgensen (eds.): *Constructing International Relations: The Next Generation* (Armonk, NY: M. E. Sharpe, 2001), pp. 179–200.

Luard, Evan: *War in International Society* (New Haven, CT: Yale University Press, 1987).

Lüdke, Martin: "The Utopian Motif is Suspended: A Conversation with Leo Lowenthal." *New German Critique* 38 (1986), pp. 105–11.

Lukács, Georg: *History and Class Consciousness* (Cambridge, MA: MIT Press, 1971).

Lukes, Steven: *Power: A Radical View*, 2nd ed. (London: Palgrave-Macmillan, 2005).

Luoma-Aho, Mika: "Political Theology, Anthropomorphism, and Person-hood of the State: The Religion of IR." *International Political Sociology* 3 (2009), pp. 293–309.

Lyall, Jason, and Isaiah Wilson III: "Rage against the Machine: Explaining Outcomes in Counterinsurgency Wars." *International Organization* 63:1 (2009), pp. 67–106.

Lynch, Marc: *State Interests and Public Spheres: The International Politics of Jordan's Identity* (New York: Columbia University Press, 1999).

Lynch, Marc: "The Dialogue of Civilizations and International Public Spheres." *Millennium* 29:2 (2000), pp. 307–330.

Lynch, Marc: "Why Engage? China and the Logic of Communicative Engagement." *European Journal of International Relations* 8:2 (2002), pp. 187–230.

Lynch, Marc: "Beyond the Arab Street: Iraq and the Arab Public Sphere." *Politics and Society* 31 (2003), pp. 55–91.

Lynch, Marc: "Transnational Dialogue in an Age of Terror." *Global Society* 19:1 (2005), pp. 5–28.

Lynch, Marc: "Critical Theory: Dialogue, Legitimacy, and Justifications for War." In Jennifer Sterling-Folker (ed.): *Making Sense of International Relations Theory* (Boulder, CO: Lynne Rienner, 2006), pp. 182–197. [2006a]

Lynch, Marc: *Voices of the New Arab Public: Iraq, Al-Jazeera and Middle East Politics Today*. (New York: Columbia University Press, 2006). [2006b]

Lynch, Marc: "After Egypt: The Limits and Promise of Online Challenges to the Authoritarian Arab State." *Perspectives on Politics* 9:4 (2011), pp. 301–310.

MacFie, A. L.: *Orientalism* (New York: Longman, 2002).

MacFie, A. L.: *Orientalism: A Reader* (Edinburgh, Scotland: Edinburgh University Press, 2000).

Machiavelli, Niccolò: *The Prince* (New York: Penguin, 1961).

Machill, Marcel, Markus Beiler, and Corinna Fisher: "Europe-Topics in Europe's Media: The Debate about the European Public Sphere: A Meta-Analysis of Media Content Analyses." *European Journal of Communications* 21:1 (2006), pp. 57–88.

Manners, Ian: "Normative Power Europe: A Contradiction in Terms?" *Journal of Common Market Studies* 40:2 (2002), pp. 235–258.

Mannheim, Karl: *Ideology and Utopia: An Introduction to the Sociology of Knowledge* (New York: Harcourt, 1936).

Mannheim, Karl: *Man and Society in an Age of Reconstruction* (Glencoe, IL: Free Press, 1940).

Mannheim, Karl: *Essays on the Sociology of Knowledge* (London: Routledge and Kegan Paul, 1952).

Manning, C. A. W.: *The Nature of International Society* (New York: John Wiley, 1962).

Manuel, Frank E.: *The Prophets of Paris* (Cambridge, MA: Harvard University Press, 1962).

Marcuse, Herbert: *Reason and Revolution: Hegel and the Rise of Social Theory* (Boston: Beacon, 1960).

Marcuse, Herbert: *One-Dimensional Man* (Boston: Beacon, 1964).

Marcuse, Herbert: *Negations: Essays in Critical Theory* (London: Free Association Books, 1988).

Margalit, Avishai: "Political Theology: The Authority of God." *Theoria* 52: 106 (April 2005), pp. 37–50.

Markovits, Andrei S., and Warren W. Oliver III: "The Political Sociology of Integration and Social Development: A Comparative Analysis of Emile Durkheim and Karl W. Deutsch." In Richard L. Merritt and Bruce M. Russett (eds.): *From National Development to Global Community: Essays in Honor of Karl W. Deutsch* (London: George Allen & Unwin, 1981), pp. 165–83.

Marks, Michael P.: *Metaphors in International Theory* (London: Palgrave, 2011).

Martin, William: "The Christian Right and American Foreign Policy." *Foreign Policy* 114 (1999), pp. 66–80.

Marx, Karl: *Capital, Vol. 1* (New York: Penguin, 1976).

Masterman, Margaret: "The Nature of a Paradigm." In Imre Lakatos and Alan Musgrave (eds.): *Criticism and the Growth of Knowledge* (Cambridge: Cambridge University Press, 1970), pp. 59–89.

Matthews, Jessica Tuchman: "Redefining Security." *Foreign Affairs* 68:2 (1989), pp. 162–177.

Mayo, Deborah G.: *Error and the Growth of Experimental Knowledge* (Chicago: University of Chicago Press, 1996).

Mazur, G. O. (ed.): *One Hundred Year Commemoration to the Life of Hans Morgenthau* (New York: Semenenko Foundation, 2004).

McAlister, Melani: *Epic Encounters: Culture, Media and US Interests in the Middle East, 1945–2000* (Berkeley: University of California Press, 2001).

McCormick, John P.: "Political Theory and Political Theology: The Second Wave of Carl Schmitt in English." *Political Theory* 26:6 (1998), pp. 830–854.

McNeill, William H.: *The Pursuit of Power* (Chicago: University of Chicago Press, 1982).

McNeill, William H: *The Rise of the West: A History of the Human Community; with a Retrospective Essay* (Chicago: University of Chicago Press, 1992).

McShea, Robert J.: *The Political Philosophy of Spinoza* (New York: Columbia University Press, 1968).

McSweeney, Bill: *Security, Identity and Interests: A Sociology of International Relations.* (Cambridge: Cambridge University Press, 1999).

McQueen, Alison Elizabeth Jennifer: *Political Realism in Apocalyptic Times.* (Unpublished Doctoral Dissertation, Cornell University Department of Political Science, 2012).

Mearsheimer, John J.: "Back to the Future: Instability in Europe after the Cold War." *International Security* 15:1 (1990), pp. 5–56.

Mearsheimer, John J.: *The Tragedy of Great Power Politics* (New York: Norton, 2001).

Mearsheimer, John J.: "Power and Fear in Great Power Politics." In G. O. Mazur (ed.): *One Hundred Year Commemoration to the Life of Hans J. Morgenthau* (New York: Semenenko Foundation, 2004), pp. 184–96.

Mearsheimer, John J.: "Reckless States and Realism." *International Relations* 23:2 (2009), pp. 241–256.

Meinecke, Friedrich: *Machiavellism: The Doctrine of* Raison d'État *and Its Place in Modern History* (New Haven, CT: Yale University Press, 1957).

Meinecke, Friedrich: *Historism: The Rise of a New Historical Outlook* (New York: Herder and Herder, 1972).

Mercado, Raymond: "Keep on Muddling Through?" *International Theory* 1:3 (2009), pp. 455–465.

Merritt, Richard L., and Bruce M. Russett (eds.): *From National Development to Global Community: Essays in Honor of Karl W. Deutsch* (London: George Allen & Unwin, 1981).

Merton, Robert K.: *Social Theory and Social Structure* (Glencoe, IL: Free Press, 1963).

Mi'Ari, Mahmoud: "Attitudes of Palestinians toward Normalization with Israel." *Journal of Peace Research* 36:3 (1999), pp. 339–348.

Milgram, Stanley: "Behavioral Study of Obedience." *Journal of Abnormal and Social Psychology* 67:4 (1963), pp. 371–378.

Miller, Aaron David: "The False Religion of Middle East Peace." *Foreign Policy* 179 (May–June 2010), pp. 50–57.

Milner, Helen V.: "The Assumption of Anarchy in International Relations: A Critique." *Review of International Studies* 17:1 (1991), pp. 67–85.

Milward, Alan: *The European Rescue of the Nation-State* (London: Routledge, 2000).

Misselwitz, Philipp, and Tim Rieniets: *City of Collision: Jerusalem and the Principles of Conflict Urbanism* (Basel and Boston: Birkhäuser, 2006).

Mitchell, Timothy: *Colonizing Egypt* (Cambridge: Cambridge University Press, 1988).

Mitrany, David: *The Progress of International Government* (New Haven, CT: Yale University Press, 1933).

Mitrany, David: *American Interpretations: Four Political Essays* (London: Contact, 1946).

Mitrany, David: "Mental Health and World Unity." In *Proceedings of the First World Congress on Mental Health*, 4 vols. (New York: Columbia University Press, 1948), pp. 4:71–85.

Mitrany, David: *Marx against the Peasant: A Study in Social Dogmatism* (Chapel Hill: University of North Carolina Press, 1951).

Mitrany, David: *A Working Peace System* (Chicago: Quadrangle, 1966).

Mitrany, David: "The Functional Approach in Historical Perspective." *International Affairs* 47:3 (1971), pp. 532–543.

Mitrany, David: *The Functional Theory of Politics* (London: Martin Robertson, 1975). [1975a]

Mitrany, David: "A Political Theory for the New Society." In A. J. R. Groom and Paul Taylor (eds.): *Functionalism: Theory and Practice in International Relations* (New York: Crane, Russak, 1975), pp. 25–37. [1975b]

Mitzen, Jennifer: "Ontological Security in World Politics: State Identity and the Security Dilemma." *European Journal of International Relations* 12:3 (2006), pp. 341–370.

Modelski, George: "Agraria and Industria: Two Models of the International System." *World Politics* 14:1 (1961), pp. 118–143.

Molloy, Seán: "Realism: A Problematic Paradigm." *Security Dialogue* 34:1 (2003), pp. 71–85.

Molloy, Seán: "Truth, Power, Theory: Hans Morgenthau's Formulation of Realism." *Diplomacy and Statecraft* 15:1 (2004), pp. 1–34.

Molloy, Seán: *The Hidden History of Realism* (London: Palgrave, 2006).

Mommsen, Wolfgang J.: *Max Weber and German Politics* (Chicago: University of Chicago Press, 1984).

Monk, Daniel Bertrand: *An Aesthetic Occupation: The Immediacy of Architecture and the Palestine Conflict* (Durham, NC: Duke University Press, 2002).

Montag, Warren: *Bodies, Masses, Power: Spinoza and His Contemporaries* (London: Verso, 1999).

Montag, Warren, and Ted Stoltz (eds.): *The New Spinoza* (Minneapolis: University of Minnesota Press, 1997).

Monteiro, Nuno, and Kevin Ruby: "IR and the False Promise of Philosophical Foundations." *International Theory* 1:1 (2009), pp. 15–48. [2009a]

Monteiro, Nuno and Kevin Ruby: "The Promise of Foundational Prudence: A Response to Our Critics." *International Theory* 1:3 (2009), pp. 499–512. [2009b]

Moore, Barrington: *The Social Origins of Dictatorship and Democracy* (Boston: Beacon, 1993).

Moravcsik, Andrew: "Liberal Intergovernmentalism and Integration: A Rejoinder." *Journal of Common Market Studies* 33:4 (1995), pp. 611–628.

Moravcsik, Andrew: "Taking Preferences Seriously: A Liberal Theory of International Politics." *International Organization* 51:4 (1997), pp. 513–555.

Moravcsik, Andrew: *The Choice for Europe* (Ithaca, NY: Cornell University Press, 1998).

Moravcsik, Andrew: "Liberal International Relations Theory: A Scientific Assessment." In Colin Elman and Miriam Fendius Elman (eds.): *Progress in International Relations Theory: Appraising the Field* (Cambridge, MA: MIT Press, 2003), pp. 159–204.

Moravcsik, Andrew: "Robert Keohane: Political Theorist." In Helen Milner and Andrew Moravcsik (eds.): *Power, Interdependence and Non-State Actors in World Politics: Research Frontiers* (Princeton, NJ: Princeton University Press, 2009), p. 243–263.

Moravcsik, Andrew: "Tilting at Windmills: A Final Reply to Jahn." *International Theory* 2:1 (2010), pp. 157–173. [2010a]

Moravcsik, Andrew: "'Wahn, Wahn, Überall Wahn': A Reply to Jahn's Critique of Liberal Internationalism." *International Theory* 2:1 (2010), pp. 113–139. [2010b]

Morgan, Patrick: *Deterrence: A Conceptual Analysis* (Thousand Oaks, CA: Sage, 1977).

Morgan, Patrick: *Deterrence Now* (Cambridge: Cambridge University Press, 2003).

Morgenthau, Hans J.: *La Notion du 'Politique' et la Théories des Différends Internationaux* (Paris: Librairie du Recueil Sirey, 1933).

Morgenthau, Hans J.: *La Réalité des Normes, en Particulier des Normes du Droit International: Fondements d'une Théorie des Normes* (Paris: Librairie Felix Alcan, 1934).

Morgenthau, Hans J.: *Scientific Man versus Power Politics* (Chicago: University of Chicago Press, 1946).

Morgenthau, Hans J.: "Reflections on the State of Political Science." *Review of Politics* 17:4 (1955), pp. 431–460.

Morgenthau, Hans J.: *The Purpose of American Politics* (New York: Vintage, 1960).

Morgenthau, Hans J.: "Death in the Nuclear Age." *Commentary* 32 (1961), pp. 231–234.

Morgenthau, Hans J.: "Love and Power." *Commentary* (March 1962), pp. 247–251.

Morgenthau, Hans J.: "Introduction." In David Mitrany: *A Working Peace System* (New York: Quadrangle, 1966), pp. 7–11. [1966a]

Morgenthau, Hans J.: "The Purpose of Political Science." In James C. Charlesworth (ed.): *A Design for Political Science: Scope, Objectives, and Methods* (Philadelphia: American Academy of Political and Social Science, 1966), pp. 63–79. [1966b]

Morgenthau, Hans J.: "Common Sense and Theories of International Relations." *Journal of International Affairs* 21 (1967), pp. 207–214. [1967a]

Morgenthau, Hans J.: *Politics among Nations: The Struggle for Power and Peace*, 4th ed. (New York: Alfred A. Knopf, 1967). [1967b]

Morgenthau, Hans J.: Untitled [Review Essay on *Thucydides and the Politics of Bipolarity*], *Journal of Politics* 30:1 (1968), pp. 238–240.

Morgenthau, Hans J.: *Truth and Power* (New York: Praeger, 1970).

Morgenthau, Hans J.: *Science: Servant or Master?* (New York: Norton, 1972).

Morgenthau, Hans J.: "The Organic Relationship between Ideology and Political Reality." In George Schwab (ed.): *Ideology and Foreign Policy: A Global Perspective* (New York: Cyrco, 1976), pp. 117–123.

Morgenthau, Hans J.: "Hannah Arendt on Totalitarianism and Democracy." *Social Research* 44 (1977), pp. 127–131.

Morgenthau, Hans J.: "Fragment of an Intellectual Autobiography." In Kenneth Thompson and Robert J. Myers: *Truth and Tragedy: A Tribute to Hans J. Morgenthau* (New Brunswick, NJ: Transaction, 1984), pp. 1–17.

Morgenthau, Hans J.: *Political Theory and International Affairs* (Westport, CT: Praeger, 2004).

Morrice, David: "The Liberal-Communitarian Debate in Contemporary Political Philosophy and Its Significance for International Relations." *Review of International Studies* 26 (2000), pp. 233–251.

Morris, Benny: *The Birth of the Palestinian Refugee Problem Revisited* (Cambridge: Cambridge University Press, 2004).

Morse, Edward L.: "Managing International Commons." *Journal of International Affairs* 31:1 (1977), pp. 1–21.

Moskos, Charles, et al.: *The Postmodern Military* (New York: Oxford University Press, 2000).

Mosser, Michael W.: "Puzzles versus Problems: The Alleged Disconnect between Academics and Military Practitioners." *Perspectives on Politics* 8:4 (2010), pp. 1077–86.

Most, Benjamin A., and Harvey Starr: *Inquiry, Logic and International Relations* (Columbia: University of South Carolina Press, 1989).

Mueller, John: *The Retreat from Doomsday: The Obsolescence of Major War* (New York: Basic Books, 1990).

Mufti, Aamir R.: *Enlightenment in the Colony: The Jewish Question and the Crisis of Postcolonial Culture* (Princeton, NJ: Princeton University Press, 2007).

Müller, Harald: "International Relations as Communicative Action." In Karin Fierke and Knud Erik Jørgensen (eds): *Constructing International Relations. The Next Generation* (Armonk, NY: M. E. Sharpe, 2001), pp. 160–178.

Müller, Harald: "Arguing, Bargaining and All That: Communicative Action, Rationalist Theory and the Logic of Appropriateness in International Relations." *European Journal of International Relations* 10:3 (2004), pp. 395–435.

Müller, Jan-Werner: "Fear and Freedom: On 'Cold War Liberalism.'" *European Journal of Political Theory* 7:1 (2008), pp. 45–64.

Murray, A. J. H.: "The Moral Politics of Hans Morgenthau." *Review of Politics* 58:1 (1996), pp. 81–107.

Mutimer, David: "My Critique is Bigger than Yours: Constituting Exclusions in Critical Security Studies." *Studies in Social Science* 3:1 (2009), pp. 9–22.

Nakarada, Radmila: "The Uncertain Reach of Critical Theory." In Paul Wapner and Lester Edwin J. Ruiz (eds.): *Principled World Politics: The Challenge of Normative International Relations* (New York: Rowman and Littlefield, 2000), pp. 65–78.

Nardin, Terry: "Ethical Traditions in International Affairs." In Terry Nardin and David R. Mapel: *Traditions of International Ethics* (Cambridge: Cambridge University Press, 1992), pp. 1–22.

Narizny, Kevin: *The Political Economy of Grand Strategy* (Ithaca, NY: Cornell University Press, 2007).

Naumann, Friedrich: *Central Europe*, tr. Christabel M. Meredith (New York: Knopf, 1917).

Navari, Cornelia: "David Mitrany and International Functionalism." In David Long and Peter Wilson (eds.): *Thinkers of the Twenty Years' Crisis: Inter-War Idealism Reassessed* (Oxford: Clarendon, 1995), pp. 214–46.

Navon, Immanuel: "The 'Third Debate' Revisited." *Review of International Studies* 27 (2001), pp. 611–625.

Neacsu, Mihaela: *Hans J. Morgenthau's Theory of International Relations* (New York: Palgrave Macmillan, 2010).

Neufeld, Mark: "Reflexivity and International Relations Theory." *Millennium* 22:1 (1993), pp. 235–251.

Neufeld, Mark: *The Restructuring of International Relations Theory* (Cambridge: Cambridge University Press, 1995).

Neufeld, Mark: "What's Critical about International Relations Theory?" In Richard Wyn Jones: *Critical Theory and World Politics* (Boulder, CO: Lynne Rienner, 2001), pp. 127–46.

Neumann, Iver B.: "Beware of Organicism: The Narrative Self-View of the State." *Review of International Studies* 30 (2004), pp. 259–267.

Newman, David: "Citizenship, Identity and Location: The Changing Discourse of Israeli Geopolitics." In Klaus Dodds and David Atkinson (eds.): *Geopolitical Traditions: A Century of Geopolitical Thought* (London: Routledge, 2000), pp. 302–331.

Newman, David: "From National to Post-National Territorial Identities in Israel-Palestine." *Geopolitics* 53 (2001), pp. 235–246.

Newman, David: "The Geopolitics of Peacemaking in Israel-Palestine." *Political Geography* 21 (2002), pp. 629–646.

Nexon, Daniel H.: *The Struggle for Power in Early Modern Europe* (Princeton, NJ: Princeton University Press, 2009).

Niebuhr, Reinhold: *The Children of Light and the Children of Darkness* (New York: Scribner's, 1944).

Niemann, Arne: "The PHARE Programme and the Concept of Spillover: Neofunctionalism in the Making." *Journal of European Public Policy* 5:3 (1998), pp. 428–446.

Nisbet, Robert: *The Sociological Tradition* (New York: Basic Books, 1966).

Nitzan, Jonathan, and Shimshon Bichler: *The Global Political Economy of Israel* (London: Pluto, 2002).

Norrie, Alan: "From Critical to Socio-Legal Studies: Three Dialectics in Search of a Subject." *Social & Legal Studies* 9:1 (2000), pp. 85–113.

Norrie, Alan: "A Fateful Inversion." *Social & Legal Studies* 12:1 (2003), pp. 121–132.

North, Douglas C.: *Institutions, Institutional Change and Economic Performance* (Cambridge: Cambridge University Press, 1990).

North, Douglas C., and Robert Paul Thompson: *The Rise of the Western World* (Cambridge: Cambridge University Press, 1973).

Norton, Anne: "Political Science as a Vocation." In Ian Shapiro, Rogers M. Smith, and Tarek E. Masoud (eds.): *Problems and Methods in the Study of Politics* (Cambridge: Cambridge University Press, 2004), pp. 67–82.

Nye, Joseph S.: *Peace in Parts: Integration and Conflict in Regional Organization* (Boston: Little, Brown, 1971).

Nye, Joseph S.: *Nuclear Ethics* (New York: Free Press, 1986).

Nye, Joseph S.: *Bound to Lead* (New York: Basic Books, 1990).

Nye, Joseph S.: *Understanding International Conflicts* (New York: Longman, 1997).

Oakeshott, Michael: *The Social and Political Doctrines of Contemporary Europe* (Cambridge: Cambridge University Press, 1939).

Ochoa-Espejo, Paulina: "On Political Theology and Possibility of Superseding It." *Critical Review of International Social and Political Philosophy* 13:4 (2010), pp. 475–494.

Odysseos, Louiza, and Fabio Petito (eds.): *The International Political Thought of Carl Schmitt* (London: Routledge, 2007).

O'Hanlon, Michael: *Technological Change and the Future of Warfare* (Washington, DC: Brookings, 2000).

Ollman, Bertell: *Alienation: Marx's Conception of Man in Capitalist Society* (Cambridge: Cambridge University Press, 1971).

Olson, Mancur: "Toward a Unified View of Economics and the Other Social Sciences." In James E. Alt and Kenneth A. Shepsle (eds.): *Perspectives on Positive Political Economy* (Cambridge: Cambridge University Press, 1990), pp. 212–231.

Olson, William C., and A. J. R. Groom: *International Relations Then and Now* (London: Harper-Collins, 1991).

Onuf, Nicholas G.: *World of Our Making* (Columbia: University of South Carolina Press, 1989).

Onuf, Nicholas G.: *The Republican Legacy in International Thought* (Cambridge: Cambridge University Press, 1998).

Onuf, Nicholas G.: "Worlds of Our Making: The Strange Career of Constructivism in International Relations." In Donald J. Puchala (ed): *Visions of International Relations* (Columbia: University of South Carolina Press, 2002), pp. 119–141.

Onuf, Nicholas G.: "Structure? What Structure?" *International Relations* 23:2 (2009), pp. 183–199.

Onuf, Nicholas G., and Thomas J. Johnson: "Peace in the Liberal World: Does Democracy Matter?" In Charles W. Kegley Jr.: *Controversies in International Relations Theory: Realism and the Neoliberal Challenge* (New York: St. Martin's, 1995), pp. 179–197.

Oren, Ido: *Our Enemies and US* (Ithaca, NY: Cornell University Press, 2003).

Oren, Ido: "The Unrealism of Realism: The Tension between Realist Theory and Realists' Practice." *Perspectives on Politics* 7 (2009), pp. 283–301.

Oren, Michael B.: *Power, Faith and Fantasy: America in the Middle East, 1776 to the Present* (New York: Norton, 2007).

Ó Tuathail, Gearóid: *Critical Geopolitics: The Politics of Writing Global Space* (Minneapolis: University of Minnesota Press, 1996).

Owens, Bill: *Lifting the Fog of War* (Baltimore: Johns Hopkins University Press, 2001).

Owens, Patricia: *Between War and Politics: International Relations and the Thought of Hannah Arendt* (New York: Oxford University Press, 2007).

Oye, Kenneth A. (ed.): *Cooperation under Anarchy* (Princeton, NJ: Princeton University Press, 1986).

Parker, Geoffrey: *Western Geopolitical Thought in the Twentieth Century* (New York: St. Martin's, 1985).

Parker, Geoffrey: *The Military Revolution: Military Innovation and the Rise of the West, 1500–1800* (Cambridge: Cambridge University Press, 1996).

Parkinson, G. H. R.: *Georg Lukács* (London: Routledge, 1977).

Parsons, Talcott: *The Structure of Social Action* (New York: McGraw-Hill, 1937).

Passerin d'Entrèves, Maurizio, and Seyla Benhabib (eds.): *Habermas and the Unfinished Project of Modernity* (London: Polity, 1996).

Patomäki, Heikki: "How to Tell Better Stories about World Politics." *European Journal of International Relations* 2:1 (1996), pp. 105–133.

Patomäki, Heikki: *After International Relations: Critical Realism and the (Re)construction of World Politics* (London: Routledge, 2002).

Patomäki, Heikki: "A Critical Realist Approach to Global Political Economy." In Justin Cruickshank (ed.): *Critical Realism: The Difference that It Makes* (London: Routledge, 2003), pp. 197–220.

Patomäki, Heikki, and Colin Wight: "After Postpositivism? The Promises of Critical Realism." *International Studies Quarterly* 44 (2000), pp. 213–237.

Patterson, Eric (ed.): *Christianity and Power Politics Today: Christian Realism and Contemporary Political Dilemmas* (New York: Palgrave Macmillan, 2008).

Pempel, T. J.: *Remapping East Asia: The Construction of a Region* (Ithaca, NY: Cornell University Press, 2005).

Pensky, Max (ed.): *Globalizing Critical Theory* (New York: Rowman and Littlefield, 2005).

Pentland, Charles: *International Theory and Political Integration* (New York: Free Press, 1973).

Pentland, Charles: "Functionalism and Theories of International Political Integration." In A. J. R. Groom and Paul Taylor (eds.): *Functionalism: Theory and Practice in International Relations* (New York: Crane Russak, 1975), pp. 9–24.

Peres, Shimon: *The New Middle East* (New York: Henry Holt, 1993).

Peres, Shimon: *The Imaginary Voyage: With Herzl in the Holy Land* (New York: Arcade, 1999).

Perkovitch, George, and James M. Acton (eds.): *Abolishing Nuclear Weapons: A Debate* (New York: Carnegie Endowment, 2009).

Person, Ethel Spector: "Hans J. Morgenthau and the New York Years." In G. O. Mazur (ed.): *One Hundred Year Commemoration to the Life of Hans Morgenthau* (New York: Semenenko Foundation, 2004), pp. 148–67.

Petersen, Ulrik Enemark: "Breathing Nietzsche's Air: New Reflections on Morgenthau's Concepts of Power and Human Nature." *Alternatives* 24:1 (1999), pp. 83–118.

Philpott, Daniel: *Revolutions in Sovereignty* (Princeton, NJ: Princeton University Press, 2001).

Pichler, Hans-Karl: "The Godfathers of 'Truth': Max Weber and Carl Schmitt in Morgenthau's Theory of Power Politics." *Review of International Studies* 24 (1998), pp. 185–200.

Pin-Fat, Véronique: "The Metaphysics of the National Interest and the 'Mysticism' of the Nation-State: Reading Hans J. Morgenthau." *Review of International Studies* 31 (2005), pp. 217–236.

Pin-Fat, Véronique: *Universality, Ethics and International Relations: A Grammatical Reading* (London: Routledge, 2010).

Pippin, Robert B.: *Kant's Theory of Form* (New Haven, CT: Yale University Press, 1982).

Polanyi, Karl: *The Great Transformation: The Political and Economic Origins of Our Time* (Boston: Beacon, 2001 [1944]).

Polanyi, Michael: "The Republic of Science: Its Political and Social Theory." *Minerva* (September 1962), pp. 54–73.

Popper, Karl R.: *The Open Society and Its Enemies: Hegel and Marx, Vol. 2* (Princeton, NJ: Princeton University Press, 1966).

Portugali, Juval: *Implicate Relations: Society and Space in the Israeli-Palestinian Conflict* (Boston: Kluwer, 1993)

Posen, Barry R.: "Command of the Commons." *International Security* 28:1 (2003), pp. 5–46.

Posen, Barry R.: *The Sources of Military Doctrine* (Ithaca, NY: Cornell University Press, 1984).

Powell, Walter W., and Paul J. DiMaggio (eds.): *The New Institutionalism in Organizational Analysis* (Chicago: University of Chicago Press, 1991).

Prewitt, Kenneth: "Can Political Science Be a Policy Science?" In Gary King et al. (eds.): *The Future of Political Science* (London: Routledge, 2009), pp. 255–7.

Price, Richard (ed.): *Moral Limit and Possibility in International Relations* (Cambridge: Cambridge University Press, 2008).

Price, Richard, and Christian Reus-Smit: "Dangerous Liaisons? Critical International Theory and Constructivism." *European Journal of International Relations* 4:3 (1998), pp. 259–294.

Prokhovnik, Raia: *Spinoza and Republicanism* (New York: Palgrave Macmillan, 2004).

Pusca, Anca: "Walter Benjamin: A Methodological Contribution." *International Political Sociology* 3 (2009), pp. 238–254.

Putnam, Robert D.: "Diplomacy and Domestic Politics: The Logic of Two-Level Games." *International Organization* 42:3 (1988), pp. 427–460.

Putnam, Robert D.: *Bowling Alone: The Collapse and Revival of American Community* (New York: Simon & Schuster, 2000).

Quine, Willard Van Orman: *From a Logical Point of View* (Cambridge, MA: Harvard University Press, 1961).

Rabin, Yitzhak: *The Rabin Memoirs* (Berkeley: University of California Press, 1996).

Rafshoon, Ellen Glaser: "A Realist's Moral Opposition to War: Hans J. Morgenthau and Vietnam." *Peace & Change* 26:1 (2001), pp. 55–77.

Rajaram, Prem Kumar: "Theodor Adorno's Aesthetic Understanding: An Ethical Method for IR?" *Alternatives* 27 (2002), pp. 351–372.

Rajaram, Prem Kumar: "Dystopic Geographies of Empire." *Alternatives* 31 (2006), pp. 475–506.

Ram, Uri: *The Globalization of Israel* (London: Routledge, 2008).

Rapoport, Anatol: *Strategy and Conscience* (New York: Harper and Row, 1964).

Rathenau, Walther: *The New Society* (New York: Harcourt, Brace, 1921).

Ravitzky, Aviezer: *Messianism, Zionism and Jewish Religious Radicalism* (Chicago: University of Chicago Press, 1996).

Reiter, Dan and Allan C. Stam: *Democracies at War.* (Princeton, NJ: Princeton University Press, 2002).

Rengger, Nicholas: "Going Critical? A Response to Hoffman." *Millennium* 17:1 (1988), pp. 81–89.

Rengger, Nicholas: "A City Which Sustains All Things? Communitarianism and International Society." *Millennium* 21:3 (1992), pp. 353–369.

Rengger, Nicholas: *Political Theory, Modernity and Postmodernity* (Oxford: Blackwell, 1999).

Rengger, Nicholas: "Negative Dialectic? The Two Modes of Critical Theory in International Relations." In Richard Wyn Jones (ed.): *Critical Theory and World Politics* (Boulder, CO: Lynne Rienner, 2001), pp. 91–109. [2001a]

Rengger, Nicholas: "The Boundaries of Conversation: A Response to Dallmayr." *Millennium* 30:2 (2001), pp. 357–364. [2001b]

Rengger, Nicholas: "Realism, Tragedy, and the Anti-Pelagian Imagination." In Michael C. Williams (ed.): *Realism Reconsidered: The Legacy of Hans J. Morgenthau in International Relations* (New York: Oxford University Press, 2007), pp. 118–36.

Rengger, Nicholas, and Ben Thirkell-White: "Still Critical after All These Years? The Past, Present and Future of Critical Theory in International Relations." *Review of International Studies* 33 (2007), pp. 3–24.

Reus-Smit, Christian: *The Moral Purpose of the State* (Princeton, NJ: Princeton University Press, 1999).

Reus-Smit, Christian: "Struggles for Individual Rights and the Expansion of the International System." *International Organization* 65 (2011), pp. 207–42.

Reus-Smit, Christian, and Duncan Snidal: "Between Utopia and Reality: The Practical Discourses of International Relations." In Christian Reus-Smit and Duncan Snidal: *The Oxford Handbook of International Relations* (New York: Oxford University Press, 2008), pp. 3–37.

Rice, Daniel: "Reinhold Niebuhr and Hans Morgenthau: A Friendship with Contrasting Shades of Realism." *Journal of American Studies* 42:2 (2008), pp. 255–291.

Ricoeur, Paul: *Hermeneutics and the Human Sciences*, ed. John B. Thompson (Cambridge: Cambridge University Press, 1981).

Riker, William H.: *The Theory of Political Coalitions* (New Haven, CT: Yale University Press, 1972).

Ringmar, Erik: *Identity, Interest and Action: A Cultural Explanation of Sweden's Intervention in the Thirty Years' War* (Cambridge: Cambridge University Press, 1996).

Risse, Thomas: "Let's Argue! Communicative Action in World Politics." *International Organization* 54:1 (2000), pp. 1–39.

Risse, Thomas: "An Emerging European Public Sphere? What We Know and How to Make Sense of It." In *Europe Transformed: The European Union and Collective Identity Change.* Papers presented for the ARENA/IDNET International Policy Conference, Oslo, October 2002.

Risse, Thomas: "Global Governance and Communicative Action." *Government and Opposition* 39:2 (2004), pp. 288–313.

Roach, Steven C.: "Critical International Theory and Meta-Dialectics." *Millennium* 35:2 (2007), pp. 321–342.

Roach, Steven C. (ed.): *Critical Theory and International Relations: A Reader* (London: Routledge, 2008).

Robin, Ron: *The Making of the Cold War Enemy: Culture and Politics in the Military-Industrial Complex* (Princeton, NJ: Princeton University Press, 2001).

Robinson, Fiona: *Globalizing Care: Ethics, Feminist Theory and International Relations* (Boulder, CO: Westview, 1999).

Robinson, Fiona: "Methods of Feminist Normative Theory: A Political Ethic of Care for International Relations." In Brooke A. Ackerley et al. (eds.): *Feminist*

Methodologies for International Relations (Cambridge: Cambridge University Press, 2006), pp. 221–240.

Robinson, Glenn: *Building a Palestinian State: The Incomplete Revolution* (Bloomington: Indiana University Press, 1997).

Robinson, Glenn: "The Politics of Legal Reform in Palestine." *Journal of Palestine Studies* 27:1 (1997), pp. 51–60.

Rohde, Christoph: "Current Forms of Foreign Policy Realism in Morgenthau's Tradition: Reflections on Political Realism in Germany." In Christian Hacke et al. (eds.): *The Heritage, Challenge and Future of Realism: In Memoriam, Hans J. Morgenthau (1904–1980)* (Göttingen, Germany: V & R Unipress, 2005), pp. 49–69.

Rorty, Richard: "Habermas, Derrida and the Functions of Philosophy." In Lasse Thomassen (ed.): *The Derrida-Habermas Reader* (Chicago: University of Chicago Press, 2006), pp. 46–65.

Rosa, Hartmut: "Social Acceleration: Ethical and Political Consequences of a Desynchronized High-Speed Society." *Constellations* 10:1 (2003), pp. 3–33.

Rosamond, Ben: *Theories of European Integration* (New York: St. Martin's, 2000).

Rosamond, Ben: "The Uniting of Europe and the Foundation of EU Studies: Revisiting the Neofunctionalism of Ernst B. Haas." *Journal of European Public Policy* 12:2 (2005), pp. 237–254.

Rose, Gideon: "Neoclassical Realism and Theories of Foreign Policy." *World Politics* 51:1 (1998), pp. 144–172.

Rose, Gillian: *The Melancholy Science* (New York: Columbia University Press, 1978).

Rose, Gillian: "How Is Critical Theory Possible? Theodor W. Adorno and Concept Formation in Sociology." In Jay Bernstein (ed.): *The Frankfurt School: Critical Assessments, Vol. 3* (London: Routledge, 1994), pp. 154–72.

Rosecrance, Richard, and Arthur A. Stein (eds.): *The Domestic Bases of Grand Strategy* (Ithaca, NY: Cornell University Press, 1993).

Rosen, Howard: "Free Trade Agreements as Foreign Policy Tools: The US-Israel and US-Jordan FTAs." In Jeffrey J. Schott (ed.): *Free Trade Agreements: US Strategies and Priorities* (Washington, DC: Institute for International Economics, 2004), pp. 51–77.

Rosen, Stanley: "Benedict Spinoza." In Leo Strauss and Joseph Cropsey (eds.): *History of Political Philosophy* (Chicago: University of Chicago Press, 1972), pp. 431–50.

Rosenau, James: *Along the Domestic-Foreign Frontier: Exploring Governance in a Turbulent World* (Cambridge: Cambridge University Press, 1997).

Rosenberg, Justin: *The Empire of Civil Society: A Critique of the Realist Theory of International Relations* (London: Verso, 1994).

Ross, Andrew A. G.: "Coming in from the Cold: Constructivism and Emotions." *European Journal of International Relations* 12:2 (2006), pp. 197–222.

Ross, Dorothy: *The Origins of American Social Science* (Cambridge: Cambridge University Press, 1991).

Rotberg, Robert I.: *Israeli and Palestinian Narratives of Conflict: History's Double Helix* (Bloomington: Indiana University Press, 2006).

Roth, Ariel Ilan: "A Bold Move Forward for Neoclassical Realism." *International Studies Review* 8:3 (2006), pp. 486–488.

Roy, Sarah: "Palestinian Society and Economy: The Continued Denial of Possibility." *Journal of Palestine Studies* 30:4 (2001), pp. 5–20.

Roy, Sarah: "The Palestinian-Israeli Conflict and Palestinian Socioeconomic Decline: A Place Denied." *International Journal of Politics, Culture and Society* 17:3 (2004), pp. 365–403.

Rubin, Barry: *The Transformation of Palestinian Politics* (Cambridge, MA: Harvard University Press, 1999).

Ruggie, John Gerard: "International Responses to Technology: Concepts and Trends." *International Organization* 29:3 (1975), pp. 557–583.

Ruggie, John Gerard: "International Regimes, Transactions, and Change: Embedded Liberalism in the Postwar Economic Order." *International Organization* 36:2 (1982), pp. 379–415.

Ruggie, John Gerard: "Review: Continuity and Transformation in the World Polity: Toward a Neorealist Synthesis." *World Politics* 35:2 (1983), pp. 261–85.

Ruggie, John Gerard: "Territoriality and Beyond: Problematizing Modernity in International Relations." *International Organization* 47:1 (1993), pp. 139–174.

Ruggie, John Gerard: "The Past as Prologue: Interests, Identity, and American Foreign Policy." *International Security* 21:4 (1997), pp. 89–125.

Ruggie, John Gerard, et al.: "Transformations in World Politics: The Intellectual Contributions of Ernst B. Haas." *Annual Review of Political Science* 8 (2005), pp. 271–296.

Rumsfeld, Donald: "Transforming the Military." *Foreign Affairs* 81:3 (2002), pp. 20–32.

Russell, Greg: "Science, Technology and Death in the Nuclear Age: Hans J. Morgenthau on Nuclear Ethics." *Ethics and International Affairs* 5 (1991), pp. 115–34.

Russett, Bruce M.: *Community and Contention* (Cambridge, MA: MIT Press, 1963).

Russett, Bruce M.: *International Regions and the International System* (Chicago: Rand McNally, 1967).

Sa'di, Ahmad, and Lila Abu-Lughod (eds.): *Nakba, 1948 and the Claims of Memory* (New York: Columbia University Press, 2007).

Said, Edward W.: *Culture and Imperialism* (New York: Vintage, 1994). [1994a]

Said, Edward W.: *Orientalism* (New York: Vintage, 1994). [1994b]

Said, Edward W.: *Representations of the Intellectual* (New York: Pantheon, 1994). [1994c]

Said, Edward W.: *The End of the Peace Process: Oslo and After* (New York: Pantheon, 2000).

Samara, Adel: "Globalization, the Palestinian Economy and the 'Peace Process.'" *Journal of Palestine Studies* 29:2 (2000), pp. 20–34.

Sasley, Brent E.: "Affective Attachments and Foreign Policy: Israel and the 1993 Oslo Accords." *European Journal of International Relations* 16:4 (2010), pp. 687–709.

Sassen, Sasskia: *Territory, Authority, Rights* (Princeton, NJ: Princeton University Press, 2006).

Savir, Uri: *The Process: 1,100 Days That Saved the Middle East* (New York: Random House, 1998).

Scham, Paul: "Israeli-Arab Research Cooperation, 1995–1999: An Analytical Study." *Middle East Review of International Affairs* 4:3 (2000), pp. 1–16.

Scham, Paul, et al. (eds.): *Shared Histories: A Palestinian-Israeli Dialogue* (Walnut Creek, CA: Left Coast Press, 2005).

Schechter, Michael G.: "Critiques of Coxian Theory: Background to a Conversation." In Robert W. Cox (ed.): *The Political Economy of a Plural World* (London: Routledge, 2002), pp. 1–25.

Schelling, Thomas: *Micromotives and Macrobehavior* (New York: Norton, 1978).

Scheuerman, William E.: *Carl Schmitt: The End of Law* (Lanham, MD: Rowman & Littlefield, 1999).

Scheuerman, William E.: *Liberal Democracy and the Social Acceleration of Time* (Baltimore: Johns Hopkins University Press, 2005).

Scheuerman, William E.: "Carl Schmitt and Hans Morgenthau." In Michael C. Williams (ed): *Realism Reconsidered: The Legacy of Hans J. Morgenthau in International Relations* (New York: Oxford University Press, 2007), pp. 62–92. [2007a]

Scheuerman, William E.: "Was Morgenthau a Realist? Revisiting *Scientific Man vs. Power Politics.*" *Constellations* 14:4 (2007), pp. 506–530. [2007b]

Scheuerman, William E.: "Realism and the Left: The Case of Hans J. Morgenthau." *Review of International Studies* 34 (2008), pp. 29–51.

Scheuerman, William E.: "Realism and the Critique of Technology." *Cambridge Review of International Affairs* 22:4 (2009), pp. 563–584. [2009a]

Scheuerman, William E.: "A Theoretical Missed Opportunity? Hans J. Morgenthau as Critical Realist." In Duncan Bell (ed.): *Political Thought and International Relations* (New York: Oxford University Press, 2009), pp. 41–62. [2009b]

Schimmelfennig, Frank: "The Community Trap: Liberal Norms, Rhetorical Action, and the Eastern Enlargement of the European Union." *International Organization* 55:1 (2001), pp. 47–80.

Schmidt, Brian C.: *The Political Discourse of Anarchy: A Disciplinary History of International Relations* (Albany: State University of New York Press, 1998).

Schmitt, Carl: *Political Theology* (Chicago: University of Chicago Press, 2005 [1985]).

Schmitt, Carl: *The Concept of the Political* (Chicago: University of Chicago Press, 1996).

Schmitt, Carl: *The Nomos of the Earth and the Concept of the* Jus Publicum Europaeum, tr. G. L. Ulmen (St. Louis, MO: Telos, 2003).

Schmitter, Philippe C.: "Three Neo-Functional Hypotheses about European Integration." *International Organization* 23:1 (1969), pp. 161–166.

Schmitter, Philippe C.: "A Revised Theory of Regional Integration." *International Organization* 24:2 (1970), pp. 836–868.

Schmitter, Philippe C.: "Neo-Neofunctionalism." In Antje Wiener and Thomas Diez (eds.): *European Integration Theory* (New York: Oxford University Press, 2004), pp. 45–74.

Schneck, Stephen F. (ed.): *Letting Be: Fred Dallmayr's Cosmopolitan Vision* (Notre Dame, IN: Notre Dame University Press, 2006).

Scholem, Gershom: *On the Possibility of Jewish Mysticism in Our Time* (Philadelphia: Jewish Publication Society, 1997).

Schoolman, Morton: "Towards a Politics of Darkness: Individuality and Its Politics in Adorno's Aesthetics." *Political Theory* 25:1 (1997), pp. 57–92.

Schroeder, Paul: "Historical Reality vs. Neo-Realist Theory." *International Security* 19:1 (1994), pp. 108–148.

Schuett, Robert: "Freudian Roots of Political Realism: The Importance of Sigmund Freud to Hans J. Morgenthau's Theory of International Power Politics." *History of the Human Sciences* 20:4 (2007), pp. 53–78.

Schweller, Randall: *Deadly Imbalances: Tripolarity and Hitler's Strategy of World Conquest* (New York: Columbia University Press, 1998).

Schweller, Randall: *Unanswered Threats: Political Restraints on the Balance of Power* (Princeton, NJ: Princeton University Press, 2006).

Schwenger, Peter: "Writing the Unthinkable." *Critical Inquiry* 13:1 (1986), pp. 33–48.

Scott, James C.: *Seeing Like a State: How Certain Schemes to Improve the Human Condition Have Failed* (New Haven, CT: Yale University Press, 1998).

Scott, John, and Gordon Marshall (eds.): *A Dictionary of Sociology* (New York: Oxford University Press, 2009).

See, Jennifer W.: "A Prophet without Honor: Hans Morgenthau and the War in Vietnam, 1955–65." *Pacific Historical Review* 70:3 (2001), pp. 419–447.

Senghaas, Dieter: *The Clash within Civilizations: Coming to Terms with Cultural Conflict* (London: Routledge, 2002).

Sennett, Richard: *The Corrosion of Character* (New York: Norton, 1998).

Sewell, James Patrick: *Functionalism and World Politics* (Princeton, NJ: Princeton University Press, 1966).

Shafir, Gershon, and Yoav Peled: *Being Israeli: The Dynamics of Multiple Citizenship* (Cambridge: Cambridge Universityi Press, 2002).

Shain, Yossi, and Gary Sussman: "From Opposition to State-Building: Palestinian Political Society Meets Palestinian Civil Society." *Government and Opposition* 33:3 (1998), pp. 275–396.

Shannon, Vaughn P.: "Judge and Executioner: The Politics of Responding to Ethnic Cleansing in the Balkans." *Journal of Genocide Research* 7:1 (2005), pp. 47–66.

Shapcott, Richard: "Conversation and Coexistence: Gadamer and the Interpretation of International Society." *Millennium* 23:1 (1994), pp. 57–83.

Shapcott, Richard: "IR as Practical Philosophy: Defining a 'Classical Approach.'" *British Journal of Politics and International Relations* 6 (2004), pp. 271–294.

Shapcott, Richard: "Critical Theory." In Christian Reus-Smit and Duncan Snidal (eds.): *The Oxford Handbook of International Relations* (New York: Oxford University Press, 2008), pp. 327–45.

Shapira, Anita (ed.): *Israeli Identity in Transition* (London: Praeger, 2004).

Shapiro, Gary, and Alan Sica (eds.): *Hermeneutics: Questions and Prospects* (Amherst: University of Massachusetts Press, 1984).

Shenhav, Yehouda: *The Arab Jews: A Post-Colonial Reading of Nationalism, Religion and Ethnicity* (Stanford, CA: Stanford University Press, 2006).

Shepsle, Kenneth A.: "Why?" In Gary King et al. (eds.): *The Future of Political Science* (London: Routledge, 2009), pp. 244–45.

Sherratt, Yvonne: *Adorno's Positive Dialectic* (Cambridge: Cambridge University Press, 2002).

Shikaki, Halil: "Palestinians Divided." *Foreign Affairs* 81:1 (2002), pp. 89–105.

Shilliam, Robbie: "Morgenthau in Context: German Backwardness, German Intellectuals and the Rise and Fall of a Liberal Project." *European Journal of International Relations* 13:3 (2007), pp. 299–327.

Shilliam, Robert: "The 'Other' in Classical Political Theory: Recontextualizing the Cosmopolitan/Communitarian Debate." In Beate Jahn (ed.): *Classical Theory in International Relations* (Cambridge: Cambridge University Press, 2006), 207–32.

Shklar, Judith N.: *After Utopia* (Princeton, NJ: Princeton University Press, 1957).

Shklar, Judith N.: *Political Thought and Political Thinkers* (Chicago: University of Chicago Press, 1998).

Shlaim, Avi: *War and Peace in the Middle East: A Critique of American Policy* (New York: Viking, 1994).

Shlaim, Avi: *The Iron Wall* (New York: Norton, 2000).

Shohat, Ella: *Israeli Cinema: East-West and the Politics of Representation* (Austin: University of Texas Press, 1989).

Shore, Sean: "No Fences Make Good Neighbors: The Development of the US-Canadian Security Community, 1871–1940." In Emanuel Adler and Michael Barnett (eds.): *Security Communities* (Cambridge: Cambridge University Press, 1998), pp. 333–367.

Sil, Rudra: "Against Epistemological Absolutism: Toward a 'Pragmatic' Center?" In Rudra Sil and Eileen M. Doherty (eds.): *Beyond Boundaries? Disciplines, Paradigms and Theoretical Integration in International Studies* (Albany: State University of New York Press, 2000), pp. 145–75. [2000a]

Sil, Rudra: "The Foundations of Eclecticism: The Epistemological Status of Agency, Culture and Structure in Social Theory." *Journal of Theoretical Politics* 12:3 (2000), pp. 353–387. [2000b]

Sil, Rudra: "Problems Chasing Methods, or Methods Chasing Problems? Research Communities, Constrained Pluralism, and the Role of Eclecticism." In Ian Shapiro, Rogers M. Smith, and Tarek E. Masoud (eds.): *Problems and Methods in the Study of Politics* (Cambridge: Cambridge University Press, 2004), pp. 307–331.

Sil, Rudra, and Eileen M. Doherty (eds.): *Beyond Boundaries? Disciplines, Paradigms and Theoretical Integration in International Studies* (Albany: State University of New York Press, 2000).

Silver, Beverly: "The Contradictions of Semiperipheral Success: The Case of Israel." In William G. Martin (ed.): *Semiperipheral States in the World-Economy* (New York: Greenwood, 1990), pp. 161–81.

Simmel, Georg: *The Philosophy of Money* (London: Routledge, 2004).

Singer, J. David: "The Level-of-Analysis Problem in International Relations." *World Politics* 14:1 (1961), pp. 77–92.

Sjoberg, Laura: "Gendered Realities of the Immunity Principle: Why Gender Analysis Needs Feminism." *International Studies Quarterly* 50 (2006), pp. 889–910.

Slaughter, Anne-Marie, and Walter Mattli: "Europe before the Court: A Political Theory of Legal Integration." In Beth A. Simmons and Richard H. Steinberg (eds.): *International Law and International Relations* (Cambridge: Cambridge University Press, 2006), pp. 457–485.

Slyomovics, Susan: *The Object of Memory: Arab and Jew Narrate the Palestinian Village* (Philadelphia: University of Pennsylvania Press, 1998).

Smith, Michael Joseph: *Realist Thought from Weber to Kissinger* (Baton Rouge: Louisiana State University Press, 1986).

Smith, Norman Kemp: *A Commentary to Kant's* Critique of Pure Reason (New York: Palgrave Macmillan, 2003).

Smith, Steve: "The Self-Images of a Discipline." In Ken Booth and Steve Smith (eds.): *International Relations Theory Today* (University Park: Pennsylvania State University Press, 1995), pp. 1–37.

Smith, Steve: "Positivism and Beyond." In Steve Smith, Ken Booth, and Marysia Zalewski (eds.): *International Theory: Positivism and Beyond* (Cambridge: Cambridge University Press, 1996), pp. 11–44.

Smith, Steve: "The Contested Concept of Security." In Ken Booth (ed.): *Critical Security Studies and World Politics* (Boulder, CO: Lynne Rienner, 2005), pp. 27–62.

Smith, Tony: *America's Mission: The United States and the Worldwide Struggle for Democracy in the Twentieth Century* (Princeton, NJ: Princeton University Press, 1995).

Snidal, Duncan, and Alexander Wendt: "Why There Is *International Theory* Now." *International Theory* 1:1 (2009), pp. 1–14.

Snyder, Jack: *The Ideology of the Offensive: Military Decision-Making and the Disasters of 1914* (Ithaca, NY: Cornell University Press, 1984).

Snyder, Jack: *Myths of Empire: Domestic Politics and International Ambition* (Ithaca, NY: Cornell University Press, 1991).

Snyder, Timothy: "Holocaust: The Ignored Reality." *New York Review of Books* 56:12 (2009), http://www.nybooks.com/articles/archives/2009/jul/16/holocaust-the-ignored-reality/ (last accessed 20 April 2012), np.

Söllner, Alfons: "German Conservatism in America: Morgenthau's Political Realism." *Telos* 72 (1987), pp. 161–177.

Solomon, Ty: "Hans Morgenthau on Love and Power." Paper delivered at the International Studies Northeast Region conference, Baltimore, 2010.

Somit, Albert, and Joseph Tanenhaus: *The Development of American Political Science: from Burgess to Behavioralism* (Boston: Allyn and Bacon, 1967).

Sorensen, Ted: *Decisionmaking in the White House: The Olive Branch or the Arrows* (New York: Columbia University Press, 1963).

Spector, Stephen: *Evangelicals and Israel: The Story of American Christian Zionism* (New York: Oxford University Press, 2009).

Speer, James P.: "Hans Morgenthau and the World-State." *World Politics* 20:2 (1968), pp. 207–227.

Spegele, Roger D.: *Political Realism in International Theory* (Cambridge: Cambridge University Press, 1996).

Spinelli, Altiero: *The Eurocrats* (Baltimore: Johns Hopkins University Press, 1966).

Spinoza, Benedict de: *A Theologico-Political Treatise*, tr. R. H. M. Elwes (New York: Dover, 1951)

Sprout, Harold, and Margaret Sprout: *The Ecological Perspective, with Special Reference to International Politics* (Princeton, NJ: Princeton University Press, 1965).

Spruyt, Hendryk: *The Sovereign State and its Competitors* (Princeton, NJ: Princeton University Press, 1994).

Steele, Brent: "Eavesdropping on Honored Ghosts: From Classical to Reflexive Realism." *Journal of International Relations and Development* 10:3 (2007), pp. 272–276.

Steele, Brent: "Irony, Emotions and Critical Distance." *Millennium* 39:1 (2010), pp. 89–107.

Stein, Rebecca L., and Ted Swedenburg: *Palestine, Israel and the Politics of Popular Culture* (Durham, NC: Duke University Press, 2005).

Sterling-Folker, Jennifer (ed.): *Making Sense of International Relations Theory* (Boulder, CO: Lynne Rienner, 2006).

Sterling-Folker, Jennifer, and Rosemary Shinko: "Discourses of Power: Traversing the Realist-Postmodern Divide." In Felix Berenskoetter and M. J. Williams (eds.): *Power in World Politics* (London: Routledge, 2007), pp. 244–64.

Stirk, Peter: "John H. Herz: Realism and the Fragility of the International Order." *Review of International Studies* 31 (2005), pp. 235–306.

Stoessinger, John: "Memories of Hans J. Morgenthau as a Fellow Survivor." In G. O. Mazur (ed.): *One Hundred Year Commemoration to the Life of Hans Morgenthau* (New York: Semenenko Foundation, 2004), pp. 132–47.

Strauss, Leo: *Spinoza's Critique of Religion.* (Chicago: University of Chicago Press, 1997).

Strauss, Leo: "What Can We Learn from Political Theory?" *Review of Politics* 69:4 (2007), pp. 515–529.

Strong, Tracy B., and David B. Owen: "Introduction." In Max Weber: *The Vocation Lectures* (Indianapolis, IN: Hackett, 2004), ix-lxxv.

Sucharov, Mira: *The International Self: Psychoanalysis and the Search for Israeli-Palestinian Peace* (Albany: State University of New York Press, 2005).

Sylvester, Christine: *Feminist Theory and International Relations in a Postmodern Era* (Cambridge: Cambridge University Press, 1994).

Sylvester, Christine: *Feminist International Relations: An Unfinished Journey* (Cambridge: Cambridge University Press, 2002).

Taliaferro, Jeffrey W.: "Security Seeking under Anarchy: Defensive Realism Revisited." *International Security* 25:3 (2000–01), pp. 128–161.

Taliaferro, Jeffrey W.: *Balancing Risks: Great Power Intervention in the Periphery* (Ithaca, NY: Cornell University Press, 2004).

Tamari, Salim (ed.): *Jerusalem 1948: The Arab Neighborhoods of the New City and Their Fate in the War* (Washington, DC: Institute for Palestine Studies, 1999).

Tamari, Salim: *Mountain against the Sea: Essays in Palestinian Society and Culture* (Berkeley: University of California Press, 2008).

Tarrow, Sidney G.: *The New Transnational Activism* (Cambridge: Cambridge University Press, 2005).

Tarrow, Sidney G., and Donatella della Porta (eds.): *Transnational Protest and Global Activism* (Lanham, MD: Rowman and Littlefield, 2005).

Taubes, Jacob: *The Political Theology of Paul*, tr. Dana Hollander (Stanford, CA: Stanford University Press, 2004).

Taylor, Paul: "The Concept of Community and the European Integration Process." *Journal of Common Market Studies* 7:2 (1968), pp. 83–101.

Taylor, Paul: "The Politics of the European Communities: The Confederal Phase." *World Politics* 27:3 (1975), pp. 336–360.

Taylor, Paul: *The Limits of European Integration* (New York: Columbia University Press, 1983).

Telhami, Shibley, and Michael Barnett (eds.): *Identity and Foreign Policy in the Middle East* (Ithaca, NY: Cornell University Press, 2002).

Tellis, Ashley Joachim: *The Drive to Domination* (Ph.D. dissertation, University of Chicago, 1994), 2 vols. Available in ProQuest Digital Dissertations database (publication AAT 9419842).

Tennyson, Alfred Lord: *Poems* (London: Scholar Press, 1976).

Teschke, Benno: *The Myth of 1648: Class, Geopolitics and the Making of Modern International Relations* (London: Verso, 2003).

Teti, Andrea: "Bridging the Gap: IR, Middle East Studies and the Disciplinary Politics of the Area Studies Controversy." *European Journal of International Relations* 13:1 (2007), pp. 117–145.

Thompson, H. Edward III: "The Fallacy of Misplaced Concreteness: Its Importance for Critical and Creative Inquiry." *Interchange* 28:2–3 (1997), pp. 219–230.

Thompson, Kenneth W., and Robert J. Myers: *Truth and Tragedy: A Tribute to Hans J. Morgenthau*, augmented ed. (New Brunswick, NJ: Transaction, 1984).

Thomson, Alex: *Adorno: A Guide to the Perplexed* (London: Continuum, 2006).

Tickner, Ann: "Hans Morgenthau's Principles of Political Realism: A Feminist Reformulation." *Millennium* 17:3 (1988), pp. 429–440.

Tickner, J. Ann: "On Taking Religious Worldviews Seriously." In Helen Milner and Andrew Moravcsik (eds.): *Power, Interdependence and Nonstate Actors in World Politics* (Princeton, NJ: Princeton University Press, 2009), pp. 223–240.

Tilly, Charles: *Coercion, Capital and European States, AD 990–1992* (London: Blackwell, 1992).

Tjalve, Vibeke Schou: *Realist Strategies of Republican Peace* (London: Palgrave, 2008).

Toffler, Alvin, and Heidi Toffler: *War and Anti-War: Making Sense of Today's Global Chaos* (New York: Warner, 1993).

Tönnies, Ferdinand: *Community and Society* (New York: Harper Torchbooks, 1957).

Trachtenberg, Marc: *The Craft of International History* (Princeton, NJ: Princeton University Press, 2006).

Treitschke, Heinrich von: *Politics*, 2 vols., tr. Blanche Dugdale and Torben de Bille (New York: Macmillan, 1916).

Tuchman, Barbara: *Bible and Sword: England and Palestine from the Bronze Age to Balfour* (New York: Ballantine, 1984).

Tucker, Robert C. (ed.): *The Marx-Engels Reader* (New York: Norton, 1978).

Turner, Stephen P.: "Morgenthau as a Weberian." In G. O. Mazur (ed.): *One Hundred Year Commemoration to the Life of Hans Morgenthau* (New York: Semenenko Foundation, 2004), pp. 88–114.

Turner, Stephen P.: "Hans J. Morgenthau and the Legacy of Max Weber." In Duncan Bell (ed.): *Political Thought and International Relations* (New York: Oxford University Press, 2009), pp. 63–82.

Turner, Stephen P., and George Mazur: "Morgenthau as a Weberian Methodologist." *European Journal of International Relations* 15:3 (2009), pp. 477–504.

Tversky, Amos, and Daniel Kahneman: "Rational Choice and the Framing of Decisions." *Journal of Business* 59:4, part 2 (1986), pp. S251–S278.

Van Creveld, Martin: *The Rise and Decline of the State* (Cambridge: Cambridge University Press, 1999).

Van Creveld, Martin: *The Sword and the Olive: A Critical History of the Israel Defense Force* (New York: Public Affairs, 2002).

Van Creveld, Martin: *The Changing Face of War* (New York: Presidio, 2007).

Van de Steeg, Marianne: "An Empirical Approach to the Public Sphere in the EU." *Europe Transformed: The European Union and Collective Identity Change.* Papers presented for the ARENA/IDNET International Policy Conference, Oslo, October 2002. [2002a]

Van de Steeg, Marianne: "Rethinking the Conditions for a Public Sphere in the European Union." *European Journal of Social Theory* 5:4 (2002), pp. 499–519. [2002b]

Van de Steeg, Marianne: "Does a Public Sphere Exist in the European Union? An Analysis of the Content of the Debate on the Haider Case." *European Journal of Political Research* 45 (2006), pp. 609–634.

Van Evera, Stephen: *Causes of War: Power and the Roots of Conflict* (Ithaca, NY: Cornell University Press, 1999).

Van Gelderen, Martin, and Quentin Skinner: *Republicanism: A Shared European Heritage*, 2 vols. (Cambridge: Cambridge University Press, 2002).

Van Waganen, Richard W.: "The Concept of Community and the Future of the United Nations." *International Organization* 19:3 (1965), pp. 812–827.

Vasquez, John A.: *The Power of Power Politics* (Cambridge: Cambridge University Press, 1998).

Vasquez, John A., and Colin Elman (eds.): *Realism and the Balance of Power: A New Debate* (Upper Saddle River, NJ: Prentice-Hall, 2003).

Viner, Jacob: *The Role of Providence in the Social Order: An Essay in Intellectual History* (Philadelphia: American Philosophical Society, 1972).

Virilio, Paul: *Speed and Politics* (Cambridge, MA: MIT Press, 1986).

Vitalis, Robert: "The Birth of a Discipline." In David Long and Brian C. Schmidt (eds.): *Imperialism and Internationalism in International Relations* (Albany: State University of New York Press, 2005), pp. 159–82.

Vitalis, Robert: "The Noble American Science of Imperial Relations and its Laws of Race Development." *Comparative Studies in Society and History* 52:4 (2010), pp. 909–38.

Vucetic, Srdjan: *The Anglosphere: A Genealogy of a Racialized Identity in International Relations* (Stanford, CA: Stanford University Press, 2011).

Waever, Ole: "Securitization and Desecuritization." In Ronnie D. Lifschutz (ed.): *On Security* (New York: Columbia University Press, 1995), pp. 46–86.

Waever, Ole: "European Security Identities." *Journal of Common Market Studies* 34:1 (1996), pp. 103–132.

Waever, Ole: "Insecurity, Security and Asecurity in the West European Non-War Community." In Emanuel Adler and Michael Barnett (eds.): *Security Communities* (Cambridge: Cambridge University Press, 1998), pp. 69–118.

Waever, Ole: "Waltz's Theory of Theory." *International Relations* 23:2 (2009), pp. 201–222.

Waever, Ole: "Politics, Security, Theory." *Security Dialogue* 42:4–5 (2011), pp. 465–80.

Wagar, W. Warren: *The Open Conspiracy: H. G. Wells on World Revolution* (Westport, CT: Greenwood, 2002).

Walker, R. B. J.: *Inside/Outside: International Relations as Political Theory* (Cambridge: Cambridge University Press, 1992).

Walker, Thomas C.: "The Perils of Paradigm Mentalities: Revisiting Kuhn, Lakatos, and Popper." *Perspectives on Politics* 8:2 (2010), pp. 433–451.

Wallerstein, Immanuel: *The Modern World-System I* (New York: Academic Press, 1974).

Wallerstein, Immanuel: *World-System Analysis: An Introduction.* (Durham, NC: Duke University Press, 2004).

Walt, Stephen M.: *The Origins of Alliances* (Ithaca, NY: Cornell University Press, 1987).

Walt, Stephen M.: "The Renaissance of Security Studies." *International Studies Quarterly* 35 (1991), pp. 211–239.

Walt, Stephen M.: "International Relations: One World, Many Theories." *Foreign Policy* 110 (1998), pp. 29–32 and 34–46.

Waltz, Kenneth N.: "Political Philosophy and the Study of International Relations." In William T. R. Fox (ed.): *Theoretical Aspects of International Relations* (Notre Dame, IN: Notre Dame University Press, 1959), pp. 51–69.

Waltz, Kenneth N.: *Theory of International Politics* (Boston: Addison-Wesley, 1979).

Waltz, Kenneth N.: "Reflections on *Theory of International Politics*: A Response to My Critics." In Robert O. Keohane (ed.): *Neorealism and Its Critics* (New York: Columbia University Press, 1986), pp. 322–345.

Waltz, Kenneth N.: "Realist Thought and Neo-Realist Theory." In Robert L. Rothstein (ed.): *The Evolution of International Theory: Essays in Honor of William T. R. Fox* (Columbia: University of South Carolina Press, 1992), pp. 21–38.

Waltz, Kenneth N.: "Evaluating Theories." *American Political Science Review* 91:4 (1997), pp. 913–917.

Waltz, Kenneth N.: *Man, the State and War: A Theoretical Analysis* (New York: Columbia University Press, 2001).

Waltz, Kenneth N.: "Morgenthau and Neorealist Theory." In G. O. Mazur (ed.): *One Hundred Year Commemoration to the Life of Hans Morgenthau* (New York: Semenenko Foundation, 2004), pp. 168–83.

Waltz, Kenneth N., and Harry N. Kreisler: "Theory and International Politics: Conversation with Kenneth N. Waltz." *Conversations with History* (Institute of International Studies, University of California, Berkeley, February 10, 2003), http://globetrotter.berkeley.edu/people3/Waltz/waltz-con0.html.

Walzer, Michael: *Spheres of Justice* (New York: Basic Books, 1983).

Waxman, Dov: *The Pursuit of Peace and the Crisis of Israeli Identity: Defending/Defining the Nation* (New York: Palgrave-Macmillan, 2006).

Weber, Max: "Science as a Vocation." In H. H. Gerth and C. Wright Mills (eds.): *From Max Weber: Essays in Sociology* (New York: Galaxy, 1958), pp. 129–56. [1958a]

Weber, Max: "'Objectivity' in Social Science and Social Policy." In Edward A. Shils and Henry A. Finch (eds.): *Max Weber on the Methodology of the Social Sciences* (Glencoe, IL: Free Press of Glencoe, 1949), pp. 49–112.

Weber, Max: *The Protestant Ethic and the Spirit of Capitalism*, tr. Talcott Parsons (New York: Scribners, 1958). [1958b]

Weber, Max: *Economy and Society, Vol. 1* (Berkeley: University of California Press, 1978).

Weizman, Eyal: "Walking through Walls: Soldiers as Architects in the Israeli-Palestinian Conflict." *Radical Philosophy* 136 (2006), pp. 8–22.

Welch, Michael: "The Centenary of the British Publication of Jean de Bloch's *Is War Now Impossible?* (1899–1999)." *War in History* 7:3 (2000), pp. 273–294.

Weldes, Jutta: "Constructing National Interests." *European Journal of International Relations* 2 (1996), pp. 275–318.

Wellmer, Albrecht: "Communication and Emancipation: Reflections on the Linguistic Turn in Critical Theory." In John O'Neill (ed.): *On Critical Theory* (New York: Seabury, 1976), pp. 231–63.

Wells, H. G.: *Anticipations of the Reaction of Mechanical and Scientific Progress upon Human Life and Thought* (New York: Harper, 1901).

Wells, H. G.: *The World Set Free: A Story of Mankind* (London: Macmillan, 1914).

Wells, H. G.: *The Idea of the League of Nations* (Boston: Atlantic Monthly, 1919).

Wells, H. G.: *The Open Conspiracy.* Edition from 1933, reprinted in W. Warren Wagar (ed.): *The Open Conspiracy: H. G. Wells on World Revolution* (Westport, CT: Greenwood, 2002).

Wendt, Alexander: "The Agent-Structure Problem in International Relations Theory." *International Organization* 41:3 (1987), pp. 335–370.

Wendt, Alexander: "Anarchy Is What States Make of It: The Social Construction of Power Politics." *International Organization* 46 (1992), pp. 391–425.

Wendt, Alexander: "Constructing International Politics." *International Security* 20:1 (1995), pp. 71–81.

Wendt, Alexander: "On Constitution and Causation in International Politics." *Review of International Studies* (1998), pp. 101–117.

Wendt, Alexander: *Social Theory of International Politics* (Cambridge: Cambridge University Press, 1999).

Wendt, Alexander: "On the *Via Media*: A Response to the Critics." *Review of International Studies* 26 (2000), pp. 165–180.

Wendt, Alexander: "What Is International Relations For? Notes toward a Postcritical View." In Richard Wyn Jones: *Critical Theory and World Politics* (Boulder, CO: Lynne Rienner, 2001), pp. 205–224.

Wendt, Alexander: "Why a World State Is Inevitable." *European Journal of International Relations* 9:4 (2003), pp. 491–542.

Wendt, Alexander: "The State as Person in International Theory." *Review of International Studies* 30 (2004), pp. 289–316.

Wendt, Alexander: "*Social Theory* as Cartesian Social Science: An Auto-Critique from a Quantum Perspective." In Stefano Guzzini and Anna Leander (eds.): *Constructivism and International Relations: Alexander Wendt and His Critics* (London: Routledge, 2006), pp. 178–215.

Wendt, Alexander, and Raymond Duvall: "Sovereignty and the UFO." *Political Theory* 36:4 (2008), pp. 607–633.

Wendt, Alexander, and Daniel Friedheim: "Hierarchy under Anarchy: Informal Empire and the East German State." *International Organization* 49:4 (1995), pp. 689–721.

Wernick, Andrew: *Auguste Comte and the Religion of Humanity* (Cambridge: Cambridge University Press, 2001).

West, Cornel: *The American Evasion of Philosophy* (Madison: University of Wisconsin Press, 1989).

West, Cornel: *The Ethical Dimensions of Marxist Thought* (New York: Monthly Review, 1991).

Wheatland, Thomas: *The Frankfurt School in Exile* (Minneapolis: University of Minnesota Press, 2009).

Whitehead, Alfred North: *Science and the Modern World* (New York: Macmillan, 1925).

Whitehead, Alfred North: *Process and Reality* (New York: Free Press, 1978).

Wiener, Norbert: *Cybernetics: Or Control and Communication in the Animal and the Machine* (New York: John Wiley and the Technology Press, 1948).

Wiener, Norbert: *The Human Use of Human Beings* (Boston: Houghton-Mifflin, 1950).

Wiggershaus, Rolf: *The Frankfurt School: Its Histories, Theories and Political Significance* (Cambridge, MA: MIT Press, 1994).

Wight, Colin: "State Agency: Social Action without Human Activity?" *Review of International Studies* 30 (2004), pp. 269–280.

Wight, Colin: *Agents, Structures and International Relations: Politics as Ontology* (Cambridge: Cambridge University Press, 2006).

Wight, Martin, and Hedley Bull (eds.): *Diplomatic Investigations: Essays in the Theory of International Politics* (Cambridge, MA: Harvard University Press, 1966).

Williams, Howard, and Ken Booth: "Kant: Theorist beyond Limits." In Ian Clark and Iver B. Neumann: *Classical Theories of International Relations* (London: Macmillan, 1996), pp. 71–98.

Williams, Michael C.: "Why Ideas Matter in International Relations: Hans Morgenthau, Classical Realism, and the Moral Construction of Power Politics." *International Organization* 58 (2004), pp. 633–665.

Williams, Michael C.: *The Realist Tradition and the Limits of International Relations* (Cambridge: Cambridge University Press, 2005).

Williams, Michael C. (ed.): *Realism Reconsidered: The Legacy of Hans J. Morgenthau in International Relations* (New York: Oxford University Press, 2007).

Williams, Michael C.: "Waltz, Realism and Democracy." *International Relations* 23:3 (2009), pp. 328–340.

Williams, Michael C., and Keith Krause: *Critical Theory in International Relations: Concepts and Cases* (Minneapolis: University of Minnesota Press, 1997).

Willis, Kirk: "The Origins of British Nuclear Culture, 1895–1939." *Journal of British Studies* 34:1 (1995), pp. 59–89.

Winch, Peter: *The Idea of a Social Science* (London: Routledge and Kegan Paul, 1958).

Wivel, Anders: "Explaining Why State X Made a Certain Move Last Tuesday: The Promise and Limitations of Realist Policy Analysis." *Journal of International Relations and Development* 8 (2005), pp. 355–380.

Wohlforth, William Curti, et al.: "Testing Balance of Power Theory in World History." *European Journal of International Affairs* 13:2 (2007), pp. 155–185.

Wohlforth, William Curti: *The Elusive Balance: Power and Perceptions During the Cold War.* (Ithaca: Cornell University Press, 1993).

Wolf, Eric R.: *Europe and the People without History*, 2nd ed. (Berkeley: University of California Press, 1997).

Wolfers, Arnold: *Discord and Collaboration: Essays on International Politics* (Baltimore: Johns Hopkins University Press, 1962).

Wolin, Sheldon: "Political Theory as a Vocation." In Martin Fleischer (ed.): *Machiavelli and the Nature of Political Thought* (New York: Antheneum, 1972), pp. 23–75.

Wolin, Sheldon: "What Time Is It?" *Theory and Event* 1:1 (1997).

Wolin, Sheldon: *Politics and Vision* (Princeton, NJ: Princeton University Press, 2004).

Wolin, Sheldon: *Democracy Incorporated: Managed Democracy and the Specter of Inverted Totalitarianism* (Princeton, NJ: Princeton University Press, 2008).

Wong, Benjamin: "Hans Morgenthau's Anti-Machiavellian Machiavellianism." *Millennium* 29 (2000), pp. 389–409.

Woolf, Leonard: *The War for Peace* (London: Routledge, 1940).

Wright, Quincy: *A Study of War* (Chicago: University of Chicago Press, 1942).

Wright, T. R.: *The Religion of Humanity* (Cambridge: Cambridge University Press, 1986).

Wyn Jones, Richard: "'Message in a Bottle?' Theory and Praxis in Critical Security Studies." *Contemporary Security Policy* 16:3 (1995), pp. 299–319.

Wyn Jones, Richard: *Security, Strategy and Critical Theory* (Boulder, CO: Lynne Rienner, 1999).

Wyn Jones, Richard: "On Emancipation: Necessity, Capacity, and Concrete Utopias." In Ken Booth: *Critical Security Studies and World Politics* (Boulder, CO: Lynne Rienner, 2005), 215–35.

Wyn Jones, Richard (ed.): *Critical Theory and World Politics* (Boulder, CO: Lynne Rienner, 2001).

Xenakis, Dimitris K., and Dimitris N. Chryssochoou: *The Emerging Euro-Mediterranean System* (Manchester, England: Palgrave-Macmillan, 2001).

Yanow, Dvora, and Peregrine Schwartz-Shea (eds.): *Interpretation and Method* (Armonk, NY: M. E. Sharpe, 2006).

Yiftachel, Oren: *Ethnocracy: Land and Identity Politics in Israel/Palestine* (Philadelphia: University of Pennsylvania Press, 2006).

Young, Oran R.: "International Regimes: Problems of Concept Formation." *World Politics* 32:3 (1980), pp. 331–356.

Young-Bruehl, Elisabeth: *Hannah Arendt: For Love of the World* (New Haven, CT: Yale University Press, 2004).

Yovel, Yirmiahu: *Kant and the Philosophy of History* (Princeton, NJ: Princeton University Press, 1980).

Yovel, Yirmiahu: *Spinoza and Other Heretics* (Princeton, NJ: Princeton University Press, 1989).

Zakaria, Fareed: *From Wealth to Power* (Princeton, NJ: Princeton University Press, 1998).

Zehfuss, Maja: *Constructivism in International Relations: the Politics of Reality* (Cambridge: Cambridge University Press, 2002).

Zehfuss, Maja: "Remembering to Forgive: The 'War on Terror' in a Dialogue between German and US Intellectuals." *International Relations* 19:1 (2005), pp. 91–102.

Zerubavel, Yael: *Recovered Roots: Collective Memory and the Making of Israeli National Tradition* (Chicago: University of Chicago Press, 1995).

Zuidervaart, Lambert: "Metaphysics after Auschwitz: Suffering and Hope in Adorno's *Negative Dialectics*." In Donald A. Burke et al. (eds.): *Adorno and the Need in Thinking* (Toronto: University of Toronto Press, 2007), pp. 133–63. [2007a]

Zuidervaart, Lambert: *Social Theory after Adorno* (Cambridge: Cambridge University Press, 2007). [2007b]

Zürn, Michael, and Jeffrey T. Checkel: "Getting Socialized to Build Bridges: Constructivism and Rationalism, Europe and the Nation-State." *International Organization* 59:4 (2005), pp. 1045–1079.

Index

liberal institutionalism, ix, 1n2, 12, 24, 31,
186, 192–3, 207–9, 211–14, 257
liberalism of fear, 211
lifeworld, 22n81, 34, 93, 96n67, 97, 113,
159, 185
Lindblom, Charles, 3–4
Linklater, Andrew, 37, 45n8, 56n45, 66,
70n94, 76, 80–3, 84, 85nn20–1,
87n32, 88–93, 95–6, 98, 99n74,
153n8, 251n56
Lippmann, Walter, 78
looping effects, 20
Luckmann, Thomas, 7n24, 14–15
Lukács, Georg, 15, 33n100, 48n21, 50n26,
56n45, 66nn78 and 80, 67, 71n97,
76n119
Lukes, Steven, 180
Luttwak, Edward, 107
Lynch, Marc, 34, 84, 87nn29–30, 94n55,
243–4n37, 250n54

Maastricht, treaty of, 34
Macchiavelli, Niccolò, 20, 51, 95, 105,
106n104, 138
Mali Republic, 173
Mannheim, Karl, 3–5, 8n28, 23, 76n118,
102n90, 170, 238–9
Marcuse, Herbert, 15n54, 42, 44,
45n10, 49nn23–4, 51n29, 54, 69,
73n106, 82–3, 84, 89–91, 94, 113, 117,
180, 204
Marx, Karl, 5, 15, 24n90, 53, 71, 83n11, 84,
142, 147n122, 178
Marxism, 6–7, 8n27, 15, 23, 73, 88–90,
142, 178n99, 197
Mattli, Walter, 199, 200nn26 and 30
McNeill, William, 2n4, 85n22, 242,
248n42
McSweeney, Bill, 11, 99
Mearsheimer, John, 77n122, 120n7,
142n97, 144n107, 242, 247n41
méga thaumázein, 124, 129

Meinecke, Friedrich, 92n52, 126, 133
Melian Dialogue, 61
metaphysical methodologies,
see methodology
methodology, 1–2n2, 4, 12–15, 18, 25–9,
31–2, 35n109, 37–8, 42, 45n8, 63,
82n8, 99, 101, 102, 104, 115–6, 122,
136, 137, 152, 159, 170, 174, 182, 184,
188, 190, 193–4, 213, 214, 215, 217,
219, 223, 225–6, 228, 229,
232, 240, 241
approaches to, and role in paradigms,
xi, 1–2n2, 14, 15, 25–9, 31–2, 37–8,
101, 116, 152, 159
Middle East, 186, 228, 235n12, 236, 242,
244, 247, 254
middle ground, *see via media*
middle-range methodologies,
see methodology
Mill, James, 250
Milner, Helen, 65
Mitrany, David, viii, 4, 8n27, 9, 30, 38,
128n41, 161–3, 165n42, 166–173,
176, 178n99, 179, 183–4, 187, 192,
195–7, 198–201, 231, 246
Moore, Barrington, 62
Moravcsik, Andrew, 30, 38, 63n73, 151,
156n20, 190n2, 194, 211n80, 213n86,
215–217, 220–1
Morgan, Patrick, 65
Morgenthau, Hans J., viii, 4, 5n12, 8n28,
9–10, 22n79, 30, 37, 42, 48n19,
52n35, 56–7, 77n122, 78, 81, 83,
105n97, 116, 118, 120–35, 136–7, 139,
142, 144, 148, 150, 161, 172n76, 173,
180n105, 206, 213, 226, 230, 231,
246, 253
multiparadigmatism, ix, 31, 38, 63, 109,
192, 194, 215–224, 227–8, 232, 237,
253; *see also* analytical eclecticism;
'two-step' approach
'Munich analogy', 255–6